IFIP Advances in Information and Communication Technology 329

T0224023

IFIP – The International Federation for Information Processing

IFIP was founded in 1960 under the auspices of UNESCO, following the First World Computer Congress held in Paris the previous year. An umbrella organization for societies working in information processing, IFIP's aim is two-fold: to support information processing within its member countries and to encourage technology transfer to developing nations. As its mission statement clearly states,

> *IFIP's mission is to be the leading, truly international, apolitical organization which encourages and assists in the development, exploitation and application of information technology for the benefit of all people.*

IFIP is a non-profitmaking organization, run almost solely by 2500 volunteers. It operates through a number of technical committees, which organize events and publications. IFIP's events range from an international congress to local seminars, but the most important are:

- The IFIP World Computer Congress, held every second year;
- Open conferences;
- Working conferences.

The flagship event is the IFIP World Computer Congress, at which both invited and contributed papers are presented. Contributed papers are rigorously refereed and the rejection rate is high.

As with the Congress, participation in the open conferences is open to all and papers may be invited or submitted. Again, submitted papers are stringently refereed.

The working conferences are structured differently. They are usually run by a working group and attendance is small and by invitation only. Their purpose is to create an atmosphere conducive to innovation and development. Refereeing is less rigorous and papers are subjected to extensive group discussion.

Publications arising from IFIP events vary. The papers presented at the IFIP World Computer Congress and at open conferences are published as conference proceedings, while the results of the working conferences are often published as collections of selected and edited papers.

Any national society whose primary activity is in information may apply to become a full member of IFIP, although full membership is restricted to one society per country. Full members are entitled to vote at the annual General Assembly, National societies preferring a less committed involvement may apply for associate or corresponding membership. Associate members enjoy the same benefits as full members, but without voting rights. Corresponding members are not represented in IFIP bodies. Affiliated membership is open to non-national societies, and individual and honorary membership schemes are also offered.

Mike Hinchey   Bernd Kleinjohann
Lisa Kleinjohann   Peter A. Lindsay
Franz J. Rammig   Jon Timmis
Marilyn Wolf (Eds.)

Distributed, Parallel and Biologically Inspired Systems

7th IFIP TC 10 Working Conference, DIPES 2010 and
3rd IFIP TC 10 International Conference, BICC 2010
Held as Part of WCC 2010
Brisbane, Australia, September 20-23, 2010
Proceedings

 Springer

Volume Editors

Mike Hinchey
Lero, University of Limerick, Limerick, Ireland
E-mail: mike.hinchey@lero.ie

Bernd Kleinjohann
University of Paderborn / C-Lab, Germany
E-mail: bernd@c-lab.de

Lisa Kleinjohann
University of Paderborn / C-Lab, Germany
E-mail: lisa@c-lab.de

Peter A. Lindsay
University of Queensland, St.Lucia, Australia
E-mail: p.lindsay@uq.edu.au

Franz J. Rammig
University of Paderborn, Heinz Nixdorf Institute, Germany
E-mail: franz@upb.de

Jon Timmis
University of York, Heslington, UK
E-mail: jtimmis@cs.york.ac.uk

Marilyn Wolf
Georgia Institute of Technology, Atlanta, USA
E-mail: marilyn.wolf@ece.gatech.edu

CR Subject Classification (1998): D.2, C.2, I.2, F.3, H.4, C.3

ISSN	1868-4238
ISBN-10	3-642-42292-6 Springer Berlin Heidelberg New York
ISBN-13	978-3-642-42292-8 Springer Berlin Heidelberg New York

springer.com

© IFIP International Federation for Information Processing 2010
Softcover re-print of the Hardover 1st edition 2010

Typesetting: Camera-ready by author, data conversion by Scientific Publishing Services, Chennai, India
Printed on acid-free paper   06/3180

IFIP World Computer Congress 2010 (WCC 2010)

Message from the Chairs

Every two years, the International Federation for Information Processing (IFIP) hosts a major event which showcases the scientific endeavors of its over one hundred technical committees and working groups. On the occasion of IFIP's 50th anniversary, 2010 saw the 21st IFIP World Computer Congress (WCC 2010) take place in Australia for the third time, at the Brisbane Convention and Exhibition Centre, Brisbane, Queensland, September 20–23, 2010.

The congress was hosted by the Australian Computer Society, ACS. It was run as a federation of co-located conferences offered by the different IFIP technical committees, working groups and special interest groups, under the coordination of the International Program Committee.

The event was larger than ever before, consisting of 17 parallel conferences, focusing on topics ranging from artificial intelligence to entertainment computing, human choice and computers, security, networks of the future and theoretical computer science. The conference History of Computing was a valuable contribution to IFIPs 50th anniversary, as it specifically addressed IT developments during those years. The conference e-Health was organized jointly with the International Medical Informatics Association (IMIA), which evolved from IFIP Technical Committee TC-4 "Medical Informatics".

Some of these were established conferences that run at regular intervals, e.g., annually, and some represented new, groundbreaking areas of computing. Each conference had a call for papers, an International Program Committee of experts and a thorough peer reviewing process of full papers. The congress received 642 papers for the 17 conferences, and selected 319 from those, representing an acceptance rate of 49.69% (averaged over all conferences). To support interoperation between events, conferences were grouped into 8 areas: Deliver IT, Govern IT, Learn IT, Play IT, Sustain IT, Treat IT, Trust IT, and Value IT.

This volume is one of 13 volumes associated with the 17 scientific conferences. Each volume covers a specific topic and separately or together they form a valuable record of the state of computing research in the world in 2010. Each volume was prepared for publication in the Springer IFIP Advances in Information and Communication Technology series by the conference's volume editors. The overall Publications Chair for all volumes published for this congress is Mike Hinchey.

For full details of the World Computer Congress, please refer to the webpage at http://www.ifip.org.

June 2010   Augusto Casaca, Portugal, Chair, International Program Committee
Phillip Nyssen, Australia, Co-chair, International Program Committee
Nick Tate, Australia, Chair, Organizing Committee
Mike Hinchey, Ireland, Publications Chair
Klaus Brunnstein, Germany, General Congress Chair

Preface

This volume contains the proceedings of two conferences held as part of the 21st IFIP World Computer Congress in Brisbane, Australia, 20–23 September 2010.

The first part of the book presents the proceedings of DIPES 2010, the 7th IFIP Conference on Distributed and Parallel Embedded Systems. The conference, introduced in a separate preface by the Chairs, covers a range of topics from specification and design of embedded systems through to dependability and fault tolerance.

The second part of the book contains the proceedings of BICC 2010, the 3rd IFIP Conference on Biologically-Inspired Collaborative Computing. The conference is concerned with emerging techniques from research areas such as organic computing, autonomic computing and self-adaptive systems, where inspiraton for techniques derives from exhibited behaviour in nature and biology. Such techniques require the use of research developed by the DIPES community in supporting collaboration over multiple systems.

We hope that the combination of the two proceedings will add value for the reader and advance our related work.

July 2010

Mike Hinchey
Bernd Kleinjohann
Lisa Kleinjohann
Peter Lindsay
Franz J. Rammig
Jon Timmis
Marilyn Wolf

Organization

7th IFIP TC 10 Working Conference on Distributed and Parallel Embedded Systems (DIPES 2010)

General Chair

Marilyn Wolf   Georgia Institute of Technology, USA

Program Chair

Bernd Kleinjohann   University of Paderborn/C-LAB, Germany

Organizing Chair

Lisa Kleinjohann   University of Paderborn/C-LAB, Germany

Program Committee

Jean Arlat	LAAS-CNRS Toulouse, France
Christophe Bobda	University of Kaiserslautern, Germany
Arndt Bode	Technical University of Munich, Germany
Joao M. P. Cardoso	University of Porto, FEUP, Portugal
Luigi Carro	UFRGS, Brazil
Matjac Colnaric	University of Maribor, Slovenia
Tom Conte	Georgia Institute of Technology, USA
Alfons Crespo Lorente	TU Valencia, Spain
Nikil Dutt	UC Irvine, USA
Petru Eles	Linkoeping University, Sweden
Rolf Ernst	TU Braunschweig, Germany
Bernhard Eschermann	ABB Switzerland Ltd., Switzerland
Joao Fernandes	University of Minho, Portugal
Uwe Glässer	Simon Fraser University, Canada
Luis Gomes	University of Nova Lisboa, Portugal
Wolfgang Halang	Fernuniversität Hagen, Germany
Uwe Honekamp	Vector Informatik GmbH, Germany
Pao-Ann Hsiung	National Chung Chen University, Taiwan
Kane Kim	UC Irvine, USA
Raimund Kirner	TU Vienna, Austria
Bernd Kleinjohann	University of Paderborn/C-LAB, Germany
Lisa Kleinjohann	University of Paderborn/C-LAB, Germany

Hermann Kopetz	TU Wien, Austria
Johan Lilius	TUCS, Finland
Ricardo J. Machado	University of Minho, Portugal
Erik Maehle	University of Luebeck, Germany
Baerbel Mertsching	University of Paderborn, Germany
Vincent Mooney	Georgia Institute of Technology, USA
Carlos E. Pereira	UFRGS, Brazil
Luis Pinho	ISEP-IPP, Porto, Portugal
Peter Puschner	TU Vienna, Austria
Franz J. Rammig	University of Paderborn, Germany
Achim Rettberg	University of Oldenburg, Germany
Bernhard Rinner	Klagenfurt University, Austria
Luis-Miguel Santana Ormeno	ST Microelectronics, France
Henrique Santos	University of Minho, Portugal
Klaus Schneider	University of Kaiserslautern, Germany
Joaquin Sitte	Queensland University of Technology, Brisbane, Australia
Edwin Sha	University of Texas at Dallas, USA
Zili Shao	The Hong Kong Polytechnic University, Hong Kong
Joachim Stroop	dSPACE, Germany
Francois Terrier	CEA/Saclay, France
Lothar Thiele	TH Zurich, Switzerland
Flavio R. Wagner	UFRGS, Brazil
Klaus Waldschmidt	University of Frankfurt, Germany
Marilyn Wolf	Georgia Institute of Technology, USA
Dieter Wuttke	TU Ilmenau, Germany
Alex Yakovlev	University of Newcastle, UK
Laurence T. Yang	St. Francis Xavier University, Canada

Organizing Committee

Lisa Kleinjohann	University of Paderborn/C-LAB, Germany
Claudius Stern	University of Paderborn/C-LAB, Germany

Co-Organizing Institutions

IFIP TC10, WG 10.2, WG 10.5

3rd IFIP TC 10 International Conference on Biologically-Inspired Collaborative Computing (BICC 2010)

Program Committee

Hussein Abbas	University of New South Wales, Australia
Sven Brueckner	New Vectors LLC, USA
Yuan-Shun Dai	University of Tennessee at Knoxville, USA
Marco Dorigo	IRIDIA, Université Libre de Bruxelles, Belgium
Luca Maria Gambardella	IDSIA, Switzerland
Jadwiga Indulska	University of Queensland, Australia
Thomas Jansen	University College Cork, Ireland
Tiziana Margaria	University of Potsdam, Germany
Eliane Martins	UNICAMP, Brazil
Roy A. Maxion	Carnegie Mellon University, USA
Christian Müller-Schloer	Universität Hannover, Germany
Takashi Nanya, RCAST	University of Tokyo, Japan
Bernhard Nebel	Albert-Ludwigs-Universität Freiburg, Germany
Giuseppe Nicosia	University of Catania, Italy
Anastasia Pagnoni	Università degli Studi di Milano, Italy
Jochen Pfalzgraf	Universität Salzburg, Austria
Daniel Polani	University of Hertfordshire, UK
Ricardo Reis	Univ. Federal do Rio Grande do Sul, Brazil
Richard D. Schlichting	AT&T Labs, USA
Hartmut Schmeck	KIT, Germany
Bernhard Sendhoff	Honda Research Institute, Germany
Giovanna Di Marzo Serugendo	Birkbeck University of London, UK
Joaquin Sitte	Queensland University of Technology, Australia
Roy Sterritt	University of Ulster, Northern Ireland
Janet Wiles	University of Queensland, Australia

Table of Contents

Verification and Validation

Code-Generation, Simulation and Timing Analysis

Distributed Architectures and Design Support

Biologically-Inspired Collaborative Computing (BICC 2010) 217

Ants and Adaptive Systems

Learning Classifier Systems and Collaborative Systems

Distributed and Parallel Embedded Systems (DIPES 2010)

Edited by

Bernd Kleinjohann
Universität Paderborn / C-LAB
Germany

Lisa Kleinjohann
Universität Paderborn / C-LAB
Germany

Marilyn Wolf
Georgia Institute of Technology
USA

Preface

IFIP Working Group 10.2 was pleased to sponsor DIPES 2010, the IFIP Conference on Distributed and Parallel Embedded Systems. The conference was held in Brisbane, Australia during September 20-22, 2010 as part of the IFIP World Computer Conference.

Already when establishing this conference series in 1998, the idea of distribution, where the control task is carried out by a number of controllers distributed over the entire system and connected by some interconnect network, was emphasized in its title. This idea naturally leads to the recent research field of cyber physical systems where embedded systems are no longer seen as "closed boxes" that do not expose the computing capability to the outside. Instead networked embedded systems interact with physical processes in a feedback loop leading to ever more "intelligent" applications with increased adaptability, autonomy, efficiency, functionality, reliability, safety, and usability. Examples like collision avoidance, nano-tolerance manufacturing, autonomous systems for search and rescue, zero-net energy buildings, assistive technologies and ubiquitous healthcare cover a wide range of domains influencing nearly all parts of our lives.

Hence, the design of distributed embedded systems interacting with physical processes is becoming ever more challenging and more than ever needs the interdisciplinary research of designers and researches from industry and academia. DIPES provides an excellent forum for discussing recent research activities and results.

DIPES 2010 received 37 submissions: 30 from Europe, 4 from South America, 2 from Asia/Australia, and 1 from Africa. From these submissions, the Program Committee accepted 18 papers for presentation at the conference. The contributions present advanced design methods for distributed embedded systems, starting from specification and modelling over verification and validation to scheduling, partitioning and code generation, also targeting specific architectures such as upcoming multi-core systems or reconfigurable systems.

We would like to thank all authors for their submitted papers and the Program Committee for their careful reviews. Our thanks also go to Rolf Ernst for his inspiring keynote speech on mastering the conflicting trends safety, efficiency and autonomy in embedded systems design. We gratefully acknowledge the superb organization of this event by the WCC Committee. Furthermore, we also thank our colleague Claudius Stern for his valuable support in preparing the camera-ready material for this book.

Marilyn Wolf
Bernd Kleinjohann
Lisa Kleinjohann

Safety, Efficiency and Autonomy - Mastering Conflicting Trends in Embedded Systems Design

Rolf Ernst

Technische Universitt Carolo-Wilhelmina zu Braunschweig
Institute of Computer and Network Engineering
Hans-Sommer-Str. 66,
38106 Braunschweig, Germany
r.ernst@tu-bs.de

Extended Abstract

Embedded systems have developed from single microcontrollers to networked sys-tems and are moving further on to large open systems. As an example, automotive electronics started as a single microcontroller for engine control to develop into a local network of 50 and more electronic control units connected via several network standards and gateways which are found in current cars. These networks will be ex-tended by open wireless car-to-car or car-to-infrastructure communication enabling completely new functionality, such as advanced driver assistance systems that report approaching cars that could cause an accident. Other examples are found in health-care, where patients are monitored at home connected to a hospital data base and monitoring system rather than staying in the hospital for that purpose, or in smart buildings where different control functions are integrated to minimize energy con-sumption and adapt consumption to the available energy, or in energy supply net-works that are optimized to include renewable energy production. In all these cases we observe a transition from local closed networks with a single systems integrator controlling all design aspects (such as an automotive manufacturer) to larger open networks with many independent functions and different integrators following differ-ent design objectives. The Internet plays an important role supporting that trend. Unlike closed networks with a defined topology, such systems change over the life-time of a system.

As a consequence, there is no single design process any more that controls all components and subsystems. There is no single "product" that is replicated in produc-tion, but every open networked system is somewhat different both in implemented services and in topology. Updates and upgrades change the system over its lifetime. Lab test and maintenance become increasingly difficult as neither execution platform nor system function are fully defined at design time. Many deeply embedded nodes are hard to reach or become so large in their numbers that a centrally controlled maintenance process becomes infeasible. To handle such challenges, autonomous, self learning and evolutionary system functions have been proposed which automatically adapt to changing environments

M. Hinchey et al. (Eds.): DIPES/BICC 2010, IFIP AICT 329, pp. 5–6, 2010.

and requirements. Unfortunately, this reduces system predictability which is a main requirement to guarantee system properties such as real-time and safety.

A second consequence is the convergence of system functions with different de-pendability and safety requirements. Patient monitoring at home is certainly a safety critical task that runs in a home environment that was intended for home office, entertainment and home appliances with lower safety requirements. So, if we want to use the IT environment at home for monitoring, it must be able to handle higher safety requirements. A similar requirement holds for car-to-car communication if safety critical driver assistance functions shall be implemented this way. A future traffic assistance system is likely to include pedestrians and bicyclists using their mobile devices to communicate with cars and warn of hazardous situations. This will be particularly helpful for senior persons. Now, the mobile device and its communication channels will become safety critical which is a completely new requirement.

This host of conflicting requirements is likely to become a showstopper for many advanced embedded applications if system and service providers are not able to give guarantees and assume liability. One approach is isolation of resources. Most promi-nently, time triggered protocols and architectures have been proposed that assign unique time slots to each application in order to minimize side effects. This is a con-sistent but conservative approach which has a major impact on the autonomous development and evolution of a system. Unfortunately, current hardware components have a deep state space (caches, dynamic predictions) that affects execution timing beyond even longer time slots. That makes complete isolation in time rather difficult. Multicore based systems with shared resources are a good exam-ple for the upcoming challenges.

As an alternative or complement, formal methods have been proposed that analyze system properties, such as timing and safety. Today, they are typically used in support of embedded system simulation and prototyping, but in future autonomous systems they could run automatically since test cases and evaluation are not needed. First examples have been presented in research demonstrating feasible computation requirements.

Even if the upcoming systems integration challenges can be handled with autono-my, suitable computer architectures, and formal methods, they will not be for free. Lack of cost and power efficiency could still prevent their introduction, in particular where energy resources are scarce. So, systems integration and control of autonomous embedded systems should be seen as a global optimization problem using a separate global control function, much like the control layer of a classical communication network, but requiring guarantees that are far beyond the current state.

Rialto 2.0: A Language for Heterogeneous Computations

Johan Lilius[1], Andreas Dahlin[1,2], and Lionel Morel[3]

[1] Center for Reliable Software Technology, Åbo Akademi University, Finland
[2] Turku Centre for Computer Science, Finland
{jolilius,andalin}@abo.fi
[3] Université de Lyon, France
lionel.morel@insa-lyon.fr

Abstract. Modern embedded systems are often heterogeneous in that their design requires several description paradigms, based on different models of computation and concurrency (MoCCs). In this paper we present Rialto, a formal language intended at expressing computations in several MoCCs. The distinguishing features of Rialto and its implementation are 1) A formal semantics: the language is formalized using SOS (structured operational semantics) rules; 2) Encapsulation of models of computation into policies: we thus distinguish between the syntactic elements of the language (parallelism, interrupts) and its semantics; 3) efficient implementation algorithms. Policies are expressed in the language itself, which allows for more expressive power and a sounder semantics.

1 Introduction

A model of computation (MoC) is a domain specific, often intuitive, understanding of how the computations in that domain are done: it encompasses the designer's notion of physical processes, or as Edward A. Lee [1] puts it, the "laws of physics" that govern component interactions. Many different computational models exist: Hardware is often seen as having a synchronous model of computation in the sense that everything is governed by a global clock, while software has an asynchronous MoC. A system that is described using several MoCs is called heterogeneous, and the computations it makes are *heterogeneous computations*.

We are interested in understanding what the combination of models of computation means. The need for combining several models of computation arises often when modelling embedded systems. Our specific interest is in understanding the combination of models of computation from an operational perspective. Figure 1 shows an example of a system modeled in two different models of computation: One of the states in a state machine is refined by a Synchronous dataflow (SDF) graph. While in state wait, the program can take a transition to state process and start processing events using the algorithm in the SDF diagram. However several questions need to be answered before this description can be implemented. For example: what happens if a second e1 arrives while the system is in state process?

M. Hinchey et al. (Eds.): DIPES/BICC 2010, IFIP AICT 329, pp. 7–18, 2010.

Fig. 1. A state machine, with one state refined by an SDF graph

In practice one does not program in a model of computation but in a programming language and we have therefore taken a slightly broader definition and view a model of computation as consisting of both a language and a corresponding semantics. The goal of our research can now be stated as twofold: 1. The development of a unified operational mathematical model of models of computation, and 2. the development of a textual language, in which it will be possible to program these kinds of models using a standard set of syntactic elements to represent entities in the different models of computation.

The second goal is motivated by the fact that many of the languages we have looked at (e.g. UML state machines [2], ESTEREL [3] and Harel's Statecharts [4]), use the same syntactic concepts but with different semantics. What we would like to do is pinpoint the semantic differences to certain syntactic concepts. For example the notion of parallelism exists in all three languages above, but there is certainly a difference in the semantics of parallelism between UML state machines and ESTEREL. On the other hand all languages also have a notion of interrupt (the trap-construct in ESTEREL and hierarchical transitions in both variants of Statecharts) that have very similar semantics.

To address this issue, we propose a language for expressing computations in several models of computation. The distinguishing features of Rialto and its implementation are: 1. *A formal semantics*: The language is formalized using SOS rules, 2. *Encapsulation of models of computation into policies*: This technique makes it possible to distinguish between the syntactic elements of the language (like parallelism, interrupts) and its semantics (step, interleaving, rtc, etc.) and 3. *Efficient implementation algorithms*: A Rialto program can be flattened [5]. This means that there exists a path to an efficient implementation.

The paper is structured in the following way. In section 2, we describe syntax and motivate the choice of syntactic entities. In section 3 we briefly outline the operational semantics, and the scheduling semantics of the language. Finally in the last sections, we present some examples and give a conclusion.

1.1   Related Work

The work of Lee et al. [6, 7] is a comprehensive study of different models of computation. The authors propose a formal classification framework that makes it possible to compare and express differences between models of computation. The framework is denotational and has no operational content, which means that it is possible to describe models of computation, including timed and partial order based models that we cannot model in our framework. The reason for this is that both timed and partial order based models are models that describe

program	::= **program** *name decbody*	*nullstmt*	::= **null**
	begin *body* **end;**	*body*	::= ((*label:*)? (*S*|*expr*);)*
decbody	::= (*vardec* | *owndec* | *policdec*)*	*gotostmt*	::= **goto** *label*
vardec	::= (*label:*)? **var** *name:* *Type*;	*atomicstmt*	::= [*body*]
policydec	::= **policy** *name decbody*	*returnstmt*	::= **return** *label*
	begin *body* **end;**	*suspendstmt*	::= **suspend** *label*
ifstmt	::= **if** *boolexpr* **then** *body*	*resumestmt*	::= **resume** *label*
	else *body* **endif**	*assignstmt*	::= *i* := *expr*
parstmt	::= **par** *body* || *body* **endpar**	*trapstmt*	::= **trap** *boolexpr* **do** *S*
statestmt	::= **state policy** *name*; *decbody*		*body* **endtrap**
	begin *body* **endstate**		

Fig. 2. The Rialto grammar (*S* represents any statement)

constraints on possible implementations. Although we can model dataflow in our language, we have to decide on a specific operational semantics for the dataflow. This semantics will be one of several that preserve the partial-ordering between operations described by the dataflow specification. On the other hand Girault et al. [8] present ideas for combining graphically modelled MoCs, e.g. they combine SDF graphs with finite state machines. Their idea is similar to ours in that they use state hierarchy to delineate MoCs.

We would also like to point out that in [6], Lee independently proposes an approach that is conceptually essentially the same as ours, i.e. he suggests that a language, or a set of languages, with a given abstract syntax, can be used to model very different things depending on the semantics and the model of computation connected to the syntax. More recently, Benveniste et al. have provided interesting insights on dealing with heterogeneity through so-called Tag Systems [9,10]. Their approach, which is also based on a denotational description of the possible traces of a system, provides a mathematical setting well suited for proving properties on the correctness of particular design methods. Our work, on the other hand, proposes a language for programming heterogeneous systems, letting the user designing both the hierarchical structure of the program and the scheduling policies that rule each sub-system. From a language point of view, Rialto is also close to Ptolemy [11]. Essentially, our states are Ptolemy's actors while our policies can be seen as formal descriptions of Ptolemy's directors. Central differences are that Rialto has a formal semantics and code generation, while Ptolemy is a modelling and simulation tool.

2   Syntax of the Language

In this section we define the syntax of Rialto 2.0, discuss the choice of syntactic elements and provide an example. Our language is a small language, originally designed to describe UML statecharts. Basic syntax is given in Figure 2. Each statement in a program has a unique label, given by a designer or the compiler.

The basic concept in our language is the notion of a *state*. State is seldom explicit in programming languages like VHDL or ESTEREL but many modelling languages like UML, Harel's Statecharts or Petri nets make state explicit. Rialto states can be concurrent as well as hierarchical, sequential computations inside states can be expressed in a connected action language. Syntactically a state is represented by a state - endstate block.

An *interrupt* is an event of high priority that should be reacted upon immediately, or almost immediately. In our language, a trap - endtrap block is used to monitor interrupts. Interrupts correspond to trap in ESTEREL and hierarchical transitions going upwards in the state hierarchy in UML and Harel's Statecharts. *Coroutines* are independent threads of control that can be suspended and resumed. In programming languages, threads and processes are common abstraction mechanisms for coroutines. In modelling languages coroutines play a crucial role, e.g. history states in UML and Harel's Statecharts label the thread of control in a state as a coroutine, because the state is suspended when a hierarchical transition takes the control out of the state. In Rialto 2.0, *concurrency* is indicated using the **par** statement. The parallelism is interpreted differently depending on the execution policy for the current scope.

A novelty in our language is that we make *atomicity* explicit. Atomicity defines what the smallest observable state change is. At the one extreme, in traditional programming languages, atomicity is not a part of the language itself, but is loosely defined by multiprogramming concepts like semaphores and monitors. At the other extreme, in synchronous languages like Esterel, atomicity encompasses the whole program, so that the internal workings of the program are not observable. In the middle-field between these extremes other proposals exist, e.g. the GALS (Globally Asynchronous, Locally Synchronous) semantics proposed in POLIS [12]. In GALS atomicity is confined to single state machines, while communication between state machines can be observed. In our approach we have introduced atomicity as an explicit syntactic entity, the atomic brackets [ ]. It abides to the normal rules of scoping and is thus less general than the first approach mentioned above, but using this approach we can model its interaction with other constructs at the needed level of atomicity.

The *communication policy* states how different modules of the system communicate with each other. For the moment we have taken a rather simple approach which allows us to still model many more complex approaches. We call the main communication media in our language *channels*. A channel can e.g. represent the global event queue in a UML statechart, a link in an SDF graph etc. In state diagrams, an event is an occurrence that may trigger a state transition. In UML statecharts, there is an implicit global event queue; whereas, in our language several channels can be declared and the scope of a channel declaration is the state block. The notation in our language for checking for the presence of an event on a queue is *q1.e1*, where *q1* is the queue and *e1* is an event.

Data handling is not our primary concern at the moment, as we are more interested in control-dominated programming; however, the language has a few primitive types like integers and floats. Complex types and functions are only declared in Rialto, while their implementation is deferred to the target language. This is the same approach as in ESTEREL.

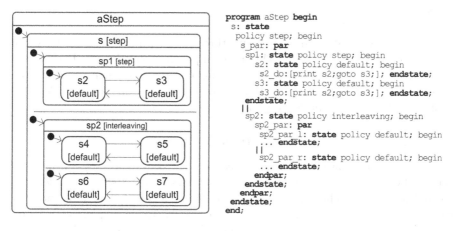

Fig. 3. A hierarchical state machine with two policies

2.1   Example

Figure 3 gives a graphical and textual representation of a simple Rialto program. This program encodes a hierarchical state machine composed of two machines sp1 and sp2 that are put in parallel with the ∥ statement. The latter is itself decomposed into two state machines put in parallel, sp2_par_l and sp2_par_r. To each state in the program is associated a scheduling policy which defines how execution is organized within the state. The default, step and interleaving policies as well as other policies are also defined in Rialto. They are discussed in section 4.

In the initial state, the state machine will be in the states s2, s4 and s6. Execution starts with the evaluation of the top-most policy shared by these three states, i.e. the policy **step** associated to s. This policy is defined (see section 4) to execute each orthogonal state. In this case both states sp1 and sp2 should be executed during the step. Our initial states are organized into partitions {s2} and {s4, s6}. The execution of s2 in the first part of the step is straightforward and it will result in a transition to the state s3. The next part of the step is to let the policy associated with {s4, s6}, namely the **interleaving** policy, decide the execution of these states. The **interleaving** policy is defined to randomly execute one of the orthogonal regions of the state it is scheduling. This means that either s4 or s6 is executed, but never both during the same step. In the scenario where s4 is executed the result of the interleaving would lead sp2 into the state {s5, s6}, while the other scenario (execution of s6) would move sp2 into {s4, s7}. The step is completed by collecting the new state of the system. The instance of the **step** policy, which is scheduling s, is responsible to collect the new observable state of the system. This state is either {s3, s5, s6} or {s3, s4, s7}. The next step will also be initiated by the policy of s, since the new state of the system also has s as its parent state.

3   Semantics

The semantics of Rialto 2.0 is split into three parts. First we define the static structure of a Rialto program. This is a graph that encodes the hierarchical and sequential relationships of statements in the program. Then we define the dynamic state of a Rialto program. Finally we explain the operational rules that are used to interpret a Rialto program.

3.1   The Static Structure of a Rialto Program

A Rialto program consists of a set of hierarchical state-machines. Each statement enclosed in a state-block has a label that acts as an "instruction address". Because of the hierarchical structure we can define a tree structure on these labels, which reflects the hierarchy of the program. There is a sequential order on some of the statements; reflected in the fact that leafs of a node in the tree may be ordered using a next relation. A program is defined as a tuple $<\mathcal{L}, \downarrow, \rightharpoonup, \mathcal{P}>$, where:

- $\mathcal{L}$ is the set of labels of the program. Labels are strings ($\mathcal{L} \subset Strings$);
- $\downarrow$ is a tree on $\mathcal{L}$;
- $\rightharpoonup$ is a partial function on $\mathcal{L}$ that defines the next relation between labels;
- $\mathcal{P}$ is the function **Label** $\rightarrow$ **Stmt**, that maps each label to a statement.

3.2   Dynamic State of a Rialto Program

The state of a Rialto program is a stack of state configurations. By default, the top element of the stack is always selected for execution. A *state configuration* is defined by $\mathcal{SC} = \mathcal{L}^* \times \mathcal{L}^*$, the set of pairs of lists of labels, representing state configurations. We have $\forall sc \in \mathcal{SC}. sc = (active, suspended)$ where: $sc.active \subseteq \mathcal{L}$ designates the set of active labels in the state configuration, while $sc.suspended \subseteq \mathcal{L}$ designates the set of suspended labels in the state configuration.

A state configuration is used to represent the dynamic state of a Rialto program, i.e. it basically contains the list of "sub-processes" that are either subject to execution (the *active* set) or that should not be executed because they have been suspended (the *suspended* set). Thus, suspend and resume actions of co-routines can easily be modelled by moving labels between the active and suspended sets.

A policy instance represents the dynamic state of execution of a particular scheduling policy associated to a particular state. It is defined as a tuple $\mathcal{P} = \mathcal{L} \times \mathcal{L} \times \mathcal{E}nv$. We have $\forall p \in \mathcal{P}. p = (callLabel, currentLabel, ownVars)$ where:

- $p.callLabel \in \mathcal{L}$ designates the label of the instance of the policy currently used (the label where the policy is "called").
- $p.currentlabel \in \mathcal{L}$ designates the label *in the policy*: the place in the policy where this instance of the policy is currently at.
- $p.ownVars \in \mathcal{E}nv$ designates the variable environments corresponding to *this* particular instance of the policy. Encodes the state of the policy.

We will use one such stack to organize the dynamic execution of a Rialto program. This stack is used to memorize execution context, in particular, when switching between user (program) and supervisor (policy) modes. Stack elements are tuples made of a *Cell*. $\mathcal{C} = \mathcal{SC} \times \mathcal{C} \times \mathcal{P}$ is the set of cells. We have: $\forall c \in \mathcal{C}.c = (sc, prevProgCtx, policyDesc)$ where:

- $c.sc \in \mathcal{SC}$ the current state configuration that gives information about suspended and active labels in the currently executing context,
- $c.policyDesc \in \mathcal{P}$ designates the current policy instance that is "leading" the execution of the current state configuration,
- $c.prevProgCtx \in \mathcal{C}$ designates the previous program context

We define *Stacks of state configurations*. $Stack(\mathcal{SC})$ denotes the type "stack of $\mathcal{SC}$ elements". We denote $top(st).active$ as $st.active$, while $top(st).suspended$ is denoted $st.suspended$. The stack $\mathcal{SC}$ can be seen as an interleaving of the program and the policy execution stacks. As we have chosen to write policies in Rialto, it is natural to use the same stack structure to represent their state. This corresponds to the normal operating system states user and supervisor. But this means that we need special functions to distinguish between these two states.

Finally we can define the *runtime state of the program* $\mathcal{RStack} : Stack \times \mathcal{Env} \times \mathcal{L}$ denotes the type "Rialto program stack". We have $\forall\ rstack \in \mathcal{RStack} = (st, env, pc)$ where st designates the program's stack, env designates the variable environment for the program and pc (program counter) is a pointer to the currently executed statement. This stack is at the heart of the semantics of the language. It is also available in the language itself. Indeed, it serves both for dealing with the basic language mechanisms (see section 3.3), and in the description of the scheduling policies.

3.3   Semantics of Statements

In this section we will discuss the operational rules for executing a Rialto program. We will assume the existence of the Rialto dynamic structures $r = (st, env, pc)$ as introduced earlier. Every statement has the same structure. The program counter points to a statement in the program array. The rule is selected by matching on this statement. There may be other conditions that have to be true. If the premise holds, then the rule is "executed". Finally the program counter is set to $\perp$ to force the control to the "enter policy" rule.

$$\frac{\mathcal{P}[\texttt{Pc}] = \text{``}stmt\text{''}\quad \text{``}otherconditions\text{''}}{\text{``}stmtstatechange\text{''}\quad \texttt{Pc} = \perp}$$

The **null** statement (0) deletes the current label from the active set and adds the successor. The **if** statement (1) is also very easily defined. We have two branches, the true and the false branch. The **par** statement (2) is a compound statement. The assumption is that all compound statements have their substatements as children in the label-tree. So the effect is to delete the label of the par-statement and to add all its children to the active set.

0	$\mathcal{P}l[Pc] = \text{``null''} \wedge Pc \neq \bot$ $st.active = st.active\backslash\{Pc\} \cup next(Pc) \wedge Pc = \bot$	6	$\mathcal{P}[Pc] = trap\ b\ do\ stmt \wedge Pc \neq \bot \wedge eval(b, Var)$ $st.active = st.active\backslash\{Pc\}\cup label(stmt) \wedge Pc = \bot$
1	$\mathcal{P}[Pc] = if\ b\ then\ stmt_1\ else\ stmt_2\ endif$ $\wedge pc \neq \bot \wedge eval(b, Var)$ $st.active = st.active\backslash\{Pc\} \cup label(stmt_1) \wedge pc = \bot$	7	$\mathcal{P}[Pc] = varname ::= expr;$ $Var[varname] = eval(expr, Var) \wedge Pc = \bot$
	$\mathcal{P}[Pc] = if\ b\ then\ stmt_2\ endif$ $\wedge pc \neq \bot \wedge \neq eval(b, Var)$ $st.active = st.active\backslash\{Pc\} \cup label(stmt_2) \wedge pc = \bot$	8	$\mathcal{P}[Pc] = state \wedge Pc \neq \bot$ $st.active = st.active\backslash\{Pc\}\cup next(Pc) \wedge Pc = \bot$
2	$\mathcal{P}[Pc] = par\ stmt(\| stmt)^*\ endpar \wedge Pc \neq \bot$ $st.active = st.active\backslash\{Pc\} \cup child(Pc) \wedge Pc = \bot$	9	$\mathcal{P}[Pc] = program \wedge Pc \neq \bot$ $st.active = st.active\backslash\{Pc\}\cup next(Pc) \wedge Pc = \bot$
3	$\mathcal{P}[Pc] = suspend\ l \wedge \exists l' \in subtree(l) : l' \in active(st)$ $\wedge Pc \neq \bot$ $st.suspended = st.suspended \cup \{st.active \cap subtree(l)\}$ $st.active = st.active\backslash\{Pc, subtree(l)\} \wedge Pc = \bot$	10	$Pc = \bot$ $Pc = lub(st.active).policyDesc$ $push(st, newC(\{Pc\}, Pc, top(st)))$
4	$\mathcal{P}[Pc] = resume\ l \wedge l \in active(st) \wedge Pc \neq \bot$ $st.suspended = st.suspended\backslash\{subtree(l)\}$ $st.active = st.active\backslash\{Pc\}$ $\cup\{st.suspended \cap subtree(l)\} \wedge Pc = \bot$	11	$Pc \neq \bot \wedge \mathcal{P}[pc] = return\ l$ $Pc = env[l] \wedge pop(st)$
5	$\mathcal{P}[Pc] = goto\ \{l_1, \ldots, l_n\} \wedge Pc \neq \bot$ $st.active = st.active\backslash\{Pc\}\cup subtree(lub(path$ $(Pc, lub(Pc, l_1, .., l_n)))) \cup \{l_1, \ldots, l_n\} \wedge Pc = \bot$	12	$Pc = \bot \wedge top(st) = \varphi$ $pop(st)$

Fig. 4. The statement (0-9) and policy rules (10-12)

The **suspend** (3) statement deletes a label from the active set and moves it into the set of suspended labels, effectively suspending the executing of the corresponding thread. There are two ways this statement can be defined. The first and the more simple one is to assume that for the statement to make sense, the label l must be active. On the other hand, when writing a scheduling policy for an operating system, it might make sense to be able to suspend a task without knowing which statement it was executing at the time. For this reason we choose a definition for **suspend** that actually suspends the subtree below it. However if this subtree is not active then the command is a "nop". **resume** (4) is the companion to **suspend**. It moves a label from the suspended set into the active set thus resuming the thread. As with the **suspend** statement we have to take care that the whole subtree is resumed.

A **goto** (5) statement should jump control from the current location to the location pointed to by the label l. For this we need to calculate the least upper bound between the goto statements label and l. Then we delete all children of lub(l, Pc) that are on the path to Pc from the active set and add all the children that are on the path to l. The **trap** (6) statement is a statement that monitors a certain condition. Anytime it is executed it checks the condition. If the condition holds the do part is executed, else nothing is done. In both cases the trap statement is reactivated. Note that for the trap statement to be effective, it should be executed at each step. However, no such execution is built into the Rialto language. Instead this has to be taken care of by the policy.

The *assignment* statement is defined in rule (7). The expression is evaluated in the environment and the resulting value is assigned to the variable. The state declaration (8) is used to delineate a hierarchical state. The nature of a state is such that the program will stay in the state until it is exited from the state explicitly, through a goto statement or by other means. Thus the execution of a **state** statement just adds the label of the first statement in the state block to the active set, while the **endstate** statement restarts the state block. Finally a **program** statement is used to start the execution of the program.

Policy Protocol. In Figure 4 the policy rules are shown. A policy controls what a step in the execution of the program consists of. It has three possible states:

1. the *initialisation*, at which point the contents of the step is calculated and the first label is selected,
2. the *execution* state, in which the policy selects the next label from a set of labels calculated in the initialisation state and
3. the *exit* state, in which the policy manipulates the stack and returns.

We define the *entry to a policy* (10) as follows. A policy execution can only start if the value of the program counter is the special label ⊥. Every rule that wants to trigger the execution of a policy must set the program counter to this special value at the end of its execution. Then we pick the top element from the state configuration stack, and find the least upper bound of this set. The label is then one whose policy we will start executing. Notice that it is not enough to select a label and then pick its policy. The state may be spread out in several hierarchical states with different policies, thus we need to pick the policy of the lowest upper bound in this hierarchy to get at the right policy. We assign the address of this policy to the program counter. Finally we add a new state configuration with only the current value of the program counter. In effect this will confine the execution to the statements of the policy.

Exiting a policy (11) is done by executing a **return** statement. The *policy return protocol* requires that the policy always returns one label, which is the next label to be executed. This label, stored in variable l, is retrieved from memory by the rule. The top of the stack is now the last label of the policy, which means that the stack must be manipulated so that this label is replaced with the next label. Finally we restore the previous *state context*.

The last rule (12) presented in Figure 4 is necessary for dealing with the special case when every active label in the current state configuration has been executed. Then we need to pop the state configuration stack to get new labels to execute. If the stack is empty the program terminates.

Some policies require "non-destructive" evaluation of statements. This situation arises e.g. in the RTC-step of UML-state-machines [2], where the RTC-step first collects all "enabled" transitions, i.e. those transitions that can be executed, because their action is on the input queue. Then this set is pruned by deleting transitions whose guard is not true, or who are disabled by some other transition higher up in the hierarchy. For this we define a function enabled : **Label** × **Var** → **Bool** that returns true if the statement attached to the label can be executed. Given the set of statements as defined above, all statements are by definition enabled all the time, except the **if** statement. For the latter, we define: enabled(**if** b **then** $stmt_1$ **else** $stmt_2$ **endif**) = eval(b, **Var**). An assumption here is that evaluation does not have any side-effects.

```
policy default
 own indefault: Boolean; var l: Label;
 begin
   l := sc.prevProgCtx.getLabelFromActiveSet();
   if indefault == true then
     indefault := false; sc.bottom().getActiveSet().add(l);
     if sc.size() > 2 then sc.popFromPrevProgCtx(); else endif;
     return __;
   else indefault := true && !sc.inPolicyMode(); return l; endif;
 end;
```

Fig. 5. The default policy

4   Policies and Examples of Models of Computation

Using Rialto, the programmer is free to program the scheduling policies, i.e. models of computations. We now illustrate the description of such policies through several examples. Due to space reasons listings of all the policies cannot be presented, but they are available in [13]. The **default policy** (Figure 5) is used for completely sequential executions. As the name suggests, the policy is used as the default choice of policy for states. Scheduling decisions cannot be made by this policy, implying that it should only be used in situations where only one label is in the active labels set for the topmost stack element, i.e. when the next statement that can be executed is unique.

The **interleaving policy** is a loose, non-deterministic execution model. For example, UML Interactions (found in communication diagrams) can be scheduled by the interleaving policy. Each time it is activated, it selects randomly *one* label among the current active labels. In Figure 6, a code listing for this policy is provided. The policy is structured according to the policy protocol in the parts: *interleaving_init*, *interleaving_exec* and *interleaving_exit*. The first part of the policy contains the necessary variable declarations and decides which part of the policy should be executed, depending on the state of the particular instance of the policy (see Figure 6a). If the policy is already in the execution step we proceed to the *interleaving_exit* part presented in Figure 6c, but if the policy is activated in the beginning of an execution step the policy enters the initialisation state. In this state, all activated labels are collected (`calculateStep(currentPc)`) and a random active label is chosen for execution. The policy will now proceed to the execution state *interleaving_exec* (Figure 6b), in which necessary modifications of stack configurations are done and the label to be executed is put on top of the stack. The execution state is always completed by a return statement; either the label to execute is returned, implying that the program counter will be set to the returned label or the ⊥ is returned, which indicates that another policy still must be invoked to decide on which statement is to be executed. In Figure 6c, the new state of the system is collected in the *exit* part of the policy. The new system state is made observable to the system by modifying the stack to reflect the new system state. Finally, the execution step is completed by returning ⊥.

The **step policy** is used when we want to allow the computation to proceed in steps. A statement is executed in each concurrent thread at each step. The step policy is suitable to use in situations where real parallelism should be allowed,

```
policy interleaving
  own instep    : Boolean;
  own stackSize: Integer;
  own lbl       : Label;
  var lfound    : Boolean;
  var step:FifoQueueOfLabel
  var l         : Label;
  var runLbl    : Label;
  var set       : SetOfLabel;
  var rLbls     : SetOfLabel;
  var scf       : StateConfig;
  var lblStr    : String;
begin
  if instep then
    goto interleaving_exit;
  else
    goto interleaving_init;
  endif;

interleaving_init:
  instep := true;
  rLbls :=sc.prevProgCtx
  .getActiveSet();
  runLbl:=sc.prevProgCtx
  .getAnyActiveSetLbl();
  step :=calculateStep(PC);
  sc.prevProgCtx
  .getActiveSet().clear();
  lbl := step.poll();
  sc.prevProgCtx
  .getActiveSet().add(lbl)
  step.poll();
```

a) initialization

```
interleaving_exec:
if step.empty() == false then
  lblStr := step.poll();
  if lblStr == __ then
    if lfound == true then
      scf.getActiveSet().add(set);
      sc.pushAbovePrevProgCtx(scf)
      scf.clear();
      rLbls.remove(set);
      lfound := false;
    else
      set.clear();
      goto interleaving_exec;
    endif;
  else
    l := lblStr;
    set.add(l);
    lfound := (lfound==false
    && l==runLbl)||lfound==true;
    goto interleaving_exec;
  endif;
else endif;

scf.getActiveSet().add(rLbls);
sc.pushToBottom(scf);
stackSize := sc.size();

if lbl == runLblthen
  return runLbl;
else
  return __;
endif;
```

b) execution

```
interleaving_exit:
instep := false;
scf:=
  sc.popFromPrevProgCtx();
scf.getActiveSet()
  .remove(lbl);
set := scf.getActiveSet();
sc.bottom().getActiveSet()
  .add(set);

if stackSize-sc.size()==1
then
  sc.popFromPrevProgCtx();
else endif;

if sc.size() > 2 then
  scf :=sc.popFromBottom();
  set:=scf.getActiveSet();
  sc.bottom().getActiveSet()
  .add(set);
else endif;

return __;
end;
```

c) exit

Fig. 6. Interleaving policy structured according to the three policy states

regardless of the chosen MoC. The policy can be seen, to some extent, as a replacement for the interleaving policy.

The **SDF policy** implements a policy for handling static dataflow. Although SDF is an abbreviation for synchronous dataflow, its underlying model is not synchronous so it can rather be described as an untimed MoC [5]. Synchronous dataflow is a special case of dataflow that requires scheduling decisions for the system can be taken already at compile time.

5   Conclusion and Future Work

We have presented Rialto, a uniform framework dedicated to the design of heterogeneous systems, based on the notion of model of computation. A MoCCs can be encoded in Rialto by writing a dedicated policy. Programs are structured using a state-based, which state being interpreted with respect to a policy that is associated to it. We have outlined several scheduling policies that are described more precisely in [13]. The latter also introduces JRialto, which is an interpreter for Rialto. Policies have been encoded and tested using JRialto.

This work can be continued in several ways. The first improvement that we are planning is to develop better abstractions for the stack manipulation. As can be seen in Figure 6 quite a lot of the code is actually housekeeping code for the stack. Better abstractions will make the writing of polices simpler and less error-prone. The main reason for the complexity is the interleaving of the policy and program contexts on the stack. A second planned extension of the work is to implement the Rialto 2.0 semantics in HOL or some other proof assistant, to be able to prove properties of programs. Finally we will need to compare Rialto with other formalisms, among those presented in section 1.1. In particular, we would like to propose Rialto as an operational implementation of the Tag Systems [10].

References

1. Lee, E.A.: Embedded software. In: Zelkowitz, M. (ed.) Advances in Computers, vol. 56. Academic Press, London (2002)
2. Lilius, J., Paltor, I.P.: Formalising UML state machines for model checking. In: France, R.B., Rumpe, B. (eds.) UML 1999. LNCS, vol. 1723, pp. 430–445. Springer, Heidelberg (1999)
3. Berry, G., Gonthier, G.: The Esterel synchronous programming language: Design, semantics, implementation. Science of Computer Programming 19(2) (1992)
4. Harel, D.: Statecharts: A visual formalism for complex systems. Science of Computer Programming 8, 231–274 (1987)
5. Björklund, D.: A Kernel Language for Unified Code Synthesis. PhD thesis, Åbo Akademi University (2005)
6. Lee, E.A., Sangiovanni-Vincentelli, A.: A framework for comparing models of computation. IEEE Transactions on Computer-Aided Design of Integrated Circuits and Systems 17(12), 1217–1229 (1997)
7. Liu, X.: Semantic Foundation of the Tagged Signal Model. PhD thesis, EECS Department, University of California, Berkeley (2005)
8. Girault, A., Lee, B., Lee, E.A.: Hierarchical finite state machines with multiple concurrency models. IEEE Transactions on Computer-Aided Design of Integrated Circuits and Systems 18(6) (June 1999)
9. Benveniste, A., Caillaud, B., Carloni, L., Sangiovanni-Vincentelli, A.: Heterogeneous reactive systems modeling: Capturing causality and the correctness of loosely time-triggered architectures (ltta). In: Proc of the Fourth Intl. Conference on Embedded Software, EMSOFT. ACM, New York (2004)
10. Benveniste, A., Caillaud, B., Carloni, L.P., Caspi, P., Sangiovanni-Vincentelli, A.L.: Composing heterogeneous reactive systems. ACM Transactions on Embedded Computing Systems, TECS (2007)
11. Eker, J., Janneck, J.W., Lee, E.A., Liu, J., Liu, X., Ludvig, J., Neuendorffer, S., Sachs, S., Xiong, Y.: Taming heterogeneity — the ptolemy approach. In: Proceedings of the IEEE, pp. 127–144 (2003)
12. Balarin, F., Giusto, P., Jurecska, A., Passerone, C., Sentovich, E., Tabbara, B., Chiodo, M., Hsieh, H., Lavagno, L., Sangiovanni-Vincentelli, A.L., Suzuki, K.: Hardware-Software Co-Design of Embedded Systems, The POLIS Approach. Kluwer Academic Publishers, Dordrecht (1997)
13. Dahlin, A.: JRialto, an implementation of the heterogeneous Rialto modelling language. Master's thesis, Åbo Akademi University (2007),
http://www.abo.fi/~andalin/mastersthesis.pdf

Scenario-Based Modeling in Industrial Information Systems

Ricardo J. Machado[1], João M. Fernandes[2], João P. Barros[3], and Luís Gomes[4]

[1] Dep. Sist. Informação, Universidade do Minho, Portugal
[2] Dep. Informática / CCTC, Universidade do Minho, Portugal
[3] Instituto Politécnico de Beja / UNINOVA-CTS, Portugal
[4] Universidade Nova de Lisboa / UNINOVA-CTS, Portugal

Abstract. This manuscript addresses the creation of scenario-based models to reason about the behavior of existing industrial information systems. In our approach the system behavior is modeled in two steps that gradually introduce detail and formality. This manuscript addresses the first step, where text-based descriptions, in the form of structured rules, are used to specify how the system is or should be regulated. Those rules can be used to create behavioral snapshots, which are collections of scenario-based descriptions that represent different instances of the system behavior. Snapshots are specified in an intuitive and graphical notation that considers the elements from the problem domain and permit designers to discuss and validate the externally observable behavior, together with the domain experts. In the second step (not fully covered in this manuscript), the system behavior is formalized with an executable model. This formal model, which in our approach is specified using the Colored Petri Net (CP-nets) language, allows the system internal behavior to be animated, simulated, and optimized. The insights gained by experimenting with the formal model can be subsequently used for reengineering the existing system.

1 Introduction

In industrial environments, reengineering an existing industrial information system, to support significant changes in the process or to improve its performance, is usually an extremely sensitive operation. In industrial environments, modifying directly the system and testing the impact of those changes on the number and quality of the produced goods is simply prohibitive, because this would imply vast losses. Additionally, some industrial information systems are intrinsically complex, since they are expected to orchestrate control, data, and communication in distributed environments, where their operation is both business- and safety-critical. Monitoring and supervision of industrial processes require huge investments in technical solutions based on real-time embedded technologies, especially developed to interconnect the production equipments with the MIS (Management Information Systems) applications [8]. Complex systems are, by their nature, hard to master and reason about. In engineering, one classical solution to this problem is to create a model, since for the specific purpose in consideration, it is simpler, safer or cheaper than the considered system. For industrial information systems, which are typically control intensive [9], this implies that we essentially need

M. Hinchey et al. (Eds.): DIPES/BICC 2010, IFIP AICT 329, pp. 19–30, 2010.

to have a model of the behavior, since this is the most critical view to take into account. This contrasts with data-centric systems, like databases or information systems, where the information and the relation among entities are the most important issues to consider.

For the majority of the existing industrial information systems in operation, there is no model with which one can immediately reason about those systems. If it does exist, typically the model does not completely reflect the system, since maintenance procedures that resulted in modifications in the system structure and behavior, were not reflected in changes in the model. This implies that techniques to obtain models for systems in use are most-needed in industrial organizations.

This manuscript presents an approach that was devised for a particular problem (i.e., an existing industrial information system), in order to obtain a behavioral model of that already existent system. This model, obtained after a careful description of the perceived behavior, permits industrial engineers (here, considered the domain experts) to reason about the system, evaluate which parts can be improved, change the model accordingly, analyze the improvements in relation to the initial version, and decide if the changes could be reflected in the industrial information system. In summary, the devised approach adopts three different artifacts:

1. Rules describe, in a textual form (written with natural language), how the system is (in an 'as-is' approach) or should be (in a 'to-be' approach) regulated, and thus implicitly specify the requirements the system is supposed to accomplish;
2. Snapshots present, in a pictorial format (by means of an intuitive and graphical notation), scenarios of the interactions among the system and the environment, illustrating application cases of the defined rules;
3. CP-nets are used to give a formal and executable nature to the snapshots, which are essential characteristics to allow reasoning capabilities.

Within a concrete reengineering problem of an existing industrial information system, the proposed approach supports the characterization of both the baseline situation (the 'as-is' system) and the future or end-state situation (the 'to-be' system). This is extremely important to allow the construction of the sequencing plan, where the strategy for changing the system from the current baseline to the target architecture is defined. It schedules multiple, concurrent, interdependent activities, and incremental builds that will evolve the industrial organization.

In this sense, the overall goal of the presented work is to simultaneously capture requirements and support animation of behavioral snapshots through Petri nets (PNs) based modeling. This manuscript focuses on the integrated usage of the first two artifacts for the considered industrial information system in an 'as-is' approach and is structured as next described. For details about the generation of CP-nets (from scenario models), please refer to [3,11,13] In Section 2, the running case study is briefly described. Section 3 presents the structuring of rules by using text-based descriptions. Section 4 illustrates the construction of snapshots by means of scenario-based descriptions. Section 5 briefly describes how CP-nets must be obtained to support reasoning activities. Section 6 is devoted to the final considerations.

2   Case Study

All artifacts presented in this manuscript are related to the production lines that manufacture car radios (Fig. 1). Each car radio is placed on top of a palette, whose track along the lines is automatically controlled. The transport system is composed of several rolling carpets that conduct the radios to the processing sites.

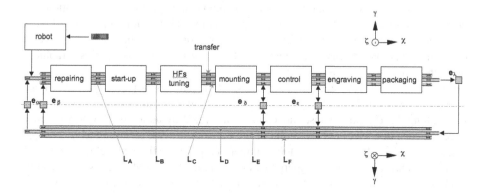

Fig. 1. The production lines of the case study

The radios are processed in pipeline by the production lines. The processing sites are geographically distributed in a sequential way, along the production lines. Each production line is composed of 6 transport tracks (that can be simply called "lines"): three on the upper level (L_A, L_B, L_C) and three on the lower level (L_D, L_E, L_F). The upper level tracks transport palettes from left to right and the lower level tracks transport palettes from right to left.

The track L_B is used to transport radios between non sequential sites. The upper tracks L_A and L_C are preferably utilized for sending the radios to the buffers of the sites (FIFOs that start at the sites). The lower tracks are used for: (1) routing malfunctioning radios to the repairing sites; (2) feed backing the sites that did not accept radios because their buffers were full; (3) transporting empty palettes to the beginning of the line. There is also a robot that receives radios from the previous production sub processes (component insertion) and puts them on track L_B. The transfers allow the change of palettes between two neighbor tracks at the same level or between a track and an elevator. The five elevators (e_α, e_β, ...) establish the linkage between the upper and the lower tracks.

3   Text-Based Descriptions

Text-based descriptions in the form of structured rules are used to specify how the system is or should be regulated. These rules constitute, from the external point of view, the functionalities of the control parts of the industrial information system.

The usage of rules at the beginning of the (re-)design phase is crucial to characterize the system, since domain experts can thus be involved to discuss, with the designers, the expected behavior for the environment elements (that constitute the plant). The option for natural language allows domain experts (frequently, persons with no scientific knowledge about specification formalisms) to effectively get involved in the definition of the rules.

Typically, the rules make reference to the elements of the environment. Taking into account the domain concepts, it is crucial to normalize the vocabulary, the notation and the graphical elements. For the case study, the graphical notation depicted in Fig. 2 was adopted, where all the basic elements of the environment (in this case, sensors and actuators), that must be sensed and controlled by the system, possess a precise graphical representation and a textual notation.

Fig. 2.a shows (1) rolling carpets that transport the palettes along the O_χ axis, whose movement is activated by actuator m_c; (2) transfers that shift palettes between transport tracks along the O_γ axis, whose movement is activated by actuator t; (3) sensors that detect palettes in a specific (x,y) point of the transport tracks, identified as i_u, $i_{l,x}$, $i_{l,y}$, i_d, i_p, $i_{r,y}$, and $i_{r,x}$; (4) bar code readers that identify the car radio that is placed on top of a palette, identified as b; (5) stoppers that block the movement of palettes in a specific (x,y) point of the transport tracks, whose state is activated by actuators s_c, s_p, s_l, and s_r; (6) processing sites, identified as $P_{n,l}$ and $P_{n,r}$.

Additionally, for each basic element of the environment, there is a tabular description that fully characterizes its functionality and its logic interface (output for sensors and input for actuators). Fig. 2.c is an example of one of these tables for one inductive sensor. The tables for the other elements in Fig. 2.a are not shown here, due to space limitations. To specify the concrete production lines, this textual notation was used to instantiate each one of the existing elements of the environment package (Fig. 2). See [10] for details, not covered in this manuscript, on how to obtain the system's components.

The notation should take into account the elements usually adopted in the problem domain, so that designers can validate the behavior with the domain experts when animating the rules with behavioral snapshots. The effort to use only elements from the problem domain (in these rule-based representations) and to avoid any reference to elements of the solution domain (in what concerns the system parts) is not enough to obtain models that can be fully understood by common domain experts. This difficulty is especially noticeable in the comprehension of the dynamic properties of the system when interacting with the environment. This means that, even with the referred efforts, those static representations should not be used to directly base the validation of the elicited requirements by the domain experts. Instead, those static representations are used to derivate behavioral snapshots.

The purpose is not to formally reason about the mathematical properties of the obtained system models, in a typical verification approach. The usage of intuitive representations of the expected system behavior, from the external point of view and in a usability driven approach, is rather preferred. The adopted tables for static characterization and pictorial representation of the plant have proven to be quite effective to accomplish the goal of simultaneously capturing requirements and supporting the animation of behavioral snapshots.

3.1   High-Level Rules

A set of generic rules (named high-level rules), that characterize the global objectives of the plant, must be defined. The concrete rules (just called rules) must contribute, either directly or indirectly, to the accomplishment of the high-level rules. For the running case study, the following high-level rule is an example:

> **[hlr 3]** Transfers and elevators must be managed as scarce resources of the environment. This implies that the time they are allocated to a given palette must be minimized and that the simultaneous accesses must be efficiently controlled.

This high-level rule of the plant is very generic and does not impose any design or implementation decision to the system. It also leaves open the way it will assure the exclusive access to the critical resources of the environment. However, although the high level rule is generic in its nature, it constitutes a proper requirement of the system, namely the need to control multiple accesses.

3.2   Rules

Due to the great complexity of the system (illustrated in the case study), it was decided to impose a functional partition that gave rise to two hierarchical levels to define the (low-level) rules: (1) level 1, where the strategic management decisions about the flows along the lines are considered; (2) level 2, where the concrete movement decisions for the palettes along the lines are taken. This 2-level partitioning guides the elicitation of the system requirements, since, for each level, a specific set of rules must be defined to specialize and refine the high-level rules.

For level 1, four sets of rules were defined: computation of the next production area (rna), site processing (rsp), buffers management (rbm), and strategic routing (rsr). In total, 15 rules of level 1 were characterized. As an example, consider one of the rules related to the site processing:

> **[rsp-2]** A car radio can be processed in a site, if the latter belongs to its processing sequence, if the task to be processed in the site was not yet accomplished over the car radio, if it is guaranteed that all the previous processing tasks were successfully executed over the car radio, and if the car radio physically arrived to the given site under coordination of the system.

For level 2, other four sets of rules were defined: transfers access (rta), elevators access (rea), fault tolerance (rft), and performance optimization (rpo). In total, 16 rules of level 2 were identified. As an example, consider one of the rules related to the elevators access:

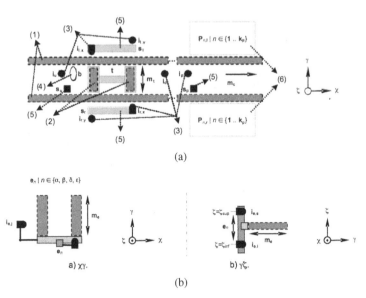

(a)

(b)

Graphical notation	Textual notation	Type	State
	$i_{line,n,site}$ $line \in \{A, B, C\}$ $n \in [0, K_p+1[$ $site \in \{u, d, p\}$	(1) inductive sensor (2) without trigger (3) two state output (**ON** e **OFF**) (4) output normally **OFF** (5) located in the upper tracks	(1) **ON**, when a kit is detected (2) **OFF**, else
	$i_{line,n,site}$ $line \in \{D, E, F\}$ $n \in [0, K_p+1[$ $site \in \{u, d\}$	(1), (2), (3), (4) the same as $i_{line,n,site} \mid line \in \{A, B, C\} \wedge site \in \{u, d, p\}$ (5) located in the lower tracks	(1), (2) the same as $i_{line,n,site} \mid line \in \{A, B, C\} \wedge site \in \{u, d, p\}$
●	$i_{line,n,site,dir}$ $line \in \{A .. F\}$ $n \in [0, K_p+1[$ $site \in \{l, r\}$ $dir = y$	(1), (2), (3), (4) the same as $i_{line,n,site} \mid line \in \{A, B, C\} \wedge site \in \{u, d, p\}$	(1), (2) the same as $i_{line,n,site} \mid line \in \{A, B, C\} \wedge site \in \{u, d, p\}$
vertical inductive sensor	$i_{line,n,site}$ $line = e$ $n = \lambda$ $site \in \{B, E\}$	(1), (2), (3), (4) the same as $i_{line,n,site} \mid line \in \{A, B, C\} \wedge site \in \{u, d, p\}$	(1), (2) the same as $i_{line,n,site} \mid line \in \{A, B, C\} \wedge site \in \{u, d, p\}$
	i_{site} $site = h$	(1), (2), (3), (4) the same as $i_{line,n,site} \mid line \in \{A, B, C\} \wedge site \in \{u, d, p\}$ (5) located at $\chi = \chi_{frt}$	(1) **ON**, when a kit is detected at $\chi = \chi_{frt}$ (2) **OFF**, else

(c)

Fig. 2. (a) Graphical notation of the case study environment; (b) Graphical notation of an elevator node; (c) Characterization of one basic element of the environment

> **[rea-2]** The routing of a palette that requires the usage of an elevator must be executed in two distinct steps; in the first one, the final destination is the transfer that is inside the elevator; in the second step, the destination is the real one and the start is the transfer inside the elevator.

This rule directly contributes to the fulfillment of high-level rule hlr-3. Nevertheless, not all high-level rules must be refined, since they are supposed to be very high-level directives to guide the development of the system. Thus, it is possible that some of them are not taken into account, especially in the early stages of system design, when functional prototyping gathers the main design effort. Typically, high-level directives that are concerned with non-functional requirements, such as fault tolerance and performance optimization, are postponed due to the need to adopt requirements prioritization techniques.

To fully characterize the interaction with the environment, all the possible rules must be elicited and documented. Thus, the system behavior is correctly and completely inferred. If this task is not properly executed, the behavioral description of the system can become incomplete and some inconsistencies may also occur.

4 Behavioral Snapshots

Scenarios are almost unanimously considered a powerful technique to capture the requirements of a given system. They are especially useful to describe the system requirements, which are typically more detailed than the user requirements. Additionally, scenarios are easier to discuss than the textual descriptions of the systems requirements, since these are inevitably interpreted in different ways by the various stakeholders, due to the usage of natural language.

UML 2.0 has several types of interaction diagrams: communication diagrams (designated collaboration diagrams in UML 1.x), sequence diagrams, interaction overview diagrams, and timing diagrams. Each type of diagram provides slightly different capabilities that make it more appropriate for certain situations. All interaction diagrams are useful for describing how a group of objects collaborate to accomplish some behavior in a given scenario. However, these diagrams are considered too technical for domain experts not able to read UML models.

In some situations, to allow a better communication with the domain experts, it is important to use a different notation, for modeling the interaction between the environment elements and the system. That notation should be based on the vocabulary of the problem domain. In the case study, the environment elements are sensors, actuators and the palettes for the car radios. If carefully selected to be as powerful and expressive as the sequence diagrams, the usage of behavioral snapshots is a proper choice, especially if the system is complex in behavioral terms and the need to discuss the system with the domain experts is paramount.

In our approach, an **instantaneous snapshot** is a static configuration of the environment elements in a sufficiently short timeframe, which assures the atomicity of the external observable system state from a behavioral point of view. A **behavioral snapshot** is a chronologically ordered collection of instantaneous snapshots that shows how elements of a system behave and react, within a given scenario. A **scenario** is a coherent sequence of actions that illustrates behaviors, starting from a well defined system configuration and in response to external stimulus. A behavioral snapshot is intended to convey the same behavior as a sequence diagram, and thus can be seen as a domain specific visual representation of a sequence diagram. Fig. 3 depicts one behavioral snapshot with four instant snapshots ($a \rightarrow b \rightarrow c \rightarrow d$), for the following rule of performance optimization:

> **[rpo 3]** If a palette, during a movement through the transfers, is in a transfer of a middle line (lines B and E, for the upper and lower nodes), it must be verified, during a pre-defined period (parameter TIME_BL), if the exit at the destination is free; if this is not the case, the palette must follow for a middle line.

In this behavioral snapshot, between instants t_1 and t_2, palette #2 is put just after the transfer C, which makes impossible for palette #1 to reach its destination. The unexpected positioning of palette #2 just after the transfer C may occur without its explicit transportation by the system, since line operators sometimes put palettes in the tracks. At instant t_3, after time TIME_BL is elapsed, the destination for palette #1 is changed to track L_B, since palette #2 is still placed just after the transfer C. In this case, track L_B is used as an alternative route, since the initial destination (track L_C) can not be reached. With this strategy, the permanence of stopped car radios at the transfers is avoided, which increases the availability of resources. This behavior maximizes the probability of car radios to have a destination to exit the node, even in situations where the initial path becomes blocked for some reason. If the track L_B is also blocked, the node is blocked until the track becomes free. At the lower tracks, the behavior is similar and track L_E is used as the alternative one.

Only for those rules that present some critical behavior requirements it is recommended to construct the corresponding behavioral snapshots. Rule rpo-3 corresponds to a critical situation. The arrows depicted in behavioral snapshots represent the final destination of palettes. Whenever the destination of a palette must be redefined, a new arrow must be drawn to represent that new destination.

The behavioral snapshots can also illustrate the application of the rules that present alternative or optional scenarios. Rule rsr-7 presents two alternative behavioral snapshots.

> **[rsr-7]** Under the request of level 2 control, level 1 control should authorize one palette to mount into one transfer, if the palette path does not present any crossing point with any other palette that is already executing its path along the same node and if the exit at the destination is free (the place just after the transfer) to receive the palette.

Fig. 4 depicts one behavioral snapshot for rule rsr-7. In this scenario, palette #2 has track L_B as its destination. At time t_1, it is possible to check that the path to track L_B is free, even though one palette (#3) is located in a transfer, while being conducted to its destination (track L_A). The movement of palette #2 can be started at time t_1, since

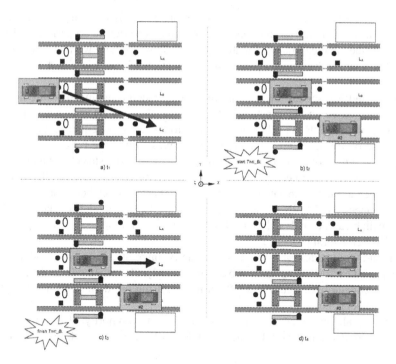

Fig. 3. A behavioral snapshot for rule rpo-3

the paths of the palettes #2, #3 and #4 do not overlap and the destination of palette #2 is free. Instants $t_2 - t_4$ show the elementary movements made simultaneously by palettes #2 and #3 to reach their destinations (palette #4 remains stopped during all the scenario).

Behavioral snapshots are a good technique for requirements elicitation. However, since they are based on scenario identification, they do not assure a complete behavior characterization and they lack semantic formalization. These characteristics justify the usage of a more formal behavioral specification to support the system detailed design, namely those based on state oriented models.

5   Specification with Colored Petri Nets

As already said, the ultimate goal of the approach partially presented here is to allow the generation of CP-nets from scenario models, in order to allow validation of the system under consideration.

The application of PNs to the specification of the behavioral view of controllers can benefit from several research results. PNs constitute a mathematical meta-model that can be animated/simulated, formally analyzed, and for which several implementation techniques are available. The designer can choose, among several PN meta-models, a specific one intentionally created to deal with the particularities of the system under consideration, like the ones referred in [4,7,15,16].

In the last years, research in scenario-based modeling is receiving a considerable attention. In this manuscript, the main general goal is to devise scenario-based modeling techniques that can be translatable to a PN model, so here we focus on previous works that address the (more generic) transformation of scenario-based models into state-based models.

Campos and Merseguer integrate performance modeling within software development process, based on the translation of almost all UML behavioral models into Generalized Stochastic PNs [1]. They explain how to obtain from sequence diagrams and statecharts a performance model representing an execution of the system.

Shatz and other colleagues propose a mapping from UML statecharts and collaboration diagrams into CP-nets [14,5]. Firstly, statecharts are converted to flat state machines, which are next translated into Object PNs (OPNs). Collaboration diagrams are used to connect these OPN models and to derive a CP-net model for the considered system, which can be analysed by rigorous techniques or simulated to infer properties some of its behavioral properties.

Pettit and Gomaa describe how CP-nets can be integrated with object-oriented designs captured by UML communication diagrams [12]. Their method translates a UML software architecture design into a CP-net model, using pre-defined CP-net templates based on object behavioral roles.

Eichner at al. introduce a formal semantics for the majority of the concepts of UML 2.0 sequence diagrams by means of PNs [2]. The approach concentrates on

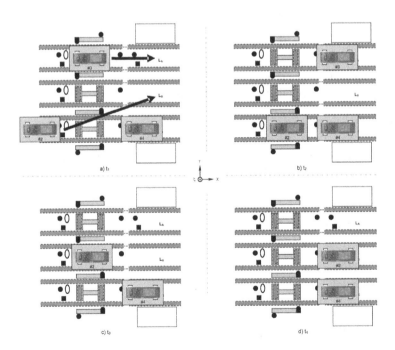

Fig. 4. First behavioral snapshot for rule rsr-7

capturing, simulating and visualizing behavior. An animation environment is reported to be under development, to allow the objects to be animated, using the PN as the main driver. Their work has some similarities with ours, namely on the usage of sequence diagrams, but uses a different PN language (M-nets) and is oriented towards sequence diagrams that describe the behavior of a set of objects.

It is important to note that the choice of which state based model to use must be made consciously, taking into account the characteristics of the system. If they have simple sequential behavior, FSMs or Statecharts are enough, but if they present several parallel activities and synchronization points, a high-level PN may be the most adequate choice to cope with the system's complexity.

In our approach, behavioral snapshots are translated into sequence diagrams to allow the application of the techniques described in [13,11,3] to allow the rigorous generation of CP-nets [6]. The transitions of these CP-nets present a strict one-to-one relationship with the messages in the sequence diagrams. So, for each message in a sequence diagram, one transition, in the corresponding CP-net, is created. In order to make that correspondence more evident, the name of each transition matches exactly the name of the corresponding message in the sequence diagram.

6 Conclusions and Future Work

In this manuscript, we present an approach that uses scenario-based descriptions and CP-net for modeling the behavior of an industrial information system. Further research is needed to investigate how the approach can be generalized, namely because the usage of an informal and intuitive notation, based on concepts and elements borrowed from the problem domain, may not have the same degree of readability.

A behavioral snapshot is an ordered collection of instant snapshots and shows how elements of a system behave and react, within a given scenario. Since the notation for the snapshots should consider the vocabulary of the problem domain, designers and domain experts can cooperate in the validation of the system behavior. The presented approach offers a client friendly scenario notation, which eases the discussion with non technical stakeholders.

Based on the sequence diagrams equivalent to the behavioral snapshots, controllers can be incrementally formalized with a state based model. CP-nets are adopted, since they are able to explicitly support the management of the environment resources in a conservative way. This incremental approach allows the completion and early correction of CP-nets by functional validation and performance optimization.

Currently, the domain concepts used in the snapshots have to be produced for each application. As a way to bridge the current gap between sequence diagrams and snapshots, the development of a domain specific meta model to describe the terms used on the sequence diagrams is under consideration.

It is also planned to incorporate into the tool workbench a mechanism to achieve the automatic generation of the animated sequence diagrams. This will allow the automatic reproduction of the very same set of scenarios that were initially described using behavioral snapshots and sequences, if the state based model is correct and complete.

References

1. Campos, J., Merseguer, J.: On the integration of UML and Petri nets in software development. In: Donatelli, S., Thiagarajan, P.S. (eds.) ICATPN 2006. LNCS, vol. 4024, pp. 19–36. Springer, Heidelberg (2006)
2. Eichner, C., Fleischhack, H., Meyer, R., Schrimpf, U., Stehno, C.: Compositional semantics for UML 2.0 sequence diagrams using Petri nets. In: Prinz, A., Reed, R., Reed, J. (eds.) SDL 2005. LNCS, vol. 3530, pp. 133–148. Springer, Heidelberg (2005)
3. Fernandes, J.M., Tjell, S., Jørgensen, J.B., Ribeiro, O.: Designing tool support for translating use cases and UML 2.0 sequence diagrams into a coloured Petri net. In: 6th Int. Workshop on Scenarios and State Machines (SCESM 2007), at ICSE 2007. IEEE CS Press, Los Alamitos (2007)
4. Gomes, L., Barros, J.P.: Structuring and composability issues in petri nets modeling. IEEE Trans. Industrial Informatics 1(2), 112–123 (2005)
5. Hu, Z., Shatz, S.M.: Mapping UML diagrams to a Petri net notation for system simulation. In: Int. Conf. on Software Engineering and Knowledge Engineering (SEKE 2004), pp. 213–219 (2004)
6. Jensen, K., Kristensen, L.M., Wells, L.: Coloured Petri nets and CPN Tools for modelling and validation of concurrent systems. Int J. on Software Tools for Technology Transfer 9(3-4), 213–254 (2007)
7. Kleinjohann, B., Tacken, J., Tahedl, C.: Towards a complete design method for embedded systems using predicate/transition-nets. In: Int. Conf. on Hardware Description Languages and Their Applications (CHDL 1997), pp. 4–23. Chapman & Hall, Boca Raton (1997)
8. Machado, R.J., Fernandes, J.M.: Heterogeneous information systems integration: organizations and tools. In: Oivo, M., Komi-Sirviö, S. (eds.) PROFES 2002. LNCS, vol. 2559, pp. 629–643. Springer, Heidelberg (2002)
9. Machado, R.J., Fernandes, J.M.: Integration of embedded software with corporate information systems. In: 1st IFIP Int. Embedded Systems Symposium (IESS 2005), pp. 169–178. Springer, Heidelberg (2005)
10. Machado, R.J., Fernandes, J.M., Rodrigues, H., Monteiro, P.: A demonstration case on the transformation of software architectures for mobile applications. In: 5th IFIP TC10 Working Conf. on Distributed and Parallel Embedded Systems (DIPES 2006), pp. 235–244. Springer, Boston (2006)
11. Machado, R.J., Lassen, K.B., Oliveira, S., Couto, M., Pinto, P.: Requirements validation: execution of UML models with CPN Tools. International Journal on Software Tools for Technology Transfer 9(3-4), 353–369 (2007)
12. Pettit, R.G., Gomaa, H.: Modeling behavioral design patterns of concurrent objects. In: 28th Int. Conf. on Software Engineering (ICSE 2006), pp. 202–211. ACM Press, New York (2006)
13. Ribeiro, O., Fernandes, J.M.: Some Rules to Transform Sequence Diagrams into Coloured Petri Nets. In: Jensen, K. (ed.) 7th Workshop and Tutorial on Practical Use of Coloured Petri Nets and the CPN Tools (CPN 2006), pp. 237–256 (2006)
14. Saldhana, J., Shatz, S.M.: UML diagrams to object Petri net models: an approach for modeling and analysis. In: Int. Conf. on Software Engineering and Knowledge Engineering (SEKE 2000), pp. 103–110 (2000)
15. Semenov, A., Koelmans, A.M., Lloyd, L., Yakovlev, A.: Designing an asynchronous processor using Petri nets. IEEE Micro 17(2), 54–64 (1997)
16. Sgroi, M., Lavagno, L., Watanabe, Y., Sangiovanni-Vincentelli, A.: Synthesis of embedded software using free-choice Petri nets. In: 36th annual ACM/IEEE Design Automation Conf. (DAC 1999), pp. 805–810. ACM, New York (1999)

An Entirely Model-Based Framework for Hardware Design and Simulation

Safouan Taha[1], Ansgar Radermacher[2], and Sébastien Gérard[2]

[1] SUPELEC Systems Sciences (E3S) – Computer Science Department, France
safouan.taha@supelec.fr
[2] LIST/LISE department of CEA (Commissariat à l'Energie Atomique), France
ansgar.radermacher@cea.fr, sebastien.gerard@cea.fr

Abstract. For a long time, the code generation from domain-specific and/or model-based languages to implementation ones remained manual and error-prone. The use of modeling was required in the early stages of development to ease the design and communicate intents, but because of the manual implementation, there were no traceability and no formal link with the final code. Model-Driven Development (MDD) was unable to win its audience.

Today, models constructed with UML have an equivalent representation in XML. And thanks to XML technologies, manipulating models for data mining, transformation or code generation becomes possible. MDD is now commonly used within the software community.

Next, for the hardware community, this work will empower the use of MDD in hardware design and simulation. It offers a completely operational framework based on OMG standards: UML and MARTE.

1 Introduction

The Object Management Group (OMG) standard UML (Unified Modeling Language) [6] is commonly used within the software community. UML has significantly improved efficiency in software development, thanks to several mechanisms, like generalization, composition, encapsulation, separation of concerns (structure/behavior), abstraction (different views), and refinement. UML is supported by many modeling tools.

By using hardware description languages like VHDL and SystemC, hardware design becomes a programming activity similar to the software development. That eases the hardware design and enables hardware simulation to avoid any risky implementations. But in practice, just like software, hardware programming is implementation-oriented and doesn't match the real issues of hardware design and architecture exploration.

Taking into account this analogy between hardware design and software, we developed an entire and operational framework that is completely based on models of concepts and constructs specific to the hardware domain. Such framework let the hardware designer benefit from all well-known features of DSLs and MDD. Our framework is composed of a standardized Hardware Resource Modeling (HRM) language and a powerful simulation engine.

M. Hinchey et al. (Eds.): DIPES/BICC 2010, IFIP AICT 329, pp. 31–42, 2010.

In this paper, we will first describe a modeling methodology which helps to resourcefully use HRM for building consistent models. This HRM methodology is a set of guidelines within an incremental process of successive hardware compositions. Then, we will illustrate the efficiency of such model-based framework on a large case study: we will apply the HRM methodology to create the model of a heterogeneous hardware platform and we will simulate it.

The paper is organized as follows. The next section introduces in brief the HRM profile. Section 3 describes the modeling methodology based on HRM. Section 4 explains how the simulation engine works. Where the last section depicts the whole design process on a case study.

2   Hardware Resource Model

The purpose of HRM is to adopt UML as a hardware design language to benefit from its features and tools, and to unify the (software/hardware) co-design process of embedded systems. Thanks to the UML extension mechanism, the HRM profile [8] extends UML with hardware concepts and semantics. HRM is part of the new OMG standard MARTE [7] (Modeling and Analysis of Real-Time Embedded systems). HRM is intended to serve for description of existing or for conception of new hardware platforms, through different views and detail levels. HRM covers a large scope:

Software design and allocation: The hardware designer may use a high level hardware description model of the targeted platform architecture, with only key properties of the available resources like the instruction set family, the memory size... Such abstract model is a formal alternative to block diagrams that are communicated to software teams and system architects.

Analysis: Analysis needs specialized hardware description model. The nature of details depends on the analysis focus. For example, schedulability analysis requires details on the processor throughput, memory organization and communication bandwidth, whereas power analysis will focus on power consumption, heat dissipation and the layout of the hardware components. HRM uses the UML ability to project different views of the same model.

Simulation: It is based on detailed hardware models (see section 4). The required level of detail depends on the simulation accuracy. The performance simulation needs a fine description of the processor microarchitecture and memory timings, whereas many functional simulators simply require entering the instruction set family.

HRM is grouping most of hardware concepts under a hierarchical taxonomy with several categories depending on their nature, functionality, technology and form. The HRM profile is composed of two sub-profiles, a logical profile that classifies hardware resources depending on their functional properties, and a physical one that concentrates on their physical nature. The logical and physical views are complementary. They provide two different abstractions of hardware that should be merged to obtain the whole model. Each sub-profile is, in turn, composed of many metamodels as shown in figure 1.

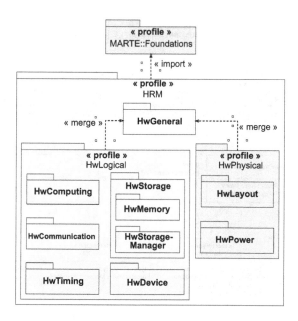

Fig. 1. HRM structure overview

Logical Model. The objective of the logical model is to provide a functional classification of hardware resources, whether if they are computing, storage, communication, timing or auxiliary devices. This classification is mainly based on services that each resource offers. As shown in figure 1, there is a specific metamodel for each hardware logical category.

HRM contains most of hardware resources thanks to a big range of stereotypes that are organized under a tree of successive inheritances from generic stereotypes to specific ones. This is the reason behind the ability of the HRM profile to cover many detail levels. For example, the *HwMemory* metamodel shown in figure 2 reveals the HRM accuracy and its layered architecture. The *HwMemory* stereotype denotes a given amount of memory. It has three attributes, *memorySize*, *addressSize* and *timings*. This latter is a datatype to annotate detailed timing durations. *HwMemory* could be an *HwProcessingMemory* symbolizing a fast and working memory, or an *HwStorageMemory* for permanent and relatively time consuming storage devices...

Physical Model. The hardware physical model represents hardware resources as physical components with physical properties. As most of embedded systems have limited area and weight, hard environmental conditions and a predetermined autonomy, this view enables layout, cost, power analysis and autonomy optimization The *HwPhysical* profile contains two metamodels: *HwLayout* and *HwPower*.

For more details on HRM, please refer to [8] and the MARTE document [7].

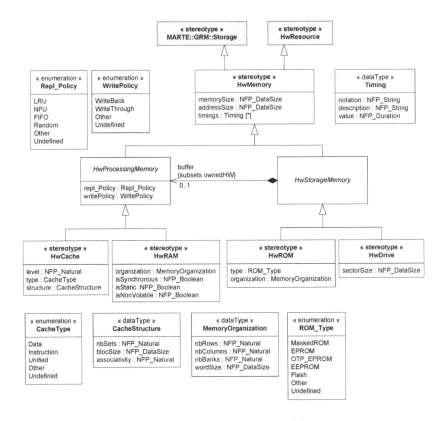

Fig. 2. HwMemory metamodel

As HRM is serialized into the OMG standard XML Metadata Interchange (XMI) [5], it can be used within most UML-based modeling tools. In our case, we use the Papyrus UML tool [3] that is developed within our laboratory (CEA LIST/LISE). Papyrus is based on the Eclipse Modeling Framework and provides a MARTE plug-in.

3   Hardware Modeling Methodology

As the HRM profile extends the generic UML kernel metaclasses, it can be used within all UML diagrams. UML offers a big amount of notations and diagrams, it also includes many variation points. Consequently, it is a common practice to adopt modeling methodologies that restrain the UML mechanisms to use, fixate their semantics and bring consistency rules. Considering that the hardware designers are not used to UML-based modeling, such a modeling methodology is quite necessary.

The HRM modeling methodology is mainly based on the UML2 Composite Structure diagram, since this latter has a clear graphical representation of composition and supports the *Part*, *Port* and *Connector* concepts that are well-adapted to hardware modeling.

The HRM modeling methodology is iterative, one iteration corresponds to the entire modeling of only one resource from the hardware platform. Each iteration is composed of many modeling steps grouped into three phases: class definition, internal structure modeling and instantiation. Our methodology is also incremental (bottom-up), it starts from modeling elementary resources, and with successive compositions, it reaches the whole platform model.

Class Definition

1. Choose the next resource to model taking into account the incremental order (partial order) of compositions. Create the corresponding class using the resource name. Specify its inheritances from previously defined classes (from previous iterations). Notice that the inheritance mechanism is an efficient way to classify hardware resources depending on their nature.

2. Apply the HRM stereotype matching the resource type. It is a key step where we extend, in a simple manner, the UML class structure and semantics with the hardware specific ones. To avoid useless decompositions, many HRM stereotypes could be applied simultaneously if the current resource plays many roles within the hardware platform (e.g. a typical chipset is either *HwMemoryManager*, *HwBridge*, *HwArbiter*...). Furthermore, stereotypes from different profiles may also be applied if necessary. UML supports these options.

3. Assign values to some of the tag definitions (stereotype attributes), especially those that match the class level and are common to all the resources represented by the current class. For example, if the instruction set of a *HwProcessor* could be assigned at this level, its frequency or its cache size should be specified later within the steps of integration and instantiation. Notice that the HRM tag definitions are optional and they should be specified only if necessary.

4. Even if HRM is very detailed, it is a standard that mainly groups generic and common properties. Therefore, if at this stage of modeling, the hardware designer still needs to specify additional properties of the current resource, he should use UML ordinary, in this step, regardless of HRM.
   - Define specific attributes. They must be strictly typed, and for this, we can exploit the UML typing mechanisms like *DataType* or Enumeration. We can also use the MARTE library of basic types *BasicNFP_Types* or define new complex types (with physical measurements and units) thanks to the NFP profile [7] of MARTE.

   - Add associations when necessary between the current class and the previously defined ones. When an association corresponds to a hardware connection, we can apply corresponding stereotypes (*HwMedia*, *HwBus*...) on it. Notice that class compositions will be defined during the next step.

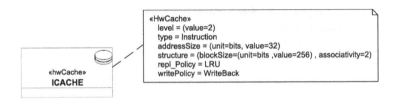

Fig. 3. ICACHE class definition

- Define operations and use the *HwResourceService* stereotype and the *providedServices* tag definition to settle if they are provided services of the current resource.

Figure 3 shows a light model of an instruction cache class that we typically obtain at the end of this first iteration phase.

Internal Structure Modeling

5. To define the internal structure of the resource being modeled, insert UML *Part*(s) typed by resources specified in previous iterations. We see here the reason behind the use of the Composite Structure diagram in our methodology and why we are following the incremental compositions order. Each *Part* has a multiplicity that is a simple and powerful mechanism for the representation of repetitive structures, very frequent in the area of hardware. Each *Part* must also display its ports, which correspond to those of its class type (see step 8).

6. Once *Part*(s) are typed as resources and taking into account their new context, it is important to reapply stereotypes and assign local values to their specific tag definitions. Indeed, if we have previously modeled resource in absolute terms regardless of its enclosing component, it should be now more specifically characterized. The hardware designer is limited to the reapplication of stereotypes previously applied to the typing class or one of its class parents. It is a rule of consistency between the nature of the resource and the roles it can play within different platforms.

7. Connect these parts by means of UML *Connector*(s) linking their ports. Such connectors must be typed by either an association defined in step 4 or a HRM meta-association. They could also be stereotyped as *HwMedia*, *HwBus* or *HwBridge* depending on their role.

8. Define boundary ports. In the UML Composite Structure diagram, a *Port* is a *Property* that is not necessarily typed but has a name and a multiplicity. Under this methodology, we require that each port and/or its class type must be stereotyped as a *HwEndPoint*.
   Use then UML *Connector*(s) to define delegations from the class ports to the ports of its subcomponents.

Figure 4 shows a model of a composite memory class that we typically obtain at the end of this second phase. It contains the ICACHE shown in figure 3.

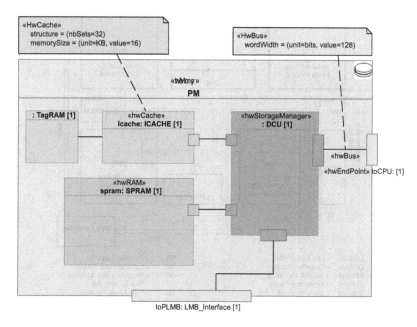

Fig. 4. PMI (Program Memory Interface) internal structure modeling

Instantiation

9. Step 9 is a test step, which unlike other steps, does nothing to the model under construction. Our methodology is iterative and incremental in the sense of composition, since the designer begins with basic resources and then iterates to resources increasingly composite. If the current class represents the entire platform, this means that the model is complete, and that normally at this stage, all resources are referenced from the current platform class. We skip therefore to step 10 for the model instantiation. Otherwise we iterate from step 1, and we choose the next resource to model from those that have all their subcomponents already modeled in previous iterations.

For example, figure 5 represents the block diagram of the complex CPU Subsystem of the *Infineon* microcontroller TC1796 [2]. Figure 6 shows its entire platform class model that was achieved through this methodology. If the first diagram is only a useless drawing, the second one is formal and may be used for analysis and simulation.

10. Finally, once the class of the whole platform is reached, instantiate the model giving values to slots (attributes, parts and ports), linking them and again applying stereotypes (if needed) on instances with assigning tag values corresponding to instance level semantics.

By the several steps of this methodology, we propose an efficient use of the HRM profile. We limit for this, the UML mechanisms to use and we give them

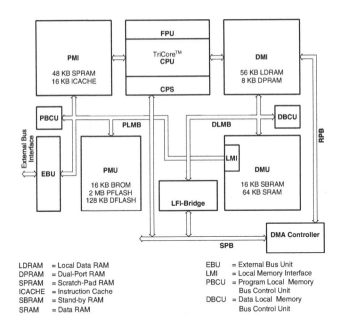

Fig. 5. TC1796 CPU Subsystem (block diagram)

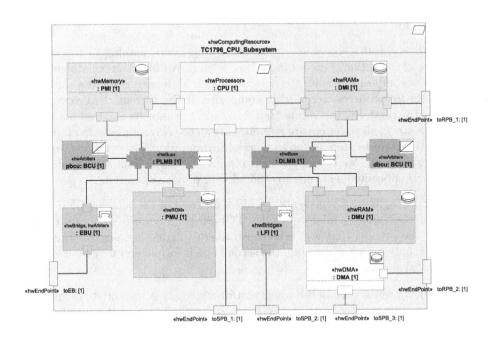

Fig. 6. TC1796 final platform class

clear semantics. However our methodology is advisory, even if it includes good practices, the use of HRM independently of it, is obviously possible. It is nevertheless adapted to new users of UML and ensures consistency of the final model. When a platform model is consistent you can use it for various manipulations, such as simulation that we will detail in the next section.

4   Hardware Simulation

The simulation of a hardware architecture to test its ability to provide an adequate execution platform for the software application, provides many benefits. It improves flexibility, accelerates the development process, saves time and money, and enables effective communication between software and hardware flows. Therefore, developers are no longer dependent on the availability of the physical hardware and they can explore in the early stages of design, several architectures, including new configurations. The simulation also offers several advances in debugging software and hardware.

Designated as one of the three HRM use cases, the idea behind our simulation engine is to use HRM/UML as a common interface to hardware simulation tools. Indeed, the user can take advantage of HRM/UML to describe a hardware architecture in a model that will be automatically translated and interpreted by simulation tools.

Most simulation tools are only Instruction Set Simulators (ISS) that simulate a processor with some RAM running assembler code. However, we simulate a whole execution platform with processors, memory, peripherals, and different means of communication. Such a simulation environment should also run complex software applications without any modification and start operating systems.

After a deep study we adopt Simics [1] as a target of our model-based simulation engine. Simics is capable of simulating the full-system. All common embedded components are available including PowerPC, ARM, SPARC, x86 processors, FLASH memories, I2C busses, serial ports and timers. Also, defining new components is feasible. Simics platform runs the same binary software as would run the real hardware target including operating systems and device drivers. Simics is at the origin a fast functional system-level simulator, it does not handle timing considerations. But recently, a Micro Architectural Interface was designed to overcome these limitations and provides cycle-accurate simulations.

Today, Simics is widely used by the telecom, networking, military/aerospace (including commercial avionics and space systems), high-performance computing, and semiconductor industries.

To start, we modeled using HRM all components supported by Simics, we get then a library of resources' models. This library will be provided to the user who will apply our HRM methodology to create his hardware platform. The user can use the resources of the library as basic components and with successive iterations in the sense of compositions, he can construct the whole hardware platform. Once done, he can automatically generate the equivalent script that will run under Simics. This process is illustrated in figure 7.

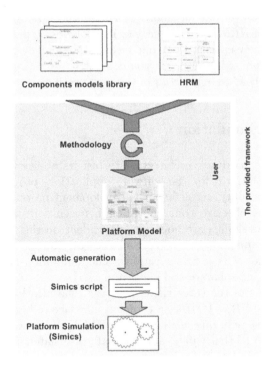

Fig. 7. Simulation engine process

Modeling the Library of Simics Components. As Simics is implemented in Python and C++, our task was easier because Simics has already an object-oriented structure. Nevertheless it has a specific terminology and semantics wider than the object paradigm ones. We had then to translate each of its concepts according to UML/HRM. In brief, the concept of *component* is central in Simics, it denotes a hardware resource that can be used in the construction of a platform (called *machine* or *configuration*), a *component* can be implemented by one or more *classes*.

Code Generation. We had primarily used Acceleo [4] that we reinforced by a set of services we have developed in Java (thanks to the Eclipse UML2 plug-in). Acceleo generates code from models by interpreting a script of declarative rules.

Our first step of code generation is to explore the platform subcomponents and generate the adequate Simics creation commands. To parametrize the Simics components, we have developed indeed a method that checks whether a stereotype is applied and gets the corresponding value of the tag definition when specified.

The second step of code generation is to produce connection commands between the Simics components created during the previous step. To do this, we take one by one all connectors of the platform that are linking the ports of the various subcomponents. We check that the ports are similar and have consistent directions. Note however that connection commands may be inappropriate for technological or generational reasons and will therefore be rejected by Simics.

The first objective of this simulation engine was to demonstrate that HRM is complete and it offers a level of detail sufficient to interface the most accurate simulation tools. The second objective was to provide the hardware designer with a rich and automated model-based tool to assist him in designing platforms. Let's illustrate it on a real complex example.

5 Case Study

For our case study shown in figure 8, we consider a highly heterogeneous hardware platform, since it combines two very different computing resources: *board* and *boardSMP*. The first is a uniprocessor from the *PowerPC* family and has a *32bits* architecture. While the second is a multiprocessor (SMP) from the *Itanium* family with a *64bits* architecture, it may contain up to 32 processors sharing a *1GiBytes* memory. We connected *board* and *boardSMP* via an *Ethernet* link *ethLink*, but it was necessary, first, to provide the *boardSMP* with an Ethernet card *CardPciEth* that we connected to a PCI port. We also have connected to

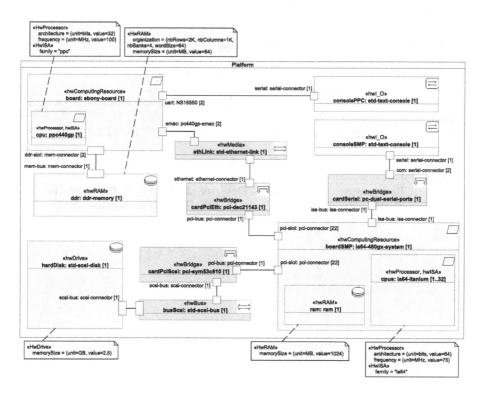

Fig. 8. Heterogeneous platform model

the *boardSMP* a *SCSI* hard disk harddisk via a *HwBridge pci-sym53c810*. *board* has a *64MiBytes ddr* memory and the exact description of its organization is specified in terms of *nbRows, nbColumns, nbBanks...*

Figure 8 shows the whole platform class that was obtained applying our methodology (within the Papyrus UML tool), we used then our simulation engine to generate the corresponding Simics script. To simulate this platform, we started two different Linux 2.4, the first on *board* was compiled for the *ppc32* instruction set and the second on *boardSMP* was compiled for the *ia64* instruction set with the SMP option activated. Both run and communicate perfectly.

6   Conclusion

Having no equals that meet the needs of high-level description of hardware architectures and with the standardization of MARTE, HRM is dedicated to a massive use within the industry. In this paper, we first describe a modeling methodology which helps to resourcefully use HRM for building consistent platform models. We developed then an innovative simulation framework that is hundred percent model-based and supports the widely-used simulator Simics.

References

1. Simics Platform, http://www.virtutech.com
2. TriCore Architecture, http://www.infineon.com/tricore
3. CEA LIST: Papyrus UML2 Tool, http://www.papyrusuml.org
4. Obeo: Acceleo Generator (2007), http://www.acceleo.org
5. Object Management Group, Inc.: MOF 2.0 XMI Mapping Specification, Version 2.1. Tech. Rep. 2005-09-01, OMG
6. Object Management Group, Inc.: OMG UML Superstructure, V2.1.2. Tech. Rep. formal/2007-11-02, OMG (2007)
7. Object Management Group, Inc.: Uml profile for marte, beta 2. Tech. Rep. ptc/08-06-09, OMG (June 2008)
8. Taha, S., Radermacher, A., Gerard, S., Dekeyser, J.L.: An open framework for detailed hardware modeling. In: SIES, pp. 118–125. IEEE, Los Alamitos (2007)

Extending the Standard Execution Model of UML for Real-Time Systems

Abderraouf Benyahia[1,2], Arnaud Cuccuru[2], Safouan Taha[1], François Terrier[2], Frédéric Boulanger[1], and Sébastien Gérard[2]

[1] SUPELEC Systems Sciences (E3S) Computer Science Department,
91192 Gif-Sur-Yvette cedex, France
[2] CEA LIST, 91191 Gif-Sur-Yvette cedex, France
{abderraouf.benyahia,safouan.taha,frederic.boulanger}@supelec.fr,
{arnaud.cuccuru,francois.terrier,sebastien.gerard}@cea.fr

Abstract. The ongoing OMG standard on the "Semantics of a Foundational Subset for Executable UML Models" identifies a subset of UML (called fUML, for Foundational UML), for which it defines a general-purpose execution model. This execution model therefore captures an executable semantics for fUML, providing an unambiguous basis for various kinds of model-based exploitations (model transformation, code generation, analysis, simulation, debugging etc.). This kind of facility is of great interest for the domain of real time systems, where analysis of system behavior is very sensible. One may therefore wonder if the general-purpose execution model of fUML can be used to reflect execution semantics concerns of real-time systems (e.g., concurrency, synchronization, and scheduling.). It would practically mean that it is possible to leverage on this precise semantic foundation (and all the work that its definition implied) to capture the precise execution semantics of real-time systems. In this paper, we show that this approach is not directly feasible, because of the way concurrency and asynchronous communications are actually handled in the fUML execution model. However, we show that introducing support for these aspects is technically feasible and reasonable in terms of effort and we propose lightweight modifications of the Execution model to illustrate our purpose.

Keywords: fUML, MDD, Model Simulation, Concurrent systems, Real-time systems.

1 Introduction

Profiles are the default UML extension mechanism for tailoring UML2 to specific application domains, from both syntactic and semantic terms. Extending UML2 syntax is well achieved, with explicit stereotype definitions capturing the syntactic extensions. Unfortunately, the semantic extensions (potentially implied by a profile) have not yet reached a similar degree of formalization. They usually take the form of a natural language description, just like the semantic description of the UML2 metamodel. The informal nature of this description leaves the door open to several (potentially contradictory) interpretations of a given model and does not lend itself to unambiguous model-based exploitations. This is particularly critical when considering

M. Hinchey et al. (Eds.): DIPES/BICC 2010, IFIP AICT 329, pp. 43–54, 2010.
© IFIP International Federation for Information Processing 2010

complex notions such as time and concurrency, which are central issues to the design of real-time and embedded software.

Things should however evolve with the ongoing OMG standard on the semantics of a foundational subset for executable UML models [2]. This standard indeed defines a formal operational semantics for a subset of UML2 called fUML (foundational UML). The operational semantics of fUML takes the form of an executable UML model called "Execution Model" (that is to say, a UML model defined with elements from the fUML subset[1]), which is precise enough to be considered as an interpreter for fUML models. While foundational, this subset includes non-trivial mechanisms carrying concurrent and asynchronous execution semantics, such as active objects (i.e., objects with their own execution thread) and asynchronous communications via signal passing. These notions are essential when considering concurrent real-time systems, such as in the MARTE profile [1] (Modeling and Analysis of Real-Time and Embedded systems) and in particular in its HLAM sub-profile (High Level Application Modeling), which provides support for designing concurrent real-time systems with extensions inspired by the concept of real-time active object [4][5][6].

Our long term objective is to reflect timed and concurrent execution semantics as introduced in HLAM by extending the general-purpose Execution Model of fUML. Ideally, this extension would first rely on fUML mechanisms for concurrency and asynchronous communications, and then add support for time. This extended Execution Model would typically provide support for model-based simulation, a design technique that has proven useful for rapid prototyping of real-time and embedded systems [7][8].

While the rationale for this approach sounds quite obvious, we believe that it cannot be directly put into practice. Our main obstacle concerns the way concurrency (i.e., active objects) and asynchronous communications (i.e., via signals) are actually supported. While the fUML specification of Execution Model leaves the door open to support some slightly different execution paradigms by including a few explicit semantics variation points (section 8.2.2 of [2]), no key variation points are defined regarding concurrency and asynchronous communications. Furthermore, the Execution Model does not identify an explicit entity responsible (such as scheduler) for the management of concurrent entities. In order to properly handle these aspects, some modifications are needed in the Execution model. The main contribution of this article is to propose such lightweight modifications. These propositions can be considered as a first step towards our long-term objective: reflecting the execution semantics of real-time systems by specializing the fUML execution model.

In section 2, we start by highlighting fUML limitations. In section 3, we discuss works related to model-based simulation of concurrent systems. We show how principles underlying these approaches could be integrated in the standard Execution Model of UML. In section 4 we propose a modification of the Execution Model, which mainly consists in introducing an explicit scheduler. Section 5 then concludes this article and sets guidelines for future research.

---

[1] In order to break circularity, some of the fUML elements have a formal axiomatic description.

2 Limitations of fUML Regarding Support for Concurrency and Asynchronous Communications

As explained in the introduction to this article, fUML [2] formalizes the execution semantics of a subset of the UML2 metamodel. Particularly, this subset contains mechanisms for the description of concurrent systems (i.e., classes can be active. See [12], section *13.3.8* for more details). It also includes support for the specification of asynchronous communications (i.e., Signal, SendSignalAction, SignalEvent, see [12], section *13.12.24*, *11.3.45* and *13.3.25*). The semantic formalization, called Execution Model, takes the form of a UML model specified with the fUML subset itself, simply by considering the fact that the fUML execution engine is a particular executable fUML model. It defines the operational procedure for the dynamic changes required during the execution of a fUML model. In the following section, we start by providing an overview of the Execution Model. Then, we discuss limitations of the Execution Model regarding the management of concurrent executions.

2.1 Overview the fUML Execution Model

The Execution Model has been defined following the Visitor design pattern [11], where almost each class of the Execution Model has a relationship with a class from the fUML syntax subset (except for a package called *Loci*, where classes *Locus*, *Executor* and *ExecutionFactory* are not visitors, and are just used for setting up the execution engine).

Each visitor class of the Execution Model basically provides an interpretation for the associated fUML class, and therefore explicitly captures the corresponding execution semantics. Globally, the Execution Model can be considered as the model of an interpreter for UML models specified with the fUML subset. Figure 1 illustrates a part of this global architecture. It represents the relationship between syntactic elements of the fUML subset (left-hand side of Figure 1) and corresponding visitors of the Execution Model (right-hand side part of Figure 1). For example, the execution semantics associated with the concept of *Class* (which is part of the fUML subset) is defined by the class *Object* from the execution model.

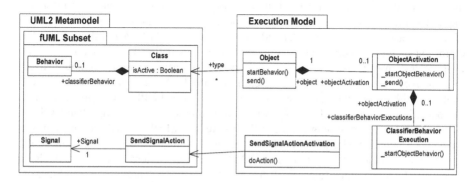

Fig. 1. The global architecture of execution model

It is important to notice that the Execution Model exploits the mechanisms provided by fUML for concurrency and asynchronous communications. For example, classes *ObjectActivation* (which encapsulates the execution of an event dispatch loop, enabling a given active object to react to event occurrences) and *ClassifierBehaviorExecution* (which encapsulates the concurrent execution of the classifier behavior associated with the type of an object) are active classes, i.e., classes whose instances have their own thread of control. In principle, the Execution Model thus explicitly captures the concurrent aspects of fUML execution semantics. In practice, however, the management of concurrency is buried inside the architecture of the fUML Execution Model. Regarding our preliminary objective, this is an important limitation of the fUML Execution Model: The place where concurrency is handled in the Execution Model must be accessible and explicit, so that it can be conveniently tailored to the needs of particular application domains. In the two following sections, we first discuss this limitation and its relationship with the usage of Java as a concrete notation for the description of behavioral aspects of the fUML Execution Model (i.e., mainly, behaviors associated with operations of classes from the Execution Model). Then, we more generally discuss the absence, in the architecture of the Execution Model, of explicit mechanisms for scheduling and synchronizing instances of concurrent entities (i.e., active objects).

2.2 On the Actual Java Specification of the Execution Model

UML activities are the only behavioral formalism supported by fUML. In the Execution Model, they are practically used to specify the implementations of every operation and/or classifier behaviors. However, for significant behaviors, these diagrams quickly become large and complex and thus hard to understand. Instead of using such complex graphical notation (or defining from scratch a new textual notation for activities), the authors of the fUML specification have used Java as a concrete textual notation for capturing behavioral aspects of the Execution Model, respecting a strict "Java to Activities" mapping (see. Appendix A of [2] for details).

In other words, Java statements should just be considered as a concrete and concise textual syntax for UML activities. Nevertheless, the positive side effect regarding the choice of Java is that the Execution Model takes an executable form, which could be used as a model interpreter for UML models respecting the fUML subset. A reference implementation is thereby provided by Model Driven Solutions [3]. However, the "Java to Activities" mapping (defined in Appendix A of [2], and followed for the definition of the Execution Model) does not consider native Java threading mechanisms. fUML mechanisms related to concurrency and asynchronous communications (e.g., active objects, signal emissions, etc.) are simply depicted using syntactic conventions, with no explicit manifestation of the Java Thread API. For example, a call to the operation _send() of class *ObjectActivation* (depicted in the right-hand side of Figure 1) is the Java mapping for a SendSignalAction, which normally corresponds to an asynchronous signal emission. Therefore, an interpreter strictly conforming to the Java implementation of the Execution Model can only interpret fUML models as sequential Java programs (e.g., a call to _send() remains a synchronous and blocking Java call).

To be clear, the fact that the resulting Java implementation is mono-threaded and purely sequential is not a fundamental issue *per se*. Indeed, as we will see in the Related Works section, most state-of-the-art simulation tools are also sequential and mono-threaded. However, these tools include explicit mechanisms for simulating concurrency, usually with a well indentified entity which is responsible for triggering the execution of the various behaviors, according to a given scheduling policy. The real issue with the current architecture of the Execution Model is that there are no equivalent mechanisms, and that executions obtained via the Execution Model are purely sequential. Let us illustrate this issue with a simple example.

The example illustrated in Figure 2 describes a simple application model that we want to simulate using the fUML Execution Model. It contains two active classes (C1 and C2) whose instances will communicate via signal exchanges (S1 and S2). The classifier behaviors of C1 and C2 are respectively described by activities C1Behavior and C2Behavior. C1 asynchronously sends a signal S1 to C2, and then waits for a reception of a signal S2 from C2. On the other side, C2 waits to receive a signal s1 from C1. After the reception, it asynchronously sends a signal S2 to C1.

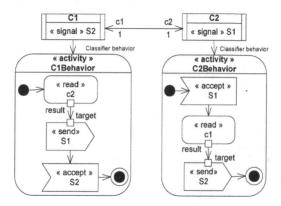

Fig. 2. fUML model of a simple asynchronous system

Figure 3 shows a sequence diagram of a sequential execution trace respecting the java statements of the operational fUML Execution Model. The hypothesis for this execution trace is that two active objects c1:C1 and c2:C2 have been created, and that c2 has been started before c1[2]. Lifelines appearing in the sequence diagram of Figure 3 represent instances of classes from the fUML execution model. The interactions between these lifelines show how the model specified in Figure 2 is actually interpreted by the fUML Execution Model (in this case, all the execution is carried out in one thread).

On the right-hand side of Figure 3, the instance of *ClassifierBehaviorExecution* represents the execution of the classifier behavior of c2. Once it is started, it performs the *AcceptEventAction*. From the Execution Model standpoint, It consists in registering an *EventAccepter* for S1 within a list of waiting event accepters (i.e., call to operation

---

[2] Another fundamental limitation of this sequential Java interpretation is that it is non-deterministic. The resulting execution trace will be different if c1 is started before c2.

register()). It captures the fact that the execution of c2 is now waiting for an occurrence of S1. However, the execution of c2 does not actually wait for an occurrence of S1 (i.e., with the strict interpretation of the Java statements, the *ClassifierBehaviorExecution* is not executed on its own thread). Instead, it returns to the main activity, which continues the execution by starting the classifier behavior of c1. The execution flow of c2's *ClassifierBehaviorExecution* will be further continued, after an explicit notification. On the left-hand side of Figure 3, when the classifier behavior of c1 starts (i.e., call to *execute()* emitted by the *ActivityExecution*), it executes the *SendSignalAction*. The semantics associated with the *SendSignalAction* is captured in the execution model by calling the operation *send()* of target object c2, which in turn calls the operation *send()* of *ObjectActivation*. It results in adding a signal instance s1 to the event pool associated with the object activation of c2.

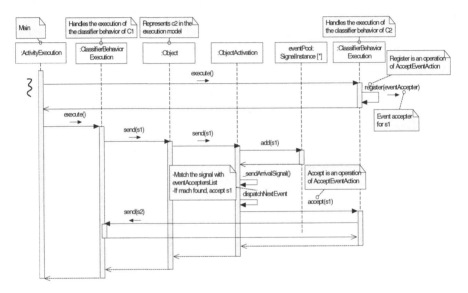

Fig. 3. Execution trace from a sequential implementation of the Execution Model

In order to notify the *ClassifierBehaviorExecution* of c2 that a signal is available for dispatch (and therefore that its execution flow can potentially be continued if there is a matching *EventAccepter*), a call to *_send(new ArrivalSignal())* is emitted, which in turn causes a call to *dispatchNextEvent()*. This operation dispatches a signal from the event pool and matches it against the list of waiting event accepters. If an event accepter matches, a call to the *accept* operation of the *AcceptEventAction* is performed and the classifier behavior of c2 continues the execution by sending signal S2 to c1. The execution of this *SendSignalAction* results in a call to operation *send()* on target object c1, which in turn implies the sequencing of operations described above.

Beyond these technical details, it is important to notice here that this sequential propagation of operation calls will finally result in a valid execution trace (i.e., an execution trace respecting control and data dependencies expressed between actions in the application model being simulated). Basically, once an action execution terminates, it will simply trigger the execution of another action that can logically be executed after it. The problem here is that the mechanisms which determine the next action to be scheduled is buried inside the implementation of each *ActionExecution* visitor class. If we want the Execution Model to be easily customizable for the real-time domain (which is our primary objective), we clearly need to extract this scheduling aspect from visitor classes, and add an explicit entity that would be responsible for scheduling the execution of actions. Once the entity which is responsible for scheduling action executions is clearly identified, it can be easily specialized to capture various execution schemes, corresponding to various execution semantics (i.e., semantics implied by a profile definition). Perceptive readers may wonder whether the need for an explicit scheduler is the consequence of the sequential Java implementation.

If we make abstraction of the actual Java statements and the way they would be interpreted by a Java compiler (i.e., sequential propagation of synchronous and blocking operation calls), the classifier behavior of each active object c1 and c2 is theoretically started asynchronously and performed on its own thread. What is important to notice is that active objects are simply started by the Execution Model, and finish their execution once their associated classifier behavior terminates. There is neither a well identified entity in the Execution Model describing scheduling rules, nor synchronization primitives that could be used by the scheduler to synchronize running active objects (e.g., operations or signal receptions that could be associated with class *Object* of the Execution Model depicted in Figure 1).

This architecture is not well suited to our primary objective: Specializing the Execution Model in order to reflect concerns of the real-time domain. For this purpose, we believe that introducing an explicit and well-identified entity responsible for scheduling active objects and/or action executions is mandatory, along with well-identified primitives for synchronizing and scheduling concurrent entities. Existing solutions (discussed in the next section) in model-based simulation of concurrent systems could inspire the modifications required by the Execution Model.

3 Related Works

In the field of Hardware Description Languages (HDLs), designers have already been facing the issue of simulating hardware systems (which are intrinsically concurrent) on design platforms which are typically not concurrent. SystemC [9, 10] is a representative example of solutions put into practice in this domain in order to solve this issue. It basically consists of a set of C++ extensions and class definitions (along with a usage methodology), and a simulation kernel for executing them. These extensions include handling of concurrent behaviors, time sequenced operations and simulation support. The core of SystemC is based on an event-driven simulator, where processes are behaviors and events are synchronization points that determine when a process must be triggered. The SystemC scheduler controls the timing, the order of process execution and handles event notifications. It provides primitives to synchronize and notify processes (e.g., *wait()* and *notify()* primitives). Concretely, similar mechanisms could be easily integrated in the fUML Execution Model, by adding a scheduler and primitives like *wait()* and *notify()* (which would be associated with class *Object*).

More generally, in the field of model-based simulation of concurrent systems, generic approaches such as Ptolemy [13] and ModHel'X [14] should also be considered. Ptolemy focuses on modeling, simulation, and design of concurrent, real-time, embedded systems. This approach is based on the notion of *actors* which communicate through an interface which hides their internal behaviour and is composed of *ports*. Models are built from actors and *relations* between their ports, with a *director* in charge of interpreting the relations between ports and the values available on the ports. The director of a model gives the execution semantics of the model as the rules used to combine the behaviors of its component actors. In fact, a director may represent a family of execution semantics and may have parameters such as a scheduling policy. Ptolemy comes with a number of directors ranging from Synchronous Data Flow for discrete time signal processing to Continuous Time for modeling physical processes. It supports a Discrete Event model of computation which is similar to the execution model of SystemC, as well as a Process Network model of computation in which asynchronous processes are synchronized on the availability of their inputs (contrary to CSP, producing data is never blocking, only getting data may block a process if the data is not yet available). In Ptolemy, actors are autonomous entities with a behavior which may be executed in its own flow of control. However, in many models of computation, actors are activated in sequence according to a static or dynamic schedule. What is important to notice here is that the Director / Actor architecture of Ptolemy is flexible enough to support multiple models of computation, that is to say multiple execution semantics. Regarding the fUML Execution Model, a similar architecture could be adopted: Active objects and/or action executions could be considered as actors, and the explicit entity responsible for scheduling their execution could be a kind of Ptolemy director. Defining a specialization of the Execution Model for a given application domain (i.e., explicitly capturing the execution semantics implied by a profile) would therefore basically come to extending corresponding classes in the execution model, and overloading or implementing some of their operations.

Like Ptolemy, ModHel'X defines a unique generic simulation engine to support all MoCs. Consequently, ModHel'X is well adapted for heterogeneous systems modeling. It adopts a model-based approach where the whole behavior is represented by a set of blocks, ports and unidirectional lines. A snapshot-based execution engine is proposed for interpreting this structure. As described in [14], a model execution is a sequence of snapshots. To compute each snapshot, the algorithm provides the model with inputs from the environment and builds an observation of the outputs, according to its current state. This process has a generic structure: first, choose a component to observe, then observe its behavior in response to its inputs, and propagate this observation according to the relations within the model structure. This generic algorithm for executing models relies on such primitive operations which can be refined for each model of computation. The semantics of these operations define the semantics of the model of computation. Indeed, ModHel'X has a more generic execution engine and provides a finer grain description of models of computation than Ptolemy. Concretely, we could also get inspiration of this architecture to modify the fUML Execution Model. A class encapsulating the snapshot-based execution engine could be integrated in the Execution Model, and specializing the Execution Model for a given application domain would basically come to provide particular implementations for the operations described above.

Coupling with existing and more static approaches such as TimeSquare [16] could also be considered. TimeSquare provides an environment for modeling and analyzing timed systems. TimeSquare supports an implementation of the Time Model introduced in the UML MARTE profile and the CCSL language (Clock Constraint Specification Language). It displays possible time evolutions as waveforms generated in the standard VCD format. These evolutions constitute a scheduling trace.

TimeSquare takes as input an UML model and a CCSL model applied to the UML model. The CCSL model is used to specify time constraints and apply a specific behavioral semantics on a model. The result produced by TimeSquare is a sequence of steps (Scheduling Map) that can be used by external tools for analysis/simulation purposes. Concretely, coupling the fUML Execution Model would mean that a CCSL model must be generated for a given application model, and that the generated model reflects the time and concurrent semantics of the application domain for which a profile is defined. Scheduling maps generated by TimeSquare could then be "played" by the Execution Model. Again, modifications in the architecture of the Execution Model would be required, and would mainly consist in adding an explicit entity responsible for triggering executions of active objects and actions, with respect to the scheduling map generated by TimeSquare.

4 Introducing an Explicit Scheduler in the fUML Execution Model

In section 2, we have shown that the executions performed by the fUML Execution Model are purely sequential. We have highlighted the absence of an explicit entity responsible for scheduling the execution of actions. We have identified in section 3 different approaches for modeling and simulation of concurrent systems. Each approach contains an entity and primitives to control behavior executions. We propose in this section a lightweight modification of the Execution Model following this general idea. The goal is to break the sequential execution and provide the ability to control the start of each action execution, in a way that can be easily overloaded (so that it is possible to cope with multiple scheduling policies). We introduce for this purpose an explicit scheduler into the Execution model, as illustrated in Figure 4.

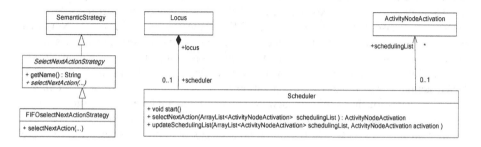

Fig. 4. Description of the Scheduler in fUML Execution Model

The class *Scheduler* manipulates a list of *ActivityNodeActivation* (i.e., this class represents the visitor class of UML::Action) depicted by the property *schedulingList*, which contains the list of all actions ready to execute (i.e., an action is ready to execute if all its control and data tokens are available). *Scheduler* offers several operations that can be used to control executions of actions. These operations are called in the body of *start ( )* which actually start the behavior of the scheduler. The operation *selectNextAction( )* determines the next action to be executed, by extracting an element from *schedulingList*, according to a given scheduling policy. The operation *updateSchedulingList ( )* determines the potential successors for the last executed action (i.e., with respect to control and data dependencies within the executed activity) and adds them to the scheduling list.

To capture several scheduling policies that could correspond to different execution semantics, we rely on the strategy pattern proposed by the Execution model, itself based on the class *SemanticStrategy* (for more details about the strategy pattern, see [11]). In the fUML execution model, *SemanticStrategy* is used to address semantic variation points of UML, with a refinement of this class for each semantic variation point of UML (e.g., there is a class called *GetNextEventStrategy*, which is introduced to address the UML semantic variation point related to the selection of an event from an object's event pool). Fixing a given semantic variation point then comes to refine the corresponding strategy class, by providing an implementation for the operation capturing the strategy.

Following this pattern, supporting different scheduling policies amounts to refine the class *SelecNextActionStrategy* (see Figure 4) for each new policy and to overload the *selectNextAction()* operation to capture the underlying behavior. In our case, we introduce the class *SelecNextActionStrategy*, whose operation *selectNextAction()* is overloaded in order to encapsulate the behavior of one particular scheduling policy. For example, *FIFOSelectNextActionStrategy* is a concrete class that implements a simple FIFO strategy (i.e., by "FIFO", we simply mean that actions are executed respecting their order of appearance in a list of action activations such as *shedulingList*). In order to plug the scheduler onto the fUML execution model, we also modify the behavior of *ActivityNodeActivation* in order to let the scheduler determine the next action to be executed after a given *ActivityNodeActivation* finishes the execution of its visited action. Figure 5 shows a sequence diagram of an interaction trace between the scheduler and an action. The scheduler executes the operation *selectNextAction ( )* that chooses one action from its scheduling list according to a certain policy. Its implementation actually consists in delegating the choice to a *SelectNextActionStrategy* class (in this case, the policy is the one of *FIFOSelectNextActionStrategy*. Note that the *Loci* class dynamically determines the various semantic strategy classes to be used, provided it has been correctly configured before launching the execution). Then, the scheduler triggers the execution of the selected action. The behavior of the selected action is performed by the operation *doAction( )*. The operation *sendOffer( )* then propagates tokens to the next actions that can logically be executed after it, but it does not trigger anymore the execution of these actions. The scheduler indeed calls *updateSchedulingList()* to add these potential successors into the scheduling list. The next action to be executed is selected by calling *selectNextAction()*. This behavior is repeated until the scheduling list becomes empty (i.e., the execution of the activity is finished).

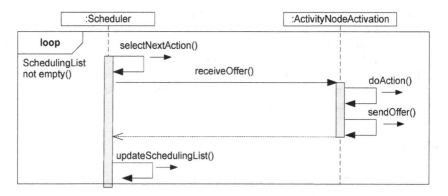

Fig. 5. Execution trace of scheduler interactions with action

5 Conclusion

The ongoing OMG standard on the semantics of a foundational subset (fUML) for executable UML models defines a general-purpose execution model for a subset of UML. This subset includes non trivial mechanisms, carrying concurrent and asynchronous execution semantics (e.g., active objects, signals, etc). Our objective was to evaluate how far the current definition of the fUML Execution Model can support formalization of concurrent and temporal semantic aspects required for real time embedded system design and analysis. As shown in the study, the current form of the fUML execution model is not suited to this objective, mainly due to the way concurrency and asynchronous communications are actually handled.

We have mainly shown that the current architecture of the fUML Execution Model suffers the lack of explicit mechanisms for manipulating and synchronizing concurrent entities. Existing solutions for embedded system simulation indicate that it is possible to provide much more adapted and realistic solutions. We proposed some concrete modifications regarding the architecture of the fUML Execution Model, inspired by these solutions. We took care of minimizing changes in the architecture, so that we can leverage as much as possible on the existing Execution Model (and all the work that its definition implied). The proposed solution is mainly intended to show that a modification of the fUML Execution Model is technically feasible and reasonable in terms of efforts. However, further experiments are still required to validate the proposed modifications. Additionally, this solution only reflects executions by a single unit of computation (i.e., mono-processor). The case of executions onto multiple processing units will be investigated in future works.

Another important aspect which has not been detailed in this article concerns the simulation of time in the Execution Model, which is currently not supported. Time is indeed considered as a semantic variation point within the fUML Specification (Subclause 2.3 of [2]). Consequently, a wide variety of time models could be adopted, including discrete or continuous time. fUML does not make any assumptions about the sources of time information and their related mechanisms. Therefore, to support timed execution semantics and underlying timing properties (e.g., ready time, period, deadline, etc.), it is necessary to extend the Execution Model with both necessary syntactic and semantic concepts. Time is a central aspect to our work. Resolving the concurrency issues of the fUML Execution Model by adopting solutions similar to those proposed in the Related Works could therefore, in the same move, provide a solution for the Time issue of the Execution Model. Ultimately, our goal is to provide a kind of methodological and tooled framework for the definition of UML profiles, where the semantic specializations of UML implied by a profile will take as much considerations as syntactic specializations.

References

1. OMG. A UML profile fore MARTE: Modeling and Analysis of Real-Time Embedded systems Version 1.0. (2009)
2. OMG. Semantics of Foundational Subset for Executable UML models FTF-Beta2 (2009)
3. Model driven solution, http://portal.modeldriven.org/content/fuml-reference-implementation-download
4. Agha, G.: Actors: a model of concurrent computation in distributed system. MIT Press, Cambridge (1986)
5. Selic, B., Ward, P.T., McGee, G.G.: Real-Time Object-Oriented Modeling. Wiley, John & Sons, Inc. (October 1994), ISBN-13: 9780471599173
6. Terrier, F., Fouquier, G., Bras, D., Rioux, L., Vanuxeem, P., Lanusse, A.: A real time object model. In: International Conference on Technology of Object Oriented Languages and Systems, TOOLS Europe 1996, Paris, France, Février (1996)
7. Eker, J., Janneck, J.W., Lee, E.A., Liu, J., Liu, X., Ludvig, J., Neuendorffer, S., Sachs, S., Xiong, Y.: Taming heterogeneity – the Ptolemy approach. Proceedings of the IEEE, Special Issue on Modeling and Design of Embedded Software 91(1), 127–144 (2003)
8. Basu, A., Bozga, M., Sifakis, J.: Modeling heterogeneous real-time systems in BIP. In: 4th IEEE International Conference on Software Engineering and Formal Methods (SEFM 2006), pp. 3–12 (2006)
9. Open SystemC Initiative. SystemC 2.0.1 Language Reference Manual (2004)
10. SystemC. Official web site of SystemC community, http://www.systemc.org/
11. Gamma, Helm, Johnson, Vlissides: Design Patterns: Elements of Resuable Object-Oriented Software, pp. 163–174, 331–344. Addison-Wesley, Reading (1995)
12. OMG. Unified Modeling Language: Superstructure. version 2.2. formal/2009-02-02 (2009)
13. Eker, J., Janneck, J.W., Lee, E.A., Liu, J., Liu, X., Ludvig, J., Neuendorffer, S., Sachs, S., Xiong, Y.: Taming heterogeneity – The Ptolemy approach. Proceedings of the IEEE, Special Issue on Modeling and Design of Embedded Software 91(1), 127–144 (2003)
14. Boulanger, F., Hardebolle, C.: Simulation of Multi-Formalism Models with Mod-Hel'X. In: Proceedings of ICSTW 2008, pp. 318–327. IEEE Comp. Soc., Los Alamitos (2008)
15. Executable UML/SYSML semantics. Model Driven Solutions. Final project report (November 2008)
16. André, C., Ferrero, B., Mallet, F.: TimeSquare: a Multiform Time Simulation Environment. In: Sophia Antipolis and Formal Analysis Workshop (Décembre 2008)

Task Migration for Fault-Tolerant FlexRay Networks

Kay Klobedanz, Gilles B. Defo, Henning Zabel, Wolfgang Mueller, and Yuan Zhi

University of Paderborn/C-LAB

Abstract. In this paper we present new concepts to resolve ECU (Electronic Control Unit) failures in FlexRay networks. Our approach extends the FlexRay bus schedule by redundant slots with modifications in the communication and slot assignment. We introduce additional backup nodes to replace faulty nodes. To reduce the required memory resources of the backup nodes, we distribute redundant tasks over different nodes and propose the migration of tasks to the backup node at runtime. We investigate different solutions to migrate the redundant tasks to the backup node by time-triggered and event-triggered transmissions.

1 Introduction

FlexRay is the emerging standard for safety-critical distributed real-time systems in vehicles [5][15]. It implements deterministic behavior and comes with high bandwidths. For increased safety, it provides redundant channels to guarantee communication if one channel is corrupted. Nevertheless, since an ECU (Electronic Control Unit) failure still often results in the malfunction of the whole system, the main question remains how to ensure the correct behavior of a safety-critical distributed system in such a case. As presented in [4], different techniques for tolerating *permanent, transient,* or *intermittent* faults are applied. In our article, we consider ECU failures based on permanent hardware faults which are compensated by means of redundancy. We focus on the replication of tasks and the activation of backup nodes. The failure results in an execution of the redundant tasks on a different node which induces changes in the communication at runtime. Unfortunately, FlexRay only supports static bus schedules where each slot is reserved for an individual sender and the slot assignments can only be changed by a bus restart, whose timing is not exactly predictable. In contrast, our approach extends bus schedules by redundant slots and considers communication dependencies already at the system design phase before network configuration. Additionally, as ECU functionalities are distributed over several ECUs, the failure of an ECU which executes several functions may have a big impact on the correct operation of the whole system. We adopt this approach and assign two functions to an ECU.[1] One implements the main ECU function; the other one is a redundant mirrored instance of another ECU function, which is activated on a failure of the other ECU (see Fig. 1 and [4]). Here, just the failure of one ECU can be compensated. A second node failure may lead to the failure of the complete system again. In Figure 1, for example, the failure of node n1 disables its own task set and the backup for node n2. The additional failure of node n4 irrecoverable corrupts the functionality of node n1. We introduce backup nodes to

---

[1] For the matter of simplicity, we presume that a function corresponds to a task.

M. Hinchey et al. (Eds.): DIPES/BICC 2010, IFIP AICT 329, pp. 55–65, 2010.

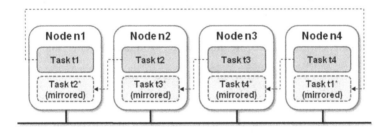

Fig. 1. Redundancy with mirrored tasks on other nodes

completely replace any faulty node and presume a homogeneous network of nodes with identical resources. This redundancy raises the fault tolerance of distributed networks and we can furher improve it by simply increasing the number of backup nodes. This approach additionally requires the migration of the main and the redundant function of the faulty ECU from other nodes and their migration to the backup node. The additional advantage is that the redundant function can immediately start executing before the migration, e.g., t1* on node n4. After the migration, the execution is resumed by the backup node. This yields to the initial setup where every node is executing only its main functionality again and keeps a redundant instance of a function from another ECU which compensates an additional failure of an arbitrary node.

In this article, we present different variants for such a task migration and evaluate them with respect to their time consumption, predictability, and impact to the communication. A detailed description of our approach is given in Section 4. The evaluation is presented in Section 5 before the final section concludes with a summary.

2 Related Work

Several approaches like [14] deal with the analysis of the FlexRay protocol and its optimization. They present several heuristics to determine proper configurations and parameterizations for the FlexRay bus based on the static [11][7][10] and the dynamic segment [14][13]. In general, their optimizations and the resulting configurations assume that the executed tasks are statically linked to the nodes of the FlexRay network. [4] considers a replication of tasks and a more flexible task to node assignment. Based on these assumptions they determine the reconfiguration capabilities of the FlexRay bus.

Task migration itself is a hot topic in current automotive research. For example, [1] describes a concept for a middleware, which uses task migration further described in [9] to increase the reliability of distributed embedded systems with soft real-time constraints, e.g., for infotainment systems. In contrast to our work, they do not consider safety-critical components and the runtime reconfiguration of FlexRay networks.

Task migration at runtime was considered in the context of mobile agents like [12] and [2]. However, we are not interested in principle architectures rather than on their technical realization and the efficient task migration in the context of FlexRay. We are not aware of other related approaches in this area.

3 FlexRay

FlexRay was introduced to implement deterministic and fault-tolerant communication systems for safety-critical distributed real-time systems like x-by-wire. The main benefits of FlexRay are:

- **Synchronous and asynchronous data transmission:** FlexRay offers cycle-based time-triggered communication complemented by an optional event-triggered transmission mode.
- **Determinism:** The time triggered transmission mode of FlexRay ensures real-time capabilities of the communication because it guarantees deterministic behavior with a defined maximum message latency.
- **Redundant communication channels with large bandwidth:** FlexRay offers two redundant channels for safety-critical systems. Each channel offers a bandwidth up to 10 $Mbit/s$ with little latency.

A communication cycle can be composed of a static and an optional dynamic segment (see Figure 2(a)). In the static segment, the time-triggered data transfer is carried out via TDMA (Time Division Multiple Access). The transmission slots of the segment are assigned to one sender node by a globally known synchronously incremented slot-counter. The static segment consists of a fixed number of equally sized static slots (2 – 1023). The event-triggered dynamic segment realizes the bus access via FTDMA (Flexible Time Division Multiple Access) and consists of dynamic slots with variable size. Dynamic slots are composed of minislots whose number depends on the length of the message to transmit (max. 7986 per cycle). The arbitration is accomplished by a priority assignment to nodes (Frame IDs). If a node has nothing to send, only one minislot is unused and the next node gets the opportunity for transmission. The size of the slots and minislots, the cycle length, the size of messages (frames) as well as several other parameters are defined through an initial setup of the FlexRay schedule, which cannot be changed during runtime. Figure 2(b) shows the basic components of a FlexRay node. A host for the functionality of the ECU and a communication controller (CC). The CC

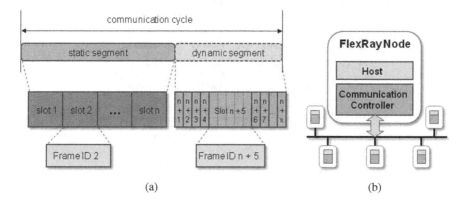

(a)   (b)

Fig. 2. Components of the FlexRay communication cycle (a) and communication controller (b)

is the core component of FlexRay because it implements the actual protocol. It provides the communication interface to the bus through a bus driver and it performs the sending/receiving and the decoding/coding of data messages (frames). For more detailed introduction to FlexRay, the reader is referred to [6].

4   Migration of Redundant Tasks in FlexRay Networks

Our concepts are based on existing approaches for redundant tasks to improve the robustness of FlexRay networks in case of a node failure. To further increase the fault tolerance of a FlexRay network, our concept extends them by the improvements outlined in the next subsection.

4.1   Overview

Our improvements for an increasing fault tolerance are:

- **Extension with additional backup node(s):** Backup nodes can completely replace any faulty node as they provide the same resources as the other nodes. To reduce the memory demand for the backup node, we migrate necessary tasks rather than storing instances of all tasks on a backup node. This results in a homogenous system topology with similar node capacity.
- **Migration to the backup node at runtime:** During the migration, the functionality is immediately executed by the redundant instance on another ECU. After the migration, the corresponding task execution is resumed on the backup node. This yields to the initial system setup where every node executes a main function and keeps an additional redundant instance from another ECU.

Additionally, we add a coordinator component, which is in charge of the communication in the system. This can be realized by two different strategies. First, the coordinator can be distributed on different nodes. Second, the coordinator can – as it is realized here – run on an extra node to keep the topology described above with ECUs executing one main function, represented as one task. Figure 3 presents the topology of a FlexRay network with an extra backup and coordinator node.

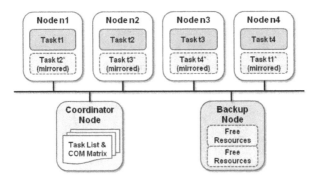

Fig. 3. Topology with backup and coordinator node before a failure of Node n1

As shown in Figure 3, the coordinator maintains a task list, with main and redundant tasks of every node and a communication matrix (see Table 1) with the corresponding transmission/reception slots. These structures will be updated when modifications in task and slot assignments are required due to node failures, execution of redundant tasks, or task migrations. The coordinator is configured to monitor messages from all slots. Using the information from the task list and the communication matrix, the coordinator detects node failures monitoring the bus traffic. If a malfunction of an ECU is detected, the coordinator sends a message to the appropriate nodes to activate the corresponding redundant task instance and to start the transmission of the particular tasks to the backup node. This message also contains information about changes in the slot assignment for receiving nodes. When the transmission is complete, this is recognized by the coordinator. Then, the coordinator activates the migrated task on the backup node at the same time it deactivates the redundant task and informs the receiving nodes about rearrangements in the slot assignments. Figure 4 illustrates this process for the system shown in Figure 3 in case of a failure of node n1. The synchronous and asynchronous data transmission of the FlexRay protocol allows different implementations of our approach. It can be realized in the static segment, in the dynamic segment, or in both. In the following we introduce alternative scenarios for the previous example.

Table 1. Example of a communication matrix for a topology with 4 nodes

		static segment				dynamic segment		
Slot	s1	s2	s3	s4	...	d1	d2	...
Node n1	t1:tx	-	t1:rx	-	...	-	-	...
Node n2	t2:rx	t2:tx	t2:rx	-	...	-	-	...
Node n3	t3:rx	-	t3:tx	t3:rx	...	-	-	...
Node n4	-	-	-	t4:tx	...	-	-	...

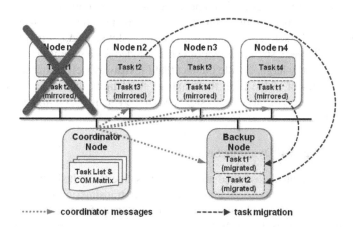

    ⋯⋯▶ coordinator messages   - - - -▶ task migration

Fig. 4. Topology with backup and coordinator node after a failure of Node n1

4.2 Exclusive Usage of Static Segment

For an exclusive usage of the static segment, additional static slots for the coordinator, the backup node, and the migrations have to be reserved. This extends the static segment as shown in Table 2. The advantage of this solution is the predictability for the transmissions of all nodes as well as the task migration. The duration $\Delta_{migration}$ of the copy process for a task with the size Φ_{task} can be computed by

$$\Delta_{migration} = \#_{cycles} \cdot \Delta_{cycle} \quad with \quad \#_{cycles} = \left\lceil \frac{\Phi_{task} \cdot gdBit}{\Delta_{slot}} \right\rceil, \tag{1}$$

where $\#_{cycles}$ is the number of cycles and Δ_{cycle} the length of a cycle. The cycle length and the nominal bit time (inverted bit rate) $gdBit$ are configured in the FlexRay schedule as well as the slot length Δ_{slot}, which is related to the number of needed cycles for a task migration ($\#_{cycles}$) (ref. (1)). Table 2 presents the static slots and the resulting assignments and changes for a failure of node n1. In addition to slots s1,..,s4 for the primarily communication between the four nodes, slots for the coordinator (s5) and the transmission of the redundant task during the migration process (s6,...,s9) – here t1* transmits in s9 – have to be reserved in the schedule. For the migration, a slot for each node (s10, ..., s13) and a slot for the backup node (s14) has to be reserved. The communication matrix shows that all nodes receive the messages from the coordinator (s5) and the coordinator monitors all slots. Node n4 uses slot s13 to copy the task t1* to the backup node (t1*:mig) and node n2 uses s11 (t2:mig). During that period, the redundant task t1* transmits its data in slot s9 and receives from slot s3. The corresponding tasks/nodes are informed via the coordinator message to listen to s5. When the migration is finished, the backup node receives the advice (bk:rx) to activate its migrated instance of t1*. Thereafter, task t1* on the backup node reads from slot s3 and sends via slot s14 whereas the receiving tasks are informed to listen to this slot. Simultaneously, node n4 stops executing its instance of task t1*. All transmissions as well as the migration are time-triggered and have a guaranteed maximum latency. But only few of the reserved slots are required in the case of a node failure. This results in a big overhead of slots. The setting of an appropriate static slot size (Δ_{slot}) makes the situation even worse. To get a small number of cycles needed for a migration ($\#_{cycles}$), slots should be considerably large. Beside the fact that FlexRay as well as system properties (e.g., sampling rates of tasks) limit the maximal slot length, this causes a significant increase of the overhead because every slot needs to be equally sized independent of its transmitted content.

4.3 Exclusive Usage of Dynamic Segment

To minimize the overhead described above, it is possible to exclusively use the event-triggered dynamic segment. To guarantee the correct transmission of data within the dynamic segment, FlexRay only allows a node to send if its frame completely fits into the remaining minislots (ref [6]). In the case that it does not fit, the node has to wait for the next cycle. This makes the communication nondeterministic, particularly if the dynamic segment is also used for other event-based messages like error codes etc. Thus, the calculation of the time needed for the migration within the dynamic segment is more complex. The value for ($\Delta_{migration}$) can be determined using equation (1). The slot size (Δ_{slot}) is dynamic and is determined by

$$\Delta_{slot} = \Delta_{dynamic} - \Delta_{hp} \ with \ \Delta_{hp} = \sum_{k=1}^{i} \Delta_{frame_i}. \tag{2}$$

Equation (2) shows that the available dynamic slot size for the migration is given by the complete length of the dynamic segment ($\Delta_{dynamic}$) decremented by the slot sizes used by frames with higher priority (Δ_{hp}). These results inserted into Equation (1) yield to the migration time derived from the segment length and the priority assignment. The communication matrix in Table 3 shows the assignment. The coordinator gets the highest priority (d1) because it transmits messages of highest priority. During the migration process task t1* running on node n4 uses d2 to send its data. The other reserved slots (d3-d5) are unused. When the migration is finished, the activated backup node blocks the dynamic slot d6 and d2 remains unused. The communication matrix also shows that the migration of the tasks gets the lowest priorities (d7,..., d10). Here, d8 is used for the migration of t2 and d10 for the migration of t1*. To permit access to the dynamic segment, the data size of the migration process must fit in the space left influenced by prior messages. Additionally, the coordinator informs the backup node how much data to transmit per cycle. This usage of the dynamic segment makes this solution more flexible than the use of the static segment. Even though the transmission is event-triggered and nondeterministic, it can be guaranteed that sufficient data are transmitted due to a proper priority assignment. The size of the dynamic segment has to be initially configured based on the system properties and the message sizes to reach the desired migration process duration $\Delta_{migration}$ along Equation (2). Because the utilization in the dynamic segment is more flexible and the static slot size is independent of the migration data, the potential overhead of this solution is considerably less than in the static version of Table 2. In particular, each unused slot in the dynamic segment only consumes one minislot. Nevertheless, the major drawback is the partial loss of determinism, which is an important requirement for safety-critical systems.

4.4   Usage of Static and Dynamic Segments

A compromise between the previous two solutions is given by the configuration given in Table 4. Here, we achieve a reduction of overhead in compliance with a deterministic communication. The communication matrix shows that the coordinator node (s5), the redundant task instances (s6,..., s9), and the backup node (s10) communicate time-triggered over reserved static slots like in the exclusive static segment solution. In contrast, the migration itself is performed via the dynamic segment (d1,...,d4), which reduces the overhead significantly as the size of the migration frames only influences the size of the dynamic segment and unused slots in the dynamic segment generate less overhead. Hence, the size of the static slots remains independent of the migration data. In summary, this yields to a higher flexibility in the schedule configuration and combines the benefits. On the one hand, we guarantee a maximum latency and a deterministic transmission for the important messages using the static segment. On the other hand,

Table 2. Communication matrix for exclusive usage of the static segment

Slot	s1	s2	s3	s4	s5	s6	s7	s8	s9	s10	s11	s12	s13	s14
Node n1	t1:tx	-	t1:tx	-	t1:rx	-	-	-	-	-	-	-	-	-
Node n2	t2:rx	t2:tx	t2:rx	-	t2:rx	-	-	-	t2:rx	-	t2:mig	-	-	t2:rx
Node n3	t3:rx	-	t3:tx	t3:rx	t3:rx	-	-	-	t3:rx	-	-	-	-	t3:rx
Node n4	-	-	t1*:rx	t4:tx	t4:rx	-	-	-	t1*:tx	-	-	-	t1*:mig	-
Coordinator	co:rx	co:rx	co:rx	co:rx	co:tx	co:rx	co:rx	co:rx	co:rx	co:rx	co:rx	co:rx	co:rx	co:rx
Backup	-	-	t1*:rx	-	bk:rx	-	-	-	-	-	mig:rx	-	mig:rx	t1*:tx

Table 3. Communication matrix for exclusive usage of dynamic segment

Slot	static segment				dynamic segment									
	s1	s2	s3	s4	d1	d2	d3	d4	d5	d6	d7	d8	d9	d10
Node n1	t1:tx	-	t1:tx	-	t1:tx	-	-	-	-	-	-	-	-	-
Node n2	t2:rx	t2:tx	t2:rx	-	t2:rx	-	-	-	t2:rx	t2:rx	-	t2:mig	-	-
Node n3	t3:rx	-	t3:tx	t3:rx	t3:rx	-	-	-	t3:rx	t3:rx	-	-	-	-
Node n4	-	-	t1*:rx	t4:tx	t4:rx	-	-	-	t1*:tx	-	-	-	-	t1*:mig
Coordinator	co:rx	co:rx	co:rx	co:rx	co:tx	co:rx	co:rx	co:rx	co:rx	co:rx	co:rx	co:rx	co:rx	co:rx
Backup	-	-	t1*:rx	-	bk:rx	-	-	-	-	t1*:tx	-	mig:rx	-	mig:rx

Table 4. Communication matrix for "mixed" usage of static segment and dynamic segment

Slot	static segment										dynamic segment			
	s1	s2	s3	s4	s5	s6	s7	s8	s9	s10	d1	d2	d3	d4
Node n1	t1:tx	-	t1:tx	-	t1:rx	-	-	-	-	-	-	-	-	-
Node n2	t2:rx	t2:tx	t2:rx	-	t2:rx	-	-	-	t2:rx	t2:rx	-	t2:mig	-	-
Node n3	t3:rx	-	t3:tx	t3:rx	t3:rx	-	-	-	t3:rx	t3:rx	-	-	-	-
Node n4	-	-	t1*:rx	t4:tx	t4:rx	-	-	-	t1*:tx	-	-	-	-	t1*:mig
Coordinator	co:rx	co:rx	co:rx	co:rx	co:tx	co:rx	co:rx	co:rx	co:rx	co:rx	co:rx	co:rx	co:rx	co:rx
Backup	-	-	t1*:rx	-	bk:rx	-	-	-	-	t1*:tx	-	mig:rx	-	mig:rx

we reduce the overhead by the exclusive assignment of the dynamic segment to the migration process. Through this, the migration time is even more predictable because the capacity required by prioritized tasks is omitted.

5   Experimental Results

We evaluated the presented alternatives by simulations with our SystemC Flex-Ray library. SystemC is a system design language providing means to model application-specific hardware and software at different levels of abstraction [3]. The implemented FlexRay CC supports the simulation of static and dynamic segments for one communication channel. All necessary modules specified in the FlexRay standard (see [6]) are also covered by the implementation. Our model consists of six modules implementing communication nodes along the topology shown in Figure 3. Each node uses an instance of the CC for the communication. All CCs are in turn connected to a transaction level (TLM) bus object. The CC model can be configured with the same controller host interface (CHI) files like hardware CCs. This file contains all necessary parameters to configure the registers and message buffers for the communication. The bus communication applies TLM 2.0 [8]. Figure 5 depicts a communication sequence between two communication controllers. The communication controllers act as initiators of the transaction during the communication process and the bus acts as the target. We use approximately timed TLM 2.0 coding style to model the communication with the bus module. The communication is divided into four phases: Begin/end request and begin/end response. As shown in Figure 5, CONTROLLER1 starts a write transaction, with a begin request. Immediately after the receipt of the transaction, the bus module notifies CONTROLLER2 about the start of the data transmission with the time required for the data transfer. Afterwards, CONTROLLER2 starts a read transaction. Both controllers then wait until they have received a confirmation from the bus about the end of the data transfer. The SystemC model consists of 6 nodes, 6 CCs, and 1 bus module in total. Nodes communicate via their respective CCs. Communication between nodes and CCs is realized via callback methods. Each node has to implement receive and transmit function, that are called by the FlexRay CC. Since we are using an abstract model for the evaluation, we did not actually implement the migration process itself. Instead we simulate the reconfiguration/migration duration since timing analysis is our main focus.

Simulation Results. In the following, we present the simulation results for one example. For that we assume a size of 1 $kByte = 8000$ bit for a task to migrate (Φ_{task}) and configure the FlexRay_Bus schedule by:

- $\Delta_{cycle} = 600\mu s$ for static solution,
- $\Delta_{cycle} = 600\mu s + 400\mu s = 1000\mu s$ for dynamic and mixed solution,
- $\Delta_{slot} = 50\mu s$ for the static segment with 14 slots,
- $gdBit = 0, 1\mu s/bit$ (equates to a bandwith of 10 $Mbit/s$).

The time needed for the migration within the static segment can be determined by means of Equation (1) as:

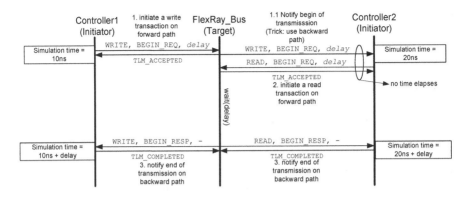

Fig. 5. Simulation of bus transmission

$$\#_{cycles} = \left\lceil \frac{\Phi_{task} \cdot gdBit}{\Delta_{slot}} \right\rceil = \left\lceil \frac{8000\,bit \cdot 0,1\,\mu s/bit}{50\mu s} \right\rceil = 16,$$

$$\Delta_{migration} = \#_{cycles} \cdot \Delta_{cycle} = 16 \cdot 600\mu s = 9,6ms$$

For the (exclusive) assignment of the dynamic segment to the migration and the usage of both transmission modes, the simulation also confirms the computed values, e.g.:

$$\#_{cycles} = \left\lceil \frac{\Phi_{task} \cdot gdBit}{\Delta_{slot}} \right\rceil = \left\lceil \frac{8000\,bit \cdot 0,1\,\mu s/bit}{400\mu s} \right\rceil = 2 \;\; with \;\; \sum_{k=1}^{i} \Delta_{frame_i} = 0,$$

$$\Delta_{migration} = \#_{cycles} \cdot \Delta_{cycle} = 2 \cdot 1000\mu s = 2ms.$$

All numbers were additionally validated by our simulations which thus confirms the applicability of our approach.

6   Conclusion and Outlook

This paper presented different alternatives of redundant tasks and slots for the compensation of node failures in safety-critical FlexRay networks. We introduced backup nodes, which can replace any faulty node when our task migration is applied. With this scalable approach, we further increase redundancy and fault tolerance through the compensation of an additional failure of an arbitrary node. We presented three different task migration strategies based on the transmission capabilities of FlexRay and evaluated them by a SystemC simulation. The comparison of the proposed solutions showed that the combined usage of static and dynamic segment improves the benefits and minimizes the disadvantages by providing deterministic communication with low overhead and flexibility for task migration. On the one hand, it results in a maximum latency for the transmission of functional relevant messages in the static segment. On the other hand, it reduces the overhead through the exclusive assignment of the dynamic segment to the migration process.

In future work, we will examine the distribution and redundancy of the coordinator component within the system. By this, we avoid the potential "single-point of failure" induced by the solution with a single coordinator ECU. The additional small memory requirement resulting from the stored task list and communication matrix on several nodes is neglectable.

Acknowledgements

The work described herein is supported by the BMBF through the ITEA2 VERDE project (01S09012H).

References

1. Anthony, R., Chen, D., Törngren, M., Scholle, D., Sanfridson, M., Rettberg, A., Naseer, T., Persson, M., Feng, L.: Autonomic middleware for automotive embedded systems. In: Autonomic Communication (2009)
2. Bic, L.F., Fukuda, M., Dillencourt, M.B.: Distributed computing using autonomous objects. Computer 29(8) (1996)
3. Donovan, J., Black, D.C.: SystemC: From the Ground Up. Kluwer Academic Publishers, New York (2004)
4. Brendle, R., Streichert, T., Koch, D., Haubelt, C., Teich, J.: Dynamic reconfiguration of flexray schedules for response time reduction in asynchronous fault-tolerant networks. In: Brinkschulte, U., Ungerer, T., Hochberger, C., Spallek, R.G. (eds.) ARCS 2008. LNCS, vol. 4934, pp. 117–129. Springer, Heidelberg (2008)
5. Broy, J., Müller-Glaser, K.D.: The impact of time-triggered communication in automotive embedded systems. In: SIES (2007)
6. FlexRay Consortium: Flexray communications system protocol specification version 2.1 rev. A. (December 2005), www.flexray.com
7. Ding, S., Tomiyama, H., Takada, H.: An effective ga-based scheduling algorithm for flexray systems. IEICE - Trans. Inf. Syst. E91-D(8) (2008)
8. Open System Initiative. Osci tlm2 user manual, software version tlm 2.0 draft 2, dcument version 1.0.0 (2007)
9. Kluge, F., Mische, J., Uhrig, S., Ungerer, T.: Building Adaptive Embeddd Systems by Monitoring and Dynamic Loading of Application Module. In: Almeida, L., et al. (eds.) Workshop on Adaptive and Reconfigurable Embedded Systems, St. Louis, MO, USA (April 2008)
10. Lukasiewycz, M., Glaß, M., Teich, J., Milbredt, P.: Flexray schedule optimization of the static segment. In: CODES+ISSS 2009. ACM, New York (2009)
11. Havet, L., Grenier, M., Navet, N.: Configuring the communication on flexray: the case of the static segment. In: ERTS 2008 (2008)
12. Peine, H., Stolpmann, T.: The architecture of the ara platform for mobile agents. In: Rothermel, K., Popescu-Zeletin, R. (eds.) MA 1997. LNCS, vol. 1219. Springer, Heidelberg (1997)
13. Pop, T., Pop, P., Eles, P., Peng, Z.: Bus access optimisation for flexray-based distributed embedded systems. In: DATE 2007 (2007)
14. Pop, T., Pop, P., Eles, P., Peng, Z., Andrei, A.: Timing analysis of the flexray communication protocol. Real-Time Syst. 39(1-3) (2008)
15. Schedl, A.: Goals and architecture of flexray at bmw. Slides presented at the Vector FlexRay Symposium (March 2007)

Flexible and Dynamic Replication Control for Interdependent Distributed Real-Time Embedded Systems

Luís Nogueira[1], Luís Miguel Pinho[1], and Jorge Coelho[2]

[1] CISTER Research Centre
[2] LIACC
School of Engineering, Polytechnic Institute of Porto, Portugal
{lmn,lmp,jmn}@isep.ipp.pt

Abstract. Replication is a proven concept for increasing the availability of distributed systems. However, actively replicating every software component in distributed embedded systems may not be a feasible approach. Not only the available resources are often limited, but also the imposed overhead could significantly degrade the system's performance.

This paper proposes heuristics to dynamically determine which components to replicate based on their significance to the system as a whole, its consequent number of passive replicas, and where to place those replicas in the network. The activation of passive replicas is coordinated through a fast convergence protocol that reduces the complexity of the needed interactions among nodes until a new collective global service solution is determined.

1 Introduction

The highly dynamic and unpredictable nature of open distributed real-time embedded systems can lead to a highly volatile environment where QoS provision needs to adapt seamlessly to changing resource levels [1].Some of the difficulties arise from the fact that the mix of independently developed applications and their aggregate resource and timing requirements are unknown until runtime but, still, a timely answer to events must be provided in order to guarantee a desired level of performance. Our previous work [2] applied concepts of cooperative QoS-aware computing to address such challenges, emerging as a promising distributed computing paradigm to face the stringent demands on resources and performance of new embedded real-time systems. Available software components can be shared among different services and can be adapted at runtime to varying operational conditions, enhancing the efficiency in the use of the available resources.

Nevertheless, it is imperative to accept that failures can and will occur, even in meticulously designed systems, and design proper measures to counter those failures [3]. Software replication has some advantages over other fault tolerance solutions in distributed environments, providing the shortest recovery delays, it is less intrusive with respect to execution time, it scales much better, and is relatively generic and transparent to the application domain [4]. However, actively replicating all software components,

M. Hinchey et al. (Eds.): DIPES/BICC 2010, IFIP AICT 329, pp. 66–77, 2010.

independently of their significance to the overall system, may be infeasible in some embedded systems due to the scale of their timing, cost, and resource constraints [5].

This paper is then motivated by the need to develop a flexible and cost-effective fault tolerance solution with a significant lower overhead compared to a strict active redundancy-based approach. The term *cost-effective* implies that we want to achieve a high error coverage with the minimum amount of redundancy. The paper proposes low runtime complexity heuristics to (i) dynamically determine which components to replicate based on their significance to the system as a whole; (ii) determine a number of replicas proportional to the components' significance degree; and (iii) select the location of those replicas based on collected information about the nodes' availability as the system progresses. To quantitatively study the effectiveness of the proposed approach an extensive number of simulation runs was analysed. The results show that even simple heuristics with low runtime complexity can achieve a reasonably higher system's availability than static offline decisions when lower replication ratios are imposed due to resource or cost limitations.

One of the advantages of passive replication is that it can be implemented without the use of complex replica consistency protocols [6,7]. Nevertheless, consider the case where the quality of the produced output of a particular component depends not only on the amount and type of used resources but also on the quality of the inputs being sent by other components in the system [8]. If a primary replica is found to be faulty, a new primary must be elected from the set of passive backup ones and the execution restarted from the last saved state. However, it is not guaranteed that the new primary will be able to locally reserve the needed resources to output the same QoS level that was being produced by the old primary. In such cases, the need of coordination arises in order to preserve the correct functionality of the service's distributed execution [9,10]. This paper proposes a distributed coordination protocol that rapidly converges to a new globally consistent service solution by (i) reducing the needed interactions among nodes; and (ii) compensating for a decrease in input quality by an increase in the amount of used resources in key components in interdependency graphs.

2   System Model

We understand a service $S = \{c_1, c_2, \ldots, c_n\}$ as a set of software components c_i being cooperatively executed by a coalition of nodes [2]. Each component c_i is defined by its functionality, is able to send and receive messages, is available at a certain point of the network, and has a set of QoS parameters that can be changed in order to adapt service provisioning to a dynamically changing environment. Each subset of QoS parameters that relates to a single aspect of service quality is named as a *QoS dimension*. Each of these QoS dimensions has different resource requirements for each possible level of service quality. We make the reasonable assumption that services' execution modes associated with higher QoS levels require higher resource amounts.

Users provide a single specification of their own range of acceptable QoS quality levels Q for a complete service S, ranging from a desired QoS level $L_{desired}$ to the maximum tolerable service degradation, specified by a minimum acceptable QoS level $L_{minimum}$, without having to understand the individual components that make up the service. Nodes dynamically group themselves into a new coalition, cooperatively allocating resources to each new service and establishing an initial Service Level Agreement (SLA) that maximises the satisfaction of the user's QoS constraints associated with the new service while minimises the impact on the global system's QoS caused by the new service's arrival [2]. Within a coalition, each component $c_i \in S$ will then be executed at a QoS level $L_{minimum} \leq Q^i_{val} \leq L_{desired}$ at a node n_i. This relation is represented by a triple (n_i, c_i, Q^i_{val}).

There may exist QoS interdependencies among two or more of the multiple QoS dimensions of a service S, both within a component and among components that may be in the same or in different nodes. Given two QoS dimensions, Q_a and Q_b, a QoS dimension Q_a is said to be dependent on another dimension Q_b if a change along the dimension Q_b will increase the needed resource demand to achieve the quality level previously achieved along Q_a [11]. Furthermore, we consider the existence of feasible QoS regions [8]. A region of output quality $[q(O)_1, q(O)_2]$ is defined as the QoS level that can be provided by a component when provided with sufficient input quality and resources. Within a QoS region, it may be possible to keep the current output quality level by compensating a decreased input quality by an increase in the amount of used resources or vice versa.

The set of QoS interdependencies among components $c_i \in S$ is represented as a connected graph $\mathcal{G}_S = (\mathcal{V}_S, \mathcal{E}_S)$, on top of the service's distribution graph, where each vertex $v_i \in \mathcal{V}_S$ represents a component c_i and a directed edge $e_i \in \mathcal{E}_S$ from c_j to c_k indicates that c_k is functionally dependent on c_j. Within $\mathcal{G}_S = (\mathcal{V}_S, \mathcal{E}_S)$, we call *cut-vertex* to a component $c_i \in \mathcal{V}_S$, if the removal of that component divides $\mathcal{G}_S$ in two separate connected graphs.

A component c_i is only aware of the set of inputs $I_{c_i} = \{(c_j, Q^j_{val}), \ldots, (c_k, Q^k_{val})\}$ describing the quality of all of its inputs coming from precedent components in $\mathcal{G}_\mathcal{W}$ and the set of outputs $O_{c_i} = \{(c_l, Q^l_{val}), \ldots, (c_p, Q^p_{val})\}$, describing the quality of all of its outputs sent to its successor components in $\mathcal{G}_\mathcal{W}$. As such, no global knowledge is required for coordinating the activation of a backup replica after a failure of a primary component c_i.

3   Towards a Flexible and Adaptive Replication Control

The possibility of partial failures is a fundamental characteristic of distributed applications, even more so in open environments. A sub-domain of reliability, fault tolerance aims at allowing a system to survive in spite of faults, *i.e.* after a fault has occurred, by means of redundancy. In this paper, we consider a failure to be when a software component stops producing output.

Replication is an effective way to achieve fault tolerance for such type of failure [12]. In fault-tolerant real-time systems, using active replication schemes, where several replicas run simultaneously, has been common [13]. Even if errors are detected in some of the replicas, the non-erroneous ones will still be able to produce results within the deadlines. On the negative side, running several replicas simultaneously is costly and can be infeasible or undesirable in distributed embedded systems [5] due to the limited resource availability and excessive overhead. Thus, a different approach is needed.

Passive replication [14] minimises resource consumption by only activating redundant replicas in case of failures, as typically providing and applying state updates is less resource demanding than requesting execution. As such, passive replication is appealing for soft real-time systems that cannot afford the cost of maintaining active replicas and tolerate an increased recovery time [15]. Nevertheless, it may still be possible to tolerate faults within deadlines, thus improving the system's reliability without using a more resource consuming fault-tolerance mechanism [16].

However, most of the existing solutions for passive fault tolerance are usually designed and configured at design time, explicitly and statically identifying the most critical components and their number of replicas, lacking the needed flexibility to handle the runtime dynamics of open distributed real-time embedded systems [6]. Distributed real-time embedded systems often consist of several independently developed components, shared across applications and whose criticality may evolve dynamically during the course of computation. As such, offline decisions on the number and allocation of replicas may be inadequate after the system has been executing for some time.

Consequently, the problem consists in finding a replication scheme which minimises the probability of failure of the most important components without replicating every software component. This involves the study of mechanisms to determine which components should be replicated, the quantity of replicas to be made, and where to deploy such replicas [17]. As such, the benefits of replication in open dynamic resource-constrained environments are a complex function of the number of replicas, the placement of those replicas, the selected replica consistency protocol, and the availability and performance characteristics of the nodes and networks composing the system. Since replica consistency protocols are relatively well understood [18,7,6], we will not consider them in the remainder of this paper.

Thus, assuming that a mechanism exists for keeping passive replicas consistent, how can we make use of passive replication for increasing the reliability of distributed resource-constrained embedded systems where it may not be possible to replicate every available component? Our approach is based on the concept of significance, a value associated to each component which reflects the effects of its failure on the overall system. Intuitively, the more a component c_i has other components depending on it, the more it is significant to the system as a whole. Then, the significance degree w_i of a component c_i can be computed as the aggregation of the interdependencies of other components on it, determining the usefulness of its outputs to all the components which depend on it to perform their tasks.

More formally, given $S_{\mathcal{G}} = \{\mathcal{G}_1, \ldots, \mathcal{G}_n\}$, the set of connected graphs of interdependencies between components for a given system, and $\mathcal{O}_{\mathcal{G}_j}(c_i)$, the out-degree of a node $c_i \in \mathcal{G}_j$, the significance wi of c_i is given by Equation 1.

$$w_i = \sum_{k=1}^{n} \mathcal{O}_{\mathcal{G}_k}(c_i) \tag{1}$$

Once the significance of each component to the system has been estimated, the decision on which components to replicate and the correspondent number of passive replicas must be taken. Equation 2 determines a number of replicas for a component c_i which is directly proportional to the component's significance degree w_i and to the maximum number of possible replicas max_{c_i}[1] and inversely proportional to the sum of the significance degree of all components in the system W.

$$n^{c_i} = \left\lceil \frac{w_i * max_{c_i}}{W} \right\rceil \qquad (2)$$

The next step is to determine a strategy for placing those replicas in the network. Consider the effects of placing replicas on unreliable nodes. The resulting unreliability of those replicas will usually require replica consistency protocols to work harder [6], increasing network traffic and processing overheads. Thus, not only will the system's performance suffer but its availability may actually decrease, despite the increased number of available components through replication [18]. However, an optimal replica placement in a distributed system can be classified as a NP-hard discrete location problem. Consequently, several heuristic strategies which do not have a guarantee in terms of solution quality or running time, but provide a robust approach to obtaining a high quality solution to problems of a realistic size in reasonable time have been investigated, independently of the followed replication approach [19,20]. Nevertheless, it is our belief that static offline approaches are inadequate for open real-time systems, where the environment dynamically changes as the system progresses. As such, a placement of a replica which was correct when a service was started may be incorrect after it has been executing for some time.

Two gross measures of the reliability of a node are its Mean Time To Failure (MTTF) and its Mean Time To Recovery (MTTR) [17]. We propose to use those measures to dynamically allocate the set of replicas of a component c_i based on the expected availability of nodes in the system. The utility $0 \leq u_k^{r_j^i} \leq 1$ of allocating a passive replica r_j^i of a component c_i to a node n_k is then defined by the probability of its availability during the system's execution, given by Equation 3. Utilities range from zero, the value of a completely unavailable node, to one, the value of a totally available node.

$$u_k^{r_j^i} = \frac{MTTF_k}{MTTF_k + MTTR_k} \qquad (3)$$

Having the utility of each possible allocation, the probability of failure of a given set of replicas $R_i = r_1^i, r_2^i, \ldots, r_{n^{c_i}}^i$ is determined by Equation 4.

$$F(R_i) = (1 - u_1^i) * (1 - u_2^i) * \ldots * (1 - u_{n^{c_i}}^i) \qquad (4)$$

The system will then allocate the set of replicas $R_i = r_1^i, r_2^i, \ldots, r_{n^{c_i}}^i$ such that its probability of failure $F(R_i)$ is minimal among all the possible allocation sets. In order to keep this allocation as up-to-date as possible, nodes have to be monitored as the system runs. If reliability of a replica set strays outside a predefined tolerance value a reconfiguration of the allocation set should be performed.

4   Coordinated Activation of Passive Backup Replicas

While passive replication is appealing for systems that cannot afford the cost of maintaining active replicas, the requirement to provide both high availability, strong state

---

[1] max_{c_i} is given by the number of nodes in a heterogeneous environment which have the needed type of resources to execute the component c_i.

consistency, and satisfactory response times during the non-failure cases is conflicting in many ways. In fact, response times perceived by applications will depend on the time taken by the primary replica to synchronise its state with that of the slowest backup replica, even if low complexity replica consistency protocols are used [6,7].

To overcome this limitation a possibility is for the backup replicas' state to be made consistent only during a failure's recovery, which significantly improves response times and saves resources during the non-failure cases. We recognise, however, that extra time must be spent to activate a new primary due to the significantly weaker consistency model. The problem is even more challenging when activating replicas in interdependent cooperative coalitions where the output produced by a component may depend not only on the amount and type of used resources but also on the quality of the received inputs [21]. Nevertheless, the complexity of the needed interactions among nodes until a new collective global service solution is determined can be reduced through a fast convergence protocol, while benefiting from a better performance on non-failure cases by only updating the backup replicas' state on a failure of a primary one.

Ideally, whenever a primary components fails it is elected as a new primary a backup which is able to obtain the needed resources to output the QoS level that was being produced by the old primary replica. However, due to the heterogeneity and dynamically varying workloads of nodes in the system, it is not guaranteed that at least one of the backups will be able to locally reserve the needed resources to output such quality level. Such feasibility is determined by the anytime local QoS optimisation algorithm of [2], which aims to minimise the impact of the activation of a new component on the currently provided QoS level of previously activated components at a particular node.

Thus, whenever the required QoS level cannot be assured by the new primary replica there is a need to ensure that individual substitutions of a component will produce a globally acceptable solution for the entire distributed interdependent service [22]. While there has been a great deal of research in several aspects of runtime coordination in embedded real-time systems [23,24,25,26], to the best of our knowledge we are the first to address the specific problem of coordinating the activation of passive replicas in interdependent distributed environments with real-time constraints. Here, the term *coordinated activation* refers to the ability of a distributed system to invoke adaptive actions on multiple nodes in a coordinated manner so as to achieve a new service configuration.

Without any central coordination entity, the collective adaptation behaviour must emerge from local interactions among components. This is typically accomplished by the exchange of multiple messages to ensure that all involved components make the same decision about whether and how to adapt [26]. One main challenge is controlling this exchange of information in order to achieve a convergence to a globally consistent solution. It may be difficult to predict the exact behaviour of the system taken as a whole due to the large number of possible non-deterministic ways in which the system can behave [27]. Whenever real-time decision making is in order, a timely answer to events suggests that after some finite and bounded time the global adaptation process converges to a consistent solution. We propose to achieve a time-bounded convergence to a global solution through a regulated decentralised coordination protocol defined by the following three phases:

1. **New primary selection.** Let Q_{val}^i be the QoS level that was being outputted by the primary replica of component $c_i \in S$ that has failed. If no passive replica of c_i is able to output the same QoS level, select the one which is able to output the QoS level $Q_{val'}^i < Q_{val}^i$ closer to Q_{val}^i. A coordination message is sent to affected partners in the coalition.

2. **Local adaptation.** Affected partners, executing any interdependent component $c_j \in S$, become aware of the new output values $Q_{val'}^i$ of c_i and recompute their local set of SLAs using the anytime QoS optimisation approach of [2]. We assume that coalition partners are willing to collaborate in order to achieve a global coalition's consistency, even if this might reduce the utility of their local optimisations.

3. **Coordinated adaptation.** Coalition partners affected by the decrease to $Q_{val'}^i$ in the path to the next cut-vertex $c_c \in S$ may be able to continue to output their current QoS level despite the downgraded input by compensating with an increased resource usage while others may not. If the next cut-vertex c_c is unable maintain its current QoS level then all the precedent components c_j which are compensating their downgraded inputs with an increased resource usage can downgrade to $Q_{val'}^j$ since their effort is useless.

Note that, if a cut-vertex c_c, despite the change in the current quality of some or all of its inputs, is able to maintain its current QoS level there is no need to further propagate the required coordination along the dependency graph $\mathcal{G}_S$, reducing the needed time to achieve a new acceptable global solution. On the other hand, if c_j is forced to downgrade its outputs due to the lower quality of its inputs, global resource usage is optimised by aborting useless compensations at precedent components in $\mathcal{G}_S$ and the coordination request is propagated. Thus, the core idea behind the proposed decentralised coordination model is to support distributed systems composed of autonomous individual nodes working without any central control but still producing the desired function as a whole. The proposed approach is sufficient to reach a new acceptable, non-optimal, service configuration in a time-bounded manner.

A formal validation of the properties and correctness of the proposed coordination model, as well as a detailed example of its operation, are available in [28].

5   Evaluation

An application that captures, compresses and transmits frames of video to end users, which may use a diversity of end devices and have different sets of QoS preferences, was used to evaluate the efficiency of the proposed passive replication mechanism with coordinated activations, with a special attention being devoted to introduce a high variability in the characteristics of the considered scenarios. The application is composed by a set of components to collect the data, a set of compression components to gather and compress the data sent from multiple sources, a set of transmission components to transmit the data over the network, a set of decompression components to convert the data into the user's specified format, and a set of components to display the data in the end device [2].

The number of simultaneous nodes in the system randomly varied, in each simulation run, from 10 to 100. For each node, the type and amount of available resources, creating a distributed heterogeneous environment. Nodes failed and recovered according to their MTTF and MTTR reliability values, which were randomly assigned when the nodes were created (it was ensured that each node had an availability between 60% and 99%). Each node was running a prototype implementation of the CooperatES framework [29], with a fixed set of mappings between requested QoS levels and resource requirements. At randomly selected nodes, new service requests from 5 to 20 simultaneous users were randomly generated, dynamically generating different amounts of load and resource availability. Based on each user's service request, coalitions of 4 to 20 components were formed [2] and a randomly percentage of the connections among those components was selected as a QoS interdependency.

In order to assess the efficiency of the proposed dynamic replication control as opposed to an offline static replication in dynamic resource-constrained environments, we considered the number of coalitions which where able to recover from failures and conclude their cooperative executions as a function of the used replication ratio. The reported results were observed from multiple and independent simulation runs, with initial conditions and parameters, but different seeds for the random values used to drive the simulations, obtaining independent and identically distributed variables. The mean values of all generated samples were used to produce the charts.

In the first study, we evaluated the achieved system's availability with the proposed dynamic replication control based on components' significance and with a static offline approach in which the components to replicate and their number of replicas is fixed by the system's designer at a coalition's initialisation phase [17]. At each simulation run, if the primary replica of a component c_i failed during operation, a new primary was selected among the set of passive backups. If this was not possible, all the coalitions depending on c_i were aborted. In this study, replicas were also randomly allocated among eligible nodes with the dynamic replication control policy.

Figure 1 clearly shows that our strategy is more accurate to determine and replicate the most significant components than a static offline one, particularly with lower replication ratios. Thus, when lower replication ratios are imposed due to resource or cost limitations, a higher availability can be achieved if the selection of which components to replicate and their number of replicas depends on their significance to the system as a whole. In open and dynamic environments, such significance can be determined online as the aggregation of all the other components that depend on a particular component to perform their tasks.

A second study evaluated the impact of the selected replicas' placement strategy on the achieved system's availability for a given replication ratio. The study compared the performance of the proposed allocation heuristic based on collected information about the nodes' availability as the system evolves with a random policy in which the placement of the generated replicas is fixed offline [30]. The decision on which components to replicate and their number of replicas followed the same dynamic and static approaches of the first study. For the dynamic allocation strategy, a tolerance value for the availability of each replica set was randomly generated at each simulation run. If this tolerance was surpassed, a reassignment of replicas was performed. The results were plotted in Figure 2.

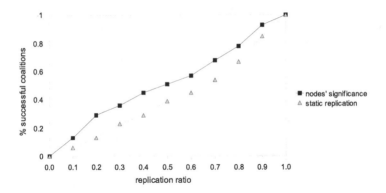

Fig. 1. Impact of the chosen replication control strategy on the system's availability

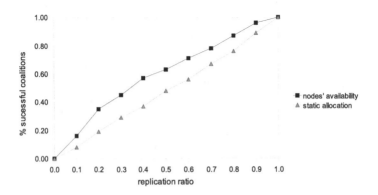

Fig. 2. Impact of the chosen replica allocation strategy on the system's availability

It is then possible to conclude that the location of replicas is a relevant factor for the system's availability as a whole. The proposed dynamic replicate allocation that takes into account the nodes' reliability over time always achieves a better performance than an offline static allocation policy in open and dynamic environments. Furthermore, a comparison of Figures 1 and 2 shows that even though an improvement in availability can be achieved by increasing the replication ratio, the impact of replicas' placement is quite significant.

A third study evaluated the efficiency of the proposed coordinated activation of inter-dependent passive replicas in comparison to a typical centralised coordination approach [31] in which a system-wide controller coordinates resource allocations among multiple nodes. The average results of all simulation runs for the different coalition sizes and percentages of interdependencies among components are plotted in Figure 3. As expected, both coordination approaches need more time as the complexity of the service's topology increases. Nevertheless, the proposed decentralised coordination model is faster to determine the overall coordination result in all the evaluated services' topologies, needing approximately 75% of the time spent by the centralised near-optimal model.

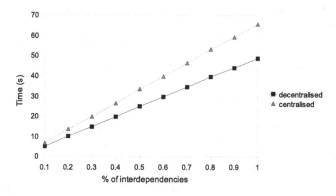

Fig. 3. Time for a coordinated replica activation

6 Conclusions

The availability and performance of open distributed embedded system is significantly affected by the choice of the replication control strategy and placement of the generated replicas. Due to its low resource consumption, passive replication is appealing for embedded real-time systems that cannot afford the cost of maintaining active replicas and need not assure hard real-time performance. The proposed heuristics based on the components' significance to the overall system and on nodes' reliability history have a low runtime complexity and achieve a reasonably higher system's availability than static offline decisions, particularly when lower replication ratios are imposed due to resource or cost limitations.

Another challenge is to transfer the state of a distributed service to a new globally acceptable configuration whenever a new elected primary cannot provide the same QoS level that was being outputted by the old primary that was found to be faulty. The proposed distributed coordination model reduces the complexity of the needed interactions among nodes and is faster to converge to a globally acceptable solution than a traditional centralised coordination approach.

Acknowledgements

This work was supported by FCT through the CISTER Research Unit - FCT UI 608 and the research project CooperatES - PTDC/EIA/71624/2006.

References

1. Anane, R.: Autonomic behaviour in qos management. In: Proceedings of the Third International Conference on Autonomic and Autonomous Systems, Athens, Greece, June 2007, p. 57 (2007)
2. Nogueira, L., Pinho, L.M.: Time-bounded distributed qos-aware service configuration in heterogeneous cooperative environments. Journal of Parallel and Distributed Computing 69(6), 491–507 (2009)

3. Kopetz, H.: Real-Time Systems: Design Principles for Distributed Embedded Applications. Kluwer, Dordrecht (1997)
4. Guerraoui, R., Schiper, A.: Software-based replication for fault tolerance. IEE Computer 30, 68–74 (1997)
5. Cai, Z., Kumar, V., Cooper, B.F., Eisenhauer, G., Schwan, K., Strom, R.E.: Utility-driven proactive management of availability in enterprise-scale information flows. In: Proceedings of the ACM/IFIP/USENIX 2006 International Conference on Middleware, pp. 382–403. Springer, Heidelberg (2006)
6. Rubel, P., Gillen, M., Loyall, J., Schantz, R., Gokhale, A., Balasubramanian, J., Paulos, A., Narasimhan, P.: Fault tolerant approaches for distributed real-time and embedded systems. In: Proceedings of the 2007 Military Communications Conference, Orlando, Florida, USA, October 2007, pp. 1–8 (2007)
7. de Juan-Marin, R., Decker, H., Munoz-Esco, F.D.: Revisiting hot passive replication. In: Proceedings of the 2nd International Conference on Availability, Reliability and Security, April 2007, pp. 93–102 (2007)
8. Shankar, M., de Miguel, M., Liu, J.W.S.: An end-to-end qos management architecture. In: Proceedings of the 5th IEEE Real-Time Technology and Applications Symposium, Washington, DC, USA, pp. 176–191. IEEE Computer Society, Los Alamitos (1999)
9. Allen, G., Dramlitsch, T., Foster, I., Karonis, N.T., Ripeanu, M., Seidel, E., Toonen, B.: Supporting efficient execution in heterogeneous distributed computing environments with cactus and globus. In: Proceedings of the 2001 ACM/IEEE conference on Supercomputing, November 2001, pp. 52–52 (2001)
10. Ensink, B., Adve, V.: Coordinating adaptations in distributed systems. In: Proceedings of the 24th International Conference on Distributed Computing Systems, Tokyo, Japan, March 2004, pp. 446–455 (2004)
11. Rajkumar, R., Lee, C., Lehoczky, J., Siewiorek, D.: A resource allocation model for qos management. In: Proceedings of the 18th IEEE Real-Time Systems Symposium, p. 298. IEEE Computer Society, Los Alamitos (1997)
12. Powell, D. (ed.): A generic fault-tolerant architecture for real-time dependable systems. Kluwer Academic Publishers, Norwell (2001)
13. Pinho, L.M., Vasques, F., Wellings, A.: Replication management in reliable real-time systems. Real-Time Systems 26(3), 261–296 (2004)
14. Budhiraja, N., Marzullo, K., Schneider, F.B., Toueg, S.: The primary-backup approach. In: Distributed systems, 2nd edn., pp. 199–216 (1993)
15. Balasubramanian, J., Tambe, S., Lu, C., Gokhale, A., Gill, C., Schmidt, D.C.: Adaptive failover for real-time middleware with passive replication. In: Proceedings of the 15th IEEE Real-Time and Embedded Technology and Applications Symposium, pp. 118–127. IEEE Computer Society, Los Alamitos (April 2009)
16. Tjora, A., Skavhaug, A.: A general mathematical model for run-time distributions in a passively replicated fault tolerant system. In: Proceedings of the 15th Euromicro Conference on Real-Time Systems, Porto, Portugal, July 2003, pp. 295–301 (2003)
17. Little, M.C., McCue, D.: The replica management system: a scheme for flexible and dynamic replication. In: Proceedings of the 2nd International Workshop on Configurable Distributed Systems, April 1994, pp. 46–57 (1994)
18. Little, M.C.: Object Replication in a Distributed System. PhD thesis, Department of Computing Science, Newcastle University (September 1991)
19. Streichert, T., Glaß, M., Wanka, R., Haubelt, C., Teich, J.: Topology-aware replica placement in fault-tolerant embedded networks. In: Proceedings of the 21st International Conference on Architecture of Computing Systems, Dresden, Germany, February 2008, pp. 23–37 (2008)

20. Fu, W., Xiao, N., Lu, X.: A quantitative survey on qos-aware replica placement. In: Proceedings of the 7th International Conference on Grid and Cooperative Computing, Shenzhen, China, October 2008, pp. 281–286 (2008)
21. Nogueira, L., Pinho, L.M.: Dynamic qos adaptation of inter-dependent task sets in cooperative embedded systems. In: Proceedings of the 2nd ACM International Conference on Autonomic Computing and Communication Systems, Turin, Italy, September 2008, p. 97 (2008)
22. Gelernter, D., Carriero, N.: Coordination languages and their significance. Communications of the ACM 35(2), 96–107 (1992)
23. Dorigo, M., Caro, G.D.: The ant colony optimization meta-heuristic. New ideas in optimization, 11–32 (1999)
24. De Wolf, T., Holvoet, T.: Towards autonomic computing: agent-based modelling, dynamical systems analysis, and decentralised control. In: Proceedings of the IEEE International Conference on Industrial Informatics, August 2003, pp. 470–479 (2003)
25. Boutilier, C., Das, R., Kephart, J.O., Tesauro, G., Walsh, W.E.: Cooperative negotiation in autonomic systems using incremental utility elicitation. In: Proceedings of the 19th Conference on Uncertainty in Artificial Intelligence, Acapulco, Mexico, August 2003, pp. 89–97 (2003)
26. Dowling, J., Haridi, S.: Reinforcement Learning: Theory and Applications. In: Decentralized Reinforcement Learning for the Online Optimization of Distributed Systems, pp. 142–167. I-Tech Education and Publishing, Vienna (2008)
27. Serugendo, G.D.M.: Handbook of Research on Nature Inspired Computing for Economy and Management. In: Autonomous Systems with Emergent Behaviour, September 2006, pp. 429–443. Idea Group, Inc., Hershey (2006)
28. Nogueira, L., Pinho, L.M., Coelho, J.: Towards a flexible and dynamic replication control for distributed real-time embedded systems with qos interdependencies. Technical report, CISTER Research Centre (February 2010), http://www.cister.isep.ipp.pt/docs/
29. Pinho, L.M., Nogueira, L., Barbosa, R.: An ada framework for qos-aware applications. In: Proceedings of the 10th Ada-Europe International Conference on Reliable Software Technologies, York, UK, June 2005, pp. 25–38 (2005)
30. On, G., Schmitt, J., Steinmetz, R.: Quality of availability: replica placement for widely distributed systems. In: Proceedings of the 11th International Workshop on Quality of Service, Monterey, CA, June 2003, pp. 325–342 (2003)
31. Rohloff, K., Schantz, R., Gabay, Y.: High-level dynamic resource management for distributed, real-time embedded systems. In: Proceedings of the 2007 Summer Computer Simulation Conference, July 2007, pp. 749–756 (2007)

Generation of Executable Testbenches from Natural Language Requirement Specifications for Embedded Real-Time Systems

Wolfgang Mueller[1], Alexander Bol[1], Alexander Krupp[1], and Ola Lundkvist[2]

[1] University of Paderborn/C-LAB, Paderborn, Germany
[2] Volvo Technology Corp., Mechatronics & Software, Gothenburg, Sweden

Abstract. We introduce a structured methodology for the generation of executable test environments from textual requirement specifications via UML class diagrams and the application of the classification tree methodology for embedded systems. The first phase is a stepwise transformation from unstructured English text into a textual normal form (TNF), which is automatically translated into UML class diagrams. After annotations of the class diagrams and the definition of test cases by sequence diagrams, both are converted into classification trees. From the classification trees we can finally generate SystemVerilog code. The methodology is introduced and evaluated by the example of an Adaptive Cruise Controller.

Keywords: Natural Language, UML, SystemVerilog, Testbenches.

1 Introduction

Since the introduction of the electronic injection control by Bosch in the 80s, we observed a rapid growth of electronic systems and software in vehicles. Today a modern car is equipped with 30-70 microcontrollers, so called ECUs (Electronic Control Units). With the acceptance of the AUTOSAR standard and its tool support there is a need for further automation in automotive systems developments, especially in the first design phases.

Currently, the model-based testing process is based on different design stages, like Model-in-the-Loop (MIL), Software-in-the-Loop (SIL), and Hardware-in-the-Loop (HIL) tests. In this context, different testing hardware and software come into application like MTest from dSPACE which compares to the Classification Tree Method for Embedded Systems (CTM/ES) which we applied in our work. While model-based testing is well supported by existing tools, one of the major challenges still remains the transformation of requirements to a first executable specification. In practice, such requirements are typically captured as unstructured text by means of tools like Rational DOORS from IBM. Today, we can identify a major gap between requirement specifications and first implementation of the executable testbench.

This article closes this gap by introducing a structured semi-automatic methodology for the generation of test environment via UML class diagrams and CTM/ES. The first phase performs a stepwise transformation of natural language sentences before

M. Hinchey et al. (Eds.): DIPES/BICC 2010, IFIP AICT 329, pp. 78–89, 2010.
© IFIP International Federation for Information Processing 2010

they are automatically translated into UML class diagrams. For automatic translation, we defined a textual normal form (TNF) as a subset of natural English sentences, where classes, attributes, functions, and relationships can be easily identified. The generated class diagrams are annotated by additional information so that we can - after the definition of test scenarios - generate a testbench. In our evaluation, we applied SystemVerilog and QuestaSim and linked it with native SystemC code and C code generated from Matlab/Simulink. Though we applied SystemVerilog for the implementation of this case study, our methodology is not limited to SystemVerilog. The introduced methodology may easily adapt to other languages like e [10] as long as they support function coverage definition and random test pattern generation.

The remainder of this article is structured as follows. The next section discusses related work including CTM/ES and principles of functional verification as basic technologies. Section 3 introduces the four steps of our methodology. Thereafter, we present experimental results in Section 4. Section 5 finally closes with a summary and a conclusion.

2 Existing Work

In embedded systems design, test processes for automotive software are based on tool support with heterogeneous test infrastructures. The model-based testing process is based on different development steps like Model-in-the-Loop (MIL), Software-in-the-Loop (SIL), and Hardware-in-the-Loop (HIL) tests. In this context, different testing environments come into application like ControlDesk, MTest, and AutomationDesk from dSPACE. Each test environment typically applies its own proprietary testing language or exchange format and we can find only very few approaches to standard languages like ETSI TTCN-3 and the OMG UML testing profile [16].

For natural language requirement specification capture and management, Rational DOORS or just MS Word or MS Excel is applied on a regular basis. In order to increase the level of automation, several XML-based formats for enhanced tool interoperabilities have been developed. For requirement captures, RIF (Requirement Interchange Format) has been defined by HIS (Hersteller Initiative Software) and is meanwhile adopted by several tools. For the exchange of test descriptions, ATML was introduced by IEEE [7] and TestML by the IMMOS project [5]. The latter provides an XML-based exchange format which supports functional, regression, Back-to-back and time partition tests where stimuli can be defined by different means like classification tree methodology for embedded systems (CTM/ES) [4], which is introduced in the next subsection.

In general, there has been early work for the formalization of text by entity relationship diagrams like [1] and multiple work for the generation of test cases from test scenarios like [13]. However, we are not aware of any work which combines those for the generation of complete test environments (i.e., testbench architectures and test cases) for real-time systems taking advantage of principles of functional verification, e.g., functional coverage and constraint based test pattern generation.

2.1 Classification Tree Method

Classification Trees were introduced by Daimler in the 90's [6]. Classification trees provide structured tree-oriented means for capturing test cases. Starting from an entry

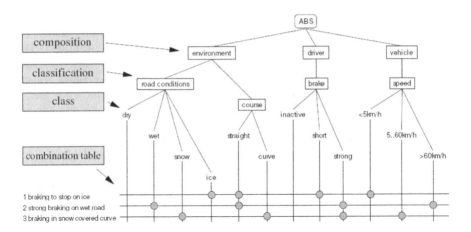

Fig. 1. Classification Tree

node, the test input is divided into compositions, classifications, and classes (see Fig. 1). A classification is divided into (equivalence) classes which represent an abstract set of test inputs each. A leaf class defines further an abstract set of possible input values. Columns and rows below define a combination table. Therein, in each row exactly one class of each classification is selected. Each row defines exactly one test step and compares to different states of the state machine which controls the test environment. The development of a classification is defined by the Classification Tree Method (CTM) [6], which is based on the Category-Partition-Method [14].

In its first introduction, classification trees described different variations of input stimuli of a System Under Test (SUT). As embedded automotive systems testing is based on sampling rates and time-based relationships between stimuli, Conrad has extended CTM to the Classification Tree Method for Embedded Systems (CTM/ES) [4]. As such, a classification tree is derived from the interface of the SUT and classifications from SUT inputs. The input domain is partitioned into different input interval classes like safety-critical ranges and corner cases. This compares to the definition of bins in the definition of a SystemVerilog functional coverage definition. For the management of more complex test suites, test cases are additionally divided into test sequences. Finally a timeline is assigned to each test sequence. That timeline is typically related to the sampling rate in automotive systems testing. Each horizontal line defines the inputs of a SUT for a specific time period where a time point stands for the activation or synchronization point of a test step. Therefore, an additional transition functions, e.g., step, ramp, sinus, has to be assigned to a synchronization point, which defines the transition between values of different synchronization points. In the combination table, different transition functions are indicated by different line styles between transition points (see Fig. 6).

2.2 Functional Verification

Our final verification environment based on the principles of functional verification. The notion of functional verification denotes the application of assertions, functional coverage, and constrained random test pattern generation in ESL and RTL designs. Such technologies are based on the application of Hardware Verification Languages like the IEEE Standards SystemVerilog [8], PSL [9] and e [10]. They support the formal and reusable definition of system properties for functional verification. Standardized APIs like the SystemVerilog DPI additionally support multi language environments and provide an interface to adapt proprietary test environments. Meanwhile, there exist several libraries and methodologies for additional support like VMM [2] and OVM [15].

3   Generation of Testbenches from Requirements Specifications

Our methodology for the derivation of executable SystemVerilog testbenches applies four different phases:

1. Formalization of Requirements
2. Transformation of Class Diagrams
3. Definition of Test Scenarios
4. Generation of the Testbench

We first provide a stepwise manual transformation of unstructured natural language English sentences into short structured English sentences. The latter can be seen as a first formal version of the requirements as they directly correspond to UML class diagrams to which they can be automatically translated. After some simple transformations of the class diagrams they are further translated into compositions, classifications, and classes of a classification tree for embedded systems. Concurrently, in Phase 3, test scenarios have to be developed. We propose the application of UML sequence diagrams though related means can be applied as well. The test scenarios compose the test sequences of the classification tree. Finally, we can automatically generate a testbench from the classification tree. In our case, we generate SystemVerilog code [8]. However, we can apply any comparable Hardware Verification Language which supports random test pattern generation and function coverage specification.

In the next paragraphs, we outline the four phases in further details. For this we apply an industrial case study from the automotive domain, i.e., an Adaptive Cruise Controllers (ACC) [3]. The ACC is a cruise controller with a radar-based distance control to a front (subject) vehicle. The ACC controls the cruise speed and the distance to the front vehicle in the same lane with the desired speed and a desired distance as input.

3.1   Formalization of Requirements

Starting from a set of unstructured English sentences, they are stepwise manually formalized into a Textual Normal Form (TNF) which is composed of unambiguous sentences which can be automatically transformed into a UML class diagram. Table 1 gives an example of some sentences before and after the transformation.

Table 1. Transformation of Unstructured Sentences

Unstructured Sentence	Transformed Sentences
The ACC system shall include a long-range radar sensor capable of detecting data about moving objects travelling in the same direction as the driven vehicle. If a vehicle is identified by the ACC a safety distance shall be kept by actuating over the throttle or applying the brakes if necessary. The ACC system shall operate under a limited speed range, between 20 and 125 km/h. The distance for detecting vehicles shall be limited to 150 meters.	*AdaptiveCruiseController is entity.*
	Radar is entity.
	AdaptiveCruiseController getsDataFrom Radar.
	AdaptiveCruiseController has currentDrivenVehicleSpeed {currentDrivenVehicleSpeed is between 20 and 125 km/h}.
	AdaptiveCruiseController has currentDistance {currentDistance is between 1 and 150 meters to SubjectVehicles}.

An unstructured textual requirement specification typically includes information about the logical description of the SUT and the environment. It identifies operational constraints and conditions but also logical components, functions, and attributes which include important information to implement test environments and test cases. The structured transformations of that information are an important step to support the traceability of requirements to their corresponding testbench components in order to guarantee the compliance of the testbench to the requirements for an advanced quality assurance.

The target of the first transformation phase is the Textual Normal Form (TNF). TNF is a machine readable presentation composed of three word sentences (plus constraints) which are later automatically transformed into UML class diagrams as an intermediate format. During the different manual transformation steps, redundancies, incompleteness, and contradictions can be much better identified by visual inspections than in the unstructured sentences. In the first step, we remove filler words and empty phrases, like *'basically'* and *'most likely'*. Thereafter, we transform long sentences into short sentences without disambiguities and incomplete information as far as possible. For instance, we split long sentences and transform subordinate clauses into main clauses and replace pronouns by proper nouns. Then, subjects and objects are transformed into identifiers, articles removed, and sentences translated into present tense. If necessary, this also means to combine or extend subjects/objects with attributes like *'Adaptive cruise controller system'* to *'AdaptiveCruiseController'*. After this, each identifier has to refer to exactly one entity, i.e., two different identifiers are not allowed to refer to the same entity and the same identifier shall not refer to different entities.

Finally, for each identifier *X*, we add an explicit sentence *'X is entity'*. This helps for later automatic translations and completeness checks by visual inspection. After the identification of entities, we have to further proceed with attributes, functions, and relationships. In details, we identify the attributes of each entity and separate it into a individual sentence of form *'<entity id> has <attribute id>'*, e.g., *'AdaptiveCruise Controller has currentDistance'* (cf. Table 1). We also associate attribute sentences with the corresponding constraints and append them enclosed in curly brackets. Thereafter, the identification of functions with constraints is similarly and results in sentences like *'Driver does applyBrakePedal'*. It is important to note here that we combine the verb with the object id for the final name of the operation in the later class diagram. Finally, all relationships between entities are identified and sentences like *'AdaptiveCruiseController getsDataFrom Radar'* are separated.

We finally arrive at a forest structured transformation relationship between original sentences at the root and TNF sentences at the leaves. When applying a simple tool like MS Excel, we can easily sort the final sentences by the first identifier (i.e., the subject), which helps to easily check for duplicates or subjects with similar meaning and even for incomplete specifications which can hardly be detected in the unstructured original text. The final TNF is nothing else than the textual representation of Class Diagrams which can thus be automatically derived along early works of Bailin [1]. For this consider the following TNF sentence examples:

- *AdaptiveCruiseController is entity..*
- *AdaptiveCruiseController has currentDistance*
- *AdaptiveCruiseController does controlCurrentDistance.*
- *AdaptiveCruiseController getsDataFrom Radar.*

We can easily see their direct correspondence to the UML Class Diagram in Fig. 2. For more details, the reader is referred to [1].

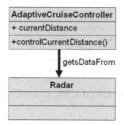

Fig. 2. UML Class Diagram

3.2 Transformation of Class Diagrams

In the second phase, Class Diagrams are structured and annotated before they are transformed into a classification tree, which is an intermediate representation for the automatic generation of the executable testbench.

As such, we first divide all classes into categories <<*environment*>> for the test environment and <<*system*>> for the SUT by assigning UML stereotypes to them. Thereafter, we analyze all attributes of all classes and divide them into: *in*, *out*, and *internal* with corresponding stereotypes. Attributes of the first category are further qualified by the delivering class as it is shown in Fig. 3. As we are dealing with distributed systems, we have to compute the same attributes by different classes. In that figure, we can also see the *out* category is actually redundant as the information is already implicitly covered by the two other categories. However, this redundancy helps to better analyze the interaction between the classes and to detect further inconsistencies as all *in* and *out* attributes of the DUT give a complete definition the DUT interface. Thereafter, we have to formalize all <<*out*>> attributes of all <<*environment*>>

classes. Let us consider *currentDrivenVehicleSpeed* of *DrivenVehicle* in Fig. 3 as an example. The original constraint defines that the ACC is only active between 20 and 125 km/h (see also the system class in Fig. 3). Considering a maximum vehicle speed of 250 km/h, we can formalize it by the definition of five intervals with 20 and 125 as corner values. In SystemVerilog syntax, this is defined as *{[0:19], 20, [21:124], 125, [126,260]}*. This example shows that several constraints can be retrieved from the original requirement specification. In practice, additional conventions and standards like IEC 61508 [13] have to be consulted to retrieve the complete set of constraints. Though our example defines closed intervals due to the limitations of SystemVerilog, without the loss of generality, we can also apply open intervals provided they are supported by the tools or verification language.

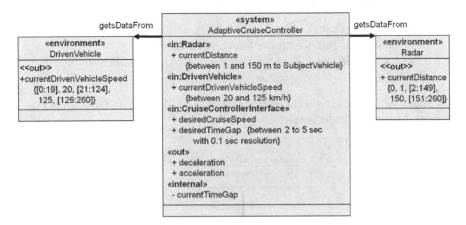

Fig. 3. Modified UML Class Diagram

The final version of the UML Class Diagram can now be directly translated into a classification tree (without a combination table) with the SUT at the root. The individual UML *environment* classes translate to the different compositions and the class attributes to classifications (cf. Fig. 4).

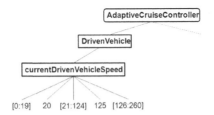

Fig. 4. Fraction of a Classification Tree for Embedded Systems

3.3 Definition of Test Scenarios

In the next step, we have to manually define test scenarios with test steps and test sequences for the completion of the classification tree. We start with the selection of one or more *environment* classes from the class diagram. The following example takes an interaction of the *Driver* and the *(Driven) Vehicle* with the ACC and defines a simplified scenario with five steps:

1. *Vehicle drives at a speed of 125 km/h.*
2. *Driver sets a new speed (desiredCruiseSpeed).*
3. *Driver sets distance to front vehicle (TimeGap).*
4. *Vehicle reaches a medium speed.*
5. *Vehicle reaches a high speed.*

We now can link the entities in the description to the classifications in the classification tree and define a UML Sequence Diagram in order to formalize the five steps. The individual steps of the description have to be mapped to message interactions with intervals as parameters. The next step is the creation of several instances of this Sequence Diagram with respect to the timeline and variations of message parameters. Fig. 5 gives an example of a possible instantiation. In this example, we assign the timeline to the time points 0s, +2s, +3s, and +5s. The vehicle starts with a speed of 125 km/h at 0s. At 3s the speed changes to an interval between 21 and 124 km/h. Hereafter, the speed increases at 5s.

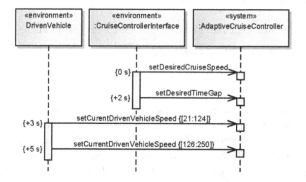

Fig. 5. Test Sequence as an UML Sequence Diagram

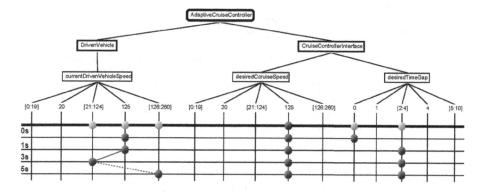

Fig. 6. Extended Classification Tree

Each of the Sequence Diagrams can be easily transformed to a test sequence of the classification tree. Fig. 5 shows part of the final classification tree, which is translated from the diagram of Fig. 5. Fig. 6 also shows some interpolation functions between synchronization points, which have to be defined before the generation of the testbench.

3.4 Testbench Generation

The final phase generates an executable testbench from the classification tree which includes the test sequences. More details of this phase can be found in [12]. Though we apply SystemVerilog here, other verification languages which support random test pattern generation and functional coverage can be taken as well. As an example, we focus on the application of SystemVerilog constraints for random test pattern generation in the following outlines.

After randomization, the input vectors with interpolation functions are applied to the specified SUT interface of the <<*system*>>. Due to the current tool support, the general execution is controlled from SystemVerilog where the SUT can be implemented in other languages like SystemC or C code generated from Matlab/Simulink. For the translation of classification tree test sequences, each test sequence is translated to a SystemVerilog class with array variables which correspond to the classifications of the classification tree, i.e., an input signal of the SUT:

```
class AdaptiveCruiseController_Sequence1;
    rand Int_class_sp
    currentDrivenVehicleSpeed[];
    ...
```

Furthermore, each array element corresponds to a test step of a classification tree test sequence for which randomization (*rand*) is applied. The array element has a data structure which includes an attribute for the time point of the test step, the value of the signal, and the individual interpolation function, like *ramp* or *sinus*. For each SystemVerilog class, we also generate a constraint block, which implements the constraints specified in the classification tree. The constraints implement the timing behavior and the selection of the equivalence class as follows:

```
constraint ctmemb{
    currentDrivenVehicleSpeed[0].t==0*SEC;
    currentDrivenVehicleSpeed[0].v==125;
    currentDrivenVehicleSpeed[1].t==
                    currentDrivenVehicleSpeed[0].t+2*SEC;
    currentDrivenVehicleSpeed[1].v==125;
    desiredTimeGap[0].t==currentDrivenVehicleSpeed[0].t;
    desiredTimeGap[0].v==0;
    desiredTimeGap[1].t==currentDrivenVehicleSpeed[1].t;
    desiredTimeGap[1].v inside {[2:4]}; ...
}
```

This example implements the constraints of the first two test steps (with index *1* and *0*) of test *Sequence1* for the two signals *currentDrivenVehicleSpeed* and *desired-TimeGap*. For each signal at each step, the time and the value is assigned. Here, *SEC* stands for the adjustment to the time unit of the simulation time. Along the classification tree specification, the second synchronization point is 2 seconds after the first one. The last line takes the interval *[2,4]* for the *desiredTimeGap* directly from the classification tree to SystemVerilog. Additionally, we define a method *pre_randomize()* for the SystemVerilog class, which instantiates array data in preparation for randomization and initializes values that are not randomized like the interpolation function.

```
function void pre_randomize
    foreach(currentDrivenVehicleSpeed[i])
        currentDrivenVehicleSpeed[i]=new();
    ...
    currentDrivenVehicleSpeed[1].ipol = ramp;
    ...
```

4 Experimental Results

We have applied the introduced the textual requirement specification of an Adaptive Cruise Controllers (ACC) in [3]. The original key requirements were composed of 23 long sentences. Those sentences were transformed by our methodology in to their Textual Normal Form (TNF) with finally 79 sentences. They were translated to a UML class diagram with 10 classes. Table 2 gives an overview of the details of the generated class diagram. The adapted class diagram had 6 classes, which were translated into a classification tree. Details of that classification tree can be found in Table 3. For our first evaluation we defined a limited set of 2 test scenarios which were related to 2 test sequences with 14 test steps each. The final test environment which was automatically generated from the classification tree was composed of 526 lines of SystemVerilog code.

Table 2. UML Class Diagram Numbers

Class	#attributes	#methods	#assoc. in	#assoc. out
AdaptiveCruiseControler	13	11	1	7
CruiseControlerInterface	3	8	2	2
Radar	5	6	1	1
Driver	0	2	1	3
SubjectVehicle	1	1	1	0
DrivenVehicle	1	0	3	0
BrakePedal	1	1	2	1
Accelerator	1	1	2	1
Brake	0	0	2	1
Throttle	0	0	2	1

Table 3. Classification Tree Numbers

Signal	# equivalence classes	component
acceleratorPosition	3	Accelerator
brakePedalPosition	3	BrakePedal
currentDistance	5	Radar
currentDrivenVehicleSpeed	5	DrivenVehicle
desiredCruiseSpeed	5	CruiseControlerInterface
desiredMode	2	CruiseControlerInterface
desiredTimeGap	5	CruiseControlerInterface
vehicleInSameLane	2	Radar

5 Conclusions and Outlook

This article presented a structured semi-automatic methodology for the generation of executable SystemVerilog testbenches from unstructured natural language requirement specification via UML and classification trees. After transformation into a Textual Normal Form (TNF), UML class diagrams are generated. After some annotations and simple adjustments they are further translated into a classification tree from which a SystemVerilog testbench is automatically generated. We successfully applied and evaluated our methodology to the requirements specification of an Adaptive Cruise Controller which was implemented in SystemC/C.

Our evaluation has shown that in the first phase until the final derivation of the TNF, several incomplete and redundant statements could be easily identified. This is a very important issue for industrial application as identification of inconsistencies and errors in very early design phases may result in a significant reduction of design respins. Due to our experience, with some extend, the detection of such errors based on manual transformations and visual inspection is currently still the most efficient and fastest method compared to a first time consuming transformation to a first formal model like finite state machines and logical formulae.

However, the main advantage of our methodology is definitely the complete traceability of each individual requirement to the corresponding objects or methods in the testbench. Though we just have used MS Excel to capture the requirements in our studies, it was easily possible to trace single requirements via subrequirements to SystemVerilog classes, methods and attributes. This greatly simplifies feedback with the customers in order to quickly resolve open design issues. Our studies have also indicated that it is very hard to achieve a complete automation of the first phase as transformations of natural language statements still require the dedicated expertise of a domain engineer. In contrast, transformations in later phases are subject of further possible automation. Our studies gave promising results and more evaluations have to follow.

Acknowledgments. The work described herein is partly funded by the BMBF through the SANITAS (01M3088) and the VERDE project (01S09012).

References

1. Bailin, S.C.: An Object-Oriented Requirements Specifications Method. Communication of the ACM 32(5) (May 1989)
2. Bergeron, J., Cerny, E., Nightingale, A., Hunter, A.: Verification Methodology Manual for System Verilog. Springer, Heidelberg (2006)
3. Bernin, F., Lundell, M., Lundkvist, O.: Automotive System Case Study, Deliverable D1.1 PUSSEE Project IST-2000-30103 (2002)
4. Conrad, M.: Modell-basierter Test eingebetteter Software im Automobil: Auswahl und Beschreibung von Testszenarien. Deutscher Universitätsverlag (2004)
5. Grossmann, J., Conrad, M., Fey, I., Krupp, A., Lamberg, K., Wewetzer, C.: TestML – A Test Exchange Language for Model-based Testing of Embedded Software. In: Automotive Software Workshop 2006, San Diego (March 2006)
6. Grochtmann, M., Grimm, K.: Software Testing, Verification and Reliability: Classification Trees for Partition Testing. John Wiley & Sons Verlag, Chichester (2006)
7. IEEE: Draft Specification for Component Standard of Automatic Test Markup Language (ATML) for Exchanging Test Results via XML (December 2004)
8. IEEE: IEEE Std.1800-2005 - Standard for SystemVerilog Unified Hardware Design, Specification and Verification Language (November 2005)
9. IEEE: IEEE Std.1850-2005 - IEEE Standard for Property Specification Language (PSL) (September 2005)
10. IEEE: IEEE Std.1647-2006 - The Functional Verification Language 'e' (March 2006)
11. IEC: Functional safety electrical/electronic/programmable electronic safety-related systems - IEC 61508 Part 1-7, Geneva, Switzerland (1998)
12. Krupp, A.: Verification Plan for Systematic Verification of Mechatronic Systems. Doctorial Thesis, Paderborn University (2008)
13. Offutt, J., Abdurazik, A.: Generating Tests from UML Specifications. In: France, R.B., Rumpe, B. (eds.) UML 1999. LNCS, vol. 1723, pp. 416–429. Springer, Heidelberg (1999)
14. Ostrand, T.J., Balcer, M.J.: The Category-Partition Method for Specifying and Generating Functional Tests. ACM, New York (1988)
15. OVM Homepage, http://www.ovmworld.org
16. Schieferdecker, I., Dai, Z.R., Grabowski, J., Rennoch, A.: The UML 2.0 Testing Profile and its Relation to TTCN-3. In: Proc. of TestCom 2003, Sophia Antipolis (2003)

Model Checking of Concurrent Algorithms: From Java to C

Cyrille Artho[1], Masami Hagiya[2], Watcharin Leungwattanakit[2],
Yoshinori Tanabe[3], and Mitsuharu Yamamoto[4]

[1] Research Center for Information Security (RCIS), AIST, Tokyo, Japan
[2] The University of Tokyo, Tokyo, Japan
[3] National Institute of Informatics, Tokyo, Japan
[4] Chiba University, Chiba, Japan

Abstract. Concurrent software is difficult to verify. Because the thread
schedule is not controlled by the application, testing may miss defects
that occur under specific thread schedules. This problem gave rise to software model checking, where the outcome of all possible thread schedules
is analyzed.

Among existing software model checkers for multi-threaded programs,
Java PathFinder for Java bytecode is probably the most flexible one. We
argue that compared to C programs, the virtual machine architecture of
Java, combined with the absence of direct low-level memory access, lends
itself to software model checking using a virtual machine approach. C
model checkers, on the other hand, often use a stateless approach, where
it is harder to avoid redundancy in the analysis.

Because of this, we found it beneficial to prototype a concurrent algorithm in Java, and use the richer feature set of a Java model checker,
before moving our implementation to C. As the thread models are nearly
identical, such a transition does not incur high development cost. Our
case studies confirm the potential of our approach.

1 Introduction

Concurrent software is often implemented using threads [26] to handle multiple active units of execution. Because the thread schedule is not controlled by
the application, the usage of concurrency introduces implicit non-determinism.
Without proper guards against incorrect concurrent access, so-called race conditions may occur, where the outcome of an two concurrent operations is no longer
well-defined for all possible interleavings in which they may occur.

In software testing, a given test execution only covers one particular instance
of all possible schedules. To ensure that no schedules cause a failure, it is desirable to model check software. *Model checking* explores, as far as computational
resources allow, the entire behavior of a system under test by investigating each
reachable system state [10], accounting for non-determinism in external inputs,
such as thread schedules. Recently, model checking has been applied directly to
software [5,6,8,11,12,13,27,28]. Initially, software model checkers were *stateless:*

M. Hinchey et al. (Eds.): DIPES/BICC 2010, IFIP AICT 329, pp. 90–101, 2010.

after backtracking, the program is restarted, and the history of visited program states is not kept [13]. This makes the model checker more light-weight, at the expense of potentially analyzing redundant states. *Stateful* model checkers keep a (possibly compressed) representation of each visited state. This allows a model checker to backtrack to a previously visited state without having to re-execute a program up to that point, and also avoids repeated explorations of equivalent (redundant) states.

Certain programming languages, such as C [17] or C++ [25], allow direct low-level memory access. *Pointer arithmetic* allows the usage of any integer offset together with a base pointer, making it impossible to guarantee memory safety in the general case. Memory safety implies that memory which is read has been allocated and initialized beforehand. Program behavior is undefined for unsafe memory accesses. More recently developed programming languages, such as Java [14], Eiffel [21], or C# [22], can restrict memory accesses to be always safe. This feature, in conjunction with garbage collection, relieves the developer from the burden of manual memory management. It also makes it easier to define the semantics of operations, and to perform program analysis.

Embedded systems may be implemented on a platform supporting either Java or C. Due to its managed memory, Java is easier to develop for, but the ease comes at the expense of a higher memory usage. Embedded systems, or core algorithms used therein, may therefore be prototyped in Java, and moved to C if resource constraints require it. In such cases, it is useful to verify the Java version in detail before translating it to C for further optimization.

In addition to memory safety, the object-oriented semantics and strong typing of many more recent programming languages facilitate the analysis of the heap structure. This enables efficient execution inside a virtual machine [20] and also allows program states to be mutated and compared easily. Software model checking benefits greatly from this, as stateful model checking can be implemented much more readily for such programming languages. Besides the promise of avoiding redundant states, the statefulness of a model checker can also be exploited for programs that utilize network communication. The results of network communication can be cached, making analysis orders of magnitude more efficient than in cases where the entire environment has to be restarted [4]. Such an input/output cache has been implemented for the Java PathFinder model checker, which analyzes Java bytecode [27]. That cache is one of about 15 available extensions for that model checker, making it much more flexible and feature-rich than its counterparts for C or C++.

Finally, it is easier to debug a concurrent implementation when memory safety is not an issue; the developer can focus on concurrency aspects without worrying about memory safety. Because of this, and the flexibility of Java model checkers, we argue that it is often beneficial to develop a concurrent algorithm in Java first. After analysis, the Java version can be readily converted to C (or C++) using the pThreads thread library. We have successfully applied this paradigm to multiple implementations of concurrent algorithms. Compared to a compilation of Java to machine code, a source-level translation has the advantage that stack memory for non-primitive data types and other optimizations are available. A verification of the resulting C code detects possible translation errors.

Translations from a higher-level language to a lower-level one are common in *model-based code generation*. However, in that domain, more abstract languages such as state charts [15] are common. High-level models prevent low-level access conflicts but cannot be optimized for fine-grained concurrency in ways that Java or C code can. Our translation is on code level, because thread-level parallelism with the explicit usage of mutual exclusion through locking is still prevalent in implementations of concurrent systems.

Related work exists in translating C code to Java [16]. That translation considers self-contained programs and mostly targets the implementation of pointer arithmetic in C as arrays in Java. For concurrent programs, manual case studies have been performed on the conversion of a space craft controller written in C, to Java [7]. The Java version was developed for analysis purposes because no suitable tools for analyzing multi-threaded C software existed at that time. We advocate the reverse direction, a translation from Java to C, because the Java version can be more readily developed, given the higher automation of low-level tasks by the run-time environment, and because more powerful concurrency analysis tools are available.

The rest of this paper is organized as follows: Section 2 introduces threads in Java and C. Section 3 shows our mapping of multi-threaded Java code to C. Experiments are described in Section 4. Section 5 concludes.

2   Thread Models in Java and C

A *thread* is an independent unit of execution, with its own program counter and stack frame, and possibly a separate memory region (thread-local memory) [26]. It typically interacts with other threads through semaphores (signals), and ensures mutual exclusion by using monitors (locks). Threads are started by a parent thread, which is the only thread of execution in a process at its creation. Execution may merge with other threads by "joining" them, waiting for their termination.

The standard version of Java has built-in support for multi-threading. In Java, a thread has its own program counter and stack frame, but shares the main memory with all other application threads. Threads may run on one or more hardware processors, potentially by using time-slicing to support more threads than available processors [14]. The C programming language has no built-in support for threads [17]. However, on most modern operating systems, threads are supported by libraries following the POSIX threads (pThreads) standard [23].

As Java threads were designed with the possibility of an underlying pThreads implementation in mind, the two thread models have much in common. The specified memory model allows each thread to hold shared data (from main memory) in a thread-local cache. This cache may be out of date with respect to the copy in main memory. Whenever a lock is acquired or released, though, values in the thread-local cache are synchronized with the main memory [14].

This behavior of Java is similar to other programming environments, in particular typical environments supporting the pThreads standard. Furthermore, there are no constraints on the thread scheduling algorithm; while it is possible to set thread priorities, both the Java and the pThreads platforms do not have to adhere to thread priorities strictly [14,23]. Most importantly, the rather unrestricted memory model used by Java does not imply the sequential consistency [18] of a sequence of actions within one thread. Instruction reorderings, which are performed by most modern hardware processors, are permitted, requiring a concurrent implementation to use locking to ensure mutual exclusion and correct execution. As a consequence of this, a concurrent program in Java needs to use the same safeguards that a concurrent program written in C uses.

Finally, variables in Java and C may be declared as `volatile`, disallowing thread-local caching of such values. Because read-and-set accesses of `volatile` values are not atomic, there exist few cases where they are actually used in practice. We do not cover `volatile` values further in this paper.

3   Mapping Java to C

We define a mapping of Java thread functions to C here. This allows a developer to write an initial version of a concurrent algorithm in Java. The version can then be transformed to C, for example, if the memory requirements of Java may not be fulfilled by an embedded platform. The translation is discussed both in terms of differences in the concepts and in the application programming interface (API) of the two implementations. A complete transformation of a program entails addressing other issues, which are mentioned at the end of this section.

3.1   Threads

Both in Java and C, threads are independent units of execution, sharing global memory. Data structures that are internal to a thread are stored in instances of `java.lang.Thread` in Java [14], and of the `pthread_t` data structure when using pThreads [23]. These data structures can be initialized via their constructor in Java or by setting attributes in pThreads. The functionality of the child thread is specified via inheritance in Java, and via a function pointer in C. These mechanisms correspond to the object-oriented paradigm of Java and the imperative paradigm of C, and can be easily transformed. Likewise, functions to start the child thread, join the execution of another thread (awaiting its termination) or terminate the current thread, are readily translated (see Table 1).

3.2   Locks

Some of the concurrent functionality of Java cannot be mapped isomorphically. Specifically, important differences exist for locking and shared conditions (semaphores). In Java, each object may be used as a lock; the initialization of the lock, and access to platform-specific lock properties, are not specified by

Table 1. Comparison between thread primitives for Java and C

Function	Java	C
Thread start	`java.lang.Thread.start`	`pthread_create`
Thread end	end of `run` method	`pthread_exit`
Join another thread	`java.lang.Thread.join`	`pthread_join`
Lock initialization	implicit with object creation	`pthread_mutex_init`
Acquire lock	`synchronized` keyword	`pthread_mutex_lock`
Release lock	`synchronized` keyword	`pthread_mutex_unlock`
Lock deallocation	implicit with garbage collection	`pthread_mutex_destroy`
Initialize condition	conditions are tied to locks	`pthread_cond_init`
Wait on condition	`java.lang.Object.wait`	`pthread_cond_wait`
Signal established cond.	`java.lang.Object.notify`	`pthread_cond_signal`
Broadcast est. cond.	`java.lang.Object.notifyAll`	`pthread_cond_broadcast`
Deallocate condition	implicit with garbage collection	`pthread_cond_destroy`

Java code and happen internally in the Java virtual machine [20]. In pThreads, on the other hand, lock objects have to be created and initialized explicitly. Locks use the opaque C data type `pthread_mutex_t`, which is initialized through `pthread_mutex_init` and managed by the library. In Java, classes derive from base class `java.lang.Object` and carry their own data, in addition to the implicit (hidden) lock; in C using pThreads, application data and lock data are separate. Therefore, locks in Java have to be transformed in two possible ways, depending on their usage:

Lock only: Instances of `java.lang.Object` carry no user-defined data and may be used for the sole purpose of locking. They can be substituted with an instance of `pthread_mutex_t` in pThreads.

Locks combined with data: In all other cases, instances are used both as data structures and as objects. They have to be split into two entities in C, where application-specific data structures and pThread locks are separate.

Similarly, the syntax with which locking is used is quite different between the two platforms: In Java, a `synchronized` block takes a lock as an argument. The lock is obtained at the beginning of the block and released at the end of it. The current thread is suspended if the lock is already taken by another thread. Locks in Java are reentrant, i.e., nested acquisitions and releases of locks are possible. Furthermore, there exists a syntactic variation of locking, by annotating an entire method as `synchronized`. This corresponds to obtaining a lock on the current instance (`this`) for the duration of a method, as if a `synchronized` block spanning the entire method had been specified.

After transforming `synchronized` methods to blocks, lock acquisitions and releases in Java can be readily mapped to C. The beginning of a `synchronized` block is mapped to `pthread_mutex_lock`, using the lock corresponding to the argument to `synchronized`. Lock releases are mapped likewise (see Table 1). Reentrancy is supported by pThreads through a corresponding attribute. Finally, locks should be explicitly deallocated in C to prevent resource leaks.

Java	C
| ```
synchronized (lock) {
  while (!condition) {
    try {
      lock.wait();
    } catch (InterruptedException e) {
    }
  }
  assert (condition);
  ... // condition established
}
``` | ```
pthread_mutex_lock (&lock);
while (!condition) {

  pthread_cond_wait (&cond_var, &lock);
  // explicit condition variable
  // of type pthread_cond_t
}
assert (condition);
... // condition established
pthread_mutex_unlock (&lock);
``` |

Fig. 1. Inter-thread conditional variables in Java and C

3.3 Conditions

Efficient inter-thread communication requires mechanisms to notify other threads about important status (condition) changes. To avoid busy-waiting loops, Java and pThreads offer mechanisms to wait for a condition, and to signal that the condition has been established. The mechanism is similar on both platforms, with one major difference: In Java, locks are used as a data structure to signal the status of a shared condition. In pThreads, there is a need for a separate *condition variable*, in addition to the lock in question.

In Java, due to the absence of condition objects, there always exists a one-to-one relationship between locks and condition variables. In pThreads, several condition variables may relate to the same lock, a fact that is further elucidated below. Figure 1 shows how shared conditions are mapped. The condition itself is expressed through a boolean variable or a complex expression. If the condition is not established, a thread may suspend itself using wait, awaiting a signal. Both in Java and C, a lock has to be held throughout the process; Java furthermore requires to check for the presence of an InterruptedException, because a waiting thread may optionally be interrupted by another thread.

3.4 Possible Implementation Refinements for pThreads

There are a couple of differences between Java threads and POSIX threads that allow for a more efficient implementation in C, by exploiting low-level data structures that are not accessible in Java. This may be exploited when translating an algorithm from Java to C. As such a translation cannot always be done automatically, another verification against concurrency defects is advisable when optimizing the C/pThreads implementation.

- When using pThreads, the function executing in its own thread may return a pointer to a thread waiting for its termination. This allows a thread to return data directly, rather via other ways of sharing.
- Separate condition variables in pThreads (pthread_cond_t) enable a decoupling of related but distinct conditions. In the experiments, we describe a case where the Java version uses one lock to signal the emptiness or fullness

of a queue. In C, the two cases can be separated, which sometimes yields performance improvements.

- The pThreads library has a function `pthread_once`, for which no direct equivalent exists in Java. This mechanism allows a function to be executed at most once, resembling the way static initializers are used in Java to initialize class-specific data. Unlike static initializers, the execution of `pthread_once` is not tied to another event, such as class initialization.
- In pThreads, it is possible to forgo the acquisition of a lock when the lock is already taken, by using `pthread_mutex_trylock`. In some cases, the same effect may be achieved in newer versions of Java by checking if a particular thread already holds a lock (by calling `Thread.holdsLock`, available from Java version 1.4 and higher).

Furthermore, both platforms offer ways to fine-tune the performance of thread scheduling using specific API calls in Java, and via attributes in pThreads. This does not affect the correctness of algorithms, and is elided here.

Finally, newer versions of Java (1.5 and later) offer read-write locks (`java.util.concurrent.lock.ReentrantReadWriteLock`), and barriers (`java.util.concurrent.CyclicBarrier`), which facilitate the implementation of certain distributed algorithms. Equivalent facilities are provided by pThreads, as `pthread_rwlock_t` and `pthread_barrier_t`, respectively. The translation of these and other similar functions resemble the translations shown above, and are not described in further detail here.

3.5 Other Mappings

It is possible to compile Java to machine code, or to automate the mapping of Java programs to C, but the result will not be efficient. Java allocates all non-primitive data on the heap, while C allows complex data to be allocated on the stack. Stack-based allocation requires no explicit memory management or garbage collection, and is more efficient than heap memory. Furthermore, if Java heap memory is emulated in C, that memory has to be managed by garbage collection as well. A manual translation therefore yields better results.

Among library functionality other than multi-threading, Java offers many types of complex data structures such as sets, maps, and hash tables. These have to be substituted with equivalent data structures in C, provided by third-party libraries. In our experiments, we used a publicly available hash table [9] as a substitute for the hash table provided by the Java standard library.

Finally, for programs using input/output such as networking, the corresponding library calls have to be translated. In these libraries, the Java API offers some "convenience methods", which implement a sequence of low-level library calls. The C version may require additional function calls and data structures.

4   Experiments

In our experiments, we verify two concurrent algorithms, and one concurrent client/server program. To our knowledge, no higher-level code synthesis approach supports all types of parallelism used, so we advocate a verification of the implementation itself. We verified the Java and C versions using Java PathFinder [27], and inspect [28], respectively. At the time of writing, they were the only model checkers to support enough of the core and thread libraries to be applicable.

4.1 Example Programs

We originally tried to obtain multi-threaded programs written in Java and C from a well-known web page hosting benchmarks for various problems, implemented in different programming languages [1]. Unfortunately, the quality of the implementations is not sufficient for a scientific comparison. The different implementations are not translations from one language to another, but completely independent implementations. Their efficiency, due to differences in the algorithm, may vary by orders of magnitudes.

Hash. The first example is provided by a source that strives for a faithful translation of a benchmark from Java to C++ [24]. We then translated the C++ version to C, and implemented a concurrent version in C and Java.

The program counts the number of matching strings for numbers in hexadecimal and decimal notation, up to a given value. It uses a hash table to store the strings, and worker threads to compute the string representations of each number. While the concurrent implementation is not faster than the sequential one, due to contention on the lock guarding the global data structure, it is still a useful benchmark for model checking. The program utilizes the typical worker thread architecture with fork/join synchronization, which is also found in mathematical simulations and similar problems.

Queue. This example implements a blocking, thread-safe queue that offers atomic insertions and removals of n elements at a time. The queue uses a fixed-size buffer, and obeys the constraints that the removal of n elements requires at least n elements to be present, and that the buffer size may not be exceeded. When these constraints cannot be fulfilled, the queue blocks until the operation can be allowed. The queue uses a circular buffer, which wraps around when necessary.

The C version of the queue is used in an ongoing project about model checking networked software [19]. The algorithm has originally been developed and verified in Java, before it has been translated to C, inspiring this paper.

Alphabet client/server. The last benchmark is a client/server program. The alphabet client communicates with the alphabet server using two threads per connection: a producer and a consumer thread. The server expects a string containing a number, terminated by a newline character, and returns the corresponding character of the alphabet [3]. In this case, both the client and the server are multi-threaded, and were model checked in two steps; in each step, one side is run in the model checker, using a cache layer to intercept communication between the model checker and peer processes [4]. For the alphabet server, we used both a correct and a faulty version. The faulty version included a read-write access pattern where the lock is released in between, constituting an atomicity race [2], as confirmed by an assertion failure that checks for this.

4.2   Translation to C

Translation of the Java version to the C version proceeded as described in Section 3. For the hash benchmark, we kept the optimization where the C version allocates a single large buffer to hold all strings [24]. This optimization is not (directly) possible in Java. In the Java version, locking was used implicitly by wrapping the global hash table (of type `java.util.HashMap`) in a synchronized container, using `java.util.Collections.synchronizedMap`. A corresponding lock was used in the C translation.

In the queue example, we split the conditions for fullness/emptiness into separate condition variables, as described in Section 3. There were no special issues when translating the alphabet client/server. However, for the experiments, the execution of the peer processes had to be automated by a script, which checks for the existence of a temporary file generated whenever the C model checker inspect starts a new execution run.

4.3   Verification Results

All experiments were run on the latest stable release of Java PathFinder (4.0 r1258) and the C model checker inspect, version 0.3. We analyzed the default properties: the absence of deadlocks; assertion violations; and, for Java, uncaught exceptions. Table 2 shows the results. It lists each application (including parameters), the number of threads used, and the time and number of transitions taken for model checking the Java and C version, respectively.

Being a stateful model checker, Java PathFinder (JPF) can check if transitions lead to a new or previously visited state. In the latter case, the search can be pruned. The ratio of such pruned branches to new states grows for more complex cases. This is indicated as a percentage in Table 2; one should keep in mind that previously visited states may include entire subtrees (with additional redundant states), so the percentage is a lower bound on the potential overhead of a stateless search. The C model checker fares much better on small systems with fewer states, as its lightweight architecture can explore more execution runs in a given time than JPF does. One should note that transitions are not always equivalent in the two versions, owing to differences in the language semantics of Java and C, and in the implementations of the model checker platforms.

Inspect had an internal problem when analyzing the alphabet client. We expect such problems to disappear as the tool becomes more mature. Other than that, the alphabet server case stands out, where inspect was very fast. In the correct version of the alphabet server, there is no data flow between threads. The data flow analysis of inspect recognizes this, allowing inspect to treat these thread executions as atomic, and to skip the analysis of different orders of network messages on separate channels. After the insertion of an atomicity race [2] into the alphabet server, transitions inside a thread are broken up, resulting in

Table 2. Verification results for Java and C versions of the same programs

Application	# thr.	Java				C	
		Time [s]	Transitions			Time [s]	Trans.
			new	visited	vis./new [%]		
Hash (4 elements)	1	1.36	73	34	46	0.03	91
	2	2.76	1,237	1,500	121	0.76	1,438
	3	128.84	124,946	218,748	175	10.72	18,789
	4	> 1 h				288.02	501,576
Hash (8 elements)	1	1.41	121	58	47	0.04	147
	2	3.56	2,617	3,416	130	119.27	181,332
	3	283.90	381,233	748,583	196	> 1 h	
	4	> 1 h				> 1 h	
Hash (17 elements)	1	1.56	205	100	48	0.07	268
	2	7.25	9,882	13,709	138	> 1 h	
	3	1034.51	1,617,695	3,386,868	209	> 1 h	
Queue	2	1.45	121	72	59	0.06	77
(size 5, atomic	3	2.15	958	699	72	0.91	1,130
insert/remove with	4	23.25	47,973	81,849	170	54.67	62,952
two elements)	5	236.72	494,965	975,576	197	> 1 h	
	6	2622.14	4,982,175	12,304,490	246	> 1 h	
Alphabet Client	3	3.01	1,607	4,226	262		
(3 messages)	4	20.12	21,445	83,402	388		
	5	291.95	275,711	1,423,326	516		
Alphabet Client	3	3.83	2,354	6,032	256	Assertion failure	
(4 messages)	4	32.68	35,159	133,556	379	inside inspect	
	5	553.87	501,836	2,533,616	504	model checker	
Alphabet Client	3	4.63	3,281	8,234	250		
(5 messages)	4	50.73	53,957	201,122	372		
	5	972.50	843,521	4,182,406	495		
Correct	3	8.08	589	1,164	197	0.14	33
Alphabet Server	4	21.29	12,635	36,776	291	0.15	42
(3 messages)	5	124.75	89,590	351,517	392	0.19	51
Correct	3	8.61	959	1,903	198	0.14	36
Alphabet Server	4	30.48	22,560	65,617	290	0.15	46
(4 messages)	5	253.93	179,197	704,855	393	0.19	61
Correct	3	9.23	1,455	2,894	198	0.14	39
Alphabet Server	4	44.55	37,327	108,466	290	0.17	50
(5 messages)	5	391.17	326,862	1,287,935	394	0.21	61
Atomic-race	3	7.45	141	225	159	1.83	2,633
Alphabet Server	4	9.63	146	333	228	43.64	76,502
(3 messages)	5	11.79	158	457	289	2905.33	3,565,667
Atomic-race	3	7.60	183	304	166	1.79	2,747
Alphabet Server	4	9.82	190	453	238	44.43	79,213
(4 messages)	5	12.04	204	619	303	2542.21	3,667,525
Atomic-race	3	7.76	231	395	170	1.86	2,861
Alphabet Server	4	10.04	240	591	246	45.20	81,924
(5 messages)	5	12.26	256	805	314	2541.16	3,769,383

an explosion of the state space. JPF has an advantage in that case, because the caching of network input/output [4] enables the model checker to generate most interleavings of network messages in memory, as opposed to having to execute the peer process many times (up to 113,400 times for five messages).

5   Conclusions

Nowadays, embedded systems may be developed either in Java or C. Java offers easier development, but a translation to C may be necessary if system constraints require it. We show that a development approach where a concurrent core algorithm is developed in Java and then translated to C. Concurrency primitives in Java can be readily mapped to POSIX threads in C. A direct, automatic translation from Java to C is theoretically possible, but a manual translation may yield a more efficient program. Areas where the C code can be optimized include memory allocation and a more fine-grained treatment of condition variables.

Because concurrent software is difficult to verify, we believe that software model checking is an invaluable tool to analyze multi-threaded code. Software model checkers for Java are currently more flexible and powerful than for C. Because of this, it can be beneficial to develop a concurrent algorithm in Java first. Our case studies confirm the viability of the approach.

Acknowledgements

We would like to thank the research team developing *inspect* for their feedback and advice on using their tool.

This work was supported by a *kakenhi* grant (2030006) from JSPS.

References

1. The computer language benchmarks game (2010),
   http://shootout.alioth.debian.org/
2. Artho, C., Biere, A., Havelund, K.: Using block-local atomicity to detect stale-value concurrency errors. In: Wang, F. (ed.) ATVA 2004. LNCS, vol. 3299, pp. 150–164. Springer, Heidelberg (2004)
3. Artho, C., Leungwattanakit, W., Hagiya, M., Tanabe, Y.: Efficient model checking of networked applications. In: Proc. TOOLS EUROPE 2008. LNBIP, vol. 19, pp. 22–40. Springer, Heidelberg (2008)
4. Artho, C., Leungwattanakit, W., Hagiya, M., Tanabe, Y., Yamamoto, M.: Cache-based model checking of networked applications: From linear to branching time. In: Proc. ASE 2009, Auckland, New Zealand, pp. 447–458. IEEE Computer Society, Los Alamitos (2009)
5. Artho, C., Schuppan, V., Biere, A., Eugster, P., Baur, M., Zweimüller, B.: JNuke: Efficient dynamic analysis for Java. In: Alur, R., Peled, D.A. (eds.) CAV 2004. LNCS, vol. 3114, pp. 462–465. Springer, Heidelberg (2004)

6. Ball, T., Podelski, A., Rajamani, S.: Boolean and Cartesian abstractions for model checking C programs. In: Margaria, T., Yi, W. (eds.) TACAS 2001. LNCS, vol. 2031, pp. 268–285. Springer, Heidelberg (2001)
7. Brat, G., Drusinsky, D., Giannakopoulou, D., Goldberg, A., Havelund, K., Lowry, M., Pasareanu, C., Visser, W., Washington, R.: Experimental evaluation of verification and validation tools on Martian rover software. Formal Methods in System Design 25(2), 167–198 (2004)
8. Chaki, S., Clarke, E., Groce, A., Jha, S., Veith, H.: Modular verification of software components in C. IEEE Trans. on Software Eng. 30(6), 388–402 (2004)
9. Clark, C.: C hash table (2005), http://www.cl.cam.ac.uk/~cwc22/hashtable/
10. Clarke, E., Grumberg, O., Peled, D.: Model checking. MIT Press, Cambridge (1999)
11. Clarke, E., Kroening, D., Sharygina, N., Yorav, K.: SATABS: SAT-based predicate abstraction for ANSI-C. In: Halbwachs, N., Zuck, L.D. (eds.) TACAS 2005. LNCS, vol. 3440, pp. 570–574. Springer, Heidelberg (2005)
12. Corbett, J., Dwyer, M., Hatcliff, J., Pasareanu, C., Robby, Laubach, S., Zheng, H.: Bandera: Extracting finite-state models from Java source code. In: Proc. ICSE 2000, Limerick, Ireland, pp. 439–448. ACM Press, New York (2000)
13. Godefroid, P.: Model checking for programming languages using VeriSoft. In: Proc. POPL 1997, Paris, France, pp. 174–186. ACM Press, New York (1997)
14. Gosling, J., Joy, B., Steele, G., Bracha, G.: The Java Language Specification, 3rd edn. Addison-Wesley, Reading (2005)
15. Harel, D.: Statecharts: A visual formalism for complex systems. Sci. Comput. Program 8(3), 231–274 (1987)
16. Kamijima, Y., Sumii, E.: Safe implementation of C pointer arithmetics by translation to Java. Computer Software 26(1), 139–154 (2009)
17. Kernighan, B., Ritchie, D.: The C Programming Language. Prentice-Hall, Englewood Cliffs (1988)
18. Lamport, L.: How to Make a Multiprocessor that Correctly Executes Multiprocess Programs. IEEE Transactions on Computers 9, 690–691 (1979)
19. Leungwattanakit, W., Artho, C., Hagiya, M., Tanabe, Y., Yamamoto, M.: Introduction of virtualization technology to multi-process model checking. In: Proc. NFM 2009, Moffett Field, USA, pp. 106–110 (2009)
20. Lindholm, T., Yellin, A.: The Java Virtual Machine Specification, 2nd edn. Addison-Wesley, Reading (1999)
21. Meyer, B.: Eiffel: the language. Prentice-Hall, Upper Saddle River (1992)
22. Microsoft Corporation. Microsoft Visual C#.NET Language Reference. Microsoft Press, Redmond (2002)
23. Nichols, B., Buttlar, D., Farrell, J.: Pthreads Programming. O'Reilly, Sebastopol (1996)
24. W^3 Systems Design. C++ vs Java (2009), http://www.w3sys.com/pages.meta/benchmarks.html
25. Stroustrup, B.: The C++ Programming Language, 3rd edn. Addison-Wesley Longman Publishing Co., Inc, Boston (1997)
26. Tanenbaum, A.: Modern operating systems. Prentice-Hall, Englewood Cliffs (1992)
27. Visser, W., Havelund, K., Brat, G., Park, S., Lerda, F.: Model checking programs. Automated Software Engineering Journal 10(2), 203–232 (2003)
28. Wang, C., Yang, Y., Gupta, A., Gopalakrishnan, G.: Dynamic model checking with property driven pruning to detect race conditions. In: Cha, S(S.), Choi, J.-Y., Kim, M., Lee, I., Viswanathan, M. (eds.) ATVA 2008. LNCS, vol. 5311, pp. 126–140. Springer, Heidelberg (2008)

Integrate Online Model Checking into Distributed Reconfigurable System on Chip with Adaptable OS Services

Sufyan Samara, Yuhong Zhao*, and Franz J. Rammig

Heinz Nixdorf Institute, University of Paderborn
Fürstenallee 11, 33102 Paderborn, Germany
sufyan@mail.uni-paderborn.de

Abstract. This paper presents a novel flexible, dependable, and reliable operating system design for distributed reconfigurable system on chip. The dependability and reliability are achieved by integrating online model checking technique. Each OS service has different implementations which are further partitioned into small blocks. This operating system design allows the OS service to be adapted at runtime according to the given resource requirements and response time. Such adaptable services may be required by real time safety-critical applications. The flexibility introduced in executing adaptable OS services also gives rise to a potential safety problem. Thus, online model checking is integrated to the operating system so as to improve the dependability, reliability, and fault tolerance of these adaptable OS services.

Keywords: Online Model Checking, Distributed Reconfigurable System on Chip, OS Adaptable Service.

1 Introduction

The vast growing need for powerful yet small and customized systems encouraged the development of embedded systems. These now are most likely to contain more than one computational element on a single chip forming what so called a System on Chip (SoC). An addition of a Field Programmable Gate Array (FPGA) gives SoC the ability of reconfiguration. FPGAs are known of their computational power and dynamic behavior in comparison with General Purpose Processors (GPP). Many applications such as signal processing, encryption/decryption, and multimedia encoding/decoding are in need for such systems. However, the complexity of these systems is no longer easily manageable, especially if they are distributed. This raises the necessity for embedded Operating System (OS).

---

* This work is developed in the course of the Collaborative Research Center 614 - Self-Optimizing Concepts and Structures in Mechanical Engineering - Paderborn University, and is published on its behalf and funded by the Deutsche Forschungsgemeinschaft (DFG).

M. Hinchey et al. (Eds.): DIPES/BICC 2010, IFIP AICT 329, pp. 102–113, 2010.

An OS working on distributed Reconfigurable SoCs (RSoC) can also benefit from the dynamic behavior and the computational power provided by their FPGAs. These benefits involve adaptability, runtime safety checking and recovery, etc. This adaptable OS is capable of changing its resource requirements and execution behavior in order to accommodate the variety of applications highly expected in distributed systems.

The underlying OS services usually play a critical role in order to safely execute real time applications/tasks on distributed RSoCs. This is reflected in ensuring the executions of these services *correct* without violating any deadlines or safety constraints. In order to achieve this goal, we make OS services be accompanied with a runtime checker to predict possible errors or constraints violation. In case that an error or constraint violation is found, the presented novel OS service design allows the service to recover. The recovery process allows the OS service to continue execution from the point the error occurred with as minimum losses as possible and without violating any constraints. This is achieved by recalculating and finding another configuration efficiently [1,2].

In this paper we present a novel flexible and dependable OS design that can adapt at runtime its services according to applications/tasks desired QoS, i.e., the actual resource requirements and response time, on the one hand; meanwhile online check at model level the safety constraints of these adaptable services and then recover if necessary from the detected errors or constraints violation on the other hand. We make this design feasible by partitioning OS services and integrating online model checking [3,4] into the operating system.

The rest of this paper is organized as follows: Section 2 introduces the distributed system topology and discusses the adaptable OS design; in Section 3 the online model checking is introduced as follows: Subsection 3.1 explains application scenario; Subsection 3.2 describes how to generate an abstract model for an adaptable OS service; the model checking paradigm and the pre and post- checking are presented in Subsection 3.3 and 3.4 respectively; the integration of the online model checker with the OS design is discussed in Section 4; in Section 5 some related work is introduced and finally we conclude the work in Section 6.

2   Distributed Reconfigurable System on Chip with Adaptable OS Services

The distributed system under consideration is a *hybrid* one between a centralized and fully distributed system. The RSoCs are distributed and allowed to operate and communicate freely without central coordination. However, at the initialization stages and for the sake of OS services distribution, a unique central RSoC exists. This central RSoC is assumed to have enough resources to hold and manage a whole copy of the OS and acts as OS Services Repository (OSR), see Figure 1. After distributing the services, this central RSoC existence is no more important, but beneficent. This is because the used distribution algorithm supports encoding which allows the retrieval of any OS services and provides for some fault tolerance.

Each RSoC in the distributed system has at least an FPGA and GPP. For an OS service to be able to fully or partially utilize FPGA and GPP on each

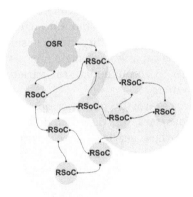

Fig. 1. RSoCs distribution

RSoC, the service exists in two implementations. One implementation is to run on FPGA while the other one is to run on GPP. Further, each of the two implementations is divided into the same number of blocks, where each block is called a Small Execution Segment (SES), see Figure 2. Each SES with the same index has the same functional behavior. For instance, the second SES in all the implementations of the given OS service will have the same functional behavior. If we input identical data to the second SES in any implementation of this OS service, we should get identical output. However, the time of getting these outputs, the power consumed, and the area/utilization required for each SES differ.

These similarities and differences give us much flexibility in executing an OS service. For example, if we have one service with two implementations each with just two SESs, we would have four possibilities to execute the service, each with different resource requirements and response time. Our previous work, [1] and [2], prove the feasibility of this design to execute and adapt an OS service to run on RSoC even with very limited resources without violating any demanded constraints. Further, a complete formal description of the design and a linear algorithm to schedule such service were presented.

As aforesaid, the RSoCs are distributed in a hybrid topology network where a central RSoC management node exists but the RSoCs can work without central RSOC. This central RSoC contains the whole set of OS services. It is used in the initialization stage to balance the distribution of the services/SESs over all the available RSoCs in the system. Depending on resources and distribution, an execution of a service can be either carried out on a single RSoC or as collaboration of more than one RSoC. This requires an evaluation at runtime to find a suitable configuration for the service to execute on available resources without violating any constraint. Due to dynamic changes in applications/tasks, the resources or the constraints may change accordingly at runtime. This may lead to change/adjustment in service configuration. Due to the sensitivity of the process, as this may be a service requested by a real time application/task, dependability and fault tolerance of the underlying operating system is highly expected.

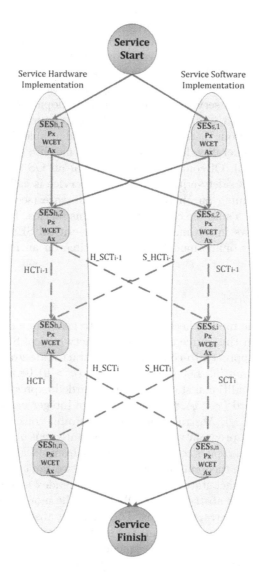

Fig. 2. Two implementations of OS service with execution order of the SES's. Here S stands Software, H: for Hardware, C for Communication, T for Time, P for power and A for Area. For example SCT denotes Software Communication Time.

3   Online Model Checking

3.1   Application Scenario

Given an adaptable service with n (> 1) implementations and each implementation with m (> 1) SES's, then we have m^n different combination ways to configure the SES's of this OS service. The actual configuration of the SES's has to be determined at runtime with respect to the resource requirements and the response time. There is no way to know in advance which configuration of the SES's should be selected. In essence, each configuration of the SES's can be seen as a different implementation of this service. Due to the huge time and space complexity, it is impossible to verify the safety properties of all the m^n different implementations of this service at the systems development phase. Therefore, online model checking [3,4] might be a good choice to improve the dependability and fault tolerance of our distributed RSoC with adaptable OS services.

Without loss of generality, let's suppose that some SES's of a given OS service are safety-critical. Of course, all the SES's of an OS service can be conservatively labeled as safety-critical. When this service is called by a real-time application/task running on an RSoC, the middleware (see Section 4) of the RSoC will figure out a suitable configuration of this service. Therefore, the middleware always knows in advance when a safety-critical SES will be executed and thus can trigger online model checking in time on an RSoC with enough resource.

3.2   Abstract Model

In order to do online model checking, we need to generate a sufficiently precise abstract model from the source code of each safety-critical SES of a service at first. A promising approach to construct an abstract state graph automatically is *predicate abstraction* [5]. Let $\{\varphi_1, \varphi_2, \cdots, \varphi_k\}$ $(k > 0)$ be a set of predicates induced from the conditional statements and guarded expressions of the source code. E.g., for a guard $(x < y)$, where x and y are Integer variables, we can get a predicate $\varphi = (x < y)$. Abstract states are the evaluations of these predicates $\varphi_1, \varphi_2, \cdots, \varphi_k$ on the program variables at each statement of the source code.

The abstract state graph is constructed starting from the abstract initial state. With the help of some theorem prover (e.g., PVS), we can compute the possible successors of any abstract state by deciding for each index i whether φ_i or $\neg\varphi_i$ is a *post* condition of this abstract state. Obviously, the more predicates we have, the more precise the abstract model is. The resulting abstract model is an over approximation of the concrete system. For every concrete state sequence, there exists a corresponding abstract state sequence.

The relations between concrete states and abstract states are defined by means of two functions: *abstraction* function α maps every set of concrete states to a corresponding abstract state; *concretization* function γ maps every abstract state to a set of concrete states that it represents.

In this way, for each safety-critical SES_i of a service, we can get the corresponding abstract model $\widehat{SES_i}$ as well as the abstraction function α_i and concretization function γ_i.

3.3   Model Checking Paradigm

Online model checking runs on an RSoC in parallel with the SES's to be checked. The abstract model of the checked SES is explored with respect to the given

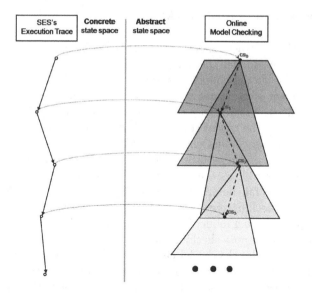

Fig. 3. Online Model Checking

safety property. Here we consider such a kind of the safety properties that can be formally specified as invariants or LTL formulas. Since our model checking is done online, the current (concrete) states of the SES's execution can be monitored and reported to the model checker from time to time (see Subsection 4.1). By mapping these concrete states to the corresponding abstract states at model level through the abstraction function, the online model checker needs only to explore such a partial state space reachable from these abstract (current) states as shown in Fig 3. Initially, when the current starting state is not available, online model checking will explore all the possible behaviors from the abstract starting state. Once a current state is available, the state space to be checked will be shrunk to the part reachable from the corresponding abstract state. If this partial abstract model is checked *safe* against the given property, then we have more confidence to the safety of the actual execution trace. It doesn't matter even though there might be some errors lurked outside the partial abstract state space. If an error is detected within the partial state space, the recovery process will be triggered (see Subsection 4.2). Notice that the detected error might not really exist in the source code, because we check at (abstract) model level, which usually contains more behaviors than the corresponding source code. To avoid the error really to happen, it is necessary for safety-critical systems to trigger recovery process.

We have done some experiments to estimate the performance of our online model checking for invariants and LTL formulas [4]. The experimental results are promising and demonstrate that the maximal out-degree of a model has a larger influence on look-ahead performance than the average degree of the model.

3.4   Pre-checking and Post-checking

Since we check the abstract model instead of the concrete source code, the execution of our online model checker is loosely bound to the execution of the source code. Online model checking is able to explore the abstract state space even when a current state is not yet monitored. In fact, the current states are only used to reduce the state space to be checked. From this point of view, there exists a race between the model checker and the source code to be checked.

Ideally, we wish that model checker could always run enough (time) steps ahead the execution of the source code. This depends on the complexity of the checking task as well as the underlying hardware architecture. In reality, model checker might fall behind the execution of the source code. Therefore, we introduce two checking modes: *pre-checking* and *post-checking*. The model checking is in pre-checking mode, if it runs ahead of the execution of the source code; otherwise, it is in post-checking mode.

In pre-checking mode, the model checker can predict violations before they really happen. In post-checking mode, it seems at first sight that the violations could only be detected after they have already happened. However, it is still possible to "predict" violations even in post-checking mode because our on-line checking works at the model level. If an error is detected at some place other than the monitored execution trace in the partial state space, then we can "predict" that there might be an error in the model which has not happened yet. In this sense, both checking modes are useful for safety-critical systems.

Of course, we hope that the model checker can take the leading position against the source code for as long time as possible. We need to find a sophisticated strategy to make the model checking have more chance or higher probability to *win* against the source code. Recall that the source code is usually validated by means of simulation and testing. Currently we are looking to find some heuristic knowledge at the system testing phase so that the abstract model can be enriched with more useful information. The heuristic information can thus guide on-line model checker to further reduce the state space to be explored whenever necessary.

4   Integrate Online Model Checking into Distributed RSoC with Adaptable OS Services

Recall that every RSoC in the distributed system is assumed to have at least one FPGA and one GPP. In order to hide the complexity and provide some transparency to applications, a middleware is introduced to each RSoC. The middleware can prepare the services needed by applications, coordinate the communication between applications and OS services, monitor the resources availability, and manages the SES's. It can also cooperate with the online Model Checker (MC), see Figure 4-A, to provide for fault tolerance and recovery as discussed bellow.

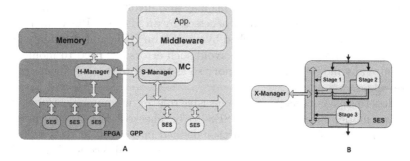

Fig. 4. A) An overview of an RSoC with one FPGA and GPP and the communications between SESs, MC, and memory. B) An insight of the SES stages and the communication with the X-manager.

4.1 Communication between the MC and SES's

Online model checker needs to communicate with SES's running on FPGA as well as on GPP. For the implementations of an adaptable service, all the SES's with the same index have the same functional behavior, i.e., given the same input, we will get the same output from the SES's with the same index. However, the SES's with the same index might be implemented by different algorithms in different languages on different platforms. They might be executed in a parallel or sequential way depending on the underlying architecture. As a result, the SES's with the same index are distinctive in terms of execution time and resource usage. This makes it unrealistic to synchronously schedule the communication between the model checker and an SES to be checked, e.g., every T time. Fortunately, an event driven approach is a suitable solution. This can be done at the design phase by defining triggering points at which communication is initiated. The triggering points depends on the functional behavior and states of each OS service and can be obtained by analyzing the source code. When the communication is triggered, a decoded message with the required information is sent to the model checker. These are normally global data and conditional values.

The model checker is usually running on GPP. This eases data transferring between SES's running on GPP and the model checker. It can be achieved by coping/accessing the address space of the SES or using shared memory. Because we also consider to check the SES's running on FPGA, an X-manager is introduced, where X is either H for hardware or S for software. The X-manager is working as complementary part to the model checker. It consists of two parts: the H-manager which works on FPGA and the S-manager which runs with the model checker on GPP, see Figure 4-A. All the SES's communications involving reading or writing memory are done through the X-manager. In doing so, the X-manager can monitor all the modifications and synchronize the SES's to get an updated value to any memory request. Without the X-manager the memory requested by SES may not be up to date, because FPGA can normally access the physical memory directly. In addition, anything running on GPP accesses memory using a memory manager. This may also involve caching and/or virtual memory usage. In this case, memory accessed by an SES on FPGA might not be up to date if that memory was cached by an SES on GPP, and no update occurs to the physical original memory. To avoid such errors, we need to monitor and synchronize any modification to memory so as to ensure that we always read up to date values.

Needless to say, X-manager plays a decisive role in the communication between the online model checker and the SES to be checked. For this purpose, the internal structure of each SES is further defined into stages at design phase as shown in Figure 4-B. A stage is a logical grouping of a SES code after which the MC is triggered. Any access to the memory from every stage is monitored by the X-manager. At the end of each stage, an event will be sent to the X-manager. On receiving the event, the X-manager will provide the model checker with a snap shot of the memory just modified by the so far executed stage of the SES to be checked. This minimizes the time needed to transfer data to the model checker. Thus, the model checker might have more chance to run in pre-checking mode, i.e., look ahead in the near future at the model level. This is important as it allows the recovery process to happen without violating any constraints.

4.2 Recovery Process

When an application/task running on an RSoC requests a service to be executed, the middleware of the RSoC evaluates the available resources and the real time demands of the application/task to find a suitable configuration. This process may require coordination with other RSoCs or if applicable with an Operating Systems Repository (OSR) (see Fig. 1). It is just at this time that the configuration of the service to be executed is known. This configuration is then administrated by the the middleware of the RSoC for execution. The online model checker is triggered whenever an SES marked with safety-critical is known to be executed. The model checker runs in parallel with the SES to be checked. In case that a possible violation is detected in the abstract model of the SES to be checked, a recovery process is initiated as shown in Fig 5.

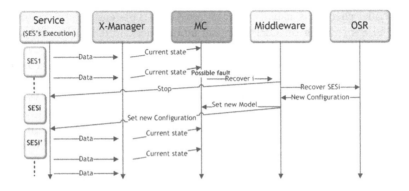

Fig. 5. Recovering a possible fault in OS service execution

The recovery process is initiated by sending a recovery message from the model checker to the RSoC middleware which coordinates the process of OS service execution. This can be the same RSoC where the model checker is being executed or different RSoC in the distributed system. The message contains information about the possible incorrect SES and the current state of this SES. The middleware then evaluates a new suitable configuration and if necessary acquires any missing SES from OSR. Meanwhile, it raises a stop signal to the incorrect service. The middleware afterwards initialize the new configuration and redirect the further execution of the service to it. The middleware also sends the model checker a message to set a new model associated with the new SES to be executed if necessary.

5   Related Work

The benefits of implementing OS partially on RSoC is well recognized [6,7]. Many researches have been carried out in the direction for an OS design to support RSoC [8,9,10]. The idea of multiple implementations was also presented in [11] and [12]. Every Service were assumed to have one implementation as a whole for GPP and another for FPGA. Both implementations co-exist at the same time on an RSoC to allow context switching. Doing so wastes too much resources on each RSoC and makes the underlying OS design unfeasible for distributed systems. Moreover, this OS design uses an algorithm based on Binary Integer Programming (BIP), whose computational complexity is $O(n^2)$. We present an OS design specially for distributed systems. It is fault tolerant and it can adapt according to the QoS requirements of the applications. Further, the adopted algorithm [1,2] has a linear complexity.

For distributed systems, correctness and temporal analysis of the underlying OS are desirable, because most SoC systems have real-time and dependability requirements [13]. This analysis includes more and more formal verification techniques like model checking [14]. Model checking has the advantage of being fully automated and inherently includes means for diagnosis in case of errors. On the other hand, model checking is substantially confronted with the so called state explosion problem. Numerous approaches to overcome this deficiency have been developed, like partial order reduction [15], compositional reasoning [16], and other simplification and abstraction techniques, which aim to reduce the state space to be explored by *over-approximation* [17] or *under-approximation* [18] techniques.

In recent years, runtime verification is presented as a complementary approach to the static checking techniques. The basic idea of the state-of-the-art runtime verification [19,20,21,22] is to monitor the execution of the source code and afterwards to check the so far observed execution trace against the given properties specified usually by LTL formulas. The checking progress always falls behind the execution of the source code because the checking procedure can continue only after a new state has been observed. In contrast, our runtime verification is applied to the model level. The states observed from the execution trace are mainly used to reduce the state space to be explored at the model level. If the checking speed is fast enough, our online model checking could keep looking certain time steps ahead of the execution of the source code and then predict how many time steps in the near future are safe.

6   Conclusion

We present a novel OS design which allows OS services to have flexible QoS, fault tolerance, and recovery ability in distributed RSoC environment. Each OS service may have different implementations, which can be configured at runtime. This dynamic feature makes it difficult to check the safety of such OS services at design phase. Therefore, online model checker is integrated so as to make error prediction and recovery available. In [1] and [2], we have proved the feasibility of this OS design to execute and adapt an OS service running on RSoC even with very limited resources without violating any demanded requirements. We have done some experiments to estimate the performance of our online model checking for invariants and LTL formulas [4]. The experimental results are promising and demonstrate that the maximal out-degree of a model has a larger influence on look-ahead performance than the average degree of the model.

References

1. Samara, S., Tariq, F.B., Kerstan, T., Stahl, K.: Applications adaptable execution path for operating system services on a distributed reconfigurable system on chip. In: ICESS 2009: Proceedings of the 2009 International Conference on Embedded Software and Systems, Washington, DC, USA, pp. 461–466. IEEE Computer Society, Washington (2009)
2. Samara, S., Schomaker, G.: Self-adaptive os service model in relaxed resource distributed reconfigurable system on chip (rsoc). In: Proceedings of the 2009 Computation World: Future Computing, Service Computation, Cognitive, Adaptive, Content, Patterns, Washington, DC, USA, pp. 1–8. IEEE Computer Society, Washington (2009)
3. Zhao, Y., Rammig, F.J.: Model-based runtime verification framework. Electronic Notes in Theoretical Computer Science 253(1), 179–193 (2009)
4. Rammig, F.J., Zhao, Y., Samara, S.: On-line model checking as operating system service. In: Lee, S., Narasimhan, P. (eds.) SEUS 2009. LNCS, vol. 5860, pp. 131–143. Springer, Heidelberg (2009)
5. Graf, S., Saidi, H.: Construction of abstract state graphs with pvs. In: Grumberg, O. (ed.) CAV 1997. LNCS, vol. 1254, pp. 72–83. Springer, Heidelberg (1997)
6. Engel, F., Kuz, I., Petters, S.M., Ruocco, S.: Operating systems on socs: A good idea? National ICT Australia Ltd. (2004)
7. Wigley, G., Kearney, D.: Research issues in operating systems for reconfigurable computing. In: Proceedings of the International Conference on Engineering of Reconfigurable System and Algorithms (ERSA), pp. 10–16. CSREA Press (2002)
8. Donato, A., Ferrandi, F., Santamberogio, M., Sciuto, D.: Operating system support for dynamically reconfigurable soc. architectures. Politecnico di Milano (2006)

9. Nollet, V., Coene, P., Verkest, D., Vernalde, S., Lauwereins, R.: Designing an operating system for a heterogeneous reconfigurable soc. In: Proceedings of the RAW 2003 workshop (2003)

10. Walder, H., Platzner, M.: A runtime environment for reconfigurable hardware operating systems. In: Becker, J., Platzner, M., Vernalde, S. (eds.) FPL 2004. LNCS, vol. 3203, pp. 831–835. Springer, Heidelberg (2004)

11. Götz, M., Rettberg, A., Pereira, C.E.: Run-time reconfigurable real-time operating system for hybrid execution platforms. In: Information Control Problems in Manufacturing, IFAC (2006)

12. Götz, M., Rettberg, A., Pereira, C.E.: Towards run-time partitioning of a real time operating system for reconfigurable systems on chip. In: IFIP International Federation for Information Processing (2005)

13. Gajski, D.D., Vahid, F.: Specification and design of embedded hardware-software systems. IEEE, Design & Test of Computers 12, 53–67 (1995)

14. Clark, E.M., Grumberg Jr., O., Peled, D.A.: Model Checking. MIT Press, Cambridge (1999)

15. Godefroid, P.: Partial-Order Methods for the Verification of Concurrent Systems: An Approach to the State-Explosion Problem, Secaucus, NJ, USA. Springer, New York (1996), Foreword By-Wolper, Pierre

16. Berezin, S., Campos, S.V.A., Clarke, E.M.: Compositional reasoning in model checking. In: de Roever, W.-P., Langmaack, H., Pnueli, A. (eds.) COMPOS 1997. LNCS, vol. 1536, pp. 81–102. Springer, Heidelberg (1998)

17. Clarke, E.M., Grumberg, O., Long, D.E.: Model checking and abstraction. ACM Trans. Program. Lang. Syst. 16(5), 1512–1542 (1994)

18. Lee, W., Pardo, A., Jang, J.Y., Hachtel, G., Somenzi, F.: Tearing based automatic abstraction for ctl model checking. In: ICCAD 1996: Proceedings of the 1996 IEEE/ACM international conference on Computer-aided design, Washington, DC, USA, pp. 76–81. IEEE Computer Society, Los Alamitos (1996)

19. Barnett, M., Schulte, W.: Spying on components: A runtime verification technique. In: Leavens, G.T., Sitaraman, M., Giannakopoulou, D., eds.: Workshop on Specification and Verification of Component-Based Systems. October 2001, Published as Iowa State Technical Report 01-09a (October 2001)

20. Arkoudas, K., Rinard, M.: Deductive Runtime Certification. In: Proceedings of the 2004 Workshop on Runtime Verification (RV 2004), Barcelona, Spain (April 2004)

21. Chen, F., Rosu, G.: Towards Monitoring-Oriented Programming: A Paradigm Combining Specification and Implementation. In: Proceedings of the 2003 Workshop on Runtime Verification (RV 2003), Boulder, Colorado, USA (2003)

22. Havelund, K., Rosu, G.: Java PathExplorer — a runtime verification tool. In: Proceedings 6th International Symposium on Artificial Intelligence, Robotics and Automation in Space (ISAIRAS 2001), Montreal, Canada (June 2001)

Efficient Mutation-Analysis Coverage for Constrained Random Verification

Tao Xie[1], Wolfgang Mueller[1], and Florian Letombe[2]

[1] University of Paderborn /C-LAB, Fürstenallee 11,
33098 Paderborn, Germany
{tao,wolfgang}@c-lab.de
[2] SpringSoft, 340 rue de l'Eygala
38430 Moirans, France
florian_letombe@springsoft.com

Abstract. Constrained random simulation based verification (CRV) becomes an important means of verifying the functional correctness of the increasingly complex hardware designs. Effective coverage metric still lacks for assessing the adequacy of these processes. In contrast to other coverage metrics, the syntax-based Mutation Analysis (MA) defines a *systematic correlation* between the coverage results and the test's ability to reveal design errors. However, it always suffers from extremely high computation cost. In this paper we present an efficient integration of mutation analysis into CRV flows, not only as a coverage gauge for simulation adequacy but also, a step further, to direct a dynamic adjustment of the test probability distribution. We consider the distinct cost model of this MA-based random simulation flow and try to optimize the coverage process. From the probabilistic analysis of the simulation cost, a heuristics for steering the test generation is derived. The automated flow is implemented by the SystemC Verification Library and by Certitude[TM] for mutation analysis. Results from the experiment with an IEEE floating point arithmetic design show the efficiency of our approach.

Keywords: Verification Coverage, Constrained Random Verification, Mutation Analysis.

1 Introduction

Simulation has still a dominant role in the verification of the functional correctness of electronic and embedded systems. Today, designs are increasingly complex, on the one hand, driven by the need to fill the Moore's Law driven capacity of integrated circuits and, on the other hand, thanks to our eager promotion of the design capability. Model-based, system-level methodologies and more extensive IP reuse are adopted. However, our verification ability lags behind. By [13], many current development projects have already a verification team sized over 2:1 to the design team.

To accommodate this growing complexity of designs, random simulation is applied to ease the labor cost of writing directed test vectors. It generates test input automatically and, therefore, reinforces the scalability of simulation-based approaches.

M. Hinchey et al. (Eds.): DIPES/BICC 2010, IFIP AICT 329, pp. 114–124, 2010.
© IFIP International Federation for Information Processing 2010

Constraints and biases on the inputs domain can be imposed additionally on the randomness to overcome its shortage and exercise the design more extensively. By the nature of focusing on the boundary, the constrained random simulation based verification (CRV) processes need particularly an effective metric, or a suite of them, to assess their adequacy. On the whole, the effectiveness and reliability of such an adequacy guard should be judged by its ability to detect potential design errors.

Code coverage like *statement coverage* or *branch coverage* is the most intuitive metrics and long being used for both software testing and hardware design simulation. It is also supported by most Hardware Description Languages (HDLs) simulation tools. However, though a necessary step, high code coverage solely reflects the completion progress very limitedly. The *functional coverage* mechanism [20, 21] provided by the recently popular hardware verification languages like *SystemVerilog* requires the explicit definition of variable value ranges to hit, which is then recorded during simulation. A major drawback is the enforcement of verification engineers to thoroughly understand the design and extra effort to define the coverage points or applying libraries as a *subjective* metric.

Originally proposed for software testing, Mutation Analysis (MA) is a fault-based test data selection technique. A so-called *mutation* is a *single syntactic* change to the original program source code under test, such as replacing an *add* arithmetic operator with a *minus*, as an artificially injected bug. Such a program mutant is said to be *killed* by a test when it under the test produces a different output from that of the original program. When applied to generate or assess an adequate set of tests, MA creates a bunch of mutants from the original program, each by a single, different mutation. Then the percentage of the mutants killed by the testing process is measured as the adequacy of the coverage.

The possible syntactic changes, as *mutation operators*, obviously depend only on the description language of the objects. As testing is a requirement with many computer-aided artifacts, subsequent research work extends mutation analysis to other languages. Particularly, HDLs share similar syntaxes with programming languages and have alike execution means as software. As an industrial EDA tool, Certitude[TM] [7,14] from *SpringSoft* implements the mutation analysis mechanism on Verilog and VHDL. Mutation operators specifically for HDLs are defined like:

```
    sign <= opa(63) xor opb(63) ;

Δ   sign <= opa(63) xnor opb(63) ;
```

where Δ is by convention used to indicate the only mutated statement.

Design errors, at various levels of descriptions, are essentially any of its deviation from the specification. Different from other fault-based methods like [10,11,12] for test data selection, MA defines a *systematic correlation* between the coverage results and the test's ability to reveal design errors. This is done in two steps. First, a coverage point is defined directly as if a test exposes a potential mistake by the designer. Second, MA hypothesizes and experimentally establishes a *coupling-effect* [1,4], which states that a set of tests capable of killing those mutants with simple faults injected will also be effective at exposing other more complex errors. As such, MA serves as a reliable guard for testing or verification processes ensuring the detection of design errors.

However, though with extensive study, mutation analysis suffers from extremely high computation cost, which becomes the main challenge for any MA application. Considering a hardware design with L lines under the simulation which is guarded by a mutation analysis with M mutation operators, we will have a mutant set with approximately a size $(M * L)$ as the coverage metric. M as a constant and assuming the simulation cost linear to the design size, calculation of one test case against the metric will have a cost to $O(L * L)$ and the overall coverage evaluation a cost to $O(T * L^2)$ for T test cases. This is a high computation requirement with increasingly complex designs. With a CRV flow, the situation is even worse, since T will be enlarged as randomness is used to reach the adequacy. This cost efficiency issue should be addressed. Therefore, in this work, we experiment with the use of MA coverage for CRV, consider the accurate cost model of such a flow, and try to develop an efficient algorithm to tackle the coverage cost problem.

2 Related Work

MA is a fault-based verification technique. Analogously, the fault models at gate-level, e.g. the stuck-at, is used to guide the selection of product test data for exposing defects that may be introduced during the manufacturing processes. Manufacturing defects can be viewed as the deviation of a product circuit from the designed structure. Automatic test pattern generation (ATPG) algorithms like PODEM (Path-Oriented Decision Making) and FAN (FAN-out-oriented test generation algorithm) generate test vectors targeting the gate-level modeled faults. Although theoretically, when hardware designs are concerned, we can always translate higher level faults to gate-level and apply an ATPG there to generate test vectors that correspondingly expose the high-level faults. This mapping imposes high complexity and inefficiency, especially with complex designs. Successful application of ATPGs relies on *Design-for-Testability* techniques [8], with which ATPG algorithms can assume a small portion of the circuit as their input, and output effective tests for the *structural testing*. In contrast, simulation vector generation for functional verification, similar to *functional testing*, concerns the overall functionality of the design. They are supposed to take the whole design as the algorithm input.

Fault models for automatic test generation at higher levels, such as the behavioral level or RTL, has also been considered in [9,11], for instance. [9] also mentions the use of MA for hardware designs. The designs are transformed to FORTRAN programs and then fed as the standard input into software mutation analysis tool Mothra [2]. Faults analysis and tests generation are then the task of Mothra [2,5]. However, neither the language translation is efficient, nor does the Mothra system handle complex objects. [11] first transforms the original and faulty VHDL descriptions to Binary Decision Diagram (BDD) based representations, with a different BDD for each output bit. Then each pair of these bits is compared to extract the symbolic test vector. Here, scalability is the main challenge.

Other coverage metrics have been used to direct random test generation. Code coverage, more specifically branch coverage is considered in [15]. A Genetic Algorithm, with the branch coverage degree as a *fitness* measurement, is developed to guide simulation sequences generation and evaluated on some VHDL design. The method in

[17] begins with a test planning and the coverage is defined as the amount of pre-planned verification tasks that have been simulated, e.g., specific transactions from a CPU unit. Then an evolving Bayesian Network is constructed to model the correlation between test generation directives and the coverage. [16] employs a so-called *tag-coverage*. A *tag* is defined as some symbolic disturbance to a variable value assignment and is said to be covered if this disturbance is propagated to any observation point in the simulation. A Markov Chain derived from the hardware design is built and tuned according to this tag-coverage. Probability distribution of the random input is then optimized by the chain.

We consider the distinct cost model of a MA-based random simulation flow and try to optimize the coverage by dynamically adjusting the probability distribution of the random test generation.

3   Mutation-Analysis Directed Constrained Random Simulation

Our CRV flow is built with three components. First, the SystemC Verification Library (SCV) [18] presents a standard constrained-random test generation (CRTG) facility, with a handy interface for defining input constraints associated with weighted ranges. Second, the ModelSim^{TM} simulator is employed due to its ability to simulate mixed SystemC/VHDL/Verilog designs. Third, as a key enabling factor, the Certitude^{TM} defines a comprehensive model of design errors on VHDL and Verilog for mutation analysis.

Originally, the identification of mutants is defined by observation and comparison at the boundary of the object under test. Another concept *weak mutation* is developed in [3] by allowing this observation at any intermediate points between the mutation point and the design output, e.g. immediately after the execution of the mutated expression, or statement. In contrast, the classical MA with the mutant identification at the output, can be denoted as *strong mutation analysis*. In Certitude^{TM}, the option for distinguishing mutants' behaviors ranges from directly after the mutation line, to any subcomponent ports, and to the top design output ports. Further, Certitude^{TM} applies another so-called *schema-based mutation* technique [6], which encodes all independent mutants into a single design copy. Compilation of mutants becomes a one-time job and, at the same time, the statement-based weak mutation analysis for all mutants, i.e. whether a mutant produces a locally different behavior, requires only *a single simulation* of this instrumented design by in-time comparison with the execution of the original statement.[1]

3.1   The Simulation Flow and Its Cost

Figure 1 depicts the general design flow. The three bold arrows represent simulations and behavior monitoring, either on the original DUV (Design Under Verification) or the mutants. We start with some initial test constraints for the DUV and a CRTG. At the beginning and any time the DUV is changed the design files are copied and instrumented by the mutation operators. This process is determinate and the product is

---

[1] Certitude introduces a layer called *functional qualification* [19], which gives the test bench a good credit when its monitor is vigilant enough and flags a failure when a mutant does produce a distinguishable behaviour at the observation point.

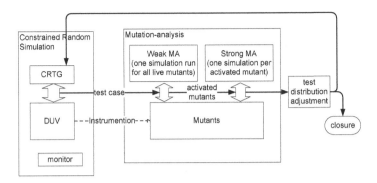

Fig. 1. The CRV loop and closure directed by the coverage of mutation analysis

the mutants. We should also note that some mutants remain *functionally unchanged*, which always produce the same output as in the original program. These so-called *equivalent mutants* are eliminated from the mutants box. Each time the CRTG generates a test case and the monitor flags a pass to the DUV simulation result, this test case is sent to be assessed by the mutation analysis.

In this work, we use *strong mutation analysis results as the final coverage measurement*. However, putting a weak mutation phase at the front saves simulation effort definitely and significantly, as herewith we only need to simulate the *locally already exposed* mutants, though each one against the test case. As previously described, this requires only *one* extra simulation under Certitude^{TM}.

Killed mutants are removed from the mutants box. The accumulated results from mutation analysis are used for a runtime calculation of some reasonable adjustment to the test distribution, and if any, to be fed back to the CRTG. At the same time, a certain percentage of dead mutants is used to break the loop and end the flow. This does not apply a 100% killing of mutants, which can rarely be the case for complex designs. Without loss of generality, we consider here the cost model for an 100% mutant-killing coverage.

Although constraint solving, source code instrumentation for creating mutants, and equivalent mutants identification all consume computation resources, most time of the flow will be spent on simulation. Basically this is due to the nature of mutation analysis of feeding each test case to individual mutants for simulation. Since the single simulation cost scales linearly with the design size, the complexity of the proposed flow is decided by the number of simulation runs. In the following, we make a detailed analysis on the required simulations. Consider D the design in the flow under verification and $M(D) = \{M_1, M_2, ..., M_N\}$ as the set of non-equivalent mutants generated. At any time in the CRV loop we have a probability distribution φ over the input variable value domain $I(D)$. With MW_i the random variable for the weak mutation analysis outcome on M_i and MS_i for the strong analysis, for any φ we can define $pw_{\varphi,i} \stackrel{\text{def}}{=} \Pr(MW_i = 1)$ and $ps_{\varphi,i} \stackrel{\text{def}}{=} \Pr(MS_i = 1)$.

Then the simulation runs on M_i in the strong mutation phase can be represented by a random number X_i as the times of $(MW_i = 1)$ happening until the first success of $(MS_i = 1)$. Noting that for $\forall i \ (MS_i = 1) \subseteq (MW_i = 1)$, we can derive by geometric distribution the expected value of X_i as

$$E_\varphi(X_i) = \frac{1}{\Pr(MS_i = 1 | MW_i = 1)}$$
$$= \frac{1}{\dfrac{ps_{\varphi,i}}{pw_{\varphi,i}}}$$
$$= \frac{pw_{\varphi,i}}{ps_{\varphi,i}}$$

denoted by $Cost_{\varphi,i,strong}$. Further, as the weak MA phase costs one simulation for all remained mutants, $Cost_{\varphi,weak}$ as the total weak mutation runs, i.e., the flow loop count until the last live mutants being killed, can be simply estimated by $\max_i(1/ps_{\varphi,i})$. Therefore, we calculate $Cost_\varphi$ as the total simulation effort needed to kill all mutants under distribution φ, expectedly, as

$$Cost_\varphi = Cost_{\varphi,weak} + \sum_{1 \le i \le N} Cost_{\varphi,i,strong}$$
$$= \max_{1 \le i \le N}(1/ps_{\varphi,i}) + \sum_{1 \le i \le N} \frac{pw_{\varphi,i}}{ps_{\varphi,i}} \qquad (1)$$

I other words, a high activation rate of mutants with low propagation probability leads to high simulation costs. For instance, assuming a set of 100 design mutants and under a certain test distribution φ_1 each of $pw_{\varphi_1,i}$ having a same value of 0.01, and all $ps_{\varphi_1,i}$ a value of 0.005, we can calculate then $Cost_{\varphi_1}$ as a cost estimation of 400 simulation runs. For another φ_2 with all $pw_{\varphi_2,i}$ having a value 0.5 and $ps_{\varphi_2,i}$ 0.01, *though the mutants have a higher probability to be exposed*, they give more costs with a total of 5100 simulation runs, expectedly.

As another example, under selective mutation operators an RTL FFT design module with 29811 lines derives already $M(D)$ of 26758 non-equivalent mutants. $Cost_\varphi$ becomes extremely high with growing design sizes. Symbolic methods traditionally used for mutation-based test generation [5, 2] assume at most time $(MW_i = 1) \rightarrow (MS_i = 1)$, i.e., a mutant when activated then propagates to the output. This is not the case if we apply mutation analysis to the simulation of large designs. This cost problem can be addressed and, next, we present a heuristics as our first effort towards an efficient mutant-killing coverage for the CRV flow.

3.2 Dynamic Distribution Adjustment for More Efficient Coverage

We note that Equation (1) can be simply applied to a subset of $M(D)$. At some point during the CRV flow in Figure 1, $M(D)$ is reduced by dead mutants and only those hard-to-kill under the current test distribution are left. Then if we adjust φ, a newly estimated computation cost is defined in the same manner. This adjustment should be based on the cost estimation in Equation (1), so as to *reach more quickly a high mutant-killing coverage*. For this, a heuristics as described in Figure 2 is developed.

The algorithm for the heuristics assumes that the test input domain can be segmented into some discrete ranges. Then, basically, it *utilizes the past analysis information to estimate the effectiveness of those ranges and re-distributes the probability*.

Mutation analysis results $\sum_{1\leq i\leq N} ms_i\,(tc)/\sum_{1\leq i\leq N} mw_i\,(tc)$ as given in Line 3 are used to represent the $\sum ps_i/pw_i$ under the current distribution. The effectiveness is then measured relatively to a value $effective\_^{ps}/_{pm}$ through Lines 6 to 11 and used to flag a range as effective by adding it to an $effective\_distrib$ array, if its n_{ms}/n_{mw} surpasses $effective\_^{ps}/_{pm}$. If no mutant is killed, we add it to an $ineffective\_distrib$ array. Initially $effective\_^{ps}/_{pm}$ is assigned a parameter value $initial\_effective\_^{ps}/_{pm}$. This relative measure always relaxes in Line 19 as live mutants decrease and the remaining ones become harder to kill.

Heuristics   *#for the distribution adjustment box in Figure 1.*

Parameters: *starting_heuristic,* initial_good_$^{ps}/_{pm}$, *adjustment_threshold*

   #Assume the input value domain can be segmented as a set of ranges
   $I(D) : \{I_1, I_2, \dots, I_H \mid \cup_i I_i = I\}$. *For each mutant* M_i, mw_i, $ms_i : I \to \{0,1\}$
   as
   the weak and strong mutation analysis result, respectively.

(1) $effective\_^{ps}/_{pm} := initial\_effective\_^{ps}/_{pm}$

(2) $mark := 0$

(3) $\left(tc \in I_k, n_{mw} := \sum_{1\leq i\leq N} mw_i\,(tc), n_{ms} := \sum_{1\leq i\leq N} ms_i\,(tc)\right)$
   as received from CRTG and mutation analysis

(4) Enter the following loop if the previous total happening of event ($n_{ms} = 0$) already reaches *starting_heuristic*.

(5) **Loop** until the killed mutants reach a certain ratio predefined, or the verification cost budget is reached

(6)   **If** $\left(n_{ms}/n_{mw} \geq effective\_^{ps}/_{pm}\right)$

(7)   Add pair (k, n_{ms}) into an array $effective\_distrib$

(8)   **Elseif** $(n_{ms} = 0)$

(9)   Add k into another array $ineffective\_distrib$

(10)   Increase $mark$ by 1

(11) **End if**

(12) **If** $(mark \geq adjustment\_threshold)$

(13)   **If** $effective\_distrib$ is not empty, set test distribution as:

(14)   For each (k', n'_{ms}) in $effective\_distrib$, set
         $Pr(I_{k'}) := n'_{ms}/(sum\ of\ all\ n_{ms}\ in\ effective\_distrib)$

(15)   **Else**, set the distribution as

(16)   Uniformly distributed on $(\cup\,I_{k'} \mid k' \notin ineffective\_distrib)$

(17)   **End if**

(18)   Empty arrays $effective\_distrib$, $ineffective\_distrib$, set $mark := 0$

(19)   Lower $effective\_^{ps}/_{pm} := effective\_^{ps}/_{pm}\,/\,2$

(20) **End if**

(21) **End loop**

Fig. 2. Heuristics for mutant-killing by utilizing past analysis information

This establishes a *macro* relation between the test input domain and the overall mutant-killing. Our hypothesis is that if an input range is assessed to be effective at killing mutants, we expect it to be further capable of killing mutants and adjust the test distribution towards it. Otherwise, the distribution is steered away. Lines 13 to 17 are for this purpose. After this adjustment the arrays are emptied.

Furthermore, a threshold parameter *adjustment_threshold* is defined to trigger an adjustment procedure in Line 12, when the loop iteration killing none of the mutants, recorded by a variable *mark*, reaches this amount. We have not considered an optimal setting for this parameter. It could be set initially to a value of 1 and also loosens while the remaining mutants become more stubborn.

Since at this level 100 percent killing of the mutants could be infeasible under some time restriction, the whole flow should also be controlled by a *simulation cost budget* which terminates at a reasonably high *certain ratio* of killed mutants.

The presence of a *starting_heuristic* parameter is the last to notice. The dynamic distribution adjustment is not necessary at the beginning phase of the CRV flow, when many of the easy-to-kill mutants are still alive. This trigger is controlled by parameter *starting_heuristic*.

4 Results

We have chosen a VHDL implementation of the IEEE binary double-precision floating point arithmetic unit from *opencores.org* for our experiments in our MA-directed CRV flow. Figure 3 shows the architecture of that example.

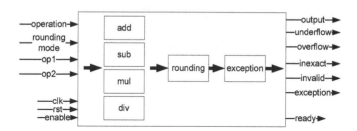

Fig. 3. The floating point arithmetic under CRV

The test domain of the DUV is composed of its major input ports including the arithmetic operator, rounding mode, and two operands. To execute the heuristics, this domain is segmented by the number classification of the operands, *norm*, *infinity*, *denormal*, etc. For strong mutation analysis, the mutant-distinguishing point is set at the output ports of the core including the arithmetic output and exception signals. Further, though not the focus of this experiment, a software implementation of the floating point standard is used in the simulation as an oracle, to compare and assess the correctness of the DUV output.

Figure 4 gives a summary of the experimental results. The design with a total number of 2492 lines-of-code derives 2257 mutants, which have the mutation points scattered over all the major sub-components. 58 of them are detected by the tool as equivalent mutants. We then executed the flow in Figure 1 with two setups, one fixed with a uniform input distribution, another *also starting with a uniform distribution* but self-tuning directed by the heuristics. Each setup is executed twice for 200 loop iterations, i.e., 200 test cases as shown in the figure to provide more evident data. The adjustment threshold parameter of the heuristics is set to 1, and $initial\_good\_^{ps}/_{pm}$ set to 0.01. Our studies also compared the simulation time with and without memory utilization and found no significant difference. To conduct the two experiments with uniform distribution, it took us 89460 and 101681 simulation runs for about 85 and 96 hours, respectively, which killed 1301 and 1289 mutants. The other two experiments with the heuristics took 78460 and 78849 simulations for around 75 and 77 hours with a mutant killing coverage of 1679 and 1668, respectively. The original test bench delivered with the arithmetic core, simulating all the operations, rounding modes, and corner cases, is also exercised with the mutation analysis. It killed 1440 mutants.

In summary, experiments gave a clear improvement by the heuristics against the single uniform distribution, in terms of a higher total mutant-killing coverage and less simulation effort. This means that our heuristics significantly advances the current state of mutation-based verification automation. Although the deterministic test bench exposes a certain amount of mutants more rapidly, it is the advantage of the CRV to avoid the manual, labour intensive writing and improving of test cases.

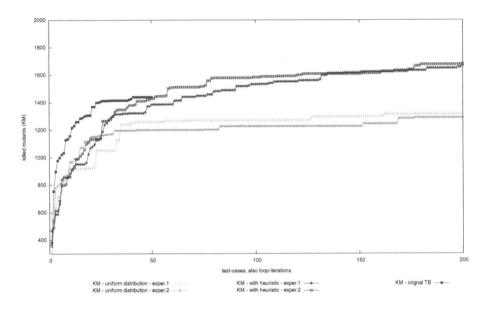

Fig. 4. Experimental results

5 Conclusion

We primarily considered the cost model when applying mutation analysis as the coverage metric to measure the completeness of a CRV flow. Basically, the simulation effort is $O(T * L^2)$, where T stands for the number of test cases and L the size of the design. L representing the design complexity grows rapidly along with the Moore's Law driven capacity of integrated circuits. In CRV, T is further enlarged as the amount of test cases required to reach an adequacy is based on random generation. More accurately, with some probability analyses $(\max_i 1/ps_i + \sum_i pw_i/ps_i)$ is found to be the expected simulation runs. Based on this, a heuristics is developed that collects the past analysis information to estimate the effectiveness of test domain ranges and re-distributes the probability.

The CRV flow equipped with the dynamic distribution adjustment heuristics has been implemented and experimented with Certitude^{TM} and a VHDL floating point arithmetic unit. The results are encouraging and show the efficiency improvement in terms of *reaching more rapidly a higher mutant-killing coverage*. With more, yet automated simulation effort, it also surpasses the manual test bench that is carefully composed by the author of the arithmetic core.

In future work, we will investigate different architecture and their impact on the heuristics with a focus on control-oriented circuits like microprocessors. Since the verification flow is based on simulation, it also scales well to large designs.

In contrast to other fault-based test generation approaches, MA systematically correlates the mutant-killing and the test's capability of revealing design errors. This can be key technology for solving the verification bottleneck today. The work presented in this paper is established on the macro relation between the test input domain and the overall mutant killing. It promotes coverage efficiency but specific, even-harder-to-expose mutants may remain. Here, future work will also consider the automatic, deterministic test generation for exposing an individual mutant. Existing solutions rely on symbolic execution and constraint solving with the assumption that mutant behaviors propagate to the output if activated. This is a limitation when the algorithms face complex SW/HW/system designs. More efficient, light-weight solutions have to be developed to enable a practical deployment. Nevertheless, the MA directed CRV will remain a necessary step to obtain a first mutant killing coverage, since it sieves out the easy-to-kill mutants, which the deterministic test generation algorithms can hardly do.

Acknowledgements. The work described herein is funded by the FP7 COCONUT project (FP7-ICT-3217069), the BMBF ITEA2 project VERDE (VERDE (01S09012H), and the DFG Sonderforschungsbereich SFB 614 (Self-Optimizing Systems for Mechanical Engineering).

References

[1] DeMillo, R.A., Lipton, R.J., Sayward, F.G.: Hints on Test Data Selection: Help for the Practicing Programmer. IEEE Computer 11(4) (April 1978)

[2] DeMillo, R.A., Offutt, A.J.: Constraint-Based Automatic Test Data Generation. IEEE Transactions on Software Engineering 17(9) (September 1991)

[3] Howden, W.E.: Weak Mutation Testing and Completeness of Test Sets. IEEE Transactions on Software Engineering 8(4) (July 1982)

[4] Offutt, A.J.: The coupling effect: fact or fiction. ACM SIGSOFT Software Engineering Notes 14(8) (December 1989)

[5] Offutt, A.J., Seaman, E.J.: Using Symbolic Execution to Aid Automatic Test Data Generation. In: Proceedings of the fifth Annual Conference on Computer Assurance, COMPASS 1990, Gaithersburg, MD, USA (June 1990)

[6] Untch, R.H., Offutt, A.J., Harrold, M.J.: Mutation Analysis Using Mutant Schemata. ACM SIGSOFT Software Engineering Notes 18(3) (July 1993)

[7] Hampton, M., Petithomme, S.: Leveraging a Commercial Mutation Analysis Tool For Research. In: Proceedings of the Testing: Academic and Industrial Conference Practice and Research Techniques- MUTATION. TAICPART-MUTATION 2007 (September 2007)

[8] Sengupta, S.: Defect-based Tests: A Key Enabler for Successful Migration to Structural Test. Intel Technology Journal (1999)

[9] Al Hayek, G., Robach, C.: From Specification Validation to Hardware Testing: A Unified Method. In: Proceedings of the IEEE International Test Conference on Test and Design Validity, ITC 1996, Washington, DC, USA (October 1996)

[10] Ghosh, S., Chakraborty, T.J.: On Behavior Fault Modeling for Digital Designs. Journal of Electronic Testing: Theory and Applications 2(2) (June 1991)

[11] Ferrandi, F., Fummi, F., Sciuto, D.: Implicit Test Generation for Behavioral VHDL Models. In: Proceedings of the 1998 IEEE International Test Conference, ITC 1998, Washington, DC, USA (October 1998)

[12] Fin, A., Fummi, F.: A VHDL Error Simulator for Functional Test Generation. In: Proceedings of the 2000 conference on Design, Automation and Test in Europe, DATE 2000, Paris, France (March 2000)

[13] International Technology Roadmap for Semiconductors (ITRS). ITRS 2009 Edition, http://www.itrs.net/Links/2009ITRS/Home2009.htm

[14] SpringSoft. Functional Qualification Tool Certitude™, http://www.springsoft.com/products/functional-qualification/certitude

[15] Corno, F., Sonza Reorda, M., Squillero, G., Manzone, A., Pincetti, A.: Automatic Test Bench Generation for Validation of RT-Level Descriptions: An Industrial Experience. In: Proceedings of the 2000 Conference on Design, Automation and Test in Europe, DATE 2000, Paris, France (March 2000)

[16] Tasiran, S., Fallah, F., Chinnery, D., Weber, S., Keutzer, K.: Coverage-Directed Generation of Biased Random Inputs for Functional Validation of Sequential Circuits. In: Proceedings of the International Workshop on Logic and Synthesis (June 2001)

[17] Fine, S., Ziv, A.: Coverage directed test generation for functional verification using bayesian networks. In: Proceedings of the 40th annual Design Automation Conference, DAC 2003, Anaheim, CA, USA (2003)

[18] Open SystemC Initiative Verification Working Group, SystemC Verification Library Standard, release 1.0p2 (2006), http://www.systemc.org/downloads/standards

[19] Bombieri, N., Fummi, F., Pravadelli, G., Hampton, M., Letombe, F.: Functional Qualification of TLM Verification. In: Proc. of the 2009 ACM/IEEE Design, Automation and Test in Europe, DATE 2009, Nice, France (April 2009)

[20] Lachish, O., Marcus, E., Ur, S., Ziv, A.: Hole Analysis for Functional Coverage Data. In: Proceedings of the 39th Conference on Design Automation, pp. 807–812 (June 2002)

[21] Asaf, S., Marcus, E., Ziv, A.: Defining coverage views to improve functional coverage analysis. In: Proceedings of the 41st Conference on Design Automation, pp. 41–44 (June 2004)

Generating VHDL Source Code from
UML Models of Embedded Systems

Tomás G. Moreira[1], Marco A. Wehrmeister[3], Carlos E. Pereira[2],
Jean-François Pétin[4], and Eric Levrat[4]

[1] Informatics Institute,
[2] Dept. Electical Engineering,
Federal University of Rio Grande do Sul – Porto Alegre, Brazil
tgmoreira@inf.ufrgs.br, cpereira@ece.ufrgs.br
[3] Department. of Computer Science
Santa Catarina State University – Joinville, Brazil
marcow@joinville.udesc.br
[4] Centre de Recherche en Automatique de Nancy
University of Nancy – Vandoeuvre-Lès-Nancy, France
{jean-francois.petin,eric.levrat}@cran.uhp-nancy.fr

Abstract. Embedded systems' complexity and amount of distinct functionalities have increased over the last years. To cope with such issues, the projects' abstraction level is being continuously raised, and, in addition, new design techniques have also been used to shorten design time. In this context, Model-Driven Engineering approaches that use UML models are interesting options to design embedded systems, aiming at code generation of software and hardware components. Source code generation from UML is already supported by several commercial tools for software. However, there are only few tools addressing generation code using hardware description languages, such as VHDL. This work proposes an approach to generate automatically VHDL source code from UML specifications. This approach is supported by the GenERTiCA tool, which has been extended to support VHDL code generation. To validate this work, a use case focused in maintenance systems attended by embedded systems is presented.

Keywords: Embedded systems, system engineering, intelligent maintenance, UML specification, VHDL code generation.

1 Introduction

Embedded systems are dedicated system designed to perform a small number of functions. It contains predominantly digital components, consisting in a hardware platform upon which software application execute [1]. Embedded systems' functionalities can be distributed over different processing nodes. Distributed Embedded Systems (DES) rely on a communication infrastructure constrained by requirements/constraints of embedded systems domain, e.g. timing and energy consumption requirements.

In the industrial domain, DES may be composed by several intelligent components, which make decisions and perform their activities autonomously [2]. Industrial DES

M. Hinchey et al. (Eds.): DIPES/BICC 2010, IFIP AICT 329, pp. 125–136, 2010.

support conventional or innovative functions. The former concerns to simple control functions, whereas the later represents more elaborated functions, e.g. maintenance and prognostic systems' functions to perform Condition Monitoring (CM), Health Assessment (HA), Prognostics (PR), etc. Components' intelligence level is defined by the amount of different services required by the end-user that are implemented as component functions [3], [4]. As machines do not suddenly fail, they usually pass through a measurable process of degradation before failing. Intelligent maintenance or prognostics systems use information provided by sensors and computing components embedded into equipments. Then, algorithms for health estimation and failure prediction are applied to assess machines' degradation level. Hence, embedded sensors, intelligent actuators and processing elements play a fundamental role in the development of intelligent maintenance systems.

The complexity of this scenario demands new tools and techniques. Increasing the design's abstraction level by using, for instance Model-Driven Engineering (MDE) [6] techniques, is an interesting approach to deal with the mentioned issues [5]. Standard graphical languages, e.g. the *Unified Modeling Language* (UML)[1], must be used to facilitate the communication of design's intentions to different teams, i.e. software and hardware teams. UML is a high-level design language and is broad enough in scope to model DES. Usually, UML-based MDE approach focus only in the software part of embedded systems by defining a mapping between high-level specification's construction down to software construction using programming languages (e.g. C/C++, Java, etc.). There are many academic works and commercial tools (e.g. Rational Rose[2] and Artisan Studio[3]) that can generate software code from UML models. However, considering embedded systems' hardware part, only few works address the use of UML to produce *Hardware Description Language* (HDL) descriptions, as in [9], [10]. In this sense, the transformation of UML models into HDL code, e.g. using VHDL (*Very High Speed Integrated Circuit HDL*), is not yet well diffused, opening room for research on this subject.

This works presents an extension to our aspect-oriented MDE approach for DES named *Aspect-Oriented Model-Driven Engineering for Real-Time systems* (AMoDE-RT) [7]. This work's main contribution is to support automatic generation of VHDL descriptions from UML models. In other words, this work extends AMoDE-RT's supporting tool GenERTiCA (*Generation of Embedded Real-Time Code based on Aspects*) [12], aiming at automatic generation of VHDL descriptions from UML models. The generated VHDL code is intended to be used in FPGA (Field Programmable Gate Array) systems. Thus, the proposed approach allows the behavior of the required system to be described (modeled) and verified (simulated) before synthesis tools translate the design into real hardware (gates and wires).

Additionally, this work proposes an engineering process, which covers from requirements analysis and UML modeling phases to VHDL code generation. The focus is to generate VHDL source code for the logical functions of an embedded system, which so far has only been implemented in software. To validate this work, this paper presents a use case focused on a distributed embedded system (i.e. DES) used for

---

[1] UML 2.2 Specification. Object Management Group, http://www.omg.org/ spec/UML/2.2/

[2] http://www.ibm.com/software/rational/

[3] http://www.artisansoftwaretools.com

maintenance systems (intelligent components), which integrates both conventional and innovative functions.

This paper is organized as follows: Section 2 provides an overview of the proposed approach to map UML specifications into VHDL source code, whereas Section 3 presents the developed mapping rules. The case study of a valve component system is presented in Section 4. Section 5 provides a review of works related. Finally, conclusion and directions for future work are presented in Section 6.

2   Overview of the Proposed Approach

The proposed approach follows the flow proposed by the Aspect-oriented Model-Driven Engineering for Real-Time systems (AMoDE-RT) [7], [15] (see Fig. 1), which uses MDE techniques combined with AO concepts to design DES. AMoDE-RT is supported by GenERTiCA [12] code generation, which uses mapping rules scripts to produce source code files for a given target platform from UML models annotated with the MARTE profile[4]. Therefore, GenERTiCA is capable of generating code for many distinct languages (Java, C/C++, etc.), since there are mapping rules for the target platforms. The process is the same to generate code for different languages and therefore it is considered generic. This work proposes an extension for the GenERTiCA tool in terms of a new set of mapping rules to map UML meta-model elements into VHDL constructs.

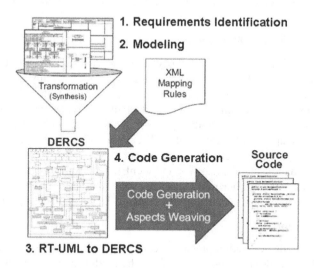

Fig. 1. General overview on the whole process

---

[4] UML Profile for Modeling and Analysis of Real-time and Embedded Systems (MARTE), http://www.omg.org/spec/MARTE/1.0

Following, a brief description of each step of AMoDE-RT design flow is presented.

1. Requirements Analysis and Identification

In the first phase, requirements and constraints of the distributed embedded real-time system are gathered. To accomplish this, the RT-FRIDA [13] requirements analysis is performed, resulting in a set of documents describing system's requirements, functionalities and constraints. Afterwards, use case diagrams are created, depicting all expected functionalities of the distributed embedded real time system, and also the external elements that interact with the system.

2. Modeling

The next step is to specify the elements to handle the functional and non-functional requirements gathered in the previous phase. To model functional requirements, designers use class diagrams to describe the structure, and sequence diagrams to describe the methods behavior. Other behavioral and structural diagrams, such as activity or state diagrams, or composite structure or deployment diagrams, can also be used. However the class and sequence diagrams are mandatory to describe the structure and behavior of all system with correctness. These UML diagrams are annotated with the stereotype of the MARTE profile to specify real-time characteristics of (some) DES' elements. During this phase, the non-functional requirements handling are specified using aspects from the Distributed Embedded Real-Time Aspects Framework (DERAF) [12]. These aspects are modeled in the Aspects Crosscutting Overview Diagram (ACOD) [15], and the points (in the UML model) in which DERAF aspects perform adaptations are specified using Join Point Designation Diagrams (JPDD).

3. UML-to-DERCS Transformation

At this point GenERTiCA transforms the system specification, i.e. the UML model, into another model called DERCS (Distributed Embedded Compact Specification) [12], which represents an embedded system PIM free of information overlapping[5]. A UML specification can contain several model elements, representing the same element that hinders the code generation process. Thus these ambiguous elements of UML model are mapped in a single DERCS element, eliminating such ambiguities that could result in code with errors. When an inconsistency is detected, the UML-to-DERCS transformation algorithm stops and GenERTiCA informs this occurrence to the designer, requesting his/her intervention to solve the issue. Interested readers are referred to [12] to have more details on this UML-to-DERCS model transformation.

4. Code Generation

In this phase the code generation process executes a set of scripts (i.e. mapping rules), which guide the GenERTiCA tool   to perform the model-to-text transformation from DERCS elements to constructions in the target platform. Furthermore, the code generation process also performs the aspects weaving. If the element under evaluation is

---

[5] Information overlapping in UML models means the same feature of the target system, which has been specified using distinct diagrams depicting different viewpoints of the same structural/behavioral characteristic.

affected by an aspect, the aspects weaving process modifies the generated code fragments according to aspects adaptations described in the mapping rules.

3 Mapping UML to VHDL

As previously mentioned, to generate code from the UML model, GenERTiCA adopts a script-based approach, in which small scripts define how to map model elements into target platform constructions, generating source code fragments that are merged to produce source code files. The script-based code generation process improves separation of concerns in mapping rules specification, as each script is concerned with the transformation of a single model element (or few of them) into source code fragment.

Table 1. Concepts Mapping

UML Element	VHDL Element
Class	Entity-Architecture pair
Public attribute	Entity Ports
Private attribute	Signals
Methods	Processes
Events and Message exchange	Entity Ports
Associations between classes	Entity Ports
Inheritance	VHDL key word "new"
Static polymorphism	Configuration structure
Objects instantiation	Component structure

In this sense, this work has proposed a set of mapping rules to allow VHDL code generation from UML models, following GenERTiCA's approach. Table 1 shows the mapping from UML concepts into VHDL ones. Scripts to accomplish these transformations have been developed and inserted in an eXtensible Markup Language (XML)[6] file, which guide GenERTiCA in the code generation process. Details on the created mapping rules are provided in the following sub-sections.

Classes are mapped into VHDL entity-architecture pairs. The class parameters are mapped to VHDL generic statements, while public attributes to VHDL entity ports and private attributes to VHDL signals. The methods are mapped to VHDL processes. The composition relationship, which describes the composition of a system from components, is mapped to a VHDL port map statements. Objects are instantiated as component structures into other entities. Events and Messages exchanges are implemented as entities ports that allow the communication between different entities and their processes (methods). Associations between classes are similar to the approach used to messages exchange, however component structures representing each associated-class (i.e. entities) are instantiated into the pair-class to accomplish the association by the mapping of signals between these two classes. Inheritance is obtained making the entity or architecture declaration with the VHDL key word "tagged", which means that the declaration is valid but still incomplete. Then, we declare a new

---

[6] eXtensible Markup Language (XML) 1.0 (Fifth Edition). http://www.w3.org/TR/2008/REC-xml-20081126/

entity/architecture using the VHDL key word "new", with the desired modifications. Static polymorphism is obtained using the VHDL configuration structure to bind the same VHDL component to different entities or architectures.

3.1 Mapping Rules

Mapping rules are specified as small scripts that create source code fragments (representing target platform constructions) from DERCS model elements. Source code files are made up from these generated code fragments. Scripts are stored and organized in one mapping rules file specified using the XML format. This XML file has a portable format allowing the specification of self-described content organized in a tree structure. XML tree organization facilitates scripts storage in terms of platform mapping rules repositories. It allows scripts to be reused in further projects that use the same target platform. Hence, the design effort to derive system implementation from an UML model is decreased.

Scripts are located in the leaf nodes of the tree. The correct script is selected based on which element is being accessed by the code generation algorithm (i.e. the leaf node must match with the DERCS element). The code generation algorithm first identifies the type of the element. Afterwards, it tries to find the tree's leaf that better represents the type of such element being evaluated. Then, it executes the script contained within the found node (i.e. leaf), which will create a VHDL code fragment to that element being evaluated.

The language used to describe the scripts is the well-known open source scripting framework called Velocity[7], which defines the Velocity Template Language (VTL) that provides all functionalities required to assist the code generation approach implementation. VTL is a Java-like scripting language, which returns a string as result of script execution. Thus, the generated source code fragment is obtained by means of accessing model information through DERCS API.

To illustrate what is a script an example is given above. This script is responsible for the code generation to the classes' methods. It generates one VHDL process for each method in the classes.

```
01  #if ($Message.Name != $Class.Name)
02    \n${Message.Name}: process(
03    #if ($Message.Name == "run")
04        clock,
05        reset,
06    #end
07    #if ($Message.ParametersCount > 0)
08        #foreach( $param in $Message.Parameters )
09            #if ($velocityCount > 1), #end
10            $param.Name
11        #end
12    #end
13    )
14    \n$Options.BlockStart
15    #if ($Message.Name == "run")
16        \n
17        \nif (reset='1') then
18        \n-- variables initialization
19        \n
20        \nelsif (clock'EVENT and clock='1') then
```

[7] http://velocity.apache.org

```
21    #end
22    \n$CodeGenerator.getVariablesDeclaration(0)
23    \n$CodeGenerator.getActionsCode(1)
24    #if ($Message.Name == "run")
25        \n
26        \nend if;
27    #end
28    \n$Options.BlockEnd process;
29    \n
30 #end
```

3.2 Concepts

The concepts used in this work to the transformation of UML structures into VHDL code are based in [9] and [14]. These works gave us some ideas on how to represent in VHDL the structure of classes, attributes, methods, association between classes, events and messages exchange, inheritance, and polymorphism.

UML Model is object-oriented, while the VHDL code is structured. This semantic gap between abstraction levels hinders the mapping between these two languages. It may be one of the main reasons why it is very rare, until the present days, to find works addressing to VHDL code generation from UML models and/or any commercial tool.

From these concepts some rules have been developed and tested to this version of the VHDL mapping rules. They represent the first version of the mapping rules to provide the VHDL code generation through GenERTiCA tool. Up to now, it has been developed and tested mapping rules to generate VHDL code from UML classes, attributes and behaviors. Their feasibility is shown in the case study of next section. The concepts of inheritance, polymorphism, associations between classes, etc, are being be implemented in the next version of this work.

4 Case Study

This section shows an example of automatic VHDL code generation from a UML model. The system under evaluation is composed by an automatic valve and the sensors that give information about the valve's states. This valve is used to regulate the water flow and is part of CISPI (*Conduite de grands systèmes industriels à risque*) experimental platform located at CRAN (*Centre de Recherche en Automatique de Nancy - France*). By applying the proposed approach, we intend to integrate new functionalities supported by a FPGA in this valve, leading to an implementation of an intelligent component. This intelligent component is part of a mechatronic system which also contains other mechanical, electronics and computational parts. The electronics and computational parts represent the control system, which is composed of logical functions executing in a hardware platform. Logical functions represent components' behavior and are usually implemented in software. This work aims at implementing these logical functions as hardware. Thus the system has been specified in UML and its implementation has been generated as VHDL code. The generated code represent the hardware description of the logical and the control system parts (logical functions), which is executed inside of a FPGA (hardware platform).

The development of this case study was compliant with the AMoDE-RT approach defined in the section III. Then, the first step was to gather the requirements and create a use case diagram to identify system's services and the actors that interact with the system. Only two actors were considered. The "User" actor request services to open and close the valve, while the "Maintenance Operator" actor requests services to know the number of times the valve performed opening and closing actions. Information about these numbers is used for assessing the component physical heath.

The second step was to create class and sequence diagrams. The class diagram has been built from the knowledge acquired in the use case. It represents the system's structure. All services have been modeled as classes. These classes work together to provide the system's services. They are enclosed by a main class responsible for all system. No DERAF aspects have been used to deal with non-functional requirements, and hence, no ACOD and JPDD diagrams have been created.

Services are modeled as sequences of actions in sequence diagrams. Sequence diagrams represent the exchange of messages between the objects that compose the system in order to represent the expected system behavior. Each service demanded by the actors results in the execution of one or many sequence diagrams. Fig. 2 depicts a part of the main sequence diagram of valve's system related to the service solicitations.

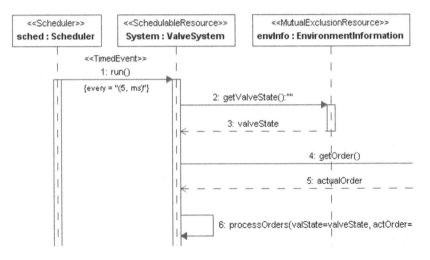

Fig. 2. Sequence diagram of the main function in the valve's system

The rule implementing the association between classes was not developed in this first version of the mapping rules. Thus, all this case study was re-modeled as just one class and one method. From these new diagrams the feasibility of the system could be tested and the 3rd and 4th steps performed. The mapping has transformed the UML class and sequence diagrams into one single VHDL file, which contains an entity-architecture pair declaration. The UML class is represented by the entity-architecture pair, while the UML behavior (method) is represented by a VHDL process inside of the architecture.

The code that appears in fig. 3 is the result of the automatic code generation performed by the mapping rules proposed in this work. This first test generated code for only one embedded component. For this component have been automatically generated 80 lines of VHDL code, covering 100% of the needed code for the application. This component is simple and its model was developed on only one UML class, however the results are encouraging for future works.

The real feasibility of the VHDL code can be tested quickly, since this code can be synthesized in the resulting bitstream uploaded in a FPGA development platform, such as Virtex-II PRO (V2-Pro) development system by Digilent[8].

```
23  architecture Behavioral of SmartComponent is
24
25          signal numberOS : INTEGER;
26          signal numberCS : INTEGER;
27          signal orderPerformed : BOOLEAN;
28          signal flagOPENING : BOOLEAN;
29          signal flagCLOSING : BOOLEAN;
30
31  begin
32
33      run: process(clock, reset, orders, fdcOPEN, fdcCLOSE)
34      begin
35      if (reset = '1') then
36      -- variables initialization
37      numberOS <= 0;
38      numberCS <= 0;
39      orderPerformed <= FALSE;
40      flagOPENING <= FALSE;
41      flagCLOSING <= FALSE;
42
43      elsif (clock'EVENT and clock = '1') then
44          if (orders = x"01" and flagCLOSING = FALSE)
45          or (flagOPENING = TRUE) then
46              if (orderPerformed = FALSE
47              and fdcOPEN = FALSE) then
48                  orderOPEN <= TRUE;
49                  orderPerformed <= TRUE;
50                  flagOPENING <= TRUE;
51                  numberOS <= numberOS+1;
52              end if;
```

Fig. 3. VHDL code representing the architecture declaration and run method initial part

5 Related Works

This section discusses some projects and commercial tools that propose transformations from UML specifications to source code VHDL. Among these works different approaches to generate source code from UML models have been found. Some use only one diagram (e.g. class diagram) to generate code, while others use a combination of

---

[8] Digilent Inc. www.digilentinc.com

distinct diagrams (e.g. class and state diagrams, sequence and/or activities diagrams) [8]. Thus the presented related works generate code ranging from classes skeletons to code containing system elements behavior.

In [9], a framework has been developed to derive VHDL specifications from UML's class and state diagrams. They use homomorphic mappings between dissimilar structures while preserving metamodel class associations in a way that resembles MDA technique. However, their generated VHDL code focuses on simulation and verification of UML models rather than on hardware synthesis.

An interesting work has been developed in [10], in which the MODCO tool is presented. It uses MDA techniques to define high-level model-based system descriptions that can be implemented in either hardware or software. Thus it can transform UML state diagrams directly into synthesizable VHDL. State machines in UML are used to describe the behavior of a part of a system. However, the complete code is generated for the behavior. Functional requirements are mapped to UML component, class, use case and state diagrams. Non-functional requirements are specified as UML annotations that describe performance constraints using property-value pairs defined by UML profiles. However, the authors targeted flat state-transition diagrams without supporting hierarchy and concurrency, and also only covering a small subset of UML state diagram constructs.

In [11], they have developed a framework for deriving VHDL specifications from UML state diagrams, and also a set of rules, which enable automated generation of synthesizable VHDL code from UML. Their engineering process is based on metamodels. Concepts of the UML state diagram metamodel are mapped onto concepts of the VHDL metamodel. There are two transformations between models, happening in the following way: the first transformation converts the main UML model into state diagram models; and the second one maps the state diagram models onto concepts in the VHDL language. A model-to-text transformation is used to generate synthesizable VHDL code from the VHDL model.

Two commercial tools to generate VHDL code could also be found. StateCAD[9] by Xilinx is a graphical entry tool for digital design that has its own graphical notation to represent state diagrams as bubble diagrams. StateCAD automatically generates HDL (VHDL and Verilog) code, for simulation and also synthesis, directly from these state diagrams. The other tool is Simulink HDL Coder[10] by MathWorks, which generates synthesizable VHDL and Verilog code from simulink models, stateflow charts, and embedded Matlab code. Simulink HDL Coder also generates simulation and synthesis scripts, enabling to simulate and synthesize quickly the developed design. These commercial tools do not generate VHDL code from UML specifications.

The approach proposed in [11] realizes the mapping between models, similarly to other MDE techniques. In [10], there is a separation of the functional and non-functional requirements in the modeling stage using distinct UML diagrams. These mentioned works are limited, because they cover a specific subset of the UML structures, and also use only the UML state diagrams. By using GenERTiCA the designer can use distinct UML diagrams, combining them to specify the full functionality in terms of structure, behavior and non-functional requirements handling, since some

---

[9] http://www.xilinx.com/

[10] http://www.mathworks.com/products/slhdlcoder/

guidelines are followed. These guidelines are simple and intuitive, allowing designers to separate the functional and non-functional requirements. Moreover, by using the extension proposed in this work, it is possible to generate code for VHDL and also for the Java and C++ languages from the same model.

6 Conclusions

This work addresses the problem of generating HDL descriptions from UML models. It presented the initial set of mapping rules to generate VHDL code from class and sequence diagrams, using GenERTiCA tool. To achieve this goal, is has been proposed a mapping from object-oriented concepts supported in UML into concepts used by VHDL. Then, a set of mapping rules (used by GenERTiCA to generate VHDL code) has been developed. These rules extend the functionality of GenERTiCA tool, allowing it to generate HDL code in addition to software source code. Besides, this paper has described all steps of the proposed approach that must be followed to generate automatically VHDL descriptions.

To demonstrate the proposed approach, a case study has been presented. It showed a small part of a maintenance system, i.e. automatic control of a valve implemented as a Smart Component. As mentioned mapping rules have been implemented and tested to produce VHDL code from UML's classes, attributes and behavior. Results shown that, for developing simple systems, 100% of the necessary code could be generated. Hence, despite the case study's size, the results are considered satisfactory since we see great potential to scale the approach to more complex systems.

To continue this work the following direction will be pursued: to complete the rules needed for the code generation of VHDL structures. The concepts of inheritance, polymorphism, associations between classes are very important to be able the modeling of complex systems; to develop the rules for the non-functional requirements implemented by aspects; to test and to prove the new rules; to perform more tests with FPGA boards; to apply the proposed approach in a complex real system, such as an industrial maintenance and prognostic systems.

References

1. Micheli, D., Gupta, R.K.: Hardware/Software Co-design. Proceedings of the IEEE 85(3), 349–365 (1997)
2. Pereira, C.E., Carro, L.: Distributed real-time embedded systems: Recent advances, future trends and their impact in manufacturing plant control. Annual Reviews in Control 31, 81–92 (2007)
3. Iung, B., Neunreuther, E., Morel, G.: Engineering process of integrated-distributed shop floor architecture based on interoperable field components. International Journal of Computer Integrated Manufacturing 14(3), 246–262 (2001)
4. Pétin, J.-F., Iung, B., Morel, G.: Distributed intelligent actuation and measurement (IAM) system within an integrated shop-floor organization. Computers in Industry 37, 197–211 (1998)
5. Sangiovanni-Vincentelli, A.: The tides of EDA. IEEE Design & Test of Computers 20(6), 59–75 (2003)

6. Mellor, S.J., Clark, A.N., Futagami, T.: Guest Editors' Introduction: Model-Driven Development. IEEE Software 20(5), 14–18 (2003)
7. Wehrmeister, M.A.: An Aspect-Oriented Model-Driven Engineering Approach for Distributed Embedded Real-Time Systems. PhD Thesis, Federal University of Rio Grande do Sul, Brazil (Apr 2009),
   http://lisha.ufsc.br/~marcow/publications/
   wehrmeister_thesis_final.pdf
8. Long, Q., et al.: Consistent Code Generation from UML Models. In: Australian Software Engineering Conference, Los Alamitos (2005)
9. McUmber, W.E., Cheng, B.H.: UML-Based Analysis of Embedded Systems Using a Mapping to VHDL. In: 4th IEEE International Symposium on High-Assurance Systems Engineering, Washington D.C (1999)
10. Coyle, F., Thornton, M.: From UML to HDL: a Model-Driven Architectural approach to hardware-software co-design. In: Information Systems: New Generations Conference (ISNG), Las Vegas (2005)
11. Wood, S.K., et al.: A Model-Driven development Approach to Mapping UML State Diagrams to Synthesizable VHDL. IEEE Transactions on Computers 57(10), 1357–1371 (2008)
12. Wehrmeister, M.A., Freitas, E.P., Pereira, C.E., Ramming, F.: GenERTiCA: A Tool for Code Generation and Aspects Weaving. In: 11th IEEE Symposium on Object Oriented Real-Time Distributed Computing (ISORC), Orlando (2008)
13. Freitas, E.P., et al.: DERAF: A high-level Aspects Framework for Distributed Embedded Real-Time Systems Design. In: Moreira, A., Grundy, J. (eds.) Early Aspects Workshop 2007 and EACSL 2007. LNCS, vol. 4765, pp. 55–74. Springer, Heidelberg (2007)
14. Ecker, W.: An object-oriented view of structural VHDL description. In: Proceedings of VHDL International Users Forum Spring 1996 Conference, Santa Clara (1996)
15. Wehrmeister, M.A., Freitas, E.P., Pereira, C.E., Wagner, F.: An Aspect-Oriented Approach for Dealing with Non-Functional Requirements in Model-Driven Development of Distributed Embedded Real-Time Systems. In: 10th IEEE Symposium on Object Oriented Real-Time Distributed Computing, pp. 428–432 (2007)

RACE: A Rapid, ArChitectural Simulation and Synthesis Framework for Embedded Processors

Roshan Ragel[1], Angelo Ambrose[2],
Jorgen Peddersen[2], and Sri Parameswaran[2]

[1] Embedded Systems and Computer Architecture Lab (ESCAL)
Department of Computer Engineering, University of Peradeniya,
Peradeniya 20400 Sri Lanka
[2] Embedded Systems Lab (ESL)
School of Computer Science and Engineering,
University of New South Wales,
Sydney 2052 Australia

Abstract. Increasingly, embedded systems designers tend to use Application Specific Instruction Set Processors (ASIPs) during the design of application specific systems. However, one of the design metrics of embedded systems is the time to market of a product, which includes the design time of an embedded processor, is an important consideration in the deployment of ASIPs. While the design time of an ASIP is very short compared to an ASIC it is longer than when using a general purpose processor. There exist a number of tools which expedite this design process, and they could be divided into two: first, tools that automatically generate HDL descriptions of the processor for both simulation and synthesis; and second, tools that generate instruction set simulators for the simulation of the hardware models. While the first one is useful to measure the critical path of the design, die area, etc. they are extremely slow for simulating real world software applications. At the same time, the instruction set simulators are fast for simulating real world software applications, but they fail to provide information so readily available from the HDL models. The framework presented in this paper, RACE, addresses this issue by integrating an automatic HDL generator with a well-known instruction set simulator. Therefore, embedded systems designers who use our RACE framework will have the benefits of both a fast instruction set simulation and rapid hardware synthesis at the same time.

Keywords: Design Automation, Simulation, Synthesis.

1 Introduction

Embedded systems are ubiquitous, and are present in low-end systems such as wireless handsets, networked sensors, and smart cards, to high-end systems such as network routers, gateways, firewalls, and servers. Embedded systems are seen as application specific equipment and they differ from general purpose computing machinery since they execute a single application or a class of applications repeatedly.

M. Hinchey et al. (Eds.): DIPES/BICC 2010, IFIP AICT 329, pp. 137–144, 2010.

The heart of an embedded system is usually implemented using either general purpose processors, ASICs or a combination of both. General Purpose Processors (GPPs) are programmable, but consume more power than ASICs. Reduced time to market and minimized risk are factors which favour the use of GPPs in embedded systems. ASICs, on the other hand, cost a great deal to design and are nonprogrammable, making upgradability impossible. However, ASICs have reduced power consumption and are smaller than GPPs.

Recently a new entrant called the Application Specific Instruction-set Processor (ASIP) has taken centre stage as an alternative contender for implementing functionalities in embedded systems. These are processors with specialized instructions, selected co-processors, and parameterized caches applicable only to a particular program or a class of programs. An ASIP will execute an application for which it was designed with great efficiency, though they are capable of executing any other program (usually with reduced efficiency). ASIPs are programmable, quick to design and consume less power than GPPs (though more than ASICs). ASIPs in particular are suited for utilization in embedded systems where customization allows increased performance, yet reduces power consumption by not having unnecessary functional units. Programmability allows the ability to upgrade, and reduces software design time. Tools and customizable processors such as ASIPmeister [1], Xtensa [2], LISATek [3], ARCtangent [4], Jazz [5], Nios [6], and SP5-flex [7] allow rapid creation of ASIPs. The advent of tools to create ASIPs has greatly enhanced the ability to reduce design turn-around time.

However, there exists a limitation. The tools listed above except the one presented in [4] will either generate the hardware description language (HDL) model of the embedded processor or a model where only Instruction Set Simulation (ISS) could be performed. The HDL models are good for precise synthesis and power measurement of the processor, but fail to provide fast simulation results such as the clock cycle count of an application that runs on such a model. The ISS models are good for faster simulation of applications, but fail to provide synthesis results which are essential in embedded system design. Even though tools such as the one from Tensilica [2] try to address this issue, they do not provide the flexibility (such as accurate power measurement using the HDL model, full control of the instruction set of the processor, etc.) expected in other ASIP design tools such as ASIPmeister.

In this paper, we present a framework, named RACE, which provides both an ISS model for fast simulation and an HDL description for fast synthesis of an embedded processor during its design. We make use of ASIPmeister [1], an automatic processor generation tool for preparing the HDL model and SimpleScalar tool-set [8] for preparing the ISS model. The detail of how these are integrated to form the RACE framework is discussed in this paper.

The rest of this paper is organised as follows. Section 2 summarizes the previous work related to embedded processor simulation and synthesis. Section 3 details our framework. Section 4 explains how our framework incorporates processor customization and Section 5 discusses a typical experimental setup of our framework. Finally, Section 6 concludes the paper.

2   Related Work

With the demand for shorter design turnaround times, many commercial and research organizations have provided base processor cores, so that fewer modifications have to be made on the design to achieve particular performance requirements. This has led to the emergence of reconfigurable and extensible processors. Xtensa [2], Jazz [5] and PEAS-III (used by ASIPmeister) [1] are examples of processor template based approaches which build ASIPs around base processors.

Xtensa [2] is a configurable and scalable RISC core. It provides both 24-bit and 16-bit instructions to freely mix at a fine granularity. The base processor supports 80 base instructions of the Xtensa Instruction Set Architecture (ISA) with a 5-stage pipe-line. New functional units and extensible instructions can be added using the Tensilica Instruction Extension (TIE) language. Synthesizable code can be obtained together with the software tools for various architectures implemented with Xtensa. However, it fails to provide the flexibility for altering the base processor.

The Jazz Processor [5] permits the modelling and simulation of a system consisting of multiple processors, memories and peripherals. Data width, number of registers, depth of hardware task queue, and addition of custom functionality are its input parameters. It has a base ISA which supports addition of extensible instructions to further optimize the core for specific applications. The Jazz processor has a 2-stage instruction pipeline, single cycle execution units and supports interrupts with different priority levels. Users are able to select between 16-bit or 32-bit data paths. It also has a broad selection of optional 16-bit or 32-bit DSP execution units which are fully tested and ready to be included in the design. However, Jazz is suitable only for VLIW and DSP architectures.

ASIPmeister [1] is able to capture a target processors specification using a GUI. A micro-operation level simulation model and RTL description for logic synthesis can be generated along with software tool chain. It provides support for any RISC architecture type and a library of configurable components. The core produced follows the Harvard style memory architecture. Even though it provides both the simulation and the synthesisable models, the simulation model could only be used with an HDL simulator such as ModelSim and therefore, real world applications will take hours (if not days) for simulation. Researchers have proposed extensions to ASIPmeister, such as the one presented in [9], so that it could be used as a fully fledged simulation system with system call support, file handling, etc. However, they failed to solve the problem of the extended simulation time taken to simulate real world applications as explained earlier.

The RACE framework we propose here uses similar techniques to that of [9] to generate the synthesis model of the processor. However, we propose to use an independent instruction set simulator which is derived from the SimpleScalar tool-set [8] for faster simulation of the same processor. We show how the instruction sets could be altered (reduced/amended/added) in both the simulation and the synthesis models of a target processor by taking PISA, the ISA used in the SimpleScalar tool-set as an example.

Therefore, in summary, the contributions are:

- a framework that performs both fast simulation and synthesis of an embedded processor model; a fully flexible and rapid ASIP design flow based on our framework; and,
- a scheme on how an instruction set could be altered to explore the design space of both the simulation and synthesisable models.

However, there exist the following limitations:

- Designing the initial models of the processors might take a longer time (a day or two to a familiar designer). However, this is a one-time process and the same model could be used later for rapid design development.
- It is assumed that the compiler tool-set is available as open source for the instruction set used in the design.

3   The RACE Framework

RACE is a hardware-software co-design framework, where both the software binary of a target application as well as the hardware model to run such a binary are designed and implemented. In this section, we explain the process of software binary generation a target ISA, and then we describe the generation of the hardware models, for instruction set simulation and for synthesis.

3.1   Software Generation

SimpleScalar cross compiler (such as *sslittle-na-sstrix-gcc*) is used to generate the instruction and the data memory dump (we call it the binary) from the application program. In the HDL models, both memories will communicate with the CPU model to function as a complete processor, executing the program. Further details on the memory generation can be found in an earlier publication [9].

Figure 1 depicts the typical software generation process. A C/C++ application is compiled to the target binary by using the SimpleScaler compiler tool-set using a cross compiler.

As depicted in Figure 1, if necessary, support for new instructions (to the ISA) is added to the assembler of the SimpleScalar cross compiler. Given that the cross compiler is a derivative of the well understood open source GNU/GCC compiler tool-chain; this task can be performed with relative ease. When the support for new instructions is available in the assembler, application programs can be written either in a higher level language like C with inline assembly (for new instructions) or in the target assembly language by using the new instructions. Here, the new instructions will both be designed and inserted (to the application) manually by the designer. Even though, this could be considered a limitation of the RACE framework (as pointed out earlier under limitations), we argue that it gives better control of the design flow to the designer. If absolutely necessary, support for such automation can be established by extending the compiler tool-set.

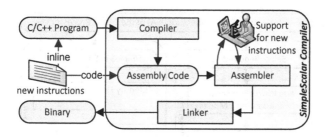

Fig. 1. The software generation process: Support for new instructions can be added to the assembler and programs can be written with either in-lined or added new assembly instructions

3.2   Hardware Generation for Simulation

Figure 2 depicts the generation process of hardware models in RACE framework. As depicted, RACE framework generates three hardware models of an ASIP from two input set of specifications.

All three models depicted as derived in Figure 2 can be used for simulation of an application program. However, as these three models vary in the level of detail used for implementing the hardware, the times taken to perform the simulation vary significantly. For example, while a typical embedded system application would take days (if not weeks) to be simulated using gate level simulation, it can be done in seconds or minutes using an instruction level simulation.

Therefore, the RACE framework uses the ISS to run complete application program simulations. Given that these simulations are cycle accurate, they will be used to count the number of clock cycles taken to simulate applications. The number of clock cycles along with the clock period (that is calculated from the synthesis discussed in the next subsection) is used to compute the execution time of an application, one of the main design metrics of any ASIP design.

SimpleSim, the ISS of the SimpleScalar tool-set is used to derive the ISS for RACE. The modular design of SimpleSim allows us to add/remove/amend instructions of the target ISA. As depicted on the right hand side of Figure 2, the machine.def file of SimpleSim is altered to change the target ISA.

3.3   Hardware Generation for Synthesis

An ASIP design tool, ASIPmeister, generates a model in HDL (both gate level and behaviour models) for a given ISA. As shown on the left side of Figure 2, to generate a processor using ASIPmeister, the first step is to create a suitable description of the processor, including the hardware resources (such as register file, ALU, divider, etc.) and pipeline stages. The instructions, their formats and addressing modes and the tasks to be performed by each instruction at run-time are defined as micro-operations (RTL operations), where each pipeline stage of the instruction is coded.

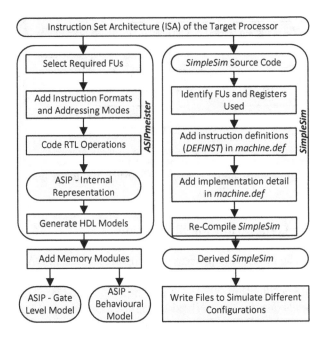

Fig. 2. The generation process of hardware models: On the left side is the HDL generation (both gate [ASIP - Gate Level Model] and behavioural [ASIP - Behaviour Model] models) with the help of ASIPmeister and on the right is the ISS generation for cycle accurate simulation

RACE uses the Portable Instruction Set Architecture (PISA: as implemented in SimpleScalar tool-set [8]) as its base processor. However, the base ISA could be of any other RISC processor. When the processor models (both gate level and behavioural) are generated, they are integrated with HDL models of memory modules to complete the ASIP models. Additional hardware can now be added to the design such as cache and memory mapped I/O.

4   Customized ASIPs

When the base models are designed in RACE, they can be customized in a number of ways either to explore the design space with different configurations or to add a totally different domain of tasks (such as instruction changes to perform security checks [11]) to the models. We discuss such customizations in this section.

Most of the applications hardly utilize the whole instruction set of a processor, thus the need for ASIPs. If an application does not need a specific instruction, it would be quite useful to turn off that instruction from the processor. This will reduce the area usage and power consumption, benefiting an embedded system [9].

ASIPs are famous for 'special instructions', instructions that are not available in the base ISA. RACE allows its users to have their own instructions. Special instructions can be utilized to add new customized hardware modules to perform repeated tasks and therefore make the processing faster [11].

5   Simulation and Synthesis Setup

Figure 3 depicts the simulation and synthesis setup used by RACE framework. The behavioural model is typically used during the design stage for debugging and testing of the ASIP (by performing simulation in ModelSim). The debugging and testing is performed by running test applications to cover all the instructions in our target ASIP. The completed gate level model is used with Synopsys Design Compiler to create the synthesized version, which is ready to be fabricated. The software binary is an input to the synthesis model, by which the memory size of the ASIP can be computed. Synthesis reports include power consumption, clock period and, area in gates and cells.

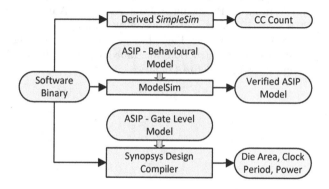

Fig. 3. Simulation and Synthesis: Simulations are performed by using the SimpleSim ISS and ModelSim. Synthesis is performed by using Synopsys Design Compiler.

Simulation is performed with SimpleSim to count the number of clock cycles (CC) particular software binaries would take. CC is multiplied by clock period (a metric computed from the synthesis using Synopsys Design Compiler) to compute the total execution time of the application.

Comparing the design time of large design problems with and without the RACE framework is currently being performed. We propose this as a future work for this paper.

6   Conclusion

In this paper, we reported RACE, a simulation and synthesis framework for rapid hardware-software co-design of ASIPs. RACE framework integrates an automatic HDL generator with a well-known instruction set simulator to support rapid processor development.

References

1. Itoh, M., Higaki, S., Sato, J., Shiomi, A., Takeuchi, Y., Kitajima, A., Imai, M.: Proceedings of 2000 International Conference on Computer Design, pp. 430–436 (2000)
2. Tensilica Inc., Xtensa Processor, http://www.tensilica.com
3. CoWare Inc., LISATek, http://www.coware.com/products/
4. ARC International, ARCtangent, http://www.arc.com
5. Improv Inc., Jazz DSP, http://www.improvsys.com
6. Altera Corp., NIOS Processor, http://www.altera.com
7. 3DSP Corp., ARCtangent, http://www.arc.com
8. Burger, D., Austin, T.M.: The SimpleScalar tool set, version 2.0. SIGARCH Computer Architecture News 25(3), 13–25 (1997)
9. Peddersen, J., Shee, S.L., Janapsatya, A., Parameswaran, S.: Rapid Embedded Hardware/Software System Generation. In: Proceedings of the 18th International Conference on VLSI Design held jointly with 4th International Conference on Embedded Systems Design (VLSID 2005), pp. 111–116 (2005)
10. Ragel, R.G., Parameswaran, S.: IMPRES: Integrated Monitoring for Processor REliability and Security. In: Proceedings of the Design and Automation Conference 2006 (DAC 2006), pp. 502–505. ACM Press, New York (2006)
11. Choi, H., Kim, J.-S., Yoon, C.-W., Park, I.-C., Hwang, S.H., Kyung, C.-M.: Synthesis of application specific instructions for embedded DSP software. IEEE Transactions on Computers 8(6), 603–614 (1999)

A Mixed Level Simulation Environment for Stepwise RTOS Software Refinement

Markus Becker, Henning Zabel, and Wolfgang Mueller

University of Paderborn/C-LAB
{beckerm,henning,wolfgang}@c-lab.de

Abstract. In this article, we present a flexible simulation environment for embedded real-time software refinement by a mixed level cosimulation. For this, we combine the native speed of an abstract real-time operating system (RTOS) model in SystemC with dynamic binary translation for fast Instruction Set Simulation (ISS) by QEMU. In order to support stepwise RTOS software refinement from system level to the target software, each task can be separately migrated between the native execution and the ISS. By adapting the dynamic binary translation approach to an efficient but yet very accurate synchronization scheme the overhead of QEMU user mode execution is only factor two compared to native SystemC. Furthermore, the simulation speed increases almost linearly according to the utilization of the task set abstracted by the native execution. Hereby, the simulation time can be considerably reduced by cosimulating just a subset of tasks on QEMU.

1 Introduction

The introduction of RTOS models raised the level of software-aware abstraction to true electronic system level designs. Today, real-time properties of even very complex designs with several CPUs can be verified efficiently. For this, RTOS models typically wrap the native execution of functionally segmented C code in a system level design language like SystemC[1] or SpecC[8]. Hereby, RTOS services are provided by means of an application programming interface (API) and task synchronization is achieved by implementing dedicated real-time scheduling policies. For timing analysis and estimation, software is partitioned into segments which are back annotated by timing information.

For this, the execution time of software tasks, functions, and basic blocks, i.e., linear code segments followed by a branch instruction, is either measured on the target CPU or retrieved from a static timing analysis. Sometimes, the timing information for the functional segments is not available as due to intellectual property protection the C code is not accessible. Then, an abstract RTOS simulation which requires the partitioning and annotation of the code cannot be applied. In such a case, the application software and RTOS has to be completely simulated by an Instruction Set Simulator (ISS). Since an ISS usually comes with a slow execution speed, it is not possible to efficiently perform detailed analysis.

Therefore, we developed a new approach to combine the benefit of the ISS with the speed of the RTOS abstraction. Our approach applies a clear separation of the software

M. Hinchey et al. (Eds.): DIPES/BICC 2010, IFIP AICT 329, pp. 145–156, 2010.

and the operating system along the natural interface of system calls and to clearly distinguish application software from the operating and its services. Application software typically runs in user space with unprivileged user mode access. Only through system calls the software can get kernel mode access to the kernel space. In contrast, system services and drivers have to run in kernel space for kernel mode access for the execution of privileged instructions for full access to the hardware.

To reach a high simulation speed, we use the open source QEMU software emulator [5] for instruction set simulation in combination with SystemC since it provides fast execution of cross-compiled target code due to an advanced dynamic binary translation. Combined with a fast execution time estimation approach and an efficient synchronization scheme, we achieve a much higher simulation speed than cosimulations of SystemC with a traditional ISS.

In the first refinement levels, the kernel space is abstracted by an abstract RTOS model. By combining it with user mode QEMU emulations, for each user space task it can be separately decided whether to be executed natively or to be coexecuted on the target Instruction Set Architecture (ISA) under QEMU. As such, software task refinement from system level towards firmware is smoothly supported as depicted by Figure 1. The task refinement starts from a) native SystemC and is then refined via b) mixed user space (i.e., subsets of tasks coexecuting on ISS) to c) the user space emulation (i.e., all tasks coexecuting on ISS) and finally arriving at d) the full system emulation including the complete target RTOS kernel and kernel space drivers.

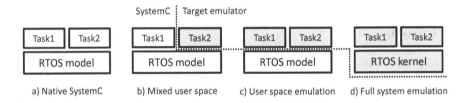

Fig. 1. RTOS software refinement

The remainder of this article is organized as follows. Section 2 describes recent research in the field of RTOS simulation. Section 3 introduces the concepts of our simulation environment providing basic concepts of the mixed level simulation. Section 4 underlines the feasibility and efficiency of our mixed level simulation levels with some experimental results. Finally, Section 5 concludes with a summary.

2   Related Work

We can find several related work in the areas of RTOS simulation and RTOS software refinement methodologies.

Early work by Hassan et al. [11] outlines a simple RTOS simulation in SystemC, where specific schedulers can be derived from a basic class. They model processes by a 1-safe Petri-Net with atomic transitions annotated by time and power consumption.

Individual state transitions are triggered by the μ-ITRON-OS-based RTOS kernel μ-Itron via round-robin scheduling, and I/O operations call hardware operations via a bus functional model. They do not consider interrupt management.

Krause et al. [12] present a tool-based approach for system refinement with RTOS generation. Stepwise refinement covers abstraction levels from CP (Communicating Processes) to CA (Cycle Accurate) models. In the context of the PORTOS (POrting to RTOS) tool, they introduce the mapping of individual SystemC primitives to RTOS functions. Mapping to different target architectures is implemented by a macro definition. PORTOS is configured by a XML specification characterizing the individual target platforms.

Destro et al. [7] introduce a refinement for multi-processor architectures in SystemC with a mapping from SystemC primitives to POSIX function calls. Starting from functional SystemC, first processor allocation and then HW/SW partitioning are performed. A final step maps SystemC to a cosimulation of hardware in SystemC and software running on top of an RTOS. After the mapping hardware threads are executed by a specific SystemC compliant hardware scheduler.

Posadas et al. [15] have published several articles on RTOS simulation. They introduce concepts of their freely available SystemC RTOS library PERFidiX, which covers approximately 70% of the POSIX standard. They report a gain in simulation speed w.r.t. ISS of more than 142 times in one of their first publications, including a 2x overhead in speed due to their operator overloading.

RTOS simulation with time annotated segments is either based on on a standard RTOS API, like the previous approach, or an abstract canonical RTOS. Gerstlauer et al. [9] implemented a canonical RTOS in SpecC. More details of that SpecC library were outlined by Yu [18], who also introduced an approach for SoC software development and evaluation of different scheduling algorithms and their impact on HW/SW partitioning in early design phases. Communication between tasks, including interrupts, is based on events. ISRs are modeled as tasks. Since task scheduling is implemented on top of the non-preemptive SpecC simulation kernel, simulations may give inaccurate results, which has most recently been resolved by Schirner and Doemer [16].

However, interrupts are still modeled as high priority tasks and have to apply the same scheduling algorithm as the software scheduler. Our SystemC RTOS model [19] follows [9] but overcomes the limited interrupt modeling accuracy by means of providing dedicated schedulers for tasks and ISRs.

In [3] we additionally proposed a four level RTOS and communication refinement flow for TLM2.0-based designs comprising our SystemC RTOS model and the QEMU system emulator for ISS cosimulation. There are some other existing approaches using QEMU dynamic binary translation for ISS. For instance, the GreenSoCs project QEMU-SystemC [14] combines SystemC and QEMU in a HW/SW cosimulation by providing a TLM interface for device driver development of memory mapped SystemC HW descriptions. In [10] the authors extend the QEMU dynamic binary translation by an approximate cycle-count estimation for fast performance evaluation in MPSoC designs. They also consider precise simulation of cache effects in MPSoCs by substituting the internal memory model of QEMU with an external cache and memory model in SystemC.

Some work can be found considering the combination of RTOS models and ISS. For instance, Krause et al. [13] combined an abstract SystemC RTOS model with the SimpleScalar ISS for target software evaluation. For this, they provide a virtual prototyping environment that abstracts the scheduling and context switching by their SystemC RTOS model whereas the residual software parts keep running on the cosimulated SimpleScalar ISS.

3   RTOS Simulation Environment

We introduce a mixed level RTOS-aware cosimulation environment with a refinement from an abstract RTOS model towards a cycle-accurate simulation of the instruction set on the basis of a per-task refinement, i.e., an independent refinement of each application task from the abstract description in SystemC towards a target-specific firmware binary. At the same time, the refinement of abstract RTOS services to the target RTOS is provided by a stepwise migration of RTOS primitives like task scheduling, I/O, and task communication from the abstract RTOS model to user mode emulation. Finally, the abstracted kernel is seamlessly replaced by the kernel of the target operating system in order to run a full system cosimulation.

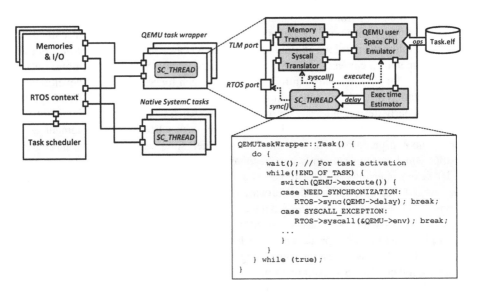

Fig. 2. Mixed level simulation by QEMU task wrapper

For mixed level cosimulation, we combine our in-house SystemC aRTOS library with the QEMU emulator at the system call interface. The abstract RTOS model abstracts the kernel space whereas QEMU emulates user space on an instruction and register accurate CPU abstraction. For this, each software task is wrapped into its own QEMU user mode emulator under control of an *SC_THREAD*.

Since QEMU has no notion of an execution time, we use a dynamic estimation approach for cycle-approximation during binary translation. Execution time estimation of each task is considered by the SystemC aRTOS model as a delay annotation for its representing *SC_THREAD*. Then, the QEMU execution is synchronized along the RTOS scheduling policy. In order to reduce the synchronization overhead due to cosimulation, context switching and task preemption is abstracted in the aRTOS model by means of an efficient synchronization scheme that still provides precise interrupt simulation.

Figure 2 depicts our mixed level cosimulation environment with non-native tasks connected with native tasks together for a common RTOS model in SystemC. For this, each non-native task is wrapped by a QEMU wrapper module providing interfaces to the RTOS model and SystemC HW models. The QEMU wrapper provides the synchronization with the RTOS model by means of task execution control, system call handling, and I/O via TLM-interfaced HW models. The core of the QEMU wrapper is the *SC_THREAD* that controls the main execution loop of a QEMU CPU. Execution delays are estimated during binary translation and used for the synchronization by calling the RTOS model *sync()* function invoking a call to the aRTOS *CONSUME_CPU_TIME()* function to define a task's execution time.

3.1 Dynamic Binary Translation

A suitable simulation model always has to consider the trade-off between accuracy and performance. Sometimes fast simulation is more important than cycle-true accuracy. This is especially during the early design phase of a complex system with a bunch of CPUs. Thus, we postpone the use of traditional cycle-accurate CPU models to a later refinement step since their use results in a slowdown in runtime by several orders of magnitude. Instead, we use QEMU as an instruction and register accurate abstraction of the target CPU to trade-off some accuracy for performance gain.

QEMU is a software emulator which is based on a dynamic binary translation for efficient conversion of a target Instruction Set Architecture (ISA) into a host ISA with the support of multiple platforms, e.g., ARM, PowerPC, MIPS, or Microblaze. The effort of porting QEMU to new target and host platforms is minimized by means of mapping instructions to an intermediate code, i.e., a canonical set of micro operations.

For the binary translation, target code is considered on Basic Block (BB) level, i.e., linear code segments until a final branch instruction. QEMU uses a dynamic code generator to translate BBs at run-time by means of concatenating precompiled host code segments. For faster execution, Translated Basic Blocks (TB) are stored in a TB cache. Then, the major translation effort is just chaining TBs from cache and patching the instruction operands.

Dynamic binary translation is widely used in a variety of hardware virtualization tools, e.g., Bochs or Sun's VirtualBox. However, QEMU supersedes them and combines some unique features that makes it particularly applicable for our purpose. In general, QEMU can operate in two system modes: user mode and full system mode. The user mode supports user space emulation of a single task on top of a Linux process. The full system mode includes an entire target platform with I/O and kernel space for an operating system and driver execution.

3.2 Dynamic Execution Time Estimation

Instruction Set Simulators are widely used to estimate target SW performance in a virtual prototyping environment. ISS can be either cycle-accurate by using CPU models on Register Transfer Level (RTL) or they can be instruction accurate by using an interpretive simulator. In contrast, QEMU uses binary translation avoiding cycle-accurate CPU models and interpretive execution.

As we can reach significantly higher simulation speeds with the binary translation compared to cycle-accurate ISS models, we do not aim at a cycle-true accuracy. Since QEMU does not provide execution times for the executed code, following the concepts of [10], we extended QEMU by an efficient dynamic estimation approach for cycle-approximate timed execution.

The estimation approach is tightly related to the binary translation. It comprises two levels. In the first phase, each time QEMU encounters a new BB, a static timing analysis of the target code is performed. For this, cycle count values are accumulated for each BB during binary translation. Cycle count values per instruction can be derived from either the CPU specification or by means of estimating average values. In order to reduce the error of dynamic instruction delays, e.g., due to branch misprediction or cache misses, special code can be inserted at the cost of an increased overhead to resolve the error during execution by means of accumulating some extra amount of cycles.

Obviously, the accuracy and efficiency of the estimation approach depends on the complexity of the target platform. In order to achieve predictable systems, most embedded platforms use simple RISC CPUs and avoid multi-staged pipelines with caches. Thus, accumulating a static amount of cycles per instruction is a reasonable abstraction to avoid complex and time-consuming cycle-accurate CPU models.

3.3 Inter-task Communication and I/O

Modern CPUs with RTOS provide several ways for tasks to communicate with their environment, e.g., inter-task communication via kernel primitives or shared memory access. I/O devices can be accessed via memory mapping, i.e., I/O registers connected to a CPU bus are mapped into the CPU address space. Some CPUs also provide special operations for direct access to I/O ports.

Our cosimulation environment supports mixed level task simulation, i.e., cosimulated ISS tasks coexecute together with native tasks on top of a SystemC aRTOS model. For task communication support, we need to define data exchange interfaces between the different simulation models. Exchanging data via kernel space primitives is covered by the syscall translator since each kernel communication invokes a call to the system call interface. Here, we catch system calls from user mode that are passed through by the QEMU by translating the Application Binary Interface (ABI) specific calls from user mode emulation and mapping them to the aRTOS model API.

Communication via shared memory is either provided at compile-time or dynamically using a kernel API. The memory access itself is performed via simple memory operations in user mode. Thus, we must provide a mechanism to redirect shared memory access to a common memory model in order to synchronize shared data between SystemC tasks and QEMU tasks. QEMU provides an API to add memory-mapped

I/O (MMIO) in order to interface HW models written in C. This feature allows to include shared memory models that can be accessed from within QEMU and also from SystemC.

Task I/O can be realized in a similar way. For MMIO, hardware models can be connected via a memory-mapped TLM transactor using the same mechanism as for shared memory simulation. Communication via I/O port accessing CPU operations can be caught and redirected to the TLM transactor via function calls that are inserted during the binary code translation.

3.4 Synchronization and Task Preemption

Precise simulation of interrupts and task preemption is crucial for a sufficient accuracy with respect to the sequence of data accesses and response times analysis. The simulation of an aRTOS model and user space emulation need to be synchronized from time to time since this is the only possibility to yield over control to the RTOS kernel thus allowing the scheduler to preempt task execution. Hence, task preemption granularity is tightly related to the synchronization scheme used by the cosimulation.

Since lock-step synchronization is usually a major reason for performance decrease in cosimulation, we partition the software code of a task into more coarse-grained segments for their timing annotation. For this, we apply our causality-true preemption scheme[4] that is comparable to the approach described in [17]. It abstracts the real preemptive behavior by enforcing a synchronization only for a task interaction, e.g., system calls, I/O, and shared memory access. Thus, the functional execution of a task can only be preempted at interaction points. The estimated execution time between two interaction points is considered in the RTOS model by means of a cycle delay annotation.

This is extremely efficient in combination with the dynamic estimation approach described in Section 3.2 since multiple TBs can be comprised in one execution segment and TB time estimations can be accumulated to a single delay annotation. In the case that all task interaction can be detected during simulation, the application of our synchronization scheme does not influence the causal order in their execution.

QEMU supports two execution modes. In single-step mode, QEMU returns from its execution loop after each target instruction to check whether there are pending interrupts to be handled. In default mode, interrupts are asynchronously triggered and QEMU checks for interrupts only at TB level. This is much more efficient due to the internal TB caching. Along our synchronization scheme, interrupts must be checked before task interaction. Thus, the BB translation must be extended in order to ensure interaction points to be always on the border of a TB. For this, we modified QEMU to finish a TB not only at branch instructions (which is the common understanding of a basic block) but also when an interaction is detected.

Figure 3 compares the different levels of functional segmentation for delay annotated simulation including our modified TB level denoted as *TB**. The difference between BB and TB* levels is that there are additional cuts whenever there is a task communication. These cuts refer to a synchronization between the ISS and the RTOS model so that all TBs in between are comprised to a single execution segment.

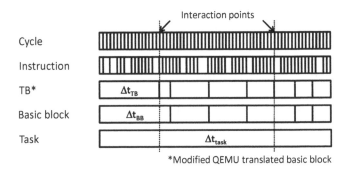

Fig. 3. Comparison of functional segmentation levels

Basically, interaction detection is covered by the task communication interfaces described in Section 3.3. Nevertheless, BB translation cannot distinguish between memory operations referring to a memory register and those referring to a I/O register since it depends on the instruction operands that are updated during TB chaining. Therefore, as our modified BB translator has no detailed knowledge about I/O, it pessimistically cuts a TB at each memory operation in order to maintain full interrupt accuracy. This may result in a performance decrease due to less efficient TB caching. However, in system level design the system communication is explicitly modeled and refined in a top-down strategy. As such I/O can be derived from a more abstract model to expose potential I/O operations to the BB translation (see Figure 4).

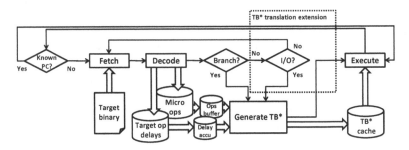

Fig. 4. Modified basic block translation (adapted from [10])

In order to obtain accurate output for scheduling analysis, the aRTOS model uses an interruptible wait algorithm to hide the abstracted preemption behavior. For this, the delay annotation of a segment is split according to the scheduling policy considering the true preemption behavior on a real target, i.e., true number of preemptions, true preemption point in time, and also the true context switching overhead.

4   Experimental Results

In order to show the feasibility and efficiency of our approach, we applied our simulation environment to the stepwise refinement of an example composed of two computation intensive software tasks running at 100% utilization of the processor. Task 1 iteratively computes prime numbers. Task 2 recursively computes faculties of n. The task set is scheduled by a fixed priority scheduler and their execution is synchronized through kernel signals.

Along the refinement introduced in Section 1, we executed several experiments (see Table 1). The first experiment executes the example on top of a native SystemC simulation using our SystemC RTOS library aRTOS. For this, the application C code is wrapped by *SC_THREADs*. For functional segmentation and time annotation, the code is instrumented with preprocessor macros at the branch level. Thus, a task's execution time is considered by means of dynamically accumulating back annotated delays during simulation. According to our synchronization scheme a task yields control to the RTOS model at interaction points. For this, some special macros additionally invoke the function which defines the time delay (*CONSUME_CPU_TIME*) which also enforces a synchronization with aRTOS and the SystemC kernel.

The next experiment runs the software tasks in a mixed level cosimulation according to the mixed level environment introduced in Chapter 3. For this, Task 2 is cross compiled for a PowerPC405 to be executed in our QEMU user mode wrapper. Task 1 remains as a native SystemC thread. At this level the mixed level task set is scheduled by the common aRTOS scheduler in SystemC. In the next step, both tasks are executed in their own QEMU user mode wrapper. The RTOS kernel is still abstract and tasks are scheduled by aRTOS. On the next level, we completely replace aRTOS by full system mode QEMU in order to introduce the actual RTOS kernel. For this, we took our in-house real-time operating system ORCOS[2].

So far, all levels apply our causality-true preemption scheme synchronizing at interaction points since it allows us to operate QEMU in the very efficient TB execution mode in order to take full advantage of the binary translation. In system mode, we switch to single instruction mode in order to achieve full interrupt accuracy. At this level, we do not cosimulate any hardware models except the ones that are provided by the QEMU full system emulator. Finally, we coupled the QEMU system emulator with a SystemC kernel for the cosimulation with SystemC HW models. For this, we synchronize with the SystemC kernel after each emulated target instruction by a SystemC *wait*() statement.

The experiments were performed on an Intel Core 2 Quad CPU @ 2.4 GHz equipped with 6 GB memory. The target code was built with the GCC 4.4 PowerPC EABI cross compiler. We adopted the QEMU user mode and system mode emulators from the QEMU 0.12.1 release. Each application task was activated 1.000.000 times. The experiments were compared by means of the task output and simulation overhead. Our experiments showed that the task output was equal for all refinement levels thus proving a functional correct simulation. Figure 5 depicts the simulation overhead which we have measured at the different refinement levels.

The plain aRTOS SystemC model required the lowest overhead with just 5.6 seconds for all task activations. Surprisingly, it turned out that migrating the application tasks from aRTOS to QEMU user mode, resulted in a slowdown of just 1.5x for one of the tasks being executed on QEMU and 2x for both tasks, respectively. This is extremely fast since traditional ISS approaches usually come with a slowdown of 4000x-40000x

Table 1. Experiments according to the refinement of the example application

Level	Description	Sim. time
aRTOS	All tasks@SystemC w. aRTOS	5.6s
Mixed tasks	Task1@SystemC/Task2@QEMU user mode w. aRTOS	7.6s
Qemu user	All tasks@QEMU user mode w. aRTOS	9.2s
Qemu system	ORCOS@QEMU full system mode	51.6s
QS cosim.	ORCOS@QEMU full system mode w. SystemC cosim.	1472.2s

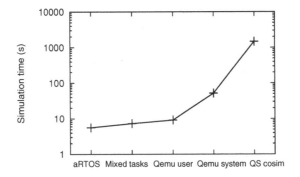

Fig. 5. Simulation overhead increase at different refinement levels

[19] compared to native executed simulation C code. Our experiments also showed that the slowdown of the QEMU execution is nearly linear to the utilization produced by the task set moved to user mode emulation. Thus, using our mixed simulation environment the simulation effort can be considerably reduced when simulating just a subset of tasks on QEMU.

Furthermore, the experiments showed that our mixed level simulation reaches a performance gain of 5.5-6.8x compared to the execution of ORCOS on the QEMU full system emulator and 150-200x compared to the cosimulation of QEMU full system emulator with SystemC, respectively. However, since CPU idle times are abstracted by aRTOS, we expect the performance gain to be even higher with a utilization of less than 100% which is the typical case in hard real-time scheduling. For instance, the worst-case CPU utilization of a task set scheduled by Rate Monotonic must not exceed 69% in order to be feasible [6]. Thus, the average utilization is typically lower.

5 Conclusion

In this article, we presented an approach for the stepwise RTOS-aware refinement of software tasks by means of a mixed level simulation combining the native speed of an abstract SystemC RTOS model and the advantage of the QEMU software emulator. For mixed level simulation, each task can be moved between host-compiled code and cross-compiled target code. Our experimental results show that user mode QEMU with integrated abstract RTOS simulation is a most efficient intermediate step for the migration of native SystemC models to full system emulation and ISS, respectively.

In this context, we can take full advantage of QEMU's efficient binary translation in combination with abstract RTOS simulation. As it makes simulation by several magnitudes faster than traditional ISS, this technology is well applicable for early design phases. Additionally, it provides an ideal intermediate refinement level to smoothly migrate from the introduction of abstract RTOS calls to full system calls of the target RTOS or OS, respectively. Future work will focus on further investigation for the correspondence of the system calls between those levels to increase the automation of the refinement.

Acknowledgments

The work described herein is partly funded by the German Ministry for Education and Research (BMBF) through the SANITAS (01M3088) and the VERDE projects (01S09012) and by the EU through the COCONUT project (FP7-ICT-3217069).

References

1. Homepage of SystemC: http://www.systemc.org/
2. Homepage of ORCOS: https://orcos.cs.uni-paderborn.de/orcos/
3. Becker, M., Di Guglielmo, G., Fummi, F., Mueller, W., Pravadelli, G., Xie, T.: Rtos-aware refinement for tlm2.0-based hw/sw designs. In: DATE 2010: Proceedings of the conference on Design, automation and test in Europe (2010)
4. Becker, M., Zabel, H., Müller, W.: Integration astrakter RTOS-Simulation in den Entwurf eingebetteter automobiler E/E-systeme. In: MBMV 2009: Proceedings of the 12th Workshop of Methoden und Beschreibungssprachen zur Modellierung und Verifikation von Schaltungen und Systemen (March 2008)
5. Bellard, F.: Qemu, a fast and portable dynamic translator. In: ATEC 2005: Proceedings of the annual conference on USENIX Annual Technical Conference, p. 41. USENIX Association, Berkeley (2005)
6. Buttazzo, G.C., Buttanzo, G.: Hard Real-Time Computing Systems: Predictable Scheduling Algorithms and Applications. Kluwer Academic Publishers, Norwell (1997)
7. Destro, P., Fummi, F., Pravadelli, G.: A smooth refinement flow for co-designing hw and sw threads. In: DATE 2007: Proceedings of Design, Automation and Test in Europe. IEEE Computer Society, New York (2007)
8. Gajski, D., Zhu, J., Dömer, R., Gerstlauer, A., Zhao, S.: SpecC: Specification Language and Methology. Kluwer Academic Publishers, Norwell (2000)
9. Gerstlauer, A., Yu, H., Gajski, D.: RTOS Modeling for System Level Design. In: DATE 2003: Design, Automation and Test in Europe (2003)
10. Gligor, M., Fournel, N., Pétrot, F.: Using binary translation in event driven simulation for fast and flexible mpsoc simulation. In: CODES+ISSS 2009: Proceedings of the 7th IEEE/ACM international conference on Hardware/software codesign and system synthesis, pp. 71–80. ACM, New York (2009)
11. AbdElSalam Hassan, H.M., Sakanushi, K., Takeuchi, Y., Imai, M.: RTK-Spec TRON: A Simulation Model of an ITRON Based RTOS Kernel in SystemC. In: DATE 2005: Proceedings of the conference on Design, Automation and Test in Europe, pp. 554–559. IEEE Computer Society, Washington (2005)
12. Krause, M., Brinkmann, O., Rosenstiel, W.: A SystemC-based Software and Communication Refinement Framework for Distributed Embedded Systems (2006)

13. Krause, M., Englert, D., Bringmann, O., Rosenstiel, W.: Combination of instruction set simulation and abstract rtos model execution for fast and accurate target software evaluation. In: CODES/ISSS 2008: Proceedings of the 6th IEEE/ACM/IFIP international conference on Hardware/Software codesign and system synthesis, pp. 143–148. ACM, New York (2008)
14. Monton, M., Portero, A., Moreno, M., Martinez, B., Carrabina, J.: Mixed SW/SystemC SoC Emulation Framework (2007)
15. Posadas, H., Adamez, J.A., Villar, E., Blasco, F., Escuder, F.: RTOS modeling in SystemC for real-time embedded SW simulation: A POSIX model. Design Automation for Embedded Systems 10(4), 209–227 (2005)
16. Schirner, G., Dömer, R.: Introducing preemptive scheduling in abstract rtos models using result oriented modeling. In: DATE 2008: Proceedings of Design, Automation and Test in Europe. IEEE Computer Society, New York (2008)
17. Wu, M.-H., Lee, W.-C., Chuang, C.-Y., Tsay, R.-S.: Automatic generation of software tlm in multiple abstraction layers for efficient hw/sw co-simulation. In: DATE 2010: Proceedings of the conference on Design, automation and test in Europe (2010)
18. Yu, H.: Software Synthesis for System-on-Chip. PhD thesis, University of California, Irvine (2005)
19. Zabel, H., Mueller, W., Gerstlauer, A.: Accurate RTOS Modeling and Analysis with SystemC. In: Hardware-dependent Software, pp. 233–260 (2009)

Global Best-Case Response Time for Improving the Worst-Case Response Times in Distributed Real-Time Systems

Steffen Kollmann, Victor Pollex, and Frank Slomka

Ulm University,
Institute of Embedded Systems/Real-Time Systems
{firstname.lastname}@uni-ulm.de

Abstract. In this paper an improvement of the schedulability analysis for fixed-priority distributed hard real-time systems is presented. During the analysis it is not sufficient to include the tasks' worst-case execution time, but also the best-case execution time has to be considered, because the lower bound of the execution has a direct impact on the event densities in the system. The presented approach improves the best-case response time analysis introduced by Redell et al. The paper shows how it is possible to calculate a lower bound for the best-case response time using an expressive event model. This new lower bound of the response time will relax the event densities in a distributed system and will therefore lead to more relaxed worst-case response times.

1 Introduction

In our daily life we are surrounded by many different computer systems. Most of them are hidden in a technical context, like an airbag control or an anti-lock system, and are called embedded systems. Some of these systems have to satisfy time constraints. In such cases we talk about embedded real-time systems which means that the correctness of the systems depends on correctly computed values as well as on the time intervals in which these values are computed.

In modern systems several CPUs are connected by several buses. Especially in the automotive industry we have large distributed systems with many different time constraints. During the design process of such systems it is desirable to prove the correctness of time constraints by a schedulability analysis. To achieve realistic results it is necessary to have tight bounds for the minimum and maximum occurrence of events in a system.

For instance, assume a sensor triggered every 5 ms. The sensor has an execution time between 1 ms and 3 ms and triggers a successive task. It is obvious that the trigger of the task depends directly on the execution time of the sensor. In the worst-case two events can occur in a time interval of 3 ms and in best-case in a time interval of 7 ms. Therefore it is not sufficient to include the worst-case execution time of tasks into the analysis, but also the best-case execution time, because the lower bound of the execution has a direct impact on the maximum event densities in the system and thus on the worst-case response times.

M. Hinchey et al. (Eds.): DIPES/BICC 2010, IFIP AICT 329, pp. 157–168, 2010.

This lower bound of execution time can be improved by considering higher priority tasks as shown in [11] where a best-case response time for tasks is introduced and the impact on the worst-case response times is shown. We will show that this best-case response time can be improved when an expressive event model is used.

2 Related Work and Contribution

In order to improve the calculation of the event densities and thereby the worst-case response times in a system it is possible to include the lower bounds of the stimulations into the real-time analysis. Some models considering these lower bounds of event densities are, for example, the periodic task model with jitter based on the busy-window approach [12] or the real-time calculus (RTC) [14].

The latter uses curves describing the arrival of events and the capacities of resources. Based on the network calculus [2] the curves are used to calculate the response times in the system. During the calculation of the outgoing event curves, the RTC considers the lower bounds of the incoming stimulations of the tasks. But the technique used cannot be applied to the busy-window approach.

The busy-window approach is very popular and many research has been done with it like a response-time analysis for Round-Robin [10] or considering offsets between tasks [9]. To calculate a best-case response time of a task was also an aim in the past. Redell et al. show in [11] how the calculation of a best-case response time can be obtained by the periodic model with jitter when lower bounds of stimulations are considered. The SymTA/S approach [12] uses this best-case response time analysis in order to relax the event densities in distributed systems. Palencia and Harbour show in [4] how a lower bound for the best-case response time can be determined. But this bound is not exact. Henderson et al. [5] improved this by a search through all possible orderings of higher priority tasks executions, but according to Redell [11], this solution leads to a numerically intractable search.

Redell's approach [11] is for some cases not exact, because it does not consider the occurrence of each single event exactly. This is founded by the fact that the periodic model with jitter is not expressive enough. For this reason, we use the event stream model from Gresser [3] which allows us to describe a wider range of task's stimulation. First we will exploit the lower bound of the stimulations in order to relax the maximum density of events in a distributed system and calculate the occurrence of each single event as accurately as possible. So we will adapt Redell's approach to the event stream model [3]. We call this approach local-best case response time.

Based on the local-best case response time we will improve the idea by means of a global context of jobs. We use the intervals between successive jobs in order to determine whether more interrupts from higher priority tasks have to be considered. We call this approach global best-case response time.

3   System Model

3.1   Task Model

Γ is the set of tasks on one resource $\Gamma := \{\tau_1, ..., \tau_n\}$. A task $\tau := (c^+, c^-, d, \phi, \Theta^+, \Theta^-)$ consists of c^+ the worst-case execution time, c^- the best-case execution time, d the deadline, ϕ the priority for the scheduling (the lower the number the higher the priority), Θ^+ defines the maximum stimulation (maximum number of events in an interval) and Θ^- the minimum stimulation (minimum number of events in an interval). An interval denotes the length of an interval. Let $\tau_{i,j}$ be the j-th job/execution of task τ_i.

In our model we assume that a task can only generate an event at the end of its execution to notify other tasks. In the following, incoming events are events triggering tasks and outgoing events are events generated by tasks. Furthermore we assume a pre-emptive fixed-priority scheduling.

3.2   Maximum Event Streams

Event streams have been first defined in [3]. The purpose was to give a generalized description for every kind of stimulation. The basic idea is to define an event function $\eta(\Delta t, \Theta^+)$ which can calculate for every interval Δt the maximum amount of events occurring within Δt. In the following, when speaking of intervals we mean the length of the interval. The idea is to describe for each number of events the minimum interval which can include this number of events. Therefore we get an interval for one event two events and so on. The interval for one event is infinitely small and therefore considered to be zero. The result is a sequence of intervals showing a non-decreasing behavior. The reason for this behavior is, that the minimum interval for n events cannot be smaller than the minimum interval for n-1 events since the first interval also includes n-1 events.

Definition 1 *(Maximum Event Stream Θ^+) A maximum event stream is a set of event stream elements $\theta : \Theta^+ = \{\theta_1, \theta_2, ..., \theta_n\}$ and each event stream element $\theta = (p, a)$ consists of an offset-interval a and a period p. The maximum event stream complies the characteristic of sub-additivity.: $\eta(\Delta t_1 + \Delta t_2, \Theta^+) \leq \eta(\Delta t_1, \Theta^+) + \eta(\Delta t_2, \Theta^+)$.*

This means that the maximum number of events of an interval cannot exceed the cumulated maximum number of events of its subintervals.

Each event stream element θ describes a set of intervals $\{a_\theta + k \cdot p_\theta | k \in \mathbb{N}\}$ of the sequence. With an infinite (∞) period it is possible to model irregular behavior. The event function is defined as follows:

Definition 2 *(Event Function $\eta(\Delta t, \Theta)$) The event function calculates an upper bound of events for a given event stream Θ and a given length of the interval Δt:*

$$\eta(\Delta t, \Theta) = \sum_{\substack{\theta \in \Theta \\ a_\theta \leq \Delta t}} \left\lceil \frac{\Delta t - a_\theta}{p_\theta} \right\rceil \tag{1}$$

As inverse function we define the interval function which denotes the minimum interval in which a given number of events can occur:

Definition 3 *(Interval Function $\Delta t(n, \Theta)$)* *The interval function gives for an event stream Θ and a number of n events the corresponding minimum interval in which these events can occur:*

$$\Delta t(n, \Theta) = inf\{\Delta t | \eta(\Delta t, \Theta) \geq n\} \tag{2}$$

A detailed definition of the concept and the mathematical foundation of the event streams can be found in [1].

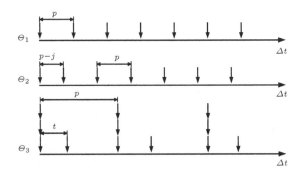

Fig. 1. Three different event streams

Example 1. In figure 1 some examples for event streams can be found. The first one $\Theta_1^+ = \{(p,0)\}$ has a strictly periodic stimulus with a period p. The second example $\Theta_2^+ = \{(\infty,0), (p,p\text{-}j)\}$ shows a periodic stimulus in which the single events can jitter within a jitter interval of size j. Since we derive the maximum occurrence of the events in an interval the worst-case is the following: The first event is delayed by $j/2$ and the following events are delayed by $-j/2$. Therefore two events can occur in a time interval of $p - j$, three events in $2p - j$ and so on. In the third example $\Theta_3^+ = \{(p,0), (p,0), (p,0), (p,t)\}$ three events occur at the same time and the fourth occurs after a time t. This pattern is repeated with a period of p.

3.3   Minimum Event Streams

Analogously we define the minimum event stream which describes for every interval Δt the minimum stimulation in such an interval.

Definition 4 *(Minimum Event Stream Θ^-)* *A minimum event stream is a set of event stream elements $\theta : \Theta^- = \{\theta_1, \theta_2, ..., \theta_n\}$ and each event stream element $\theta = (p, a)$ consists of an offset-interval a and a period p. The minimum event stream complies the characteristic of super-additivity: $\eta(\Delta t_1 + \Delta t_2, \Theta^-) \geq \eta(\Delta t_1, \Theta^-) + \eta(\Delta t_2, \Theta^-)$.*

This means that the minimum number of events of an interval can exceed the cumulated minimum number of events of its subintervals.

The event function (1) and the interval function (2) apply also for the minimum event streams.

Example 2. The corresponding minimum event streams for the examples shown in figure 1 can be described as follows: The first one $\Theta_1^- = \{(p,p)\}$. The second example $\Theta_2^- = \{(p,p+j)\}$. In the third example $\Theta_3^- = \{(p,p-t), (p,p), (p,p), (p,p)\}$.

3.4 Real-Time Analysis

Based on previous work we define the real-time analysis with event streams. As described in [13] in each global iteration step of the real-time analysis the worst/best-case response time and the outgoing maximum/minimum stimulation for each task in the system are computed until a fix-point is found. How to perform a real-time analysis with event streams is described in [7]. For the next section we will repeat how the necessary parameters to perform a real-time analysis can be computed for the event stream model.

Worst-Case Response Time. The worst-case response time of a task with event streams is bounded by the following equation:

Lemma 1. *The worst-case response time with event streams is calculated by:*

$$r^+(\tau) = \max_{k=1,\ldots,n} \{r^+(k,\tau) - \Delta t(k,\Theta_\tau^+)|r^+(k-1,\tau) > \Delta t(k,\Theta_\tau^+)\} \qquad (3)$$

$$r^+(k,\tau) = \begin{cases} c_\tau^+ & k = 0 \\ \min\{\Delta t|\Delta t = k \cdot c_\tau^+ + \sum_{\tau' \in HP} \eta(\Delta t, \Theta_{\tau'}^+) \cdot c_{\tau'}^+\} & k \geq 1 \end{cases} \qquad (4)$$

Proof. The proof is given in [8]

Equation (3) determines the maximum of the response times of each job $(r^+(k, \tau) - \Delta t(k,\Theta_\tau^+))$ in the busy window $(r^+(k-1,\tau) > \Delta t(k,\Theta_\tau^+))$. Equation (4) delivers the completion time of each job measured from the critical instance up to its finishing time. Since the calculation of the worst-case response time has not changed but only the model describing it, the proof in [8] is still valid.

Best-Case Response Time. Additionally to the worst-case response-time it is possible to determine a best-case response time, since we have minimal event streams. For this we have adapted the best-case response time from Redell [11]:

Lemma 2. *Best-Case Response Time*

$$r^-(\tau) = max\{\Delta t|\Delta t = c_\tau^- + \sum_{\tau' \in HP} \eta(\Delta t, \Theta_{\tau'}^-) \cdot c_{\tau'}^-\} \qquad (5)$$

Proof. The proof is given in [11].

Since only the model has changed to calculate the best-case response time and not the calculation itself, the proof in [11] is still valid. The equation adds to the best-case execution time of task τ the best-case execution time of higher priority tasks. How many execution times are added depends on the minimal event streams of the higher priority tasks. It is possible to find the best-case response time as well as the worst-case response time by a fix-point iteration. Since the computation of the best-case response time is done only once for all jobs, we call Redell's approach in conjunction with event streams local best-case response time.

Maximum Outgoing Event Density. To derive the outgoing event densities we give the following definition:

Definition 5 *The completion time $r^{\pm}(n, \tau)$ of the n-th job is the interval from the request of the first job up to the point in time where the n-th job has finished its execution. The response time of a job is the completion time minus the request time $\Delta t(n, \Theta_{\tau})$.*

Lemma 3. *A number of outgoing events occurs in the maximum density when the first event is delayed as much as possible and all further events occur as early as possible whereas a job can only be executed when the previous jobs have been finished. So the minimum interval between n outgoing events of a task is bounded by:*

$$\Delta t_{min}(n, \tau) = r^{\pm}(n, \tau) - r^{+}(\tau) \tag{6}$$

$$r^{\pm}(n, \tau) = \begin{cases} r^{+}(\tau) & n = 1 \\ \\ max(\Delta t(n, \Theta_{\tau}^{+}), r^{\pm}(n-1, \tau)) + r^{-}(\tau) & n > 1 \end{cases} \tag{7}$$

Proof. The proof is given in [7].

Minimum Outgoing Event Density.

Lemma 4. *A number of outgoing events occurs in the minimum density when the first event occurs as early as possible and all further events occur as late as possible. So the maximum interval between n outgoing events of a task is bounded by:*

$$\Delta t_{max}(n, \tau) = \Delta t(n, \Theta_{\tau}^{-}) + (r^{+}(\tau) - r^{-}(\tau)) \tag{8}$$

Proof. The proof is analogous to the proof of the maximum event density.

To calculate the outgoing event streams concretely, see [6] where a normalization for event streams is proposed.

4   Improved Maximum Event Density

Up to this point we have shown how to adapt the best-case response time analysis of Redell et al. [11] to the event stream model and how to conduct a real-time analysis for distributed systems. We will now introduce a methodology in order to calculate the best-case response times of each job in a global context and show how this improves the outgoing maximum event densities of tasks. Global context means here, that the order of the job execution and the time of incoming events are considered.

The idea of the approach is that between successive jobs more interference from higher priority tasks can occur than the local best-case response time ascertains. So we determine whether higher priority tasks produce more load than the interval between n outgoing events can provide. In case that the load is greater than the interval, we are able to relax the best-case response time of a job $r^-(n, \tau)$ and improve $\Delta t_{min}(n, \tau)$.

With figure 2 and equation (9), (10) and (11) we develop our new methodology.

Lemma 5. *A number of outgoing events occurs in the maximum density when the first event is delayed as much as possible and all further events occur as early as possible whereas a job can only be executed when the previous jobs have been finished and the best-case response time of the n-th job exploits the intervals between successive jobs. So the minimum interval between n outgoing events of a task is bounded by:*

$$\Delta t_{min}(n, \tau) = r^\pm(n, \tau) - r^+(\tau) \tag{9}$$

$$r^\pm(n, \tau) = \begin{cases} r^+(\tau) & n = 1 \\ \max_{l \in \mathbb{N}_0}\{r^\pm(n, \tau, l)\} + r^+(\tau) & n > 1 \end{cases} \tag{10}$$

$$r^\pm(n, \tau, l) = \begin{cases} max(\Delta t(n, \Theta_\tau^+), r^\pm(n-1, \tau)) + r^-(\tau) - r^+(\tau) & l = 0 \\ (n-1) \cdot c_\tau^- + \sum_{\tau' \in HP(\tau)} \eta(r^\pm(n, \tau, l-1) + c_{\tau'}^+, \Theta_{\tau'}^-) \cdot c_{\tau'}^- & l > 0 \end{cases} \tag{11}$$

Proof. We have to show that there exists no interval smaller than $\Delta t_{min}(n, \tau)$

Case 1 ($n = 1$): According to the lemma the first event $n = 1$ is delayed maximal. This is the worst-case response time $r^+(\tau)$ by definition and therefore the interval for one event is zero.

Case 2: ($n > 1$): For this case we have to show that the two cases in equation (11) are bounds for the completion times. The first case $l = 0$ is the lower bound shown in lemma 3. This can be obtained by inserting this case in equation (10) and we get:

$$max(\Delta t(n, \Theta_\tau^+), r^\pm(n-1, \tau)) + r^-(\tau) - r^+(\tau) + r^+(\tau)$$
$$= max(\Delta t(n, \Theta_\tau^+), r^\pm(n-1, \tau)) + r^-(\tau)$$

Second case of equation 11 assumes an interval Δt which is the earliest completion time that fulfills the lemma. So we get: $\Delta t = r^+(\tau) + \Delta t'$. If the condition $r^\pm(n, \tau, l+1) > r^\pm(n, \tau, l)$ holds, the processor is always busy in $\Delta t'$ and we get:

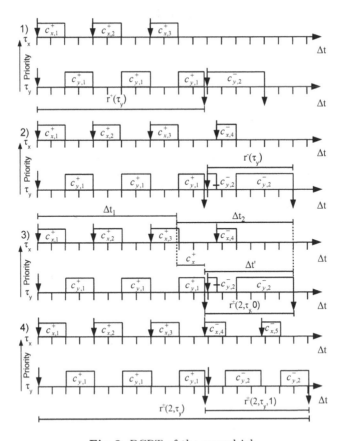

Fig. 2. BCRT of the second job

$$\Delta t = r^+(\tau) + (n-1) \cdot c_\tau^- + \sum_{\tau' \in \Gamma_{HP}} m_{\tau'} \cdot c_{\tau'}^- \qquad (12)$$

The number of events occurring in Δt are divided in the interval Δt_1 which considers all the occurrences of the events during the worst-case response time $\eta(\Delta t_1, \Theta_{\tau'}^+)$ and the rest interval Δt_2 considering the minimal occurrence of events from a task $\eta(\Delta t_2, \Theta_{\tau'}^-)$. The last possible occurrence of an event from a higher priority task during the worst-case response time is $r^+(\tau) - c_{\tau'}^+$. So it follows:

$$r^+(\tau) - c_{\tau'}^+ + \Delta t_2 = \Delta t \Leftrightarrow \Delta t_2 = \Delta t - r^+(\tau) + c_{\tau'}^+ \Leftrightarrow \Delta t_2 = \Delta t' + c_{\tau'}^+$$

This interval can be inserted into equation (12):

$$\Delta t = r^+(\tau) + (n-1) \cdot c_\tau^- + \sum_{\tau' \in \Gamma_{HP}} \eta(\Delta t' + c_{\tau'}^+, \Theta_{\tau'}^-) \cdot c_{\tau'}^-$$

The maximum interval Δt which fulfills $r^\pm(n, \tau, l+1) > r^\pm(n, \tau, l)$ can be found by a fix-point iteration and we get:

$$r^+(\tau) + (n-1) \cdot c_\tau^- + \sum_{\tau' \in \Gamma_{HP}} \eta(r^\pm(n, \tau, l) + c_{\tau'}^+, \Theta_{\tau'}^-) \cdot c_{\tau'}^-$$

So the minimal interval between n outgoing events can be calculated by lemma 5:
$\Delta t_{min}(n, \tau) = r^\pm(n, \tau) - r^+(\tau)$. $\qquad\square$

In figure 2 it is exemplarily shown how the approach works. Part one shows the event density if only the best-case execution time is considered. The second part shows the idea from Redell which is the initial value for our approach. Part three and four of figure 2 depicts the new developed fixed-point iteration. It can be seen that the load produced in interval Δt_2 is greater than the interval itself and therefore the two outgoing events have a relaxed event density.

5 Experiments and Results

To consider the improvement of the new algorithm we have used the synthetical distributed system depicted in figure 3. Due to the reversed paths we have chosen this example. The distributed system has three processing elements. All the tasks are scheduled by a fixed-priority schedule. The system has been evaluated with different utilization. The event density of the three inputs Θ_A, Θ_C, Θ_N has been varied to achieve this. In order to vary the input stimulation only the period and the jitter have been modified and mapped to the different event models.

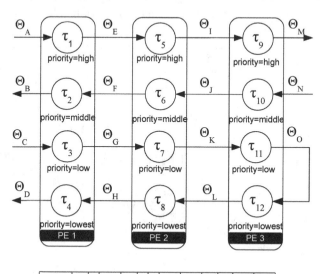

τ	τ_1	τ_2	τ_3	τ_4	τ_5	τ_6	τ_7	τ_8	τ_9	τ_{10}	τ_{11}	τ_{12}
$c^-[ms]$	200	20	1500	300	50	8	1000	500	50	4	900	1000
$c^+[ms]$	200	20	1500	300	50	16	1000	1000	150	4	1200	1100

Fig. 3. Distributed System

The jitter was up to five times the period. For each utilization step the average of 100 variations has been taken. The assumed execution demands are described in the table of figure 3.

Figure 4 depicts the average utilization of the system versus the cumulated average worst-case response time in the system. In this figure the absolute improvement of the global best-case response time versus the local best-case response time, Redell's [11] approach and the SymTA/S approach [12] can be observed. The SymTA/S approach extends Redell's methodology by a minimal distance between events. We have implemented all techniques in one framework. The SymTA/S approach is implemented as described in [12]. The improvement is especially huge for high utilization. When the utilization is low (50%-70%) it is improbable that the execution of the tasks are interrupted very often by higher priority tasks. Therefore the improvement in this range is smaller. Between the local best-case response time and global best-case response time we have also no significant improvement for high utilization (95%-99%). This is founded by the fact that we have a very high utilization and the gaps for the possible improvements are very small, because the utilization is near 100%. So in this case the local best-case response time and the global best-case response time converge. In the range (70%-95%) where the utilization is high enough for many interrupts from higher priority tasks and when enough gaps are available between successive jobs, we have good improvements concerning the worst-case response times. The relative improvement in percent is also depicted in figure 5 (left) and underlines the states above.

Figure 5 (right) gives an overview about the runtime of the implemented approaches. It is obvious that the global best-case response time approach is slower than the local best-case response time calculation. This is founded by the

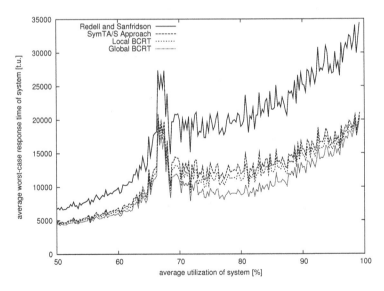

Fig. 4. Utilization vs. WCRT

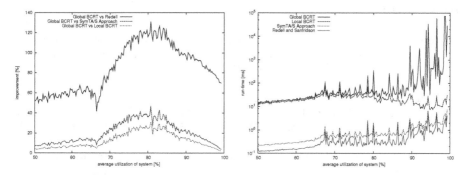

Fig. 5. Relative Improvement of the WCRT (left), Utilization vs. Runtime (right)

fact, that we have to calculate the best-case response time for each job. It is also obvious that Redell's approach and the SymTA/S approach are faster than the approaches with event streams, because not every event is calculated exactly.

Sometimes we have outliers in the runtime of the global best-case response time but not a significant improvement. In these cases we have to calculate many global best-case response times, but the effect on the worst-case response times is marginal. This occurs when the improvement over many instances is small and the relaxation has no influence on the interruption for the worst-case response times.

The experiments show that we are able to perform a real-time analysis with the global best-case response times and get tighter results than Redell's best-case response time analysis. We get up to 24% of improvement of the average worst-case response time in the system versus the local best-case response time, 41% versus the SymTA/S approach and up to 135% versus Redell's best-case response time analysis. The runtime of the global best-case response times is for lower utilization almost identical to the local best-case response time analysis. Only where the improvement is high we have higher runtime.

6   Conclusion

In this paper we have shown how to use lower bounds of stimulation in order to improve the real-time analysis of distributed systems. Two contributions are presented in this paper. The first one is the adaption of Redell's methodology [11] of the best-case response time analysis to the event stream model called local best-case response time. This technique has been improved using the intervals between successive jobs in order to determine the interrupts from higher priority task in a global context leading to best-case response times on job-level. Furthermore we have shown that this leads directly to more realistic response times of the system. Since we have only considered fixed priority pre-emptive scheduling, it would be interested in the future to consider this approach for other scheduling policies like round-robin.

References

1. Albers, K., Slomka, F.: An event stream driven approximation for the analysis of real- time systems. In: ECRTS 2004: Proceedings of the 16th Euromicro Conference on Real-Time Systems, pp. 187–195. IEEE, Los Alamitos (July 2004)
2. Boudec, J.Y.L., Thiran, P.: Network calculus: a theory of deterministic queuing systems for the internet. Springer, New York (2001)
3. Gresser, K.: An event model for deadline verification of hard real-time systems. In: Proceedings of the 5th Euromicro Workshop on Real-Time Systems, pp. 118–123 (1993)
4. Gutirrez, J., Garca, J., Harbour, M.: Best-case analysis for improving the worst-case schedulability test for distributed hard real-time systems. In: Proceedings of the 10th Euromicro Workshop on Real-Time Systems, pp. 35–44. IEEE Computer Society, Los Alamitos (1998)
5. Henderson, W., Kendall, D., Robson, A.: Improving the accuracy of scheduling analysis applied to distributed systems computing minimal response times and reducing jitter. Real-Time Syst. 20(1), 5–25 (2001)
6. Kollmann, S., Albers, K., Slomka, F.: Effects of simultaneous stimulation on the event stream densities of fixed-priority systems. In: Spects 2008: Proceedings of the International Simulation Multi-Conference, pp. 353–360. IEEE, Los Alamitos (June 2008)
7. Kollmann, S., Pollex, V., Slomka, F.: Holisitc real-time analysis with an expressive event model. In: Proceedings of the 13th Workshop of Methoden und Beschreibungssprachen zur Modellierung und Verifikation von Schaltungen und Systemen (2010)
8. Lehoczky, J.P.: Fixed priority scheduling of periodic task sets with arbitrary deadlines. In: Proceedings of the 11th IEEE Real-Time Systems Symposium, pp. 201–209 (December 1990)
9. Palencia, J.C., Harbour, M.G.: Schedulability analysis for tasks with static and dynamic offsets. In: RTSS, p. 26 (1998)
10. Racu, R., Li, L., Henia, R., Hamann, A., Ernst, R.: Improved response time analysis of tasks scheduled under preemptive round-robin. In: CODES+ISSS 2007: Proceedings of the 5th IEEE/ACM international conference on Hardware/software codesign and system synthesis, pp. 179–184. ACM, New York (2007)
11. Redell, O., Sanfridson, M.: Exact best-case response time analysis of fixed priority scheduled tasks. In: ECRTS 2002: Proceedings of the 14th Euromicro Conference on Real-Time Systems, p. 165. IEEE Computer Society, Washington (2002)
12. Richter, K.: Compositional Scheduling Analysis Using Standard Event Models - The SymTA/S Approach. Ph.D. thesis, University of Braunschweig (2005)
13. Tindell, K., Clark, J.: Holistic schedulability analysis for distributed hard real-time systems. Microprocessing and Microprogramming 40, 117–134 (1994)
14. Wandeler, E.: Modular Performance Analysis and Interface-Based Design for Embedded Real-Time Systems. Ph.D. thesis, ETH Zurich (September 2006)

Dependency-Driven Distribution
of Synchronous Programs

Daniel Baudisch, Jens Brandt, and Klaus Schneider

Embedded Systems Group,
Department of Computer Science,
University of Kaiserslautern
http://es.cs.uni-kl.de

Abstract. In this paper, we describe an automatic synthesis procedure that distributes synchronous programs on a set of desynchronized processing elements. Our distribution procedure consists of three steps: First, we translate the given synchronous program to synchronous guarded actions. Second, we analyze their data dependencies and represent them in a so-called action dependency graph (ADG). Third, the ADG is subsequently partitioned into of sub-graphs where cuts can be made horizontal (for a pipelined execution) or vertical (for a concurrent execution). Finally, we generate for each sub-graph a corresponding component and automatically synthesize a communication infrastructure between these components.

1 Introduction

Synchronous programming languages like Esterel [5], Lustre [22] or Quartz [30] are all based on the synchronous model of computation [3]. Its core is the synchronous hypothesis, which divides the program execution into *micro* and *macro steps*. Thereby, micro steps, which represent computation and communication, are all executed in zero time. Consumption of time is explicitly modeled by grouping a finite number of micro steps to macro steps, which all consume the same amount of logical time. As a consequence, all threads of the program run in lockstep, i.e. they automatically synchronize at the end of each macro step. Since all micro steps of a macro step are executed at the same point of time (at least from the semantical point of view), their ordering within the macro step is irrelevant. Therefore, values of variables are determined with respect to macro steps instead of micro steps, i.e. variables do not change within a macro-step.

This abstraction guarantees many properties which are desirable for the development of safety-critical embedded systems. It enforces *deterministic concurrency*, which has many advantages in system design, e.g. to avoid Heisenbugs (i.e. bugs that disappear when one tries to simulate/test them), and it is the key to a straightforward translation of synchronous programs to hardware circuits [4,27,30]. Furthermore, the concise formal semantics of synchronous languages makes them particularly attractive for reasoning about program properties [33,28], correctness and worst-case execution time [26,7].

However, the other side of the coin is that the synchronous model of computation makes both the compilation and synthesis quite difficult. While causality [6,36] and schizophrenia [33] problems already challenge compilers, the synthesis procedures often have to map a synchronous program to a target architecture that does not provide

M. Hinchey et al. (Eds.): DIPES/BICC 2010, IFIP AICT 329, pp. 169–180, 2010.

perfect synchrony. This mismatch between the synchronous model used for the development of a system and most real-world implementation environments poses serious problems, in particular for distributed and parallel embedded applications (as in the automotive or avionic industries), where the target architecture is a heterogeneous set of interconnected processing elements.

Using these architectures, it is often not reasonable to maintain a global clock, which synchronizes all components. In addition to communication latencies, which would slow down the execution, the varying speeds of the individual components would lead to unnecessary idle times. As the slowest component in each step defines the global speed, the resulting performance would often become unacceptable.

In general, there are many ways to partition and distribute a synchronous program into single components. The simplest approach requires that the structure of the system description corresponds to the one of the final target architecture. However, this very simple approach has several drawbacks: first, it is not in the spirit of model-based design, where the system description should be independent of the target system as long as possible. Second, it allows one only to partition the set of modules used in the system description into components, and therefore, it does not allow one to split a single module into different components. Finally, the communication among the sub-systems that correspond to the identified components has to be adapted since there is no longer a global clock.

The contribution of this paper is therefore twofold: First, it presents a partitioning of synchronous programs into concurrent, desynchronized parts. Second, it provides an automatic synthesis of a generic communication infrastructure between these components, which ensures that the implementation still complies with the synchronous semantics of the original source program.

Thereby, it integrates and extends our previous approaches: [1] extracts independent parts of a synchronous program to extract concurrent threads, whereas [2] slices chains of dependencies to create a pipelined system. In this paper, we integrate both partitioning approaches so that an arbitrary combination of concurrent and pipelined execution becomes possible. Furthermore, we do not rely on a specific synthesis target: the partitioning and the communication infrastructure are constructed in a target-independent intermediate format so that each component can be later mapped to hardware or software, as well as the communication between them can be mapped to appropriate protocols.

There is some previous work which has already considered the automatic distribution of synchronous programs to an asynchronous network of processing elements: In [20,14], a clock-driven distribution of Lustre programs is presented which partitions and distributes the system according to the clock that triggers each part. While this approach has shown to produce quite efficient implementations, it may suffer from a significant drawback: Mutual data dependencies between components may require that some component must be further decomposed into smaller components, which may require in turn additional communication and synchronization effort. In our approach, this is avoided by construction.

Related work appeared also in the implementation of digital circuits where the number of cycles required to transmit a signal from one component to another can only be done when the final layout has been derived. To this end, latency-insensitive [10,12,11] and synchronous elastic systems [18,17,24] have been proposed to make the communication between the synchronous modules independent of a global clock. We also make use of these ideas for distributing a given synchronous system description into desynchronized components.

The rest of the paper is organized as follows: Section 2 briefly introduces synchronous guarded actions, which serve as a starting point for the synthesis procedure of this paper. Section 3 explains how we analyze the data-dependencies of the guarded actions by means of an action-dependency graph (ADG), which gives rise to a partition of the guarded actions. Section 4 explains the construction of the communication infrastructure. Finally, Section 5 concludes with a short summary.

2   Synchronous Guarded Actions

Synchronous systems [3,21] as implemented by synchronous languages like Esterel [5] and Quartz [30,33,29] divide their computation into single reactions. Within each reaction, new inputs are synchronously read from all input ports, and new outputs are synchronously generated on all output ports with respect to the current state of the system and the current inputs. Furthermore, the reaction determines the state for the next reaction. It is very important for synchronous languages that *variables do not change during the macro step*. For this reason, all micro steps are viewed to be executed at the same point of time (as they are executed in the same variable environment). The instantaneous feedback due to immediate assignments to outputs can therefore lead to so-called causality problems [6,34,35]. Compilers check the causality of a program at compile time with a fixpoint analysis that essentially corresponds to those used for checking the speed-independence of asynchronous circuits via ternary simulation [9]. Besides the causality analysis, compilers for synchronous languages often perform further checks to avoid runtime exceptions like out-of-bound overflows or division by zero. Moreover, most compilers for synchronous languages also allow the use of formal verification, usually by means of model checking.

The compiler of our Averest system[1] is split into several compile phases: The frontend translates a synchronous program into an equivalent set of *(synchronous) guarded actions* [16,19,23,25] of the form $\langle \gamma \Rightarrow A \rangle$ (see [33,8,30]). The Boolean condition γ is called the guard and $\mathcal{A}$ is called the action of the guarded action, which corresponds to an action of the source language. In this paper, these are the assignments of the source language, i. e. the guarded actions have either the form $\langle \gamma \Rightarrow x = \tau \rangle$ (for an immediate assignment) or $\langle \gamma \Rightarrow next(x) = \tau \rangle$ (for a delayed assignment). In each macro step, the guards γ of all actions (of all variables) are checked simultaneously. If a guard γ is true, the right-hand side τ of the action is immediately evaluated. Immediate actions $x = \tau$ assign the computed value immediately to the variable x, while the updates of delayed actions $next(x) = \tau$ are deferred to the following macro step. If no action sets the value of a variable in the current step, it is determined by the so-called *reaction to absence*, which usually keeps the value of the previous step. In general, a different behavior (like resetting to a default value) is possible, but for the sake of simplicity, we do not elaborate these cases in the following.

---

[1] http://www.averest.org

Hence, if an immediate assignment $x = \tau$ is enabled in the current macro step, the current value of x must be equal to the value of τ. Implementations must therefore make sure that x is not read before the value of τ is evaluated so that one implements the programmer's view that the assignment was performed in zero time.

Synchronous systems are always deterministic, because there is no choice among activated guarded actions, since *all of the enabled* actions must be fired. Hence, any system is guaranteed to produce the same outputs for the same inputs. However, forcing conflicting actions to fire simultaneously may lead to causality problems. This is a well-studied problem for synchronous systems and many analysis procedures have been developed to spot and eliminate these problems [32,35,31,36]. In the following section, we assume that a program is causally correct and that for each variable at most one action is active in a macro step.

$$
\begin{bmatrix}
a = x + y & b = x - y \\
c = z \cdot z & r \Rightarrow x = p \\
s \Rightarrow next(x) = a & s \Rightarrow y = q \\
\neg s \Rightarrow y = o & next(r) = s \\
next(o) = a \cdot b & m = b + c
\end{bmatrix}
$$

Fig. 1. Synchronous Guarded Actions

Figure 1 shows a set of synchronous guarded actions, which will serve as a running example in the following. Note that the translation of synchronous programs into guarded actions is already the first step towards our distribution, since it allows us to split the system into subsets of guarded actions that will form the distributed components.

3   Partitioning System Descriptions into Components

As we already mentioned in the previous section, synchronous guarded actions must be executed according to their causal data dependencies. As we want to map the actions onto a network of asynchronous processing elements, the partition must also reflect the causal order. Before we explain our approach, we first need to give some basic definitions about the dependencies between actions and the variables accessed by them.

Definition 1 (Read and Write Dependencies). *Let* $\mathsf{FV}(\tau)$ *denote the free variables occurring in the expression* τ. *Then, the dependencies from actions to variables are defined as follows:*

$$
\begin{aligned}
\mathsf{rdVars}\,(\gamma \Rightarrow x = \tau) &:= \mathsf{FV}(\tau) \cup \mathsf{FV}(\gamma) \\
\mathsf{rdVars}\,(\gamma \Rightarrow next(x) = \tau) &:= \mathsf{FV}(\tau) \cup \mathsf{FV}(\gamma) \\
\mathsf{wrVars}\,(\gamma \Rightarrow x = \tau) &:= \{x\} \\
\mathsf{wrVars}\,(\gamma \Rightarrow next(x) = \tau) &:= \{next(x)\}
\end{aligned}
$$

The dependencies from variables to actions are determined as follows:

$$
\begin{aligned}
\mathsf{rdActs}\,(x) &:= \{\gamma \Rightarrow A \mid x \in \mathsf{rdVars}\,(\gamma \Rightarrow A)\} \\
\mathsf{wrActs}\,(x) &:= \{\gamma \Rightarrow A \mid x \in \mathsf{wrVars}\,(\gamma \Rightarrow A)\}
\end{aligned}
$$

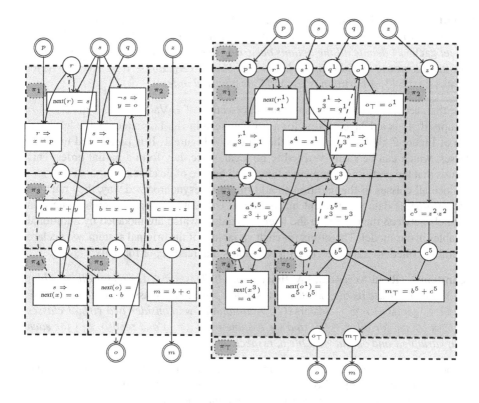

Fig. 2. Left: Partitioned ADG, Right: Partioned ADG with Intermediate Variables

For a given set of guarded actions, the dependencies between all individual elements can be illustrated by an *Action Dependency Graph (ADG)*, which is a bipartite graph consisting of vertices $\mathcal{V}$ representing variables, vertices $\mathcal{A}$ representing the guarded actions and labeled edges representing the dependencies. Thereby, a solid (or dashed) edge from $\langle \gamma \Rightarrow A \rangle$ to x denotes that action A writes x in the current step (or next step). Similarly, a solid edge from x to $\langle \gamma \Rightarrow A \rangle$ expresses that x is read in A, i.e. it appears in the guard γ or in the right-hand side of action A. Thus, this graph exactly encodes the restrictions for the execution of the guarded actions of a synchronous system. An action can be only executed if all read variables are known. Similarly, a variable is only known if all actions writing it in the current step have been evaluated before.

The dependencies encoded in the ADG give rise to possible distributions of the original synchronous system. In the following, we do not focus on the question how to find an optimal solution for a given realization (e.g. software threads or hardware circuits) or target platform. Naturally, the concrete partition generally has a significant impact on the performance of the implementation. However, the appropriate data can be only provided by an external analysis tool, which knows many internals about the target platform. We do not focus on that but provide a general method how the results of such an analysis can be exploited for desynchronization. Our approach is generally applicable and it only requires a legal partition, which is defined in the following.

Definition 2 (Legal Partition of an ADG). *A partition Π of an ADG is a mapping from actions to classes $\pi \in \Pi$. Let* class(A) *denote the class of an action $A \in \mathcal{A}$, and let* gacts(π) *denote all the actions occurring in class π. Let $\sqsubseteq$ be the reflexive and transitive closure of the following relation $R \subseteq \mathcal{A} \times \mathcal{A}$: $(A_1, A_2) \in R \Leftrightarrow$ wrVars $(A_1) \cap$ rdVars $(A_2) \neq \{\}$. A partition is legal iff $\sqsubseteq$ is a partial order.*

Note that, according to Definition 1, the intersection of wrVars (A_1) and rdVars (A_2) is empty if A_1 is a delayed action for a variable read in A_2. For example, the left hand side of Figure 2 shows the ADG of the actions of Figure 1. It is partitioned into five classes, which can be easily verified to be legal, since they form a partial order. This ensures that the partitioned implementation will be free of deadlocks.

Since all classes of the partition should run in a desynchronized way, they must be able to process data of different macro steps. This data is stored in communication channels between the classes in the later realization, which are modeled by additional variables in our model. Therefore, for each variable x of the original system, we declare several intermediate variables, one for each class that reads x, or formally:

Definition 3 (Read Access and Activity). *For all classes $\pi \in \Pi$ and for all variables $x \in \mathcal{V}$, the predicate* read(x, π) *denotes whether x is read in class π, i.e.* read$(x, \pi) = \exists G. \ G \in$ gacts$(\pi) \wedge x \in$ rdVars (G). *Additionally, we consider two virtual classes $\pi_\perp \sqsubset \pi \sqsubset \pi_\top$ for all $\pi \in \Pi$, and we assume* read$(i, \pi_\perp)$ *and* read$(o, \pi_\top)$ *for each input variable i and output variable o, respectively.*

If read(x, π) holds, an intermediate variable for x is inserted in class π, which provides the current input value of x. To distinguish all the different intermediate variables of x, we add a superscript π, where x^π represents the intermediate variable for x in class π. Among all the different copies of x, we select a set of *stable* incarnations. The stable incarnations mark the points in the partitioned system where a variable x must have become known, i.e. stable$(x) = \{\pi \mid$ read$(x, \pi) \wedge \nexists \rho \sqsubset \pi.$read$(x, \pi)\}$. Due to the concurrency of classes, there can be more than one incarnation. All write accesses to a variable will be forwarded to these stable incarnations leading to a high overhead in communication. Fortunately, each stable incarnation will get the same value for a defined macro step. Hence, communication overhead can be reduced by adding a canonical incarnation for x, written canon(x), that distributes the values for variable x to its stable incarnations.

Since all original variables have now been replaced by intermediate variables, the guarded actions must be rewritten to refer to them. Apparently, all actions (immediate and delayed) of the original system that are put in class π read variables with superscript π. Furthermore, all write accesses of a class π are forwarded to the canonical incarnation of this variable. We rewrite the actions as given in the function Transform shown in Figure 3. Thereby, let $[\gamma]^\pi$ be the operations that relabels all variables $x \in$ FV(γ) with their superscripted counterparts x^π.

However, this causes a problem since all the classes generally process different macro steps, and each class can write to the same variable. Hence, values may not arrive in-order according to their logical time so that they have to be reordered explicitly. In our approach, this is accomplished by a *merge* component Merge$_x$, which provides an input for each class that may write to x. Such a component is attached to canon(x).

function $\mathsf{Transform}(\mathcal{G})$
   $\mathcal{G}' := \{\}$
   forall $G \in \mathcal{G}$
     $\pi := \mathsf{class}(G)$
     case G :
       $\gamma \Rightarrow x = \tau$:
         $\mathcal{G}' := \mathcal{G}' \cup$
         $\langle [\gamma]^{\pi} \Rightarrow [x]^{\mathsf{canon}(x)} = [\tau]^{\pi} \rangle$
       $\gamma \Rightarrow \mathit{next}(x) = \tau$:
         $\mathcal{G}' := \mathcal{G}' \cup$
         $\langle [\gamma]^{\pi} \Rightarrow \mathit{next}([x]^{\mathsf{canon}(x)}) = [\tau]^{\pi} \rangle$
   return $\mathcal{G}'$

function $\mathsf{CreateTransport}(\mathcal{G})$
   for $\pi = 1, \ldots, N$
     forall $x^{\pi} \in \mathcal{V}$
       $\mathcal{G} := \mathcal{G} \cup \{\mathsf{true} \Rightarrow x^{\pi} = \mathsf{pre}(x^{\pi})\}$
   return $\mathcal{G}$

function $\mathsf{CreateTransport}'(\mathcal{G})$
   for $\pi = 1, \ldots, N$
     $wr_{\pi} = \bigcup_{A \in \mathsf{gacts}(\pi)} \mathsf{wrVars}(A)$
     forall $x \in wr_{\pi}$
       $guard := (\mathsf{valid}_{\mathsf{in}}(\pi) \vee \mathsf{valid}(\pi))$
         $\wedge \mathsf{stop}_{\mathsf{in}}(\pi) \wedge \neg\mathsf{fire}(\pi)$
       $\mathcal{G} := \mathcal{G} \cup \{guard \Rightarrow \mathit{next}(x) = x\}$
   return $\mathcal{G}$

function $\mathsf{DistributedSystem}(\mathcal{G})$
   $\mathcal{G} := \mathsf{Transform}(\mathcal{G})$
   $\mathcal{G} := \mathsf{CreateTransport}(\mathcal{G})$
   $\mathcal{G} := \mathsf{CreateTransport}'(\mathcal{G})$
   return $\mathcal{G}$

Fig. 3. Functions to Distribute a Synchronous System

In the current section, it does not play any role, since in a fully synchronous model, the *merge* component just implements the identity function. Its behavior is explained in detail in the next section.

Finally, we have to add the transport of the intermediate variables, which corresponds to the reaction to absence of a synchronous system: a class π that reads an intermediate variable x^{π} obtains its values from that class that precedes π and writes to x as soon as a set of variables is processed by this preceding class. The preceding class of class π is formally given by $\mathsf{classPre}(\mathsf{x}^{\pi}) = \max_{\sqsubset}\{j \mid \mathsf{read}(x^j, j) \wedge j \sqsubset \pi\}$ with $\max_{\sqsubset}(A) = \{\pi \mid \pi \in A \wedge \neg(\exists \nu \in A. : \pi \sqsubset \nu)\}$. Additionally, we define $\mathsf{pre}(x^{\pi}) = x^j, j \in \mathsf{classPre}(\mathsf{x}^{\pi})$ as an arbitrary but determined predecessor of x^{π}. Due to concurrency of classes, a class may have more than one predecessor. Each predecessor generates for each set of inputs exactly one value for x. Furthermore, all incarnations of x are copies, i. e. they contain the same value for each input set with a defined logical time step. Hence, it is sufficient to forward the values for a variable x only from one preceding incarnation of x.

Note that incarnations following the stable ones do not require a Merge_x. Due to the Merge_x, the stable incarnation obtains the variable's values in the correct temporal ordering, and it will proceed sets of variables in-order. Hence, the stable incarnations will forward a variable's values in order and as a result of this, each succeeding incarnation obtains these values also in the correct temporal ordering. The right-hand side of Figure 2 shows the transformed set of guarded actions including the transport actions for our running example. The ten original actions are rewritten so that they refer to the superscripted variables, and the remaining actions are due to the transfer of variables.

4   Communication Infrastructure

The previous section partitioned the system into a set of components, which are desynchronized in this section by introducing an appropriate communication infrastructure. Thereby, each class can be first synthesized separately and independently of the others. The individual classes are finally connected by channels that follow a generic desynchronizing protocol. We do not rely on a specific one but only require that it can model the validity of data values and the congestion of buffers (back-pressure). This is provided by latency insensitive protocols [12,15], synchronous elastic circuits [13] or almost any asynchronous communication infrastructure based on buffers.

In the following, we demonstrate how to apply the SELF protocol as described by Carmona et al. in [13] to the partitioned system to gain a synchronous elastic system. First, the classes require additional control logic for communication. The control logic guarantees the correct flow of information between the classes. The interface of each class $\pi \in \Pi$ is extended by two Boolean input signals. The input $valid_{in}(\pi)$ indicates that the current inputs of class π contain valid values, whereas the input $stop_{in}(\pi)$ tells the class whether its outputs can be processed by subsequent classes. Similarly, each class has two output signals, which drive the status signals of other classes: $valid_{out}(\pi)$ gives notice of the validity of the current outputs, while $stop_{out}(\pi)$ indicates whether the class is able to handle new inputs.

To control these flags, each class makes use of two additional variables $valid(\pi)$ and $fire(\pi)$, which memorize the validity of the current outputs and signalizes that class π can fire its actions, respectively:

1. If a class obtains valid inputs but currently has no valid outputs, it must read the inputs and fire its actions. Formally: $fire(\pi) = valid_{in}(\pi) \wedge \neg valid(\pi)$.
2. If a class obtains valid inputs or already has valid outputs, it has valid outputs in both cases. Formally: $valid_{out}(\pi) = (valid_{in}(\pi) \vee valid(\pi))$.
3. If a class has valid outputs and a stop signal comes in, the internal output validity flag has to be set for the next step. Formally: $next(valid(\pi)) = (valid_{in}(\pi) \vee valid(\pi)) \wedge stop_{in}(\pi)$.
4. If a class obtains valid inputs but already has valid outputs or obtains a stop signal, then the class must set its own stop signal. Formally: $stop_{out}(\pi) = valid_{in}(\pi) \wedge (valid(\pi) \vee stop_{in}(\pi))$.

All guarded actions are modified to take notice of the class's fire condition. The fire condition $fire(class(A))$ is added as an additional clause to the guards of all actions $A \in \mathcal{G}$ of the class's build as the conjunction of its old guard and the corresponding class's fire condition. Finally, if a class contains an action writing to a variable x and the class does not fire, but has to keep the value valid, it has to transport (copy) explicitly its value (see Function CreateTransport′ in Figure 3).

In a simple chain of classes $\pi_1, \pi_2, \ldots, \pi_N$ (as in a pipeline), the status signals can be simply connected between successive elements, i. e. $valid_{in}(\pi_{i+1}) = valid_{out}(\pi_i)$ and $stop_{in}(\pi) = stop_{out}(\pi_{i+1})$. For a general topology of the distribution, which is targeted in our approach, a more general solution is necessary. Each class that obtains its inputs from several others or sends its outputs to several others, needs to provide *join* or *fork*

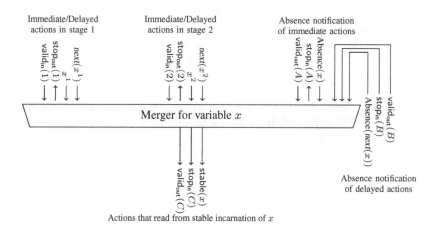

Fig. 4. Merge Component for Variable x

elements, respectively, as already explained in [13]. In the following, we explain the functioning of these elements in terms of our approach.

A join element is needed if a single class π obtains its inputs from several other classes $\pi_1, \ldots, \pi_n$. Obviously, it can only fire iff all inputs are valid. The *valid* flag of class π is set to $\mathsf{valid_{in}}(\pi) = \bigwedge_{i=1,\ldots,n} \mathsf{valid_{out}}(\pi_i)$. Values do not have to be stored internally in a join element since a valid input value is provided by the producing class until it is read, i.e. when all inputs are valid. The *stop* signals from class π to the preceding classes $\pi_1, \ldots, \pi_n$ are determined as follows: if class π stalls, the stall signal is simply broadcasted to all preceding classes. Furthermore, if some of these classes π_i already serves valid inputs but some other class π_j does not provide valid inputs yet, the class π_i must be also stalled, formally: $\mathsf{stop_{out}}(\pi_i) = \mathsf{stop_{in}}(\pi) \vee (\mathsf{valid_{in}}(\pi_i) \wedge \bigvee_{j \in \{1,\ldots,n\}, i \neq j} \mathsf{valid_{out}}(\pi_j))$.

A fork element is used if a single class π writes a variable x which is read by several other classes $\pi_1, \ldots, \pi_n$. Since $\pi_1, \ldots, \pi_n$ are unrelated, they may read x in different macro steps. Without the fork element, this leads to a critical situation: On the one hand, the value of x would have to be invalidated to prevent the reading classes to read the same value again, and on the other hand, the value of x would have to be kept valid so the stalling classes can read this value as soon as they are able to fire. Therefore, the fork broadcasts the valid signal as soon as a new value arrives from class π but individually determines the acknowledge for each class $\pi_1, \ldots, \pi_n$. Hence, each one has its own signals $\mathsf{valid_{out}}(\pi_i)$ and $\mathsf{stop_{in}}(\pi_i)$.

Join and fork elements can be also used to provide a wrapper to the environment, which reconstructs a synchronous interface. If we insert a fork element in front of all system classes (with respect to the classical order $\subseteq$ as defined in the previous section), and a join element behind of all classes, which implement two virtual classes $\pi_\perp$ and $\pi_\top$, reading and distributing all inputs and collecting and writing all outputs so that the interaction with the environment is synchronized. The right-hand side of Figure 1 shows these virtual classes.

As already mentioned, each class of the implementation may process another macro step but they all write to the same variables. Hence, for each variable x, a *merge component* Merge_x is needed to reorder values of x according to their macro steps. In principle, Merge_x waits until the value with the desired logical time arrives and forwards it. All other classes providing values which do not have the desired logical time stamp are stalled.

Figure 4 shows an exemplary structure of a Merge_x. In this example, two classes may write to x; therefore, each of these classes gets an interface to communicate with Merge_x. As the figure shows, Merge_x provides two input channels for each class - one for immediate and one channel for delayed writes to x. This distinction is necessary since immediate and delayed actions address different macro steps. However, both channels share the valid and stop signals because they stem from the same macro step.

Additionally, the interface also includes the valid and stop flags as already described above. With their help, the merge component Merge_x checks all incoming values for validity and the required logical time stamp. As long as the valid value for the required step is not available, $\text{valid}_{\text{out}}(\text{Merge}_x)$ is unset. When the requested value becomes available, it is forwarded and the validity signal is set. Whenever a valid value arrives but does not have the requested time stamp, a stop signal is sent back, i. e. the sending class is stalled until the value is read. The logical time stamp for the currently required value is determined by an internal counter. As explained Section 2, each variable is written exactly once in each macro step, i. e. if a value arrives, the counter can be safely incremented by one.

Finally, the Merge_x is also responsible for the reaction to absence of variable x. It is implemented by two special input signals $\text{Absence}(x)$ and $\text{Absence}(next(x))$, which are set iff no immediate action and delayed action can fire for a given macro step, respectively. These signals are driven by the class that succeeds the last class(es) containing immediate or delayed actions writing to x. In this case, Merge_x can assign a value to x, e. g. a default value or the value from the preceding macro step.

To the end, all required elements are available for creating the desynchronized system. The last step is to choose the correct channels, i. e. the connection of classes, in dependence of the target platform. In hardware synthesis, one would insert relay stations, and in software synthesis one can use queues with Lamport's clock synchronization to obtain a lightweight thread communication as already used in [2].

5   Summary

In this paper, we presented an approach to partition a synchronous program into desynchronized classes. The key for desynchronizing a partitioned system is the adaption of the system's classes to a defined protocol, i. e. each class must be able to wait for inputs, to signalize the validity of its outputs, and to wait for succeeding classes. In particular, the interface of each class has to be extended by four flags ($\text{valid}_{\text{in}}(\pi)$, $\text{valid}_{\text{out}}(\pi)$, $\text{stop}_{\text{in}}(\pi)$, $\text{stop}_{\text{out}}(\pi)$). Finally, attaching the join and fork elements to the classes enables us to use relay stations or queues to run our classes desynchronized. The advantage of our approach is the ability to use it in both hardware and software synthesis by only extending it by inserting corresponding channels, i. e. a hardware synthesis would insert relay stations between classes to obtain a latency insensitive system, and a software synthesis would insert queues to obtain decoupled threads.

References

1. Baudisch, D., Brandt, J., Schneider, K.: Multithreaded code from synchronous programs: Extracting independent threads for OpenMP. In: Design, Automation and Test in Europe (DATE), Dresden, Germany. EDA Consortium (2010)
2. Baudisch, D., Brandt, J., Schneider, K.: Multithreaded code from synchronous programs: Generating software pipelines for OpenMP. In: Methoden und Beschreibungssprachen zur Modellierung und Verifikation von Schaltungen und Systemen (MBMV), Dresden, Germany (2010)
3. Benveniste, A., Caspi, P., Edwards, S., Halbwachs, N., Le Guernic, P., de Simone, R.: The synchronous languages twelve years later. Proceedings of the IEEE 91(1), 64–83 (2003)
4. Berry, G.: A hardware implementation of pure Esterel. Sadhana 17(1), 95–130 (1992)
5. Berry, G.: The foundations of Esterel. In: Plotkin, G., Stirling, C., Tofte, M. (eds.) Proof, Language and Interaction: Essays in Honour of Robin Milner, MIT Press, Cambridge (1998)
6. Berry, G.: The constructive semantics of pure Esterel (July 1999),
   http://www-sop.inria.fr/esterel.org/
7. Boldt, M., Traulsen, C., von Hanxleden, R.: Compilation and worst-case reaction time analysis for multithreaded Esterel processing. EURASIP Journal on Embedded Systems, Article ID 594129 (2008)
8. Brandt, J., Schneider, K.: Separate compilation for synchronous programs. In: Falk, H. (ed.) Software and Compilers for Embedded Systems (SCOPES). ACM International Conference Proceeding Series, vol. 320, pp. 1–10. ACM, New York (2009)
9. Brzozowski, J.A., Seger, C.-J.H.: Asynchronous Circuits. Springer, Heidelberg (1995)
10. Carloni, L.P.: The role of back-pressure in implementing latency-insensitive systems. Electronic Notes in Theoretical Computer Science (ENTCS) 146(2), 61–80 (2006)
11. Carloni, L.P., McMillan, K.L., Sangiovanni-Vincentelli, A.L.: Latency insensitive protocols. In: Halbwachs, N., Peled, D.A. (eds.) CAV 1999. LNCS, vol. 1633, pp. 123–133. Springer, Heidelberg (1999)
12. Carloni, L.P., McMillan, K.L., Sangiovanni-Vincentelli, A.L.: Theory of latency-insensitive design. IEEE Transactions on Computer-Aided Design of Integrated Circuits and Systems 20(9), 1059–1076 (2001)
13. Carmona, J., Cortadella, J., Kishinevsky, M., Taubin, A.: Elastic circuits. IEEE Transactions on Computer Aided Design of Integrated Circuits and Systems 28(10), 1437–1455 (2009)
14. Caspi, P., Girault, A., Pilaud, D.: Automatic distribution of reactive systems for asynchronous networks of processors. IEEE Transactions on Software Engineering 25(3), 416–427 (1999)
15. Casu, M.R., Macchiarulo, L.: A new approach to latency insensitive design. In: Design Automation Conference (DAC), San Diego, CA, USA, pp. 576–581. ACM, New York (2004)
16. Chandy, K.M., Misra, J.: Parallel Program Design. Addison Wesley, Austin (1989)
17. Cortadella, J., Kishinevsky, M., Grundmann, B.: SELF: Specification and design of synchronous elastic circuits. In: International Workshop on Timing Issues in the Specification and Synthesis of Digital Systems, TAU (2006)
18. Cortadella, J., Kishinevsky, M., Grundmann, B.: Synthesis of synchronous elastic architectures. In: Design Automation Conference (DAC), San Francisco, CA, USA, pp. 657–662. ACM, New York (2006)
19. Dill, D.L.: The Murphi verification system. In: Alur, R., Henzinger, T.A. (eds.) CAV 1996. LNCS, vol. 1102, pp. 390–393. Springer, Heidelberg (1996)

20. Girault, A., Nicollin, X.: Clock-driven automatic distribution of Lustre programs. In: Alur, R., Lee, I. (eds.) EMSOFT 2003. LNCS, vol. 2855, pp. 206–222. Springer, Heidelberg (2003)

21. Halbwachs, N.: Synchronous programming of reactive systems. Kluwer, Dordrecht (1993)

22. Halbwachs, N.: A synchronous language at work: the story of Lustre. In: International Conference on Formal Methods and Models for Co-Design (MEMOCODE), Verona, Italy, pp. 3–11. IEEE Computer Society, Los Alamitos (2005)

23. Järvinen, H., Kurki-Suonio, R.: The DisCo language and temporal logic of actions. Technical Report 11, Tampere University of Technology, Software Systems Laboratory (1990)

24. Krstic, S., Cortadella, J., Kishinevsky, M., O'Leary, J.: Synchronous elastic networks. In: Gupta, A., Manolios, P. (eds.) Formal Methods in Computer-Aided Design (FMCAD), San Jose, California, USA, pp. 19–30. IEEE Computer Society Press, Los Alamitos (2006)

25. Lamport, L.. The temporal logic of actions. Technical Report 79, Digital Equipment Cooperation (1991)

26. Logothetis, G., Schneider, K.: Exact high level WCET analysis of synchronous programs by symbolic state space exploration. In: Design, Automation and Test in Europe (DATE), Munich, Germany, pp. 10196–10203. IEEE Computer Society, Los Alamitos (2003)

27. Rocheteau, F., Halbwachs, N.: Pollux, a Lustr-based hardware design environment. In: Quinton, P., Robert, Y. (eds.) Conference on Algorithms and Parallel VLSI Architectures II, Chateau de Bonas (1991)

28. Schneider, K.: Embedding imperative synchronous languages in interactive theorem provers. In: Conference on Application of Concurrency to System Design (ACSD), Newcastle upon Tyne, UK, pp. 143–154. IEEE Computer Society, Los Alamitos (2001)

29. Schneider, K.: Proving the equivalence of microstep and macrostep semantics. In: Carreño, V.A., Muñoz, C.A., Tahar, S. (eds.) TPHOLs 2002. LNCS, vol. 2410, pp. 314–331. Springer, Heidelberg (2002)

30. Schneider, K.: The synchronous programming language Quartz. Internal Report 375, Department of Computer Science, University of Kaiserslautern, Kaiserslautern, Germany (2009)

31. Schneider, K., Brandt, J.: Performing causality analysis by bounded model checking. In: Conference on Application of Concurrency to System Design (ACSD), Xi'an, China, pp. 78–87. IEEE Computer Society, Los Alamitos (2008)

32. Schneider, K., Brandt, J., Schuele, T.: Causality analysis of synchronous programs with delayed actions. In: Compilers, Architecture, and Synthesis for Embedded Systems (CASES), Washington, DC, USA, pp. 179–189. ACM, New York (2004)

33. Schneider, K., Brandt, J., Schuele, T.: A verified compiler for synchronous programs with local declarations. Electronic Notes in Theoretical Computer Science (ENTCS) 153(4), 71–97 (2006)

34. Schneider, K., Brandt, J., Schuele, T., Tuerk, T.: Improving constructiveness in code generators. In: Synchronous Languages, Applications, and Programming (SLAP), Edinburgh, Scotland, UK, pp. 1–19 (2005)

35. Schneider, K., Brandt, J., Schuele, T., Tuerk, T.: Maximal causality analysis. In: Desel, J., Watanabe, Y. (eds.) Application of Concurrency to System Design (ACSD), St. Malo, France, pp. 106–115. IEEE Computer Society, Los Alamitos (2005)

36. Shiple, T.R.: Formal Analysis of Synchronous Circuits. PhD thesis, University of California at Berkeley, Berkeley, CA, USA (1996)

Distributed Resource-Aware Scheduling for Multi-core Architectures with SystemC

Philipp A. Hartmann[1], Kim Grüttner[1], Achim Rettberg[2], and Ina Podolski[2]

[1] OFFIS – Institute for Information Technology, Oldenburg, Germany
{hartmann,gruettner}@offis.de
[2] University of Oldenburg
Faculty II, Department for Computer Science, Oldenburg, Germany
{achim.rettberg,ina.podolski}@iess.org

Abstract. With the rise of multi-core platforms even more complex software systems can be implemented. Designers are facing various new challenges during the development of efficient, predictable, and correct applications for such platforms. To efficiently map software applications to these architectures, the impact of platform decisions with respect to the hardware *and* the software infrastructure (OS, scheduling policies, priorities, mapping) has to be explored in early design phases.

Especially shared resource accesses are critical in that regard. The efficient mapping of tasks to processor cores and their local scheduling are increasingly difficult on multi-core architectures. In this work we present an integration of shared resources into a SystemC-based simulation framework, which enables early functional simulation and provides a refinement flow towards an implementation, covering an increasing level of platform details. We propose shared resource extensions towards multi-core platform models and discuss which aspects of the system behaviour can be captured.

Keywords: Multi-core, Resource Sharing, Platform Exploration, SystemC, Real-time, Simulation.

1 Introduction

In high-performance, desktop, and graphics processing multi- and many-core platforms are already state-of-the-art. A rise of multi-core platforms for embedded systems is not only conceivable, but is actually happening. On one hand, it enables the implementation of more functionality in software, thus exploiting the advantages of software flexibility and higher productivity. But on the other hand, this can turn into a nightmare when the new flexibility and multi-core design space needs to be limited to meet functional and non-functional system properties like real-time constraints, power consumption and cost.

To help developers during this phase of the design space exploration, efficient modelling of different architecture alternatives has to be supported by the chosen design flow. Apart from considering the underlying hardware platform, this

M. Hinchey et al. (Eds.): DIPES/BICC 2010, IFIP AICT 329, pp. 181–192, 2010.

includes the early analysis of software and (real-time) operating system (RTOS) effects on the system's overall performance. This is important especially if multiple tasks are sharing a single processor core. Real-time properties have to be analysed and explored by choosing e.g. the scheduling policies and protocols as well as task priorities to fulfil the given set of requirements like deadlines or other application specific constraints. Furthermore, the partitioning of the application in tasks and the mapping of these tasks to the cores is complex and influences the scheduling and therefore the system performance.

An important aspect from the application's point of view is the mechanism used for inter-task communication and synchronisation. Communication via global shared memory with explicit locks for mutual exclusion impairs locality and increases coupling between tasks. Especially in the real-time domain, shared resource accesses are critical, even more so on multi-core architectures. To efficiently cope with such shared (e.g. communication) resources, task dependencies have to be considered during the mapping and scheduling phase. Depending on the target platform, dedicated hardware support for such communication primitives could be beneficial.

The contribution of this paper is the extension of OSSS for modelling software on multi-core platforms. We discuss the influence of shared resources on the execution behaviour of task sets. Since we provide a framework for early design space exploration, we do not yet capture all properties of the final platform. Instead we present a basic set of representable properties like the scheduling of parallel tasks on a multi-core execution unit, task switching, and blocking on shared resources.

In Section 3, we introduce the SystemC-based OSSS Design Methodology, with a specially focus on the modelling of embedded software for multi-cores. Based on these abstract RTOS modelling capabilities of the OSSS methodology, Section 4 covers the extension of OSSS by additional features required for supporting the distributed, scheduling approach with shared resources. In Section 5 we present our first simulation results of the extended OSSS framework for multi-core scheduling with shared resources.

Before Section 6 concludes the paper with a summary and an outlook for future research directions, we discuss the capabilities of the presented approach with respect to modelling, real-time analysis, early simulation and the further refinement flow towards an implementation.

2 Related Work

Recently published work shows the importance of new programming and abstraction paradigms for multi- and many-core systems [12]. To fully exploit the possibilities of the upcoming thousand-core chips [21], workloads of the future are already discussed [18]. To encounter these trends high-level, component-based methodology and design environment for multiprocessor SoC architectures have been proposed [15].

Many different approaches to modelling embedded software in the context of SystemC have been proposed.

Abstract RTOS models, like the one presented for SpecC in [5] are suited for early comparison of different scheduling and priority alternatives. The timing accuracy and therefore the simulation performance of this approach is limited by the fixed minimal resolution of discrete time advances. Just recently, an extension deploying techniques with respect to preemptive scheduling models very similar to the ones presented in this work has been presented in [19]. The "Result Oriented Modelling" collects and consumes consecutive timing annotations while still handling preemptions accurately similar to our "lazy synchronisation" scheme presented in [8].

Several approaches based on abstract task graphs [11,14,20] have been proposed as well. In this case, a pure functional SystemC model is mapped onto an architecture model including an abstract RTOS. The mapping requires an abstract task graph of the model, where estimated execution times can be annotated on a per-task basis only, ignoring control-flow dependent durations. This reduces the achievable accuracy.

A single-source approach for the generation of embedded SW from SystemC-based descriptions has been proposed in [3,10,17]. The performance analysis of the resulting model with respect to an underlying RTOS model can be evaluated with the PERFidiX library, that augments the generated source via operator overloading with estimated execution times. Due to the fine-grained timing annotations, the model achieves a good accuracy but relatively weak simulation performance. This interesting approach aims in the same direction as our proposed software execution time annotation.

An early proposal of a generic RTOS model based on SystemC has been published in [13]. The presented abstract RTOS model achieves time-accurate task preemption via SystemC events and models time consumption via a `delay()` method. Additionally, the RTOS overhead can be modelled as well. Two different task scheduling schemes are studied: The first one uses a dedicated thread for the scheduler, while the second one is based on cooperative procedure calls, avoiding this overhead. Although in this approach explicit inter-task communication resources are required (message queue, . . .), the simulation time advances simultaneously as the tasks consume their delays.

In [9], an RTOS modelling tool is presented. Its main purpose is to accurately model an existing RTOS on top of SystemC. A system designer cannot directly use it. In this approach, the next RTOS "event" (like interrupt, scheduling event, etc.) is predicted during run-time. This improves simulation speed, but requires deeper knowledge of the underlying system.

In [23], the main focus lies on precise interrupt scheduling. For this purpose, a separate scheduler is introduced to handle incoming interrupt requests. Timing annotations and synchronisation within user tasks is handled by a replacement of the SystemC `wait()`. In [22] an annotation method for time estimation that supports flexible simulation and validation of real-time-constraints for task migration between different target processors has been presented.

In this work, we propose an extension of [7], which includes some properties of the above mentioned approaches, especially concerning a simple runtime

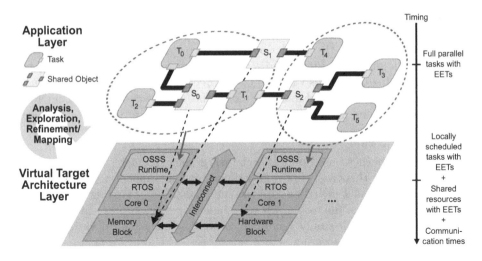

Fig. 1. Overview of the OSSS Methodology for modelling parallel Software

and RTOS model. Furthermore, our model allows a separation of application, architecture and mapping. The proposed application model allows a flexible integration of shared resources for user-defined communication mechanisms via *Shared Objects* and the handling of timing (back) annotations. Our proposed extension on the architecture model includes a configurable multitasking simulation based on SystemC that allows preemptive distributed scheduling. Tasks and *Shared Objects* can be grouped together and mapped to different cores, each of them having its own local runtime. Through simulation the effects of the chosen mapping and system configuration on the functional behaviour of the task sets can be observed.

3   The OSSS Methodology for Modelling Parallel SW

OSSS defines separate layers of abstraction for improving refinement support during the design process. The design entry point in OSSS is called the *Application Layer*. By manually applying a mapping of the system's components, the design can be refined from *Application Layer* to the *Virtual Target Architecture Layer*, which can be synthesised to a specified target platform in a separate step by the synthesis tool *Fossy* [4].

The abstraction mechanisms of OSSS allow the exploration of different implementation platforms. The separation of application and platform allows different mappings and the underlying SystemC-based simulation kernel supports model execution and monitoring.

On the *Application Layer* the system is modelled as a set of parallel, communicating processes, representing software tasks (see Listing 1). A shared resource in OSSS is called *Shared Object*, which equips a user-defined class with specific synchronisation facilities. *Shared Objects* are inspired by the Protected Objects known from Ada [1]. Synchronisation is performed by arbitrating concurrent accesses and a special feature called *Guarded Methods*, that can be used to block the execution of a method until an user-defined condition evaluates to true.

As a result, they are especially useful for modelling inter-process communication. User-defined Interface Method Calls (IMC), a concept well known from SystemC channels, performs communication between software tasks and *Shared Objects*. On the *Application Layer* this communication concept abstracts from the details of the underlying communication primitives, such as the actual implementation of channel across core and hardware/software boundaries. An in-depth description of the *Shared Object* concept, including several design examples, is part of the OSSS documentation [6].

```
class my_software_task : public osss_software_task {
 public:
  my_software_task() : osss_software_task() { /* ... */ }

  virtual void main() {
    while( some_condition )  // the following block has to be finished within 1ms
    OSSS_RET( sc_time( 1, SC_MS ) )
    {
      OSSS_EET( sc_time( 20, SC_US ) ) {
        // computation, that consumes 20μs
      }
      for( int i=0; i<max_i; ++i )  // estimate a data-dependent loop
        OSSS_EET( sc_time( 100, SC_US ) ) {
          // loop body
        }
      if( my_condition ) {
        // communication only outside of EET blocks
        result = my_port_to_shared->my_method();
      }
    } // end of RET block and loop
  }
};
```

Listing 1. Example of a software task eith estimated and required execution time annotations

A proper modelling of software requires the consideration of its timing behaviour. In OSSS, the **E**stimated **E**xecution **T**ime (EET) of a code block can be annotated within *Software Tasks* and *Shared Objects* using the OSSS_EET() block annotation. In addition to the EETs, OSSS enables the designer to specify local deadlines for a specific code block. The **R**equired **E**xecution **T**ime (RET) is specified by the OSSS_RET() block annotation, which observes the duration of the marked code block. If required, RETs can be nested at arbitrary depth. The consistency of nested RETs is checked during the simulation as well as a violation of the RETs. If such a timing constraint is violated during the simulation, it is reported. Unmet RETs may arise from (additional) delays caused by blocking guard conditions, or simply unexpectedly long estimated execution times (e.g. `max_i` ≥ 9 in Listing 1).

4   Multi-core Scheduling with Shared Resources

In this paper, we focus on the abstract modelling capabilities of OSSS for embedded software, especially targeting multi-core platforms. Here, the OSSS model is *not* meant to directly represent existing real-time operating system (RTOS) primitives. Instead, the *Software Tasks* in OSSS are meant to *run* on top of a rather generic (but lightweight) run-time system (see Fig. 1), where the synchronisation and inter-task communication is modelled with *Shared Objects*.

In a refinement step the *Application Layer* model is mapped to the *Virtual Target Architecture*. Each task is then mapped to a specific core, each of which provides a distinct run-time, to improve locality and reduce the coupling between different cores, as shown in Fig. 1. Tasks have may have statically or dynamically assigned priorities, according to a given scheduling policy for each core, an initial startup time, optional periods and deadlines.

During simulation, the tasks can be in different states as shown in Fig. 2. We distinguish between the full parallel *Application Model* and the core mapped *Virtual Target Architecture Model* task state machines. In the *Application Model* a task can either be **running**, **waiting** or **blocked**. The distinction between **blocked** and **waiting** has been introduced to ease the detection of deadlocks. A task in the **waiting** state will enter the **running** state after a given amount of time (duration), whereas a **blocked** task can only be de-blocked, once the access to a shared resource is granted. In the **running** state, a task might access a *Shared Object* through IMC. This either leads to the acquisition of its critical section (**use** state) or a suspension in the **blocked** state. In this state the task tries to reacquire the shared resource until it gets access.

The execution times of certain code blocks can be annotated flexibly, to introduce control-flow dependent time consumption, as shown in Listing 1.

In the *Virtual Target Architecture Model Software Tasks* and *Shared Objects* are grouped and mapped onto runtimes of the cores. During the simulation, the OSSS software runtime abstraction handles the time-sharing of a single processor core by several *Software Tasks*, which are bound to this OS instance. Therefore, a **ready** state has been introduced. A scheduler for handling the time-sharing is attached to the set of mapped tasks. Several frequently used scheduling policies are already provided by the simulation library, like static priorities (preemptive and cooperative), or earliest-deadline first. Additionally, arbitrary user-defined scheduling policies can be added. The RTOS overhead of context switches (assign & deassign times) and execution times of scheduling decisions can be annotated as well. With this set of basic elements, the behaviour of the real RTOS on the target platform can be modelled.

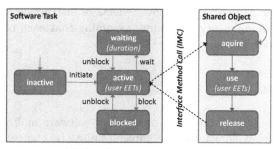

(a) Application Layer Model

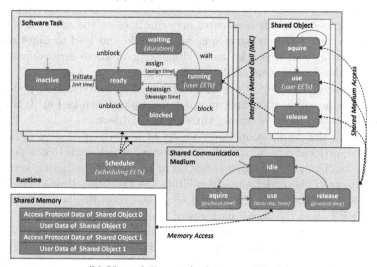

(b) Virtual Target Architecture Model

Fig. 2. Task states and transitions (terminate edges omitted)

To improve the real-time capabilities, *Guarded Methods* that can lead to arbitrary blocking times due to data-dependent conditions, are ignored. Instead, only the guaranteed mutual exclusive access to Shared Objects is used for synchronisation and communication between the tasks. Each method of such a Shared Object can then be considered as a critical section, which is executed atomically. Intra-core communication, i.e. communication between tasks mapped to the same core, can be handled as usual. Here, the accesses are ordered according to the local scheduling policy.

Moreover, the *Virtual Target Architecture Model* allows incorporating the effects of a shared memory that is connected to the cores via a shared communication medium. In an implementation on a target architecture the access protocol data, as well as the user data of a *Shared Object* are mapped to a specific location in a shared memory. Therefore, all states of the *Shared Object* include a certain overhead of shared medium acquisition, usage and release. These times could also be annotated to the proposed simulation model, but are not in the focus of this paper. We also do not cover effects of instruction and data fetches over the shared communication medium, assuming that each core has its local data and instruction memory.

5   Experiments

The main purpose of the modelling of abstract software multitasking in early design phases is the exploration of the impact of platform choices on the system's correctness and performance. In the context of multi-core architectures, accesses to shared resources (modelled as Shared Objects) have to be considered carefully. Distributed access from different cores and runtimes to the same resource has to be orchestrated. Different strategies are possible and lead to quite different behaviours during run-time. An early simulation of these cross-dependencies helps during the development of the application.

In Fig. 3, several combinations of local and distributed access policies are compared for the application and mapping example shown in Fig. 1: Six tasks are mapped on two cores, accessing three Shared Objects.

In Fig. 3(a), the Application Layer model of the system is depicted. In this initial model, no local scheduling policy is enforced, which leads to independently running tasks. The only blocking times occur in case of conflicting accesses to Shared Objects. This model already exhibits the execution times (and periods within critical regions inside the Shared Objects), according to the task arrival times, the EETs and the access patterns of tasks to resources.

Next, static priorities are assigned to the tasks ($T_0 > T_1 > T_2$, $T_3 > T_4 > T_5$) and the tasks are mapped to different cores, following Fig. 1. The scheduling policy is always assumed to be priority-based, either with or without support for local priority inheritance. Inter-core accesses to shared resources are resolved based on the set of pending requests (see Section 3). In the example, it is assumed that tasks on Core 0 have a higher priority, than those running on Core 1.

In the various scenarios, different access strategies with respect to the shared resources are compared, according to their impact on the overall system scheduling. For local resource accesses, i.e. resources that are accessed from tasks within the same core, task preemption is allowed in Fig. 3(b)–(d), and suppressed in Fig. 3(e)–(f). In case, a shared resource is currently locked by another core, the calling task can either try to do busy-waiting until the resource is available again (Spinning, in (b), (c), (e)), or stop its execution to let other tasks execute on the current core (Suspend, in (d), (f)). It is then assumed, that the runtime is able to resume the task, as soon as the blocked resource is available again.

For the given task set and mapping, the different execution traces that can be obtained by the OSSS Multi-Core Software simulation in the different scenarios are shown. Tasks are assigned to their cores according to the local priority based scheduling policy. Different run-time artefacts can be observed (in addition to potential RET violations, which are not shown here).

If a task that is currently accessing a shared resource can be preempted by the runtime system due to the arrival of a higher-priority task (or its availability due to

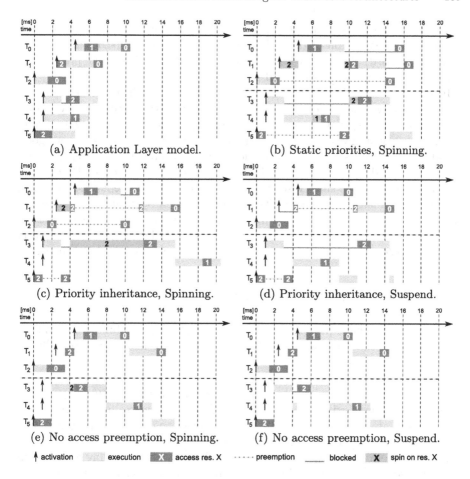

Fig. 3. Different scheduling scenarios with shared resources

resource grants), so called "priority inversion" can occur. In Fig. 3(b), this can be observed on both cores, when tasks T_2, and T_4 get access to their cores, although higher-priority tasks T_0, and T_3 are waiting for the Shared Objects S_0, and S_2, respectively. This leads to longer blocking times for these high-priority tasks.

In the context of a single core, priority inheritance [2] is known to be a solution for such scenarios. With priority inheritance, the low-priority tasks holding resources required by high-priority tasks get an elevated priority, which reduces their lock times. In the context of multi-cores, a local priority inheritance implementation may lead to even worse scenarios, as shown in Fig. 3(c). First of all, the response time of T_0 is reduced, since T_2 can continue until the release of S_0, once T_0 requests S_0. But the resource S_2 has been locked by the arrival of T_1 on Core 0, before T_3 could obtain S_2 on Core 1. Core 1 is subsequently busy waiting on S_2, which is held by the preempted task T_1 on Core 0. Overall, the response time of the latest task is now significantly worse.

An approach towards better CPU utilisation in the context of shared resources might be the suspension of tasks, blocked by conflicting inter-core accesses, as shown in Fig. 3(d). The overly long spinning time of T_3 and even the preemption of the access to S_0 by T_2 is avoided in this example.

Instead of suspending inter-core blocked tasks, an orthogonal approach to reduce blocking times between cores is to suppress the preemption of local, lower-priority tasks, that are currently accessing a shared resource. The results of this access strategy are shown in Fig. 3(e),(f). Both traces lead to very good overall response times with nearly no blocking times. The high-priority tasks are of course started with an additional delay, depending on the currently ongoing resource accesses. But since resource occupation should be kept short anyhow, this might be a feasible strategy. The spinning time on S_2, that can be observed in Fig. 3(e) is quite short. Since in case of the suspension strategy, runtime overhead costs are excluded for simplicity, the slightly better result in Fig. 3(f) might be misleading. A refined model should consider these overheads as well.

6   Conclusion and Future Work

In this paper, we have presented the current modelling capabilities for embedded software of the OSSS hardware/software design methodology, especially focussing on multi-core platforms.

OSSS features a layered approach with a separation between an abstract Application Layer which can later be mapped to a Virtual Architecture Layer. This separation enables flexible exploration of different (software) architecture variants already at early phases in the design process, e.g considering scheduling policies, priorities, resource access strategies, etc.

After a general overview of the current OSSS Software Modelling approach in Section 3, some of the required extensions to the existing methodology towards abstract, but more accurate multi-core system models have been discussed in Section 4. For a set of distributed multi-tasking systems, the OSSS approach is an expressive and suitable modelling approach for applications running on top of such platforms. Due to the explicitly visible resource sharing, expressed by using Shared Objects, the resulting synchronisation and communication overheads and conflicts can be observed already in early simulation models.

In Section 5, a simple Application Layer model has been mapped to a multi-core platform. Since distributed resource accesses are critical for the overall system behaviour, several different access strategies, both regarding local scheduling decisions (priority inheritance, atomic/nonpreemptable resource accesses) as well as the handling of remotely blocked resources (Spinning, Suspension) have been compared. It can be seen, that even for small and allegedly simple cases, the resulting system behaviour is hard to predict. Therefore, early simulation of the different alternatives is a valuable analysis tool for a designer.

Regarding an implementation on a real multi-core platform, the proposed access strategies require different platform primitives, depending on the intended implementation approach. As proposed in Section 4, an implementation purely in terms of a shared memory region with a software implementation of the access protocol is possible. For the support of an suspend-based access strategy, platform support for the reactivation of suspended tasks on a certain core is required, e.g. via sending an interrupt from the core, that releases a given resource to all cores, waiting for said resource. An initial implementation based on a Linux implementation of the OSSS runtime will be published separately.

In the context of real-time applications, it is even more difficult to give guarantees, when considering shared resources as well. We intend to further extend the presented resource access protocols to improve the static analysability of OSSS system models. This includes a restricted task/object model, e.g. by omitting user-defined guard conditions, which can lead to arbitrary, data-dependent blocking times. Future work is to study real-time scheduling approaches for multi-cores as discussed in [16]. These scheduling aspects can be integrated into the OSSS methodology.

Summarising can be said, that OSSS already provides a good starting point for modelling, exploring, refining, and implementing applications on emerging multi-core platforms. Further extensions are possible and promising to improve these capabilities even more.

References

1. Burns, A., Wellings, A.: Concurrency in Ada. Cambridge University Press, Cambridge (1997)
2. Buttazzo, G.C.: Hard Real-time Computing Systems. Kluwer Academic Publishers, Dordrecht (2002)
3. Fernandez, V., Herrera, F., Sanchez, P., Villar, E.: Embedded Software Generation from SystemC, ch. 9, pp. 247–272. Kluwer, Dordrecht (March 2003)
4. Fossy – Functional Oldenburg System Synthesiser, http://fossy.offis.de
5. Gerstlauer, A., Yu, H., Gajski, D.: RTOS Modeling for System Level Design. In: Proceedings of Design, Automation and Test in Europe, pp. 47–58 (2003)
6. Grüttner, K., Andreas, H., Hartmann, P.A., Schallenberg, A., Brunzema, C.: OSSS - A Library for Synthesisable System Level Models in SystemC^{TM} (2008), http://www.system-synthesis.org
7. Hartmann, P.A., Reinkemeier, P., Kleen, H., Nebel, W.: Modeling of Embedded Software Multitasking in SystemC/OSSS. LNEE, vol. 36, ch. 14, pp. 213–226. Springer, Heidelberg (2009)
8. Hartmann, P.A., Reinkemeier, P., Kleen, H., Nebel, W.: Efficient modelling and simulation of embedded software multi-tasking using SystemC and OSSS. In: Forum on Specification, Verification and Design Languages, FDL 2008, pp. 19–24 (September 2008)
9. He, Z., Mok, A., Peng, C.: Timed RTOS modeling for Embedded System Design. In: 11th IEEE Real Time and Embedded Technology and Applications Symposium, RTAS 2005, pp. 448–457 (March 2005)
10. Herrera, F., Villar, E.: A Framework for Embedded System Specification under Different Models of Computation in SystemC. In: Proceedings of the Design Automation Conference (2006)

11. Huss, S.A., Klaus, S.: Assessment of Real-Time Operating Systems Characteristics in Embedded Systems Design by SystemC models of RTOS Services. In: Proceedings of Design & Verification Conference and Exibition (DVCon 2007), San Jose, USA (2007)
12. Hwu, W.m., Keutzer, K., Mattson, T.G.: The concurrency challenge. IEEE Design and Test of Computers 25(4), 312–320 (2008)
13. Le Moigne, R., Pasquier, O., Calvez, J.P.: A Generic RTOS Model for Real-time Systems Simulation with SystemC. In: Proceedings of Design, Automation and Test in Europe Conference, February 16-20, vol. 3, pp. 82–87 (2004)
14. Mahadevan, S., Storgaard, M., Madsen, J., Virk, K.: ARTS: A System-Level Framework for Modeling MPSoC Components and Analysis of their Causality. In: 13th IEEE International Symposium on Modeling, Analysis, and Simulation of Computer and Telecommunication Systems, pp. 480–483 (September 2005)
15. Cesário, W.O., Lyonnard, D., Nicolescu, G., Paviot, Y., Yoo, S., Jerraya, A.A., Gauthier, L., Diaz-Nava, M.: Multiprocessor soc platforms: A component-based design approach. IEEE Design and Test of Computers 19(6), 52–63 (2002)
16. Podolski, I., Rettberg, A.: Overview of multicore requirements towards real-time communication. In: Lee, S., Narasimhan, P. (eds.) SEUS 2009. LNCS, vol. 5860, pp. 354–364. Springer, Heidelberg (2009)
17. Posadas, H., Herrera, F., Fernandez, V., Sanchez, P., Villar, E.: Single Source Design Environment for Embedded Systems based on SystemC. Transactions on Design Automation of Electronic Embedded Systems 9(4), 293–312 (2004)
18. Rabaey, J.M., Burke, D., Lutz, K., Wawrzynek, J.: Workloads of the future. IEEE Design and Test of Computers 25(4), 358–365 (2008)
19. Schirner, G., Dömer, R.: Introducing Preemptive Scheduling in Abstract RTOS Models using Result Oriented Modeling. In: Proceedings of Design, Automation and Test in Europe (DATE 2008), Munich, Germany, pp. 122–127 (March 2008)
20. Streubühr, M., Falk, J., Haubelt, C., Teich, J., Dorsch, R., Schlipf, T.: Task-Accurate Performance Modeling in SystemC for Real-Time Multi-Processor Architectures. In: Proceedings of the Design, Automation and Test in Europe Conference. pp. 480–481. European Design and Automation Association, 3001 Leuven, Belgium, Belgium (2006)
21. Yeh, D., Peh, L.S., Borkar, S., Darringer, J., Agarwal, A., mei Hwu, W.: Thousand-core chips. IEEE Design and Test of Computers 25(3), 272–278 (2008)
22. Zabel, H., Müller, W.: An Efficient Time Annotation Technique in Abstract RTOS Simulations for Multiprocessor Task Migration. In: Kleinjohann, B., Kleinjohann, L., Wolf, W. (eds.) DIPES. IFIP, vol. 271, pp. 181–190. Springer, Boston (2008)
23. Zabel, H., Müller, W., Gerstlauer, A.: Accurate RTOS Modelling and Analysis with SystemC. In: Ecker, W., Mueller, W., Doemer, R. (eds.) Hardware Dependent Software – Principles and Practice. Springer, Heidelberg (2009)

Robust Partitioned Scheduling for Real-Time Multiprocessor Systems

Frédéric Fauberteau[1], Serge Midonnet[1], and Laurent George[2]

[1] Université Paris-Est,
LIGM, UMR CNRS 8049, 5, bd Descartes,
Champs-sur-Marne, 77454 Marne-la-Vallée CEDEX 2, France
{fauberte,midonnet}@univ-mlv.fr
[2] ECE / LACSC,
37, quai de Grenelle, 75015 Paris, France
lgeorge@ieee.org

Abstract. In this paper, we consider the problem of fixed-priority partitioned scheduling of sporadic real-time tasks for homogeneous processors. We propose a partitioning heuristic that takes into account possible Worst Case Execution Time (WCET) overruns. Our goal is to maximize the duration a task can be allowed to exceed its WCET without compromising the timeliness constraints of all the tasks. This duration is denoted in the paper the *allowance* of the task and is computed with a sensitivity analysis. The partitioning heuristic we propose, assigns the tasks to the processors in order (i) to maximize the *allowance* of the tasks and (ii) to tolerate bounded execution duration overruns. Property (ii) is important as real-time applications are often prone to be subject to OS approximations or software faults that might result in execution duration overruns. We show with performance evaluations that *Allowance-Fit-Decreasing* partitioning improves the temporal robustness of real-time systems w.r.t. classical {*First-Fit/Best-Fit/Next-Fit*}-*Decreasing* partitioning.

Keywords: Real-time Scheduling, Partitioned Scheduling, Robustness.

1 Introduction

Fixed-priority scheduling of recurring real-time tasks has been largely studied for uniprocessors. In such a scheduling, a Priority Assignment (PA) assigns a fixed priority to each job of the task. For instance, Rate-Monotonic (RM) is an optimal PA for periodic tasks with *implicit-deadlines* (deadlines equal to periods) [1]. Optimality implies that if a feasible PA over a taskset exists, then the optimal PA is also feasible. A feasible taskset is a taskset such that a scheduling algorithm exists which can schedule this taskset. We focus on the more general model of tasks with *constrained-deadlines* (deadlines less than or equal to periods) for which Deadline-Monotonic (DM) is an optimal PA [2]. Recently, the optimal Robust Priority Assignment (RPA) [3] has been proposed to find the PA which maximizes the interference that a tasks system can support. These interferences

M. Hinchey et al. (Eds.): DIPES/BICC 2010, IFIP AICT 329, pp. 193–204, 2010.

can be handled by the tasks by allowing WCETs overruns while the timeliness constraints of all the tasks are respected. These tolerated WCETs overruns are denoted *allowance* of the tasks. In the same way, our motivation is to propose a robust multiprocessor scheduling which maximizes the *allowance*.

The two most studied approaches to schedule real-time tasks on a multiprocessor are *partitioned* and *global* scheduling. The first one does not allow tasks to migrate whereas the second one allows unrestricted migrations. Recent architecture have reduced the cost of migration. Nevertheless, taking into account the cost of migration in the feasibility conditions of global scheduling is still an open issue. A recent performance evaluation of partitioned and global schedulings show that partitioned scheduling outperform global scheduling, in the current state-of-the-art of feasibility conditions [4]. We therefore focus on the partitioned approach. Several algorithms for fixed-priority partitioned scheduling have been proposed [5,6,7,8,9]. The aim of the authors is to propose algorithms which improve the worst-case *utilization bound*. The worst-case utilization bound for a scheduling algorithm A is defined as the minimum utilization for which any *implicit-deadline* taskset is schedulable according to algorithm A. The utilization of an *implicit-deadline* taskset is the sum of the processor utilization (formally defined in Sect.2) of each task composing this taskset.

In this paper, our motivation is slightly different since we want to design a partitioned scheduling which improves the temporal robustness of a system i.e. to improve its capability to support variations on the system parameters at run time (WCET overruns for e.g.). Such events should not lead to a deadline violation in a hard real-time application. We focus on the WCET parameter and we propose an algorithm which allocates the tasks on the processor having the greatest capability to support WCETs overrun by maximizing the minimum *allowance* of all the tasks.

The rest of this paper is organized as follows. In Section 2, we introduce the terminology used in the rest of this paper. In Section 3, we give a definition of robustness in context of this paper. In Section 4, we discuss two manners to compute the allowance of the execution duration which is the criterion of our partitioning algorithm for the assignment of real-time tasks on the processors. In Section 5, we present our heuristic and describe how it works. In Section 6, we compare on some simulations the performance of the partitioning schedulings and we explain the benefits of our approach. We summarize the contributions of this paper in Section 7 and we give direction for our future work.

2   Terminology

In this paper, we consider an application built from a set $\tau = \{\tau_1, \tau_2, \ldots, \tau_n\}$ of n sporadic real-time tasks. A sporadic task is a recurring task for which only a upper bound on the separation between release times of the jobs is known. Each task τ_i is characterized by a minimum interarrival time T_i (also denoted period), a worst-case execution time C_i and a relative deadline D_i. This application runs on a platform $\Pi = \{\pi_1, \pi_2, \ldots, \pi_m\}$ of m identical processors (homogeneous case). We consider a fixed-priority scheduling on each processor. A fixed-priority scheduler assigns a priority to each task and all jobs of a task is released with the fixed priority of this task. We assume that tasks are indexed by decreasing priority: $\forall i = 1, \ldots, n-1$, task τ_i has a higher priority than task τ_{i+1}. A partitioning algorithm produces a partition $Part(\tau) = \{\tau^1, \tau^2, \ldots, \tau^m\}$ of m disjointed subsets where each subset τ^j of real-time tasks is executed on processor π_j. The subset τ^j composed by n_j tasks is also denoted by $\tau^j = \{\tau_1^j, \tau_2^j, \ldots, \tau_{n_j}^j\}$. In the rest of this paper, we refer to τ_i when the considered task is taken independently and to τ_i^j when it is considered assigned on processor π^j. We define u_i as the utilization of task τ_i : $u_i \equiv \frac{C_i}{T_i}$ and U^j as the utilization of the taskset τ^j : $U^j \equiv \sum_{\tau_k^j \in \tau^j} u_k$. On the processor π_j, we denote $lp^j(i)$ (respectively $hp^j(i)$) the subset of real-time tasks assigned to π^j which have a priority lower than (respectively higher than or equal to) τ_i. The response time of the task τ_i is denoted R_i. We denote R_i^k the kth iteration in the response time computation of the task τ_i.

3 Robustness

We consider the robustness in the real-time systems as the capacity of the system to handle WCET overruns faults when the WCET are estimated. If the WCET of all the tasks of the system has been well defined, a feasibility analysis shows wheter the system is feasible. But in pratice, it may possible that a task makes a fault or that the time constraints has been miscalculated. Some real-time specifications - such as Real-Time Specification for Java [10] - provide mechanism to handle cost overruns and deadline misses in the case of estimated WCET.

In this work, we consider the robustness as the capacity of a system to meet all the deadlines. We can guarantee that the system stay feasible if and only if we know the execution duration during which a task can exceed its WCET without any deadline is missed. This duration is denoted *allowance* and the more each task *allowance* has, the more robust the system regarding to our definition is.

4 Allowance Concept

The allowance of a task is used as a criterion for allocating a task on a processor by our heuristic. We define the *allowance* A_i^j of a task τ_i^j on the processor π^j as follows :

Definition 1. *Let τ^j be a given set of tasks assigned on processor π^j. The allowance A_i^j of a task τ_i^j of τ^j is the maximum duration which can be added to the WCET C_i of τ_i^j such as all tasks of τ^j meet their deadlines.*

We identified in the literature two approaches to compute the *allowance*: one based on a (Worst Case Response Time) WCRT computation and one based on a sensitivity analysis on the WCETs. The response time of a task is the duration between the time this task has been released and the time it has been

Table 1. System of 4 sporadic real-time tasks

	C_i	D_i	T_i
τ_1	10	60	70
τ_2	15	85	100
τ_3	30	190	210
τ_4	45	260	320

finished. The WCRT of a task is the response time of this task in the worst activation scheme. We use the taskset given in Tab.1 to describe the two *allowance* computation methods in the following subsections.

4.1 Allowance Computed from WCRT

One of the available approach to compute the allowance of the execution duration has been proposed by Bougueroua *et al.* [11]. For a given value of allowance A_i^j, this method consists in checking that the system remains schedulable when the execution duration of a task τ_i is equal to $C_i' = C_i + A_i^j$. In other words, this method consists in checking that the WCRT of all the tasks remains less than or equal to their deadline when their WCET is extended to $C_i + A_i^j$. The 3 following equations perform this check for the task τ_i^j on a processor π_j if τ_i^j was assigned on τ^j.

$$U^j + \frac{A_i^j}{T_i} \leq 1 \tag{1}$$

$$R_i^{k+1} = C_i + A_i^j + \sum_{\tau_h \in hp^j(i)} \left\lceil \frac{R_i^k}{T_h} \right\rceil C_h \leq D_i \tag{2}$$

$$\forall \tau_l \in lp^j(i),$$

$$R_l^{k+1} = C_l + \sum_{\tau_h \in hp^j(l)} \left\lceil \frac{R_l^k}{T_h} \right\rceil C_h + \left\lceil \frac{R_l^k}{T_i} \right\rceil A_i^j \leq D_l \tag{3}$$

The value of allowance of a real-time task τ_i is found by a binary search. Equation (1) tests if the utilization U^j of the system when the WCET of τ_i^j is extended to $C_i + A_i^j$ does not exceed processor utilization. An upper bound $A_{i,up}^j$ on the *allowance* of the task τ_i can be found from (1):

$$A_{i,up}^j = \lfloor (1 - U^j) \cdot T_i \rfloor \tag{4}$$

Equation (4) allows to bound the binary search in $[0, A_{i,up}^j]$. For the task τ_1^j of our example, $A_{1,up}^j = \lfloor (1 - 0.58) \cdot 70 \rfloor = 29$. We can carry out a binary search with $0 \leq A_1 \leq 29$. Equation (2) tests if the response time R_1 of τ_1, when its WCET has been extended to $C_1 + A_{1,j}$, does not exceed its deadline D_1. Equation (3) tests if the response times R_l of all tasks τ_l^j of lower priority than τ_1^j don't exceed their deadlines D_l when the WCET of τ_1^j is extended by $A_{1,j}$. For the value $\lfloor 29/2 \rfloor = 14$, we must check that this value satisfies (2) and (3). For $A_{1,j} = 14$, the response time of τ_1^j is $R_1 = 24 \le D_1$. We also obtain $R_2 = 39 \le D_2$, $R_3 = 69 \le D_3$ and $R_4 = 177 \le D_4$. Then $A_{1,j} = 14$ is a valid value of allowance for τ_1^j on the processor π^j. We continue the binary search until $A_{1,j} = 21$, then $A_1 = 21$ is the maximum value of allowance for $\tau_{1,j}$.

The complexity of this approach is pseudo-polynomial due to the Response Time Analysis (RTA) in (2) and in (3). This complexity is in $O(n^2)$ where n is the number of tasks. Indeed, for a task τ_i, a RTA is performed in $O(n)$ and for each task of lower priority than τ_i, a RTA is performed in $O(n)$. In the worst case, there is $n-1$ tasks of lower priority than τ_1, thus the complexity is $O(n^2)$.

4.2   Allowance Computed from Sensitivity Analysis

Another approach to compute the allowance of the execution duration is the *sensitivity analysis*. This approach has been introduced by Bini *et al.* [12]. This approach is attractive compared to the previous one because no iterative computation (such as WCRT computation) is needed. The authors propose to consider the system only at time corresponding to the activation time of the highest priority tasks in $[0, D_i]$ union time $\{D_i\}$. The maximum allowance A_i^j of a task τ_i^j on the processor π^j is computed by the following equations:

$$Sens(k) = \max_{t \in schedP_k} \frac{t - \left(C_k + \sum_{h \in hp(k)} \left\lceil \frac{t}{T_h} \right\rceil C_h \right)}{\lceil t/T_i \rceil} \tag{5}$$

$$A_i^j = \left\lfloor \min_{k \in lp(i)} Sens(k) \right\rfloor \tag{6}$$

where $schedP_k$ is the set of scheduling points defined by $schedP_k = \mathcal{P}_{i-1}(D_k)$ and $\mathcal{P}_k(t)$ is defined by :

$$\begin{cases} \mathcal{P}_0(t) = \{t\} \\ \mathcal{P}_k(t) = \mathcal{P}_{k-1}(\lfloor \frac{t}{T_k} \rfloor T_k) \cup \mathcal{P}_{k-1}(t) \end{cases} \tag{7}$$

For the task τ_1 of our example, $schedP_1 = D_1 = \{60\}$. For the other tasks in the same way, $schedP_2 = \{70, 85\}$, $schedP_3 = \{70, 100, 140, 190\}$ and $schedP_4 = \{140, 200, 210, 260\}$. The values $Sens(1) = 50$, $Sens(2) = 45$, $Sens(3) = 33.33$ and $Sens(4) = 21.66$ are computed by using Equation 5. The *allowance* $M_1 = \min_{k \in lp^j(i)} \lfloor Sens(k) \rfloor = 21$ is obtained from (5) and (6).

The complexity of this approach is exponential because $|schedP_n|$, denoted as the size of the scheduling points set computed by (7) is 2^{n-1} in the worst-case. But in practice, the size of $schedP_n << 2^{n-1}$ for a great value of n. We notice that the size of $schedP_n$ is highly sensitive to the range of task periods as seen in appendix of [13].

5   Partitioning Algorithm

5.1   Task Partitioning Problem

The task partitioning problem consists of finding a partition of a taskset τ in m subsets τ^j, $1 \leq j \leq m$ such that each subset is feasible on processor π_j. Since it has been proved that BIN-PACKING problem (NP-hard in the strong sense) can be reduced in polynomial-time to a task partitioning problem [14], no optimal algorithm exists to decide in polynomial-time if a given taskset is feasible. Fortunately, approximation algorithms and heuristics exist to find solutions for the task partitioning problem in polynomial-time. Heuristics for the tasks partitioning problem exist and are versions of the heuristics proposed for the bin-packing problem. The more cited in the literature are *First-Fit* [8] (FF), *Best-Fit* [6] (BF) and *Next-Fit* (NF) [7]. These heuristics have been initially designed to minimize the number of bins (respectively the number of processors) for the BIN-PACKING problem (respectively the tasks partitioning problem). Another heuristic *Worst-Fit* [15], is rarely used because it provides poor performance to solve the BIN-PACKING problem. On the problem of task partitioning, this heuristic allocates tasks to processors where utilization is the lowest. This approach is relevant because we want the best allocation of tasks to maximize the *allowance* of tasks. We propose in the next subsection a heuristic which allocates tasks to processors that has the greatest *allowance* rather than processors that has the lowest utilization.

5.2   Allowance-Fit-Decreasing

We propose a heuristic, denoted *Allowance-Fit-Decreasing*, to solve the task partitioning problem. We want to tolerate bounded WCET overruns, a property not considered in classical heuristics. WCETs overruns can be due to OS approximations, faults of the task or WCET under-estimation. By definition, the allowance of a processor is the minimum *allowance* for all task allocated to the processor. Our goal is to propose a partitioning scheme that assigns a task to the processor whose allowance is maximum.

We describe the *Allowance-Fit-Decreasing* heuristic with the pseudo-code given in Alg.1. The tasks are first sorted according to their utilization by function `sort_task_by_decreasing_utilization()` (line 1). For each task τ_i of the taskset τ (iteration loop at lines 2-17), the `proc` parameter, denoting the processor on which τ_i is allocated (at line 3), is initialized with a `null` value. The minimum value of *allowance* for the entire system (variable A_{min} at line 4) is first initialized to minus infinity. We then consider all processors in Π and find the processor that maximizes the processor *allowance*. For each processor π_j (iteration loop at lines 5-11), our heuristic finds the minimum value of processor *allowance* A^j_{min} computed by function `compute_allowance`(π^j, τ^j_i) when τ_i is allocated to π_j with the method described in Sect.4.2. If after the iteration loop, A_{min} is greater than or equal to 0 then, τ_i can be assigned to a processor, the one that maximizes the processor *allowance*, by construction. We then proceed with the other tasks

---

Algorithm 1. Allowance-Fit-Decreasing

---

1 sort_task_by_decreasing_utilization()
2 **foreach** τ_i *in* τ **do**
3   proc = None;
4   A_{min} = -Inf;
5   **foreach** π_j *in* Π **do**
6          $A_{min}^j = compute\_allowance(\pi_j, \tau_i^j)$
7   **if** $A_{min}^j > A_{min}$ **then**
8   proc = π_j;
9              $A_{min} = A_{min}^j$;
10   **end**
11   **end**
12   **if** $A_{min} \geq 0$ **then**
13   assign τ_i to *proc*
14   **else**
15   **return** *unschedulable*
16   **end**
17 **end**
18 **return** *schedulable*

---

until all the tasks until either all tasks have been assigned to a processor (we then return that the task set is schedulable in line 18) or one task is declared not schedulable (line 15).

5.3 Partitioned Scheduling Algorithm

A partitioned scheduling algorithm is the combination of a task partitioning algorithm with a schedulability condition. We build two partitioned scheduling algorithms, one from *Worst-Fit* and one from *Allowance-Fit-Decreasing*. For the first one, the schedulability condition is a necessary and sufficient condition implicitly given by *Allowance-Fit-Decreasing*. Indeed, our heuristic computes with the function compute_allowance(π_j, τ_i) the value of A_{min}^j, the minimum *allowance* for all the tasks assigned to processor π_j, including τ_i. If this function returns a negative value, then τ_i cannot be assigned on the processor π^j. A_{min}^j is computed from the sensitivity analysis given in Sect.4.2. For the second one, we combine *Worst-Fit* with the necessary and sufficient schedulability condition RTA [16].

During the allocation, the tasks are taken in order of their decreasing utilization. In other words, the tasks with the greater utilization are allocated first. We consider a fixed-priority assignment and we use DM priority assignment since this PA is an optimal one when the considered tasks have *constrained-deadlines* ($\forall i,\ D_i \leq T_i$) [2].

6   Simulations

6.1   Methodology

Our simulations is based on randomly generated tasksets. Because we focus on tasks with *constrained-deadlines*, we consider tasksets such that for any task τ_i, $\alpha = \frac{D_i}{T_i}$). We randomly generate 10 sets for $\alpha \in [0.1, 0.2, \ldots, 1.0]$. Each set is built from 100,000 randomly generated tasksets. Each taskset is composed by 24 tasks. A taskset is generated using the UUniFast algorithm [17] which produces a uniformly distributed set of task utilizations and which avoids bias in the generated tasksets. For a given task τ_i, the period T_i is generated with a uniform distribution between 100 and 100,000 ms. The deadline D_i is given by $D_i = \alpha \cdot T_i$ and the WCET C_i is given by $C_i = u_i \cdot T_i$. We consider an homogeneous processor composed by 8 identical processors.

6.2   Simulation Results

We show in Fig.1 the average number of iterations during the computation of *allowance*.

$$R_i^{k+1} = C_i + \sum_{\tau_h \in hp^j(i)} \left\lceil \frac{R_i^k}{T_h} \right\rceil C_h \tag{8}$$

We implement a function iteration() which computes the value given by (8). The computation of the *allowance* based on the WCRT computation calls this function in (2) and in (3). The computation of the *allowance* based on the sensitivity analysis calls this function in (5). For the two implementations of the *allowance* computation, we count the number of calls to the function iteration() for each randomly generated taskset and we keep the average of the *allowance* over all the taskset. We notice that despite the fact of the complexity of the sensitivity analysis seems greater than the complexity of the *allowance* computation based on the WCRT, the number of iterations for sensitivity analysis is well below the number of iterations for computation based on the WCRT. We therefore choose to compute *allowance* by sensitivity analysis [12].

We show in Fig.2, 3 and 5 the comparison between *First-Fit-Decreasing* (FFD), *Worst-Fit-Decreasing* (WFD) and *Allowance-Fit-Decreasing* (AFD). *Decreasing* means that these heuristics assign the tasks in order of their decreasing utilization. We voluntarily omit to show results concerning BF and NF because their behavior are very similar to FF. AFD and WFD use a necessary and sufficient condition of schedulability. Therefore we used the necessary and sufficient condition RTA [16] for the heuristics FFD.

We show in Fig.2 the number of partition found by the heuristics FFD, WFD and AFD. We notice that FFD provides a slightly better schedulability for $\alpha \geq 0.4$. This result is explained by the fact that FFD is one of the best heuristic for the task partitioning problem in terms schedulability. But the gap between FFD and the other two heuristics is not very large and may be acceptable if we want more robustness to WCETs overruns.

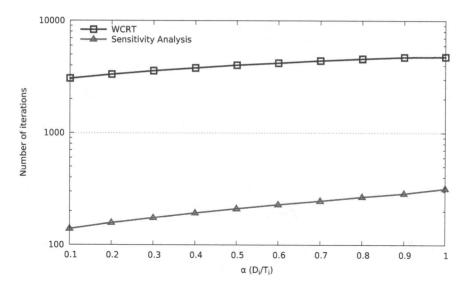

Fig. 1. Comparison of computation time for the *allowance* computation approaches

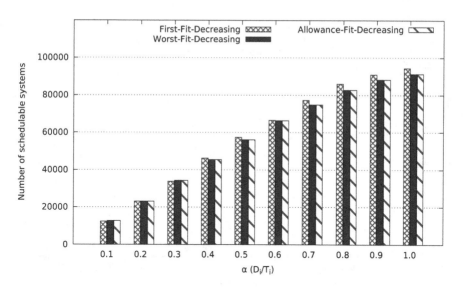

Fig. 2. Comparison of schedulability for the tasks partitioning heuristics

We compare in Fig.3 the minimum *allowance* obtained by the three heuristics on 4 processors and in Fig.4 on 8 processors. Minimum *allowance* A_{min} guarantees that any task of the system can bear an interference during A_{min} without any deadline is missed. We show that AFD and WFD outperforms largely FFD. Indeed, AFD and WFD distributes the tasks among the processors instead of fills up all the first processors. We note that AFD is slightly better than WFD.

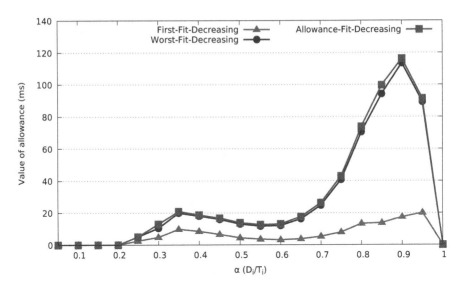

Fig. 3. Comparison of minimum *allowance* for the tasks partitioning heuristics on 4 processors

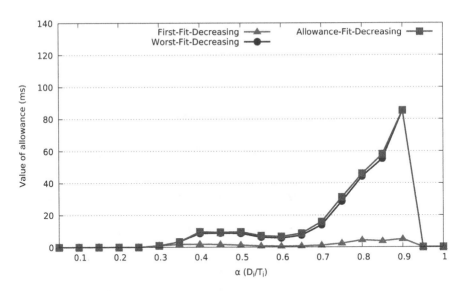

Fig. 4. Comparison of minimum *allowance* for the tasks partitioning heuristics on 8 processors

We show in Fig.5 the comparison between the computational time of the three heuristics. AFD offers better results than WFD in terms of minimum *allowance*. But the computation time of AFD is 6 to 10 greater than the computation time of WFD. For a robust allocation to the WCETs overruns, it is interesting to use AFD. But when tasks must be accepted online, WFD is a preferable choice.

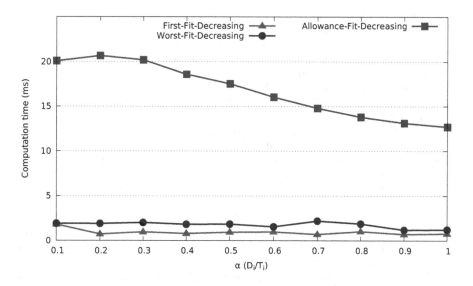

Fig. 5. Comparison of computation time of the heuristics

7   Conclusion

We have proposed a fixed-priority partitioned scheduling for homogeneous processors which maximizes the *allowance* of the execution duration. This scheduling is more robust than the others based on FF, BF or NF because during allocation of the tasks, the processor offering the greatest value of *allowance* is chosen. In terms of maximization of *allowance*, *Allowance-Fit* is slighty efficient than *Worst-Fit*. But in terms of computation time, *Worst-Fit* is largely better than *Allowance-Fit*. Thus *Worst-Fit* is a good heuristic to maximize the robustness of a partitioned system of real-time tasks. In a future work, we will extend this approach to the class of *restricted migration* scheduling to improve the schedulability of our solution. In such a scheduling, the different jobs of a recurring task can migrate from a processor to another, but no migration is allowed during the execution of the job.

References

1. Liu, C.L., Layland, J.W.: Scheduling algorithms for multiprogramming in a hard real-time environment. Journal of the ACM 20(1), 47–61 (1973)
2. Leung, J.Y.T., Whitehead, J.: On the complexity of fixed-priority scheduling of periodic, real-time tasks. Performance Evaluation 2(4), 237–250 (1982)
3. Davis, R.I., Burns, A.: Robust priority assignment for fixed priority real-time systems. In: Proceedings of the 28th Real-Time Systems Symposium (RTSS), Tucson, Arizona, USA, pp. 3–14. IEEE Computer Society, Los Alamitos (December 2007)

4. Bertogna, M.: Evaluation of existing schedulability tests for global EDF. In: Proceedings of the 38th International Conference on Parallel Processing Workshops (ICPPW), Vienna, Austria, pp. 11–18. IEEE Computer Society, Los Alamitos (September 2009); First International Workshop on Real-time Systems on Multicore Platforms: Theory and Practice (XRTS)

5. Burchard, A., Liebeherr, J., Oh, Y., Son, S.H.: New strategies for assigning real-time tasks to multiprocessor systems. IEEE Transactions on Computers 44(12), 1429–1442 (1995)

6. Oh, Y., Son, S.H.: Allocating fixed-priority periodic tasks on multiprocessor systems. Real-Time Systems 9(3), 207–239 (1995)

7. Andersson, B., Jonsson, J.: Preemptive multiprocessor scheduling anomalies. In: Proceedings of the 16th International Parallel and Distributed Processing Symposium (IPDPS), Fort Lauderdale, Florida, USA, pp. 12–19. IEEE Computer Society, Los Alamitos (April 2002)

8. Fisher, N., Baruah, S.K., Baker, T.P.: The partitioned scheduling of sporadic tasks according to static-priorities. In: Proceedings of the 18th Euromicro Conference on Real-time Systems (ECRTS), Dresden, Germany, pp. 118–127. IEEE Computer Society, Los Alamitos (July 2006)

9. Lakshmanan, K., Rajkumar, R., Lehoczky, J.P.: Partitioned fixed-priority preemptive scheduling for multi-core processors. In: Proceedings of the 21st Euromicro Conference on Real-time Systems (ECRTS), Dublin, Ireland, pp. 239–248. IEEE Computer Society, Los Alamitos (July 2009)

10. Dibble, P.: Jsr 1: Real-time specification for java (December 1998)

11. Bougueroua, L., George, L., Midonnet, S.: Dealing with execution-overruns to improve the temporal robustness of real-time systems scheduled FP and EDF. In: Proceedings of the 2nd International Conference on Systems (ICONS), Sainte-Luce, Martinique, 8 p. IEEE Computer Society, Los Alamitos (April 2007)

12. Bini, E., Di Natale, M., Buttazzo, G.C.: Sensitivity analysis for fixed-priority real-time systems. In: Proceedings of the 18th Euromicro Conference on Real-time Systems (ECRTS), Dresden, Germany, pp. 13–22. IEEE Computer Society, Los Alamitos (April 2006)

13. Davis, R.I., Zabos, A., Burns, A.: Efficient exact schedulability tests for fixed priority real-time systems. IEEE Transactions on Computers 57(9), 1261–1276 (2008)

14. Garey, M.R., Johnson, D.S.: Computers and Intractability: A Guide to the Theory of NP-Completeness (1979)

15. Coffman Jr., E.G., Garey, M.R., Johnson, D.S.: Approximation algorithms for bin packing: A survey. In: Approximation Algorithms for NP-Hard Problems, pp. 46–93. PWS Publishing Co., Boston (1996)

16. Audsley, N.C., Alan, B., Tindell, K.W., Wellings, A.J.: Applying new scheduling theory to static priority pre-emptive scheduling. Software Engineering Journal 8(5), 284–292 (1993)

17. Bini, E., Buttazzo, G.C.: Biasing effects in schedulability measures. In: Proceedings of the 16th Euromicro Conference on Real-time Systems (ECRTS), Catania, Sicily, Italy, pp. 196–203. IEEE Computer Society, Los Alamitos (June - July 2004)

An Infrastructure for Flexible Runtime Reconfigurable Multi-microcontroller Systems

Claudius Stern, Philipp Adelt, Matthias Schmitz,
Lisa Kleinjohann, and Bernd Kleinjohann

C-LAB, University of Paderborn, Paderborn, Germany
claudis@c-lab.de
http://www.c-lab.de

Abstract. Embedded systems in robotics or mechatronics need flexibility since they are working in dynamic environments. We consider an embedded modular multi-microcontroller system. Each module includes a microcontroller and special purpose hardware like a motor driver. Usually a change of the embedded software necessitates a direct access to all the devices (microcontrollers) to reload the code.

To overcome this disadvantage we introduce an infrastructure for flexible runtime reconfiguration of microcontroller modules within a system. The infrastructure enables the system to be coarse-grain reconfigurable on module level from one single point of access.

By using our infrastructure the system can remain operational during reconfiguration except the modules that actually get reconfigured. The infrastructure can cope with hardware changes during runtime like disconnection and reconnection of system parts.

1 Introduction

Embedded systems in robotics or mechatronics need flexibility since they are working in dynamic environments. We consider an embedded modular multi-microcontroller system whereby each module includes a microcontroller and special purpose hardware, e.g., a motor driver. Typically these systems are rather complex in terms of number of microcontrollers or in terms of communication structure. Nowadays those system are statically built so that an adaptation to a new environmental situation often requires a complete rebuilding of the entire system. Of course, for improvements of the algorithms used in embedded microcontrollers a reconfiguration of the according controller is also needed. If possible at all, a change of the embedded software on the embedded devices often is very difficult because a direct access to each device is necessary. In such cases a solution would be needed that provides one single point of access for reliable reconfiguration of the embedded software of a microcontroller module which is deeply embedded in the system.

As an example consider a complex mechatronic system with more than hundred microcontrollers. Given that about 20% of the microcontrollers do the same job, like motor controlling, at least 20 microcontrollers have to be reconfigured if

M. Hinchey et al. (Eds.): DIPES/BICC 2010, IFIP AICT 329, pp. 205–216, 2010.

an error is revealed or an update is necessary. Hence, besides the single point of access it would be useful to have the ability not only to reconfigure a single microcontroller but to reconfigure a functionally identical group of microcontrollers simultaneously.

Now consider a reconfigurable mechatronic system, e.g., a truck which could be equipped with different types of accessories. Each accessory for its own is a mechatronic system which is equipped with multiple microcontrollers. If, e.g., a company with several of these multi-use trucks finds an error in the height-level control of the snow plow accessory, a reconfiguration is necessary. An easy way to reconfigure these microcontrollers would be to plug a reconfiguration device in each truck equipped with the faulty snow plow. If for some reason this reconfiguration device is plugged in a truck without a snow plow the system should be able to identify its actual structure and the currently available functional units to prevent wrong reconfiguration. Furthermore, considering a necessary reconfiguration which would reconfigure microcontrollers both on an accessory as well as on the truck itself, the system should be able to reconfigure the one part without having the other part available.

As third example let us regard a production line as a mechatronic system. It could be very expensive to stop the complete system. To consider a reconfigurable system to be installed, a reconfiguration must not lead to a complete system stop. One possibility is to split the production line into sections—which already is common practice—where each section can be stopped individually. The naïve approach would bring up the non-central reconfiguration issue again. Splitting up the production line while keeping the central reconfiguration would need an architecture which ensures the reconfiguration process not to interfere with the functionality of the rest of the system.

The examples described above show that a flexible modular approach is necessary for system reconfiguration. The individual modules should represent functional units which can be combined with mechanics to create mechatronic functional units, e.g., a driving unit for robotics. The system has to be flexible enough to be used at several different places in a robotic system, e.g., as a motor controller or as a multi-servo controller. Components have to be reconfigurable without the necessity of accessing them directly. They should be reconfigurable during runtime while the rest of the system remains operational. The user should not be bothered with details of reconfiguration. The system should be able to identify its own structure.

We envision to plug a system together and when connected to a PC, a diagram of the functional unit structure appears. The user then would be able to select those parts of the system he wants to reconfigure.

In this paper we present an infrastructure for a flexible runtime reconfigurable microcontroller system, that shows the following features.

- Single point of access for reconfiguration:
  Our infrastructure provides reconfiguration-access to the complete system via a single point of access.

- Multicast reconfiguration:
  Simultaneous reconfiguration of multiple modules is possible.
- System enumerates nodes automatically and unambiguously:
  Independent from user-space communication, the system can determine its
  own structure and the system assigns unique identifiers automatically to its
  nodes.
- System recognizes changes:
  When a node is removed or added, the system recognizes this situation and
  starts a new enumeration cycle automatically.
- Separation of concerns: communication vs. reconfiguration:
  The user needs not to bother about matters of reconfiguration.
- Reconfiguration can be independent from user communication channel:
  We integrate two independent communication domains for reconfiguration
  and user-space communication. It can be selected which communication
  channel is to be used for reconfiguration.
- Runtime reconfiguration on module level:
  The reconfiguration of a module is possible without stopping the whole sys-
  tem. Only the module itself has to be stopped.

The remainder of this paper is organized as follows. In Section 2 we describe
the underlying architecture of our reconfiguration infrastructure. In Section 3 we
focus on the automatic structure determination. In Section 4 the reconfiguration
process is described. Section 5 then shows the application of our infrastructure
to a demonstration system. After that, we discuss related work in Section 6.
Finally, we conclude our work in Section 7.

2   Reconfiguration Architecture

Our intention was to create a modular system of microcontroller boards for
control purposes. A common problem nowadays is that each individual microcontroller is reconfigurable, but only at its own connector. Now imagine a large
system with 10 or more microcontrollers deeply embedded within the system.
Here a single point of access to connect to the system is desirable even if only one
microcontroller has to be reconfigured. Therefore we designed modular microcontroller boards and enhanced this design with a reconfiguration architecture.
The resulting infrastructure is depicted in Fig. 1.

In the following we use the term *node* for modules which have a specialized
logic and a dedicated microcontroller for reconfiguration and structure recognition. The architecture distinguishes three basic types of modules.

- Communication nodes
- Execution nodes (e.g., I/O nodes, calculator nodes)
- Power supply modules (no node logic)

Communication nodes hold a central position within the infrastructure. They are
the bridge between the embedded system and a controlling infrastructure. For this

purpose one Communication node is equipped with a microcontroller C_{comm} and several internal and external communication interfaces. Hence a Communication node acts as the single point of access to the system.

Execution nodes are specialized microcontroller-driven devices which are used for the actual control tasks like motor controlling, waveform generation, etc.. Each Execution node has a main microcontroller C_{main} for the actual control task and a dedicated reconfiguration microcontroller C_{config} for reconfiguring C_{main}.

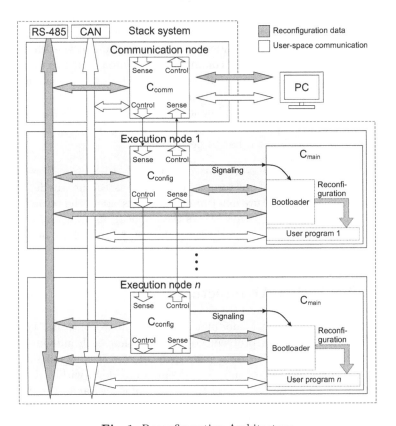

Fig. 1. Reconfiguration Architecture

Fig. 1 shows two independent communication channels throughout the system (CAN in white, RS-485 in gray). In this case the CAN bus is used for user-space communication (although it could be also used for reconfiguration) and the RS-485 bus is exclusively used for reconfiguration. The ports *Sense* and *Control* which are shown in the figure are used for the automatic structure detection. They are important during the system's initialization and whenever the system is structurally changed, e.g., because of parts of the system being switched off or on. The automatic structure determination of our architecture

which is described detailed in Section 3 enables the reconfiguration of systems
whose hardware structure can be changed. The separation of concerns between
user-space communication and reconfiguration enables a system reconfiguration
during run-time. While one microcontroller of the system is reconfigured, the
rest of the system may remain operating.

3   Automatic Structure Determination

In order to increase the flexibility of a reconfigurable microcontroller architecture, such a system should be able to determine its own physical structure and
to recognize changes to this structure. Fig. 2 depicts a simplified block diagram
of the structure of a stacked system. Actually, two connected stacks are shown.
Only one of them is equipped with a Communication node. However, in some
cases it could be useful to have more than one Communication node in the
system. Since Communication nodes act as a bridge between the internal communication architecture and an external one, more than one Communication
node could be needed. If the device which uses the system is, e.g., equipped
with an internal control PC, one Communication node would be connected to
this internal PC and another one would act as the reconfiguration access point.
Another example for a scenario with more than one Communication node would
be a setting where multiple points of access to the system are desirable, e.g., at
the front and the end of a large production line.

Unlike in Section 2 here only that part of the system is of interest which
is concerned with the actual reconfiguration. Hence, only the Communication
node, C_{comm}, and the reconfiguration microcontrollers of the Execution nodes,

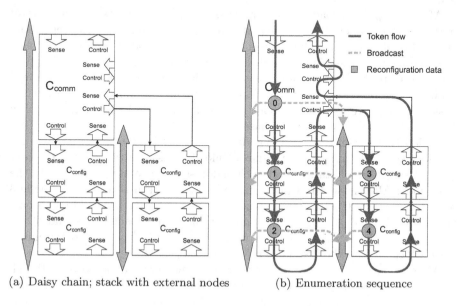

(a) Daisy chain; stack with external nodes   (b) Enumeration sequence

Fig. 2. Exemplary system configuration with enumeration

C_{config}, are shown instead of the entire nodes. While determining the structure of the system, every node gets a unique number which is later used as an address for the reconfiguration process (Section 4). The structure determination uses a depth-first search which is also used to assign the addresses at the same time.

We now describe an exemplary enumeration on the basis of the configuration shown in Fig. 2(a). Fig. 2(b) depicts the enumeration sequence and parts of the communication. Each node, except the Communication node, has two signaling ports to its logical top and the same to its logical bottom. Note another difference to Fig. 1. C_{comm} is equipped with two additional signaling ports where external stacks can be connected (see Fig. 4). *Sense* is an input port used to recognize a connected node and *Control* is an output port used to send signals to a connected node. Both signals have a predefined signal level (Control = 1, Sense = 0). Hence, initially each node is able to detect whether another node is connected. When two nodes are connected, the Control port pulls the Sense port of the other node to 1.

We defined the root node to be the one that initially has no node at its top. The initial 0 at the top Sense port is regarded as a token signaling to the root node that no other node is on top of it. In Fig. 2(a) the root node is C_{comm}. Note that any of the nodes could take this position.

All nodes hold a variable where the currently highest node address is stored (initially -1). C_{comm} gets the token (its top Sense port is 0) and therefore may take an address. It takes address 0 and broadcasts this through the system. After a node has taken an address, it then passes the token to its children. When the token returns through the bottom Sense port, it has to be passed to the next child or—if all children returned the token—it has to be passed to the parent node.

After C_{comm} has broadcasted its address, C_{comm} disables its bottom Control port (passes the token to its first child). This causes a change on the Sense port of C_{config} below C_{comm}. This signals the node below node 0 that it could now take the next address. This process is continued until no node is connected at the bottom port. In the exemplary case of Fig. 2(b) the last node in the first chain is node no. 2. It detects that no further node is connected and therefore passes the token to its parent (node 1). This signals node 1 that all nodes below have finished their enumeration phase.

Node 1 then passes the token to node 0 (C_{comm}). Node 0 recognizes the return of the token and passes it to the next child. In this case the child is the first node of the external stack. It takes the address 3 and passes the token to the next node. After node 4 has taken its address, the token is returned to node 3 and then to node 0. C_{comm} recognizes that it has no further children to pass the token to. As C_{comm} is the root node it then can broadcast the end of the enumeration phase. All nodes then return their Control ports into the initial state which enables the system to recognize changes.

After a change of the system's structure a renumeration has to be initiated. Fig. 3 depicts the two stages of the renumeration process exemplarly for a disconnect event. Since all nodes have reset their Control ports, node 1 in Fig. 3(a)

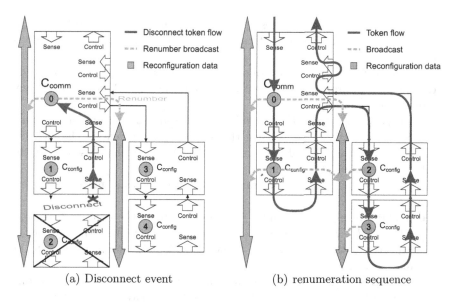

(a) Disconnect event   (b) renumeration sequence

Fig. 3. Renumeration after disconnect event

is able to detect the disconnection of node 2, as the Sense port of node 1 switches from 1 to 0. This level change is regarded as a token signaling a disconnect event to the sensing node. The token is passed to the parent until the root node has been reached. Node 0 then sends a broadcast signaling the upcoming renumeration. After that a normal enumeration process starts as shown in Fig. 3(b).

4   Reconfiguration Process

As we mentioned before, we envision a pluggable modular system whose structure is displayed when connected to a PC. After the system has determined its structure, every node has a unique address and is therefore able to reconfigure itself. Besides the two basic types Communication node and Execution node, the system is also able to distinguish between different nodes of the same basic type. The user of such a system can define groups of functionally identical nodes, e.g., motor drivers. In a structural diagram the user then would be able to identify and to select a single node as well as a group of nodes for reconfiguration. The usual reconfiguration should follow the scheme described below:

- C_{comm} of the Communication node, which wants to start a reconfiguration process, sends a message over the reconfiguration bus. The message is addressed to the C_{config} microcontrollers of those nodes that have to be reconfigured and contains the following data:
  - Desired function, e.g., *enter programming mode*
  - Desired channel for further communication, e.g., *RS485*
  - List of addressed nodes

– The reception of the initial message will be confirmed by all selected C_{config} microcontrollers. The confirmations will be sent in the order of the address list.

– All selected C_{config} microcontrollers then put their C_{main} into reconfiguration mode and prepare them for the communication with the desired communication channel.

– After C_{main} has entered the reconfiguration mode, it transmits a confirmation to the initiating C_{comm} using the selected communication channel.

– C_{comm} has to wait for all confirmation messages, which are sent over the selected communication channel.

– For every memory page to be transmitted, three types of messages are exchanged.

  • A *start message*, containing information about the content type, e.g. *EEPROM*, *FLASH*, the start address or page number, the number of expected data messages and a checksum for the complete data to be received.

  • *Data messages*, containing the actual data. Dependent on the used communication channel, these data messages can have different sizes and may be also protected by a checksum.

  • A *finishing message*, causing all recipient C_{main} microcontrollers to check the data for completeness and correctness and to write the received data to the according memory. This ensures that the reconfiguration process starts only, if all data have been received correctly. If one of the recipients reports an error, the process is restarted. Data which already have been received correctly will be ignored, so that only the erroneous nodes are reconfigured again.

– As last step, C_{comm} sends a finishing message to all selected C_{config} microcontrollers, causing them to reset their C_{main} microcontrollers into normal operation mode.

Using this communication scheme for reconfiguration ensures that single nodes as well as a group of nodes can be reliably reconfigured.

5   Realization of the Demonstrator

Fig. 4 depicts an exemplary setup of our stack system. The system consists of a Power supply module, one Communication node and two Execution nodes. The Communication node can be easily identified as it is equipped with a USB connector and two external ports to connect to other stack systems. The Power supply module has an according external connector to get connected with another stack system.

The Communication nodes hold a central position within the infrastructure. They are the bridge between the embedded system and a controlling infrastructure. For this purpose one Communication node is equipped with several internal and external communication interfaces. The internal interfaces include

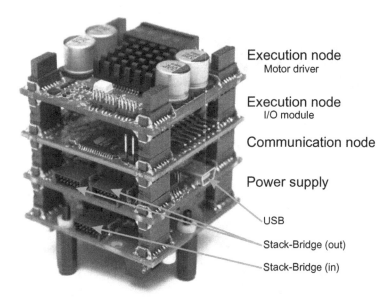

Fig. 4. Stacked sytem

two independent communication channels: a CAN bus interface for user-space communication and a RS-485 interface for reconfiguration purposes.

As external interfaces, a USB interface and a LAN interface are provided. The USB interface (FT232R) acts as a UART. The LAN interface is built on foundation of the WIZnet chip W5100, which is a hardwired TCP/IP embedded Ethernet controller. We have chosen this Ethernet controller to save program memory and CPU load on the main microcontroller. Another fact which distinguishes the Communication node from the other nodes is the different node logic controller (C_{comm}) which has two additional external interfaces for reconfiguration.

Furthermore there are different types of Execution nodes. So far, we developed a digital-analog I/O node and a motor driver node (Fig. 5). The I/O node has 16 digital outputs, 8 digital inputs and 8 analog inputs. The motor driver node is mainly based on the power motor driver VNH2SP30-E from STMicroelectronics. One specialty of the motor driver node is that its communication channels are fully optocoupled. This ensures that no electrical noise from a connected motor interferes with the communication or with the internal electrical system in general.

6   Related Work

The term reconfiguration in terms of embedded system often is related to Field Programmable Gate Arrays (FPGAs). There are many relations between an FPGA-based system and our modular multi-microcontroller system. In terms of an FPGA system coarse-granular reconfiguration means the replacement of complete system modules in contrast to only reconfiguring parts of a processor. Our

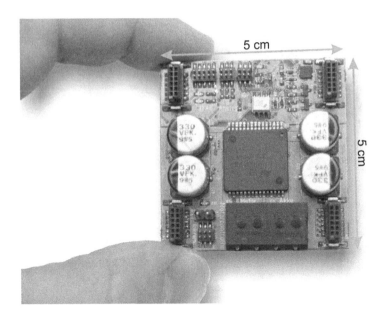

Fig. 5. One node of our stack system (motor driver node)

reconfiguration is coarse-granular in terms of only reconfiguring a complete module. Additionally, we integrate I/O-hardware, power drivers and even galvanic isolation in our modules. Masselos and Voros [5] introduce a classification of reconfigurable architectures. Our approach cannot directly be classified by their classification scheme. We have a temporal computation style, have a great post fabrication programmability and are highly flexible. Our type of reconfiguration is kind of both static—from microcontroller's point of view—and dynamic—from the system's point of view.

Wahlah and Gossens [7] propose a 3-tier reconfiguration model for FPGAs using hardwired network on chip. Besides their 3-tier architecture they use the hardwired network as a dedicated communication channel for reconfiguration. They also propose a separation of concerns as the user has no need to bother about reconfiguration details as the application manager takes over this task.

Blodget et al. [1] present an approach for dynamic reconfiguration of a special FPGA. They propose a hardware and software infrastructure to enable the FPGA to reconfigure itself using a soft microprocessor to control the reconfiguration. We also use the concept of a dedicated microcontroller to control the reconfiguration. In our case each module carries its own reconfiguration microcontroller which is also used for the automatic structure detection.

The technical term "component-based reconfiguration" is usually used for software systems but there are many related issues to a module-based system as we have proposed it in this paper. Matevska [6] "presents a model-based approach to runtime reconfiguration of component-based systems, which aims at minimising the interference caused by the reconfiguration and thus maximising system responsiveness during reconfiguration." His main goal is to maximize the system responsiveness during reconfiguration. In contrast, our main goal is to encapsulate the reconfiguration process to ease the reconfiguration. The infrastructure we proposed ensures that—except the modules that actually get reconfigured—the rest of the system remains operational.

Chen et al. [2] "propose a framework to support component-based model integration, hierarchical functionality composition, and reconfiguration of systems [...]". Their framework is more related to our future work but they also use hierarchical components to hide the implementation details. This is comparable with our separation of concerns paradigm which hides the details of reconfiguration.

David et al. [3] propose a multi-stage approach for reliable dynamic reconfiguration. They focus on a validation of the reconfiguration process to detect errors before the execution of the reconfiguration. This partly also applies to our infrastructure regarding the separation of concerns paradigm. We provide an interface to the user to reliably reconfigure a system's module. Another part of the work of David et al. is the error detection in a running system and to automatically mitigate them by reconfiguration. This part of their work is more related to our future work.

Gumzej et al. [4] propose a reconfiguration pattern for UML-based projects of embedded real-time systems. Their concept mainly regards real-time capability of the reconfiguration management. We have not analyzed the real-time capability of our infrastructure yet and in their point of view the infrastructure we proposed would only be a part of the reconfiguration management. Our infrastructure proposal would be located on the hardware level and on the middleware level.

7   Conclusion and Future Work

Our intention was to create an infrastructure for coarse-grain flexible run-time reconfiguration of multi-microcontroller systems. We have shown that the infrastructure we proposed fulfills the requirements of a flexible module-based coarse-grain run-time reconfiguration and moreover introduces a separation of concerns regarding user-space communication and reconfiguration. Our infrastructure is able to cope with structural system changes and ensures a reliable reconfiguration. Additionally, our infrastructure provides the ability to do a multicast reconfiguration of functionally identical modules.

Until now, we have tested the automatic structure detection within one stack, and we have implemented a driving unit. The driving unit includes three motor controllers realized on three Execution nodes and one Communication node. We successfully tested both the user-space communication and the reconfiguration communication. We are currently working on the bootloader code.

This infrastructure will be the foundation of future work. Both ideas, to extend the amount of modules and to more deeply integrate the stack system with complex embedded systems, will be issues in our future work. More complex functional units including embedded PCs will be developed to build a self-monitoring and self-repairing subsystem that uses in-system runtime reconfiguration to make the whole system more robust against failure.

References

1. Blodget, B., McMillan, S., Lysaght, P.: A lightweight approach for embedded reconfiguration of fpgas. In: DATE 2003: Proceedings of the conference on Design, Automation and Test in Europe, p. 10399. IEEE Computer Society, Washington (2003)
2. Chen, W., Xie, C., Shi, J.: A component-based model integrated framework for embedded software. In: Wu, Z., Chen, C., Guo, M., Bu, J. (eds.) ICESS 2004. LNCS, vol. 3605, pp. 563–569. Springer, Heidelberg (2005), http://www.springerlink.com/content/2xq8nwktc0cr7d2w/
3. David, P.C., Lger, M., Grall, H., Ledoux, T., Coupaye, T.: A multi-stage approach for reliable dynamic reconfigurations of component-based systems. In: Meier, R., Terzis, S. (eds.) DAIS 2008. LNCS, vol. 5053, pp. 106–111. Springer, Heidelberg (2008), http://www.springerlink.com/content/9j85j27363v88342/
4. Gumzej, R., Colnari, M., Halang, W.A.: A reconfiguration pattern for distributed embedded systems. Software and Systems Modeling 8(1), 145–161 (2009), http://www.springerlink.com/content/nr3t327414250784/
5. Masselos, K., Voros, N.S.: Introduction to reconfigurable hardware. In: System Level Design of Reconfigurable Systems-on-Chip, pp. 15–26. Springer, US (2005), http://www.springerlink.com/content/g76x276332511272/
6. Matevska, J.: Model-based runtime reconfiguration of component-based systems. In: WUP 2009: Proceedings of the Warm Up Workshop for ACM/IEEE ICSE 2010, pp. 33–36. ACM, New York (2009)
7. Wahlah, M., Goossens, K.: 3-tier reconfiguration model for fpgas using hard-wired network on chip. In: Proceedings of the International Conference on Field-Programmable Technology (December 2009)

Biologically-Inspired Collaborative Computing (BICC 2010)

Edited by

Mike Hinchey
Lero—the Irish Software Engineering Research Centre
University of Limerick, Ireland

Peter Lindsay
University of Queensland, Australia

Franz J. Rammig
Universität Paderborn, Germany

Jon Timmis
University of York, United Kingdom

Preface

"Look deep into nature and you will understand everything better," advised Albert Einstein. In recent years, the research communities in computer science, engineering, and other disciplines have taken this message to heart, and a relatively new field of "biologically inspired computing" has been born. Inspiration is being drawn from nature, from the behaviors of colonies of ants, of swarms of bees, and even the human body. This new paradigm in computing takes many simple autonomous objects or agents and lets them jointly perform a complex task, without having the need for centralized control. In this paradigm, these simple objects interact locally with their environment using simple rules. Applications include optimization algorithms, communications networks, scheduling and decision making, supply-chain management, and robotics, to name just a few. There are many disciplines involved in making such systems work: from artificial intelligence to energy-aware systems. Often these disciplines have their own field of focus, have their own conferences, or only deal with specialized sub-problems (e.g., swarm intelligence, biologically inspired computation, sensor networks). The Third IFIP Conference on Biologically Inspired Collaborative Computing aimed to bridge this separation of the scientific community and bring together researchers in the fields of organic computing, autonomic computing, self-organizing systems, pervasive computing, and related areas.

The contributions to the program of this conference were selected from submissions originating from North and South America, Asia, Europe, and Australia. We would like to thank the members of the Program Committee for the careful reviewing of all submissions, which formed the basis for selecting this attractive program. We are grateful to IFIP and in particular IFIP TC-10 for their support. We all enjoyed the inspiring series of talks and discussions at BICC 2010, part of a range of excellent conferences in the IFIP World Computer Conference 2010.

Peter Lindsay
Franz J. Rammig

Mike Hinchey
Jon Timmis

Model Checking the Ant Colony Optimisation

Lucio Mauro Duarte[1], Luciana Foss[2], Flávio Rech Wagner[1], and Tales Heimfarth[3]

[1] Institute of Informatics, Federal University of Rio Grande do Sul – Brazil
[2] Institute of Physics and Mathematics, DINFO, Federal University of Pelotas – Brazil
[3] Dep. of Computer Science, Federal University of Lavras - Brazil
{lmduarte,flavio}@inf.ufrgs.br, luciana.foss@ufpel.edu.br,
tales@dcc.ufla.br

Abstract. We present a model for the travelling salesman problem (TSP) solved using the ant colony optimisation (ACO), a bio-inspired mechanism that helps speed up the search for a solution and that can be applied to many other problems. The natural complexity of the TSP combined with the self-organisation and emergent behaviours that result from the application of the ACO make model-checking this system a hard task. We discuss our approach for modelling the ACO in a well-known probabilistic model checker and describe results of verifications carried out using our model and a couple of probabilistic temporal properties. These results demonstrate not only the effectiveness of the ACO applied to the TSP, but also that our modelling approach for the ACO produces the expected behaviour. It also indicates that the same modelling could be used in other scenarios.

Keywords: ant colony optimisation, self-organisation, emergent behaviour, probabilistic model checking.

1 Introduction

Biologically inspired algorithms (or simply *bio-inspired algorithms*) [1] are methods that use mechanisms that resemble behaviours observed in nature, such as food search, evolution and insect swarming. These mechanisms define solving strategies that make applications more robust, flexible and scalable. They have been successfully applied to several problems, such as sensor networks [2][3].

All bio-inspired algorithms present a decentralised control and are composed by several, simple components that act autonomously and interact with each other. The overall behaviour of the system is a result of the interactions between its components and their autonomous decisions, based on environment conditions. Therefore, bio-inspired algorithms combine self-organisation and emergence. *Self-organisation* [4] describes the ability of a system to dynamically modify its internal structure in an autonomous manner. Hence, components automatically adapt to changes without any external intervention. *Emergence* [5] means that the system's behaviour, rather than being simply the sum of the behaviours of its components, *emerges* from local interactions between these components. Systems that contain self-organisation and emergence are called *self-organising emergent systems* (SOES) and are considered one of

M. Hinchey et al. (Eds.): DIPES/BICC 2010, IFIP AICT 329, pp. 221–232, 2010.

the most promising answers to the development of massive distributed systems with decentralised control [6]. However, no appropriate support is provided by current software engineering techniques for the development of such systems.

The main problem in developing an SOES is the dynamic changes in its structure, which makes it difficult to analyse the system using traditional approaches, which require predicting all possible behaviours. Furthermore, even though components of the system and their interactions are quite simple, the great number of possibilities of interactions increases the system's overall complexity.

In this paper we investigate how to provide some guarantee that a system involving a bio-inspired algorithm – thus characterising an SOES - exhibits the expected behaviour. Though simulation is the usual technique for the analysis of these systems, we present an approach based on *probabilistic model checking* [7], which is a technique that extends the traditional model checking [8] by allowing property specification and model analysis to consider probabilities and timing information. The reason for this choice is the need of checking not only qualitative properties (i.e., properties that evaluate as either "true" or "false") but mainly *quantitative properties* regarding issues such as reliability, performance and resource usage. Moreover, modelling bio-inspired mechanisms requires different abstractions to describe the dynamics of the system and possible changes in its structure over time.

We describe a modelling strategy for a bio-inspired algorithm based on the mechanism of *pheromones*. We advocate that, since bio-inspired algorithms are naturally self-organising mechanisms, if there is a well-defined way of model-checking them, then SOESs in general could be more easily modelled and verified.

To evaluate our idea, we have developed an example involving the *travelling salesman problem* (TSP) [9] using the *ant colony optimisation* (ACO) [10] to drive the solution for the problem in a small scenario. Hence, our main goals with this study were: to propose a way of modelling the bio-inspired algorithm, to apply it to a model of the TSP and to show, through the verification of some properties, the correctness of the modelling, which means that the mechanism indeed eventually leads the system to exhibit the expected behaviour. We demonstrate how we have modelled the TSP and the ACO as a *discrete-time Markov chain* (DTMC) in the *Probabilistic Symbolic Model Checker* (PRISM) [11] and present a couple of properties specified using *probabilistic computational tree logic* (PCTL) [12] that we have checked. The results indicate that the pheromone mechanism successfully eventually leads to a behaviour that complies with requirements for solving the problem, thus demonstrating the correct modelling of the bio-inspired algorithm.

The remaining of this paper is organised as follows: Section 2 presents background information on the subject of this work; Section 3 describes how we have modelled and verified the TSP-ACO experiment and the results obtained; Section 4 presents a discussion about some related work; and Section 5 contains the conclusions.

2   Background

This section presents the basic ideas related to the problem and to the bio-inspired algorithm. It also briefly describes concepts related to probabilistic model checking.

2.1 The ACO Applied to the TSP

The *travelling salesman problem* (TSP) [9] is a classic and well-studied problem in Theoretical Computer Science that can be used to formalise a number of real-world problems. It consists in finding the shortest Hamiltonian circuit in a fully-connected graph $G=(N,E)$, where N represents a set of n cities and E describes the set of routes between pairs of cities. Each route (i,j) in E is assigned a cost $cost(i,j)$, describing the distance between cities i and j. Thus, the total cost of a certain tour $t=(c_0,c_1,...,c_n,c_0)$ is given by the sum in (1), which represents the sum of the costs of every route included in the tour. Therefore, the shortest path[1] would be the one with the lowest total cost.

$$\sum_{i=0}^{n-1} cost(i,(i+1) \bmod n). \tag{1}$$

One way proposed to help solve the TSP is by the *ant colony optimisation* (ACO) [10], which is an algorithm that simulates the behaviour of ants looking for food sources. They mark the paths they take by leaving a trail of *pheromone*, which is a natural hormone. When choosing paths, ants take into account the pheromone concentration, which indicates paths more often taken by other ants. Thus, paths leading to food sources close to the nest tend to concentrate higher levels of pheromone and become more attractive to other ants. After some time, the pheromone slowly evaporates, ensuring that paths that do not lead to good food sources (i.e., are not frequently used) will become less attractive over time. Therefore, the pheromone mechanism provides all the information ants need to choose paths and achieve the necessary organisation without external intervention. This means that the behaviour of the whole colony emerges from the interactions through pheromone.

2.2 Probabilistic Model Checking

As in any other SOES, the complexity of the ACO lies not on the behaviour of each component (ant) alone, but on the difficulty of predicting the behaviours that can emerge from local interactions. In order to provide guarantees of some sort about the emergence of a specific behaviour, we can identify two possible approaches: simulation or formal verification. *Simulations* of an abstract system model can be used to drive design choices until the required quality properties are obtained. However, system analysis based on simulation does not provide sound guarantees for the engineering of complex systems such as ACO because it is based only on approximations. In contrast to simulation, *formal verification* techniques, such as *model checking* [8], can provide precise results about the system real behaviour, at the cost of requiring more accurate abstractions.

Probabilistic model checking [7] is a model checking technique more tailored for the analysis of SOESs, as it provides means of dealing with systems that exhibit probabilistic or stochastic behaviour. It mainly differs from traditional model checking in that it involves additional information on probabilities or timing of transitions between states. Properties can involve calculations of the probability of certain events occurring during the execution of the system.

---

[1] We use the term *tour* to represent the traversal of the graph and the term *path* to describe a sequence of cities visited during a tour.

There are several commonly used model representations for probabilistic and sto-chastic systems, most of them based on Markov chains. In Markov chains, transitions between states depend on some probability distribution, where only the current state of the system influences the probability of the next transitions. A particular type of Markov chain is a *discrete-time Markov chain* (DTMC), which is represented by a transition system that defines the probability of moving from one state to another by applying discrete-time steps. The temporal logics *probabilistic computation tree logic* (PCTL) [12] is used to specify properties of a DTMC. PCTL extends the temporal logic CTL [13] with discrete time and probabilities.

One of the most used tools regarding probabilistic model checking is the *Probabilistic Symbolic Model Checker* (PRISM) [11]. Amongst some other features, it supports the specification of PCTL properties and the creation of DTMCs described using a simple, state-based language. It also provides an environment for checking the properties against the models using either simulation or verification.

3 Verification of the TSP with ACO

This section presents the results of our modelling of the ACO and how this mechanism was introduced in the TSP model to help find a solution using self-organisation and emergence. We also discuss how we specified properties based on these requirements and verified that they hold in the model.

3.1 Modelling

We modelled the problem using the PRISM language [11] to describe the symmetric version of the TSP (where routes have the same cost on both ways). The graph was composed by 4 cities, which is the minimum number of vertices necessary to introduce some complexity to the problem. To simplify the modelling, we fixed city number 1 as the initial city and modelled the solution with only one ant. This way, rather than having multiple ants travelling in parallel, there was only one ant repeatedly traversing the graph. Therefore, each tour of this sole ant represents the behaviour of a different ant, thus simulating the behaviour of several ants. This abstraction reduces the complexity of the problem but does not affect the analysis results as the effect of the pheromone mechanism works exactly in the same way.

Although we followed the original ACO algorithm [10], calculating the probabilities of paths based on both costs and desirability (amount of pheromone), we used different formulas to simplify the modelling. Our desirability component, called *preference*, refers to the amount of pheromone associated to each route between two cities, which ranges from 1 (*MIN_PREF*) to 10 (*MAX_PREF*). All routes are initialised with *MIN_PREF* and, after a tour, pheromone is deposited only on edges that are part of the path taken, causing preferences to be updated. The local updated preference value after a tour is calculated as presented in (2).

$$p_{ij}' = \min(p_{ij} + inc\_factor(tot\_dist), MAX\_PREF)). \tag{2}$$

In the formula, p_{ij} denotes the preference of route *(i,j)* and *tot_dist* is the sum of the costs of all routes comprising the most recent tour. Function *inc_factor* determines by how much the preference of a route will be increased depending on the total cost of the complete path. It assigns an increase value to paths according to their length group (short, mid-length or long). The group which a path belongs to is determined by the assignment of a cost to each route, which defines a scenario for the TSP.

The local update of routes causes a global update of probabilities. The probability of taking a certain route (i,j) is given by (3), where N_CITIES defines the number of cities involved, and $visited\_cities$ is the set of cities already visited in the current tour.

$$prob_{ij} = \frac{p_{ij}}{\sum_{k=1}^{N\_CITIES} p_{ik}} \quad s.t.\ k \in \{1,...,N\_CITIES\} - visited\_cities. \tag{3}$$

Considering a scenario with 4 cities, the probability of taking, for instance, route (1,2) when starting the tour in city 1 is given by (4).

$$prob_{12} = \frac{p_{12}}{p_{12} + p_{13} + p_{14}}. \tag{4}$$

Note that the formula guarantees that the probabilities of all possible routes from a city add up to 1. The code below presents the PRISM model of the TSP-ACO:

```
1  dtmc
2  const int N_CITIES = 4; const int MIN_PREF = 1;
3  const int MAX_PREF = 10;
4  const int D12 = 1; const int D23 = 8; const int D34 = 2;
5  const int D14 = 4; const int D13 = 4; const int D24 = 3;
6  const int MAX_DIST=(D12+D23+D34+D14+D13+D24); const double EVAP_RATE;
7  const int N_CYCLES;
8  global cont : [0..N_CYCLES] init 0;
9  global p12 : [MIN_PREF..MAX_PREF] init MIN_PREF;
10 global p13 : [MIN_PREF..MAX_PREF] init MIN_PREF;
11 global p14 : [MIN_PREF..MAX_PREF] init MIN_PREF;
12 global p23 : [MIN_PREF..MAX_PREF] init MIN_PREF;
13 global p24 : [MIN_PREF..MAX_PREF] init MIN_PREF;
14 global p34 : [MIN_PREF..MAX_PREF] init MIN_PREF;
15 formula prob12 = (p12/(p14+p13+p12));
16 formula prob13 = (p13/(p14+p13+p12));
17 formula prob14 = (p14/(p14+p13+p12));
18 formula prob123 = (p23/(p23+p24)); formula prob124 = (p24/(p23+p24));
19 formula prob132 = (p23/(p23+p34)); formula prob134 = (p34/(p23+p34));
20 formula prob142 = (p24/(p24+p34)); formula prob143 = (p34/(p24+p34));
21 formula inc_factor = (tot_dist<15) ? 7 : ((tot_dist=15) ? 4 : 1);
22 module traveller
23   loc : [1..N_CITIES+1] init 1;
24   path : [0..6] init 0;
25   tot_dist : [0..MAX_DIST] init 0;
26   [] loc=1 & path=0 -> prob12 : (loc'=2) +
27                        prob13 : (loc'=3) +
28                        prob14 : (loc'=4);
29   [] loc=2 & path=0 ->
30       prob123 : (loc'=3) &
31                 (path'=1) &
32                 (tot_dist'=D12+D23+D34+D14) +
33       prob124 : (loc'=4) &
34                 (path'=2) &
35                 (tot_dist'=D12+D24+D34+D13);
36   [] loc=3 & path=0 ->
37       prob132 : (loc'=2) &
38                 (path'=3) &
39                 (tot_dist'=D13+D23+D34+D14) +
40       prob134 : (loc'=4) &
```

```
41                    (path'=4) &
42                    (tot_dist'=D13+D34+D24+D12);
43    [] loc=4 & path=0 ->
44       prob142 : (loc'=2) &
45                    (path'=5) &
46                    (tot_dist'=D14+D24+D23+D13) +
47       prob143 : (loc'=3) &
48                    (path'=6) &
49                    (tot_dist'=D14+D34+D23+D12);
50    [] (loc=2|loc=3|loc=4) & path!=0 -> 1.0 : (loc'=5);
51    [] loc=5 & path=1 -> 1.0 :
52       (path'=0) &
53       (p12'=min(p12+inc_factor,MAX_PREF)) &
54       (p23'=min(p23+inc_factor,MAX_PREF)) &
55       (p34'=min(p34+inc_factor,MAX_PREF)) &
56       (p14'=min(p14+inc_factor,MAX_PREF)) &
57       (tot_dist'=0);
58    [] loc=5 & path=2 -> 1.0 :
59       (path'=0) &
60       (p12'=min(p12+inc_factor,MAX_PREF)) &
61       (p24'=min(p24+inc_factor,MAX_PREF)) &
62       (p34'=min(p34+inc_factor,MAX_PREF)) &
63       (p13'=min(p13+inc_factor,MAX_PREF)) &
64       (tot_dist'=0);
65    [] loc=5 & path=3 -> 1.0 :
66       (path'=0) &
67       (p13'=min(p13+inc_factor,MAX_PREF)) &
68       (p23'=min(p23+inc_factor,MAX_PREF)) &
69       (p24'=min(p24+inc_factor,MAX_PREF)) &
70       (p14'=min(p14+inc_factor,MAX_PREF)) &
71       (tot_dist'=0);
72    [] loc=5 & path=4 -> 1.0 :
73       (path'=0) &
74       (p13'=min(p13+inc_factor,MAX_PREF)) &
75       (p34'=min(p34+inc_factor,MAX_PREF)) &
76       (p24'=min(p24+inc_factor,MAX_PREF)) &
77       (p12'=min(p12+inc_factor,MAX_PREF)) &
78       (tot_dist'=0);
79    [] loc=5 & path=5 -> 1.0 :
80       (path'=0) &
81       (p14'=min(p14+inc_factor,MAX_PREF)) &
82       (p24'=min(p24+inc_factor,MAX_PREF)) &
83       (p23'=min(p23+inc_factor,MAX_PREF)) &
84       (p13'=min(p13+inc_factor,MAX_PREF)) &
85       (tot_dist'=0);
86    [] loc=5 & path=6 -> 1.0 :
87       (path'=0) &
88       (p14'=min(p14+inc_factor,MAX_PREF)) &
89       (p34'=min(p34+inc_factor,MAX_PREF)) &
90       (p23'=min(p23+inc_factor,MAX_PREF)) &
91       (p12'=min(p12+inc_factor,MAX_PREF)) &
92       (tot_dist'=0);
93    [] loc=5 & path=0 & cont<N_CYCLES -> 1.0 :
94       (p12'=(max(p12-ceil(EVAP_RATE*p12),MIN_PREF))) &
95       (p23'=(max(p23-ceil(EVAP_RATE*p23),MIN_PREF))) &
96       (p34'=(max(p34-ceil(EVAP_RATE*p34),MIN_PREF))) &
97       (p14'=(max(p14-ceil(EVAP_RATE*p14),MIN_PREF))) &
98       (p13'=(max(p13-ceil(EVAP_RATE*p13),MIN_PREF))) &
99`      (p24'=(max(p24-ceil(EVAP_RATE*p24),MIN_PREF))) &
100      (loc'=1) & (cont'=cont+1);
101   [] loc=5 & path=0 & cont=N_CYCLES -> 1.0 : true;
102   endmodule
```

A model in PRISM is described as a set of constants and global variables, a set of formulas and a set of modules. Each module describes a component of the system and consists of a set of local variables and a list of guarded transition commands. Each of these commands is described in the form [l]g -> p: <cmds>, where l is an optional label ([] for empty), g is a guard, which describes the condition on which the transition may occur, p is the probability of that transition occurring if enabled (guard is true) and <cmds> determines the effect of the transition. This effect is described in terms of changes in values of variables, which might modify values of formulas.

In our model, each constant D_{ij} determines the distance (or cost) between cities i and j. Constants *EVAP_RATE* and *N_CYCLES* are used during analysis to set the rate at which the pheromone on routes evaporates and the number of cycles to be executed, respectively. Variable *cont* controls the number of cycles executed, whereas each variable *pij* defines the preference of route *(i,j)*. Lines 15-20 describe the application of the formula in (3) to calculate the probability of travelling between cities. In the scenario proposed (lines 4-5), the distances defined for each route in the graph create 3 groups of path lengths: the longest paths have a total distance of 19, mid-length paths have a cost of 15, and the shortest paths have a total distance of 10. Therefore, we simplified the calculation by testing, according to the total distance of a path, which group this path belongs to[2]. The shortest paths receive an increase of 7, mid-length paths of 4, and the longest paths of only 1.

Module *traveller* describes the behaviour of the artificial ant moving from city to city. Variable *loc* determines the city the ant is currently in. Though *N_CITIES* limits the number of cities, we use an extra "city" to apply the necessary updates, as we will explain soon. Variable *tot_dist* determines the total distance travelled during the tour. Variable *path* determines which of the possible paths has been taken during the current tour, according to the following identification, where the sequences of numbers represent sequences of visited cities: *Path 1* = 1-2-3-4-1, *Path 2* = 1-2-4-3-1, *Path 3* = 1-3-2-4-1, *Path 4* = 1-3-4-2-1, *Path 5* = 1-4-2-3-1, and *Path 6* = 1-4-3-2-1. Considering these possible paths and the distances of each route, paths 2 and 4 are the shortest, 1 and 6 are the mid-length, and 3 and 5 are the longest ones.

From city 1 (line 26), there are three possible routes to take. Because all preferences are initialised with the minimum preference, at the beginning, the probabilities are the same for all possible routes. Depending on the next location, which is determined probabilistically, the choices for the next route are different, so that we comply with the requirement that all cities should be visited only once during a tour. For instance, consider that a transition to city 2 has been selected. Then lines 29-35 describe the behaviour at this location. If we had reached city 2 from city 1, then there would still be two cities to visit (3 and 4). Because there are only four cities involved, once the third city is chosen, we can already identify which path was taken. For example, if city 3 is selected, we know for a fact that the next city is necessarily city 4 and that, from there, we will move back to city 1 to complete the tour. Hence, the path taken was 1-2-3-4-1, which is Path 1 (line 31). Since we know the path, we can determine the total distance travelled (line 32).

We defined a special location (city number 5), which is used to apply the necessary updates. The idea is that reaching location 5 represents that a tour is completed. Depending on the path taken, the preferences of the routes involved are updated according to (2) (lines 51-92). Variables *path* and *tot_dist* are reset to signal that the

---

[2] Command *<cond> ? val1 : val2* represents a selection operation where value *val1* is returned in case the boolean expression *cond* is evaluated as true and *val2* is returned, otherwise.

preference update has been executed, which allows the evaporation update to happen. Using the defined evaporation rate, preferences are updated once again according to the formulas presented in lines 94-99. The evaporation occurs at the end of every tour until *cont* reaches the predetermined number of cycles, when the model enters a sink state (line 101). This finite behaviour is necessary to avoid state-space explosion and to allow the execution of a bounded model checking process.

3.2 Property Specification

For the TSP, considering an origin *Orig* and a destination *Dest*, such that $Orig \neq Dest$, two main requirements can be defined:

1. If an ant a_1 starts a tour at time t_1, with probability p_1 of finding the shortest path, and an ant a_2 takes off at time t_2, with a probability p_2 of finding the shortest path, such that $t_1 < t_2$, then $p_1 \leq p_2$;

2. The majority of ants travelling through the graph will eventually follow the shortest path from *Orig* to *Dest*.

Based on these requirements, we have specified properties in PCTL devised to verify whether the behaviour described in the model fulfils the requirements. These properties are presented below, where *"stopped"* is a label that represents the formula *(cont=T & loc=5)*, which defines the end of cycle *T*, where *T* is an undefined constant used during verification. Label *"R12"* represents the formula *((p12>p14) & (p12>p23))*, *"R13"* the formula *((p13>p14) & (p13>p23))*, *"R24"* the formula *((p24>p14) & (p24>p23))*, and *"R34"* the formula *((p34>p14) & (p34>p23))*. Label *"shortest_paths"* represents formula *((path=2)|(path=4))*.

P1: *P=? [F ("stopped" & "R12" & "R13" & "R24" & "R34")]*
P2: *P=? [F ("stopped" & "shortest_paths")]*

Property *P1* is based on requirement 1 and refers to the probability of the preferences of routes that compose the shortest paths being higher than those of other routes when cycle *T* ends. This property checks whether the pheromone update and pheromone evaporation processes guarantee that edges that compose the shortest paths will receive higher concentrations of pheromone, thus having higher probability of being taken. Property *P2*, based on requirement 2, asks the probability of taking one of the shortest paths when cycle *T* ends. Hence, this property can be used to identify how this probability varies from one cycle to the next.

3.3 Verification

Equipped with the model presented in Sec. 3.1 and having the properties described in Sec. 3.2, we were able to carry out experiments using the PRISM tool. Our first experiment was to compare different evaporation rates and analyse how they affect the results of our properties. The objectives were to evaluate the effect of the evaporation rate to guarantee the preference for the shortest paths (2 and 4) and to determine the minimum value of the evaporation rate that guarantees the requirements are fulfilled. For this analysis, we used a model with 20 cycles, which was enough to detect a pattern of increase or decrease of probabilities[3], and T ranging from 0 to 20. Table 1 presents the results for each property for evaporation rates ranging from 0 to 0.8 (we ignore values 0.9 and 1, as they have the same results as those of value 0.8).

Analysing the results, we can see that value 0 (i.e., preference does not decay with time) results in property $P1$ having almost 100% probability. This is because no route has its preference decreased as cycles go by, which means all routes of the scenario will reach saturation irrespective of being in the shortest paths or not. The effect of having an evaporation rate can be seen in the results of value 0.1, where already there was a clear tendency to select the shortest paths. With value 0.2 we achieved the probability that the majority of tours involve the shortest paths, but it was with value 0.3 that a consistent majority was achieved. With value 0.4 we reached the highest probability of taking the shortest paths. With values from 0.5 to 0.8, it is possible to see that the probability of the shortest paths decreased as the evaporation rate increased, resulting from an effect similar to that of not having pheromone decay.

Considering the results, we decided to adopt value 0.3 because our main objective was that routes belonging to the shortest paths had higher preference than other routes, so that ants would tend to take those routes. Hence, we needed to take into account the value of property $P1$, and its highest value, considering values 0.3, 0.4 and 0.5 (those where $P2$ is above 51%), was obtained with 0.3.

Adopting value 0.3 as the evaporation rate, we produced a model with 20 cycles and verified the results for property $P2$ at each cycle. The goal was to obtain evidence that indeed the probability of taking the shortest paths tended to grow after each cycle. The results are displayed on the graph of Fig. 1.

Table 1. Property results for different evaporation rates

Ev.	0.0	0.1	0.2	0.3	0.4	0.5	0.6	0.7	0.8
P1	0.993	0.807	0.841	0.793	0.713	0.484	0.346	0	0
P2	0.346	0.480	0.501	0.548	0.562	0.558	0.481	0.417	0.333

The graph clearly shows the expected behaviour, as the probability of the shortest paths increase continually. Hence, the behaviour described in the model leads to the global behaviour expected, where the majority of ants choose the shortest paths.

3.4 Analysis and Discussion

Our experiments showed that the model successfully fulfills the requirements of the system, considering the specification provided. We obtained numerical, accurate evidence that the majority of ants (or travellers) tended to take the shortest paths. Furthermore, we obtained results that indicate the effective action of the pheromones on paths by comparing different evaporation rates.

---

[3] In a simulation of property $P2$ considering 1000 cycles, the model reached a firm majority ($\cong 55\%$) after 20 cycles and remained around this value from that point on.

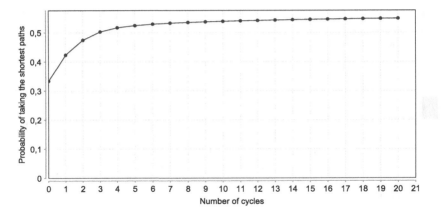

Fig. 1. Analysis of property P2 with evaporation rate 0.3 and 20 cycles

Though we worked with only four cities, we believe that the modelling could be easily extended to a higher number of cities. The limitation, however, capacity of the machine, as the number of states increases considerably just with the addition of another city. It seems that better abstractions should be defined so as to avoid state-space explosion and allow the verification of larger models. Nevertheless, we are confident that the effectiveness of the ACO modelling is not limited to four cities.

Considering our requirements, requirement 1 can be checked by verifying the result of property *P1*, since it is possible to obtain the probability of higher concentrations being deposited on routes composing the shortest paths along a certain number of cycles (by varying the value of *T*). Requirement 2 can be verified using property *P2*, analysing whether the result reaches a value higher than 50% and tends to not go below this value during the subsequent cycles.

4   Related Work

Considering the modelling of bio-inspired mechanisms, there are a few approaches worth mentioning. In [14], the authors present bio-inspired techniques for self-organisation and self-governance for autonomic networks. Simulation is used to analyse properties like traffic- and node-load and the amount of bandwidth in each route in the network (self-management of resources). In [15], the authors propose self-organising mechanisms based on properties of cellular systems to model hardware systems that can grow, self-replicate and self-repair. Hardware simulation is performed to show how the artificial organisms evolve.

Formalisms like Brane Calculus [16] and P Systems [17] are inspired by the structure and dynamics of biological membranes and used to model biological processes. There are some approaches proposing the application of model checking to these formalisms, but they are still quite restrictive.

With respect to using ACO to solve the TSP, some approaches have been proposed, such as [10], [18], [19] and [20]. In all these approaches, simulation is used to check the solution to compare it with those of other approaches. Though simulation is in general faster than model checking, it provides only approximate results. Model checking, on the other hand, provides a solid confidence on the results, which is particularly important when dealing with behaviours that cannot be easily predicted beforehand and may violate critical properties. As far as we are aware of, there is no work on applying model checking to verify properties of the TSP-ACO.

5 Conclusions

We presented a probabilistic modelling of the ACO, a bio-inspired mechanism, applied to the TSP. The ACO attributes a self-organising characteristic to the system as it adjusts the probabilities of paths automatically and autonomously, deriving emergent behaviours. Results of experiments show that our model, when checked against a couple of quantitative properties, indeed presents the expected behaviour. This behaviour corresponds to guaranteeing that most of the times the shortest paths are probabilistically taken. We analysed the effect of the pheromone evaporation rate on the variations of path probabilities and determined the most appropriate value for this rate. We also presented a comparison of path probabilities during multiple cycles of execution, representing multiple ants travelling from city to city to complete tours.

We explored the use of model checking because it can provide a higher degree of confidence when compared with other techniques, such as simulation, where results are only approximate. However, we had to apply some simplifications during the modelling phase so as to avoid state-space explosion. These restrictions did not affect the results of our experiments, but might be an issue in other applications. As problems grow more complex, creating abstractions precise enough to guarantee a good level of confidence and yet sufficiently coarse to prevent intractability becomes an even harder task. We still need more experience in applying this modelling approach, considering other scenarios, so that we can better understand the real limits of modelling characteristics as self-organisation and emergent behaviours.

Though our scenario was quite simple, it was enough to demonstrate that the application of the pheromone mechanism leads the system to the expected behaviour. From this result, we intend to study how to apply the same mechanism to other known problems where it can be useful (e.g., routing in sensor networks). We aim to define a modelling pattern for this mechanism to facilitate its use.

We also plan to study how other bio-inspired mechanisms could be modelled and used for the verification of quantitative properties, such as modelling ideas used in swarm intelligence. As bio-inspired mechanisms are essentially self-organising mechanisms, it seems that having a modelling approach for these mechanisms could be a step towards providing support for the verification of self-organising emergent systems in general.

Acknowledgments. This work was supported by grant MCT/CNPq/CT-INFO 551031/2007-7.

References

1. Olariu, S., Zomaya, A.: Handbook of Bioinspired Algorithms and Applications. Oxford University Press, Oxford (2007)
2. Heimfarth, T., Danne, K., Rammig, F.: An OS for Mobile Ad hoc Networks Using Ant Based Hueristic to Distribute Mobile Services. In: ICAS-ICNS, p. 77 (2005)

3. Janacik, P., Heimfarth, T., Rammig, F.: Emergent Topology Control Based on Division of Labour in Ants. In: AINA 2006, vol. 1, pp. 733–740 (2006)
4. Camazine, S., Deneubourg, J., Franks, N., et al.: Self-Organization in Biological Systems. Princeton University Press, Princeton (2001)
5. Lewes, G.: Problems of Life and Mind. Kessinger Publishing (2004)
6. De Wolf, T., Holvoet, T.: Emergence Versus Self-Organisation: Different Concepts But Promising When Combined Engineering. In: Brueckner, S.A., Di Marzo Serugendo, G., Karageorgos, A., Nagpal, R. (eds.) ESOA 2005. LNCS (LNAI), vol. 3464, pp. 1–15. Springer, Heidelberg (2005)
7. Vardi, M.: Automatic Verification of Probabilistic Concurrent Finite State Programs. In: 26th Annual Symp. on Found. of Comp. Sci., pp. 327–338 (1985)
8. Clarke, E.M., Grumberg, O., Peled, D.A.: Model Checking. The MIT Press, Cambridge (1999)
9. Applegate, D.L., Bixby, R.E., Chvátal, V., Cook, W.J.: The Traveling Salesman Problem: A Computational Study. Princeton University Press, Princeton (2006)
10. Dorigo, M., Gambardella, L.: Ant Colony System: A Cooperative Learning Approach to the Traveling Salesman Problem. IEEE Trans. on Evol. Comp. 1, 53–66 (1997)
11. Kwiatkowska, M., Norman, G., Parker, D.: PRISM: Probabilistic Symbolic Model Checker. In: Field, T., Harrison, P.G., Bradley, J., Harder, U. (eds.) TOOLS 2002. LNCS, vol. 2324, pp. 200–204. Springer, Heidelberg (2002)
12. Hansson, H., Jonsson, B.: A Logic for Reasoning About Time and Reliability. Formal Aspects of Computing 6, 512–535 (1994)
13. Ben-Ari, M., Manna, Z., Pnueli, A.: The Temporal Logic of Branching Time. Acta Informatica 20, 207–226 (1983)
14. Balasubramaniam, S., Botvich, D., Donnelly, et al.: Biologically Inspired Self-Governance and Self-Organisation for Autonomic Networks. In: 1st Intl. Conf. on Bio-Inspired Mod. of Net., Inform. and Comp. Sys., pp. 1–30 (2006)
15. Stauffer, A., Mange, D., Rossier, J., Vannel, F.: Bio-inspired Self-Organizing Cellular Systems. BioSystems 94, 164–169 (2008)
16. Cardelli, L.: Brane Calculi. In: Danos, V., Schachter, V. (eds.) CMSB 2004. LNCS (LNBI), vol. 3082, pp. 257–278. Springer, Heidelberg (2005)
17. Păun, G.: Computing with Membranes. Journal of Computing and System Sciences 61(1), 108–143 (2000)
18. Shang, G., Lei, Z., Fengting, Z., et al.: Solving Traveling Salesman Problem by Ant Colony Optimization Algorithm with Association Rule. In: 3rd Int. Conf. on Natural Computation, pp. 693–698 (2007)
19. Li, Y., Gong, S.: Dynamic Ant Colony Optimization for TSP. Int. J. Adv. Manuf. Technol. 22, 528–533 (2003)
20. Ugur, A., Aydin, D.: An Interactive Simulation and Analysis Software for Solving TSP using Ant Colony Optimization Algorithms. Adv. in Eng. Soft. 40, 341–349 (2009)

Feature Selection for Classification Using an Ant System Approach

Nadia Abd-Alsabour

School of Information Technology, Bond University, Australia
nadia.abdalsabour@ieee.org

Abstract. Many applications such as pattern recognition and data mining require selecting a subset of the input features in order to represent the whole set of features. The aim of feature selection is to remove irrelevant, redundant or noisy features while keeping the most informative ones. In this paper, an ant system approach for solving feature selection for classification is presented. The results we got are promising in terms of the accuracy of the classifier and the number of selected features in all the used datasets.

Keywords: Ant colony optimization, pattern recognition, support vector machine and feature selection.

1 Introduction

Pattern recognition is the assignment of an input pattern to one of several predefined categories/classes [1]. The basic component of any pattern recognition system is the classifier whose task is to partition the feature space into class-labeled decision regions. The performance of the classifiers is sensitive to the choice of the features that are used for constructing those classifiers. The choice of the features that are presented to the classifiers affects the following important things:

- The accuracy of the classifiers,
- The time needed for learning the classification function, and
- The number of examples needed for learning the classification function [2].

Some research suggests increasing the examples amount of training data, but this affects the time needed for the learning. It is here that feature selection becomes important. The assumption that more features can offer more information about the inputs is not always valid in practice. It has been found that including more features can be time consuming and may lead to finding a less optimal solution. This makes feature selection from the original set of features is highly desirable in many situations [1], [3].

Feature selection (FS) is the problem of selecting a subset of features without reducing the accuracy of representing the original set of features [3]. Feature selection (the most general term is variable selection) is used in many applications to remove irrelevant and redundant features where there are high dimensional datasets. These datasets can contain high degree of irrelevant and redundant features that may decrease the performance of learning algorithms.

M. Hinchey et al. (Eds.): DIPES/BICC 2010, IFIP AICT 329, pp. 233–241, 2010.

The main approaches that are used for solving feature selection problem can be classified into filter or wrapper approach depending on whether or not feature selection is done independently of the learning algorithm. Some researchers use a hyprid approach to take the advantage of these 2 approaches and to handle large datasets.

Feature selection can be seen as an optimization problem that involves searching the space of possible feature subsets to identify the optimal one. Many optimization techniques such as genetic algorithms (GA) [2], tabu search (TS), simulated annealing (SA) and ant colony optimization algorithms (ACO) have been used for solving feature selection.

Real ants are able to find the shortest path between their nest and food sources because of the chemical substance (pheromone) that they deposit on their way. The pheromone evaporates over time so the shortest paths will contain much pheromone and subsequently will attract more ants in future.

Ant colony optimization algorithms simulate the foraging behavior of some ant species [5]. ACO algorithms are guided search algorithms that use 2 factors for guiding the search process. These factors are: 1) the pheromone values (numerical values as a simulation for the pheromone that real ants deposit on their way from/to their nest). 2) Heuristic information that is crucial for good performance of the system when we can not use local search. There are 2 types of heuristic information used by ACO algorithms; static heuristic information (that is computed at the initialization time and then remains unchanged throughout the whole algorithm's run such as the distances between cities in traveling salesman problem) and dynamic heuristic information (that depends on the partial solution constructed so far and therefore it is computed at each step of an ant's walk).

One of the recent trends in ACO is to apply them in solving new optimization problems such as applying them in solving many industrial problems proving that these algorithms are useful in real-world applications [6]-[8]. Recently, many researchers adopted some ACO algorithms for the solutions of feature selection problem such as in [9]-[12].

The traditional ACO algorithms were designed for solving ordering problems such as traveling salesman problem and quadratic assignment problem [11]. Feature selection problem is different from these optimization problems in terms of there is no prior information known about the features such as in TSP where the distances between the cities are known in advance for guiding the search process besides the pheromone values.

In order to solve an optimization problem using an ACO algorithm, the problem should be represented as a fully connected construction graph and 2 factors are used for guiding the search process. These factors are the heuristic information (known in advance about the given problem) and the pheromone values.

In the traditional ACO algorithms, the pheromone values are associated with the nodes or the edges of the construction graph representing the problem (depending on the chosen problem representation), which may also contain heuristic information representing prior information about the given problem [6]-[7].

In the proposed algorithm, we did not use the graphical representation hence; there is no concept of path. We associate the pheromone with each feature. Although there is no heuristic information known in advance in this type of problems, we used heuristic information in computing the moving probability that is used by each ant to select a particular feature in each construction step. We used the proportional of the ants chose a particular feature as heuristic information so the proposed algorithm does not need prior knowledge of features. We also used a new equation for the pheromone update as we will explain in the following sections.

The rest of this paper is organized as follows. Section 2 addresses the fundamentals of 4 ACO algorithms based on which we developed the proposed algorithm. The third section explains the proposed algorithm. Section 4 details the experiments carried out and presents the obtained results. The discussion of the results is presented in section 5. Section 6 highlights future work in this area. And finally, section 7 concludes this paper.

2 Related Work

In this section, we explain ant system (AS) and ant colony system (ACS) in solving traveling salesman problem since we used many aspects of these approaches. We will then explain briefly 2 ACO algorithms for solving feature selection.

The first ant colony optimization algorithm is AS as proposed in the early nineties [13]. Since its appearance, it became the basis for many successive ACO algorithms and it is known as the original ACO algorithm. AS is an iterative algorithm where in each iteration each ant selects the next city to be visited using the following equation:

$$\rho_{ij}^{k} = \frac{\tau_{ij}^{\alpha} \cdot \eta_{ij}^{\beta}}{\sum_{c_{ij \in N}(s^{p})} \tau_{il}^{\alpha} \cdot \eta_{il}^{\beta}} \qquad \text{if } c_{ij} \in N(s^{p}) \text{ and } 0 \text{ otherwise} \qquad (1)$$

where $N(s^{p})$ is the set of feasible components. The parameters α and β control the relative importance of the pheromone versus the heuristic information η_{ij} that is equal to $\frac{1}{d_{ij}}$ where d_{ij} is the distance between city i and city j.

At the end of each iteration, the pheromone values (numerical values associated with each solution components- here are the edges) are updated by all ants that have built solution according to the following equation:

$$\tau_{ij} = (1 - \rho) \cdot \tau_{ij} + \sum_{k=1}^{m} \Delta \tau_{ij}^{k} \qquad (2)$$

Where ρ is the evaporation rate, m is the number of ants and $\Delta \tau_{ij}^{k} = Q / L_{k}$ where Q is a constant and L_{k} is the length of the tour constructed by ant k.

Ant colony system (ACS) is considered one of the most successful ACO algorithms [14]. Since its appearance, it has been using for solving many optimization problems. ACS is an iterative algorithm where at each iteration, each ant chooses the next city to be visited (j) using pseudorandom proportional rule that is computed according to the following equation:

$$\arg \max_{C_{il} \in N(s^p)} \{ \tau . \eta_{il}^{\beta} \} \tag{3}$$

This equation is used by each ant at each construction step to choose the next city depending on a random variable q and a parameter q_0 and it is used if $q <= q_0$.

After each construction step, the local pheromone update is performed by all ants to the last edge traversed according to the following equation:

$$\tau_{ij} = (1 - \varphi) . \tau_{ij} + \varphi . \tau_0 \tag{4}$$

Where $\varphi \in (0,1]$ and τ_0 is the initial pheromone.

Local pheromone update leads to decreasing the pheromone values on the edges that encourages subsequent ants to choose other edges and subsequently produce different solutions.

At the end of each iteration, the pheromone values are updated by only the best ant according to the following equation:

$$\tau_{ij} = \begin{cases} (1 - \rho) . \tau_{ij} \\ \tau_{ij} \quad otherwise \end{cases} + \rho . \Delta \tau_{ij} \quad if \ (i, j) \ belongs \ to \ best \ tour, \tag{5}$$

Where $\Delta \tau_{ij} = 1 / L_{best}$ and L_{best} is the length of the tour constructed by the best ant.

An ACO approach called antselect for variable selection in quantitative structure-activity relationship (QSAR) has been developed in [9]. In antselect, a weight is associated with each feature and used for calculating the probability with which the feature is randomly selected by an ant. Initially, the weights and the probabilities are equal for all variables. The moving probability is calculated according to the following equation:

$$\rho_k = \frac{\omega_k}{\sum_k \omega_k} \tag{6}$$

where ω_k is the weight associated with feature k.

The weights are updated according to the following equation:

$$\omega_k = (1 - \rho) . \omega_k + \frac{\Delta \omega}{L} \tag{7}$$

where ρ is the evaporation rate, $\Delta \omega$ is a constant factor, and L is the length of ant k's path. In [10], antselect was used with artificial neural networks for variable selection with different dataset.

A modified ant colony optimization algorithm for solving feature selection in QSAR [11] expresses the feature selection problem in a binary notation where an ant moves in an N-dimensional search space of N variables. The pheromone levels on each feature are divided into two kinds, τ_{i0} and τ_{i1}.

The pheromone levels are updated according to the appropriate one of the following two updating rules:

$$\tau_{i0}(new) = \rho\tau_{i0}(old) + \Delta\tau_{i0} \tag{8}$$

or

$$\tau_{i1}(new) = \rho\tau_{i1}(old) + \Delta\tau_{i1} \tag{9}$$

$$\text{where} \quad \Delta\tau_{i0} = \sum_{k=1}^{m}\Delta\tau_{i0}^{k} \tag{10}$$

$$\text{And} \quad \Delta\tau_{i1} = \sum_{k=1}^{m}\Delta\tau_{i1}^{k} \tag{11}$$

The moving probability for any feature is 0 or 1, where 1 means that this feature will be selected and 0 means the inverse. The moving probability is calculated according to the following equation:

$$\rho_{i}^{k} = \frac{\tau_{i1}}{\tau_{i1} + \tau_{i0}} \tag{12}$$

This algorithm has also been used for solving feature selection problem in different dataset in [12].

3 The Proposed Algorithm

The proposed algorithm is a wrapper-based system that deals with the problem of feature selection as a binary problem where a set of binary bits (of a length equivalent to the number of the features in a given dataset) is associated with each ant. If the nth bit is a 1 this means that feature number n in the dataset is selected, otherwise this feature is not selected. Thus, the concept of path in the traditional ACO algorithms does not pertain here. At the start of the algorithm, the bits are randomly initialized to zeros and ones.

The pheromone values are associated with the features. At each construction step, each ant selects a feature out of all the features with the probability computed according to the following equation:

$$\rho_{i} = \tau_{i}.\Delta\tau_{i} \tag{13}$$

where τ_{i} is the pheromone value associated with feature i and $\Delta\tau_{i}$ = proportion of the ants that selected this feature and acts as heuristic information that represents the desirability of feature i. In ACO algorithms, the design of the moving probability is critical. Here, we used both the pheromone values and heuristic information to compute it.

At the end of each iteration, the pheromone values are updated according to the following equation:

$$\tau_i = ((1-\rho) \cdot \tau_i) \quad + \quad \left(\rho \cdot \sum_{k=1}^{m} \frac{Q}{L_k} \right)^{\beta} \tag{14}$$

where L_k = no. of features selected by ant k and p is the evaporation rate. This equation is used by all ants at the end of each iteration to all features that have been chosen.

The updating of the pheromone values is important to reinforce those features that lead to high quality feature subsets. Features that belong to good solutions will contain larger pheromone. Consequently, these features tend to be selected more often.

The pseudo code of the proposed algorithm is as follows:

Procedure of the proposed algorithm

```
Initialization
While (not terminate) do
    construct ant solution
    build SVM
    update statistics
    update pheromone values by all ants
  end while
end.
```

4   Tests and Results

In order to test the proposed algorithm, we used it with a Support Vector Machine (SVM) learning algorithm, which is considered one of the most popular, powerful and efficient classification and regression methods. Although not all machine learning algorithms require the phase of feature selection, feature selection is important in building SVM-based regression and classification as well [1], [3]. We used the number of correct classification / the whole number of observations as a fitness function where each ant evaluates its solution based on its ratio of correct classifications.

4.1   Datasets

In order to test the proposed algorithm, we did several experiments using several datasets. In our experiments, we did not do any modifications to these datasets before using them rather than converting them into a suitable format for our systems. In our experiments, we used 5-fold cross validation (CV). The used datasets here are: backache, prnn_virus3, prnn_viruses, analcatdata_authorship, and analcatdata_marketing from statistical datasets available in .arff format from the Website of Waikato University [15].

4.2   Methods

In our experiments, we developed the following 2 systems:
- SVM: that uses the entire set of features (without the phase of feature selection), and
- SVM-FS: that uses subset of features selected by the proposed algorithm (with the phase of feature selection).

In this paper, we focus on testing the effect of feature selection on the performance of the classifier. So we did not optimize the performance of SVM although further investigation is highly required since it affects the performance of the whole system. We used the default values to its parameters in both cases, with and without the use of feature selection. We used C-classification SVM of package (e1071) of R language with the default values to its parameters (cost, gamma, and epsilon).

In these 2 systems, we used 5-fold CV. The number of ants was set to the number of the features in any dataset. The initial pheromone was set at 1. The number of iterations is 10 iterations. P was set at 0.3. β was set at 0.3. Q was set at 4.

4.3 Results

Table 1 shows the results of these 2 systems using the above mentioned datasets. The results for the proposed algorithm represent the average of 5 independent runs. These systems are implemented using R language [16]-[17] and WEKA machine learning tool [18]-[19]. All the experiments were run on a personal PC with 2 GHz CPU and 2 GB RAM.

Table 1. The accuracy of SVM with and without the use of feature selection

	Dataset Name	No. of original features	Avg. no. of selected features	SVM (without FS)	SVM (with FS)
1	backache	32	20.2	0.9	0.9222
2	prnn_virus3	17	13.2	0.9474	0.9789
3	prnn_viruses	17	10.8	0.0164	0.9016
4	analcatdata_authorship	70	33	1	1
5	analcatdata_marketing	32	27.2	0.6401	0.6561

5 Discussion

The proposed algorithm deals with feature selection problem as a binary one but uses many concepts from ant system although it does not have the concept of path.

The previous results show that SVM-FS with the proposed algorithm for performing feature selection outperforms SVM that uses all the features in all the used datasets (the accuracy of SVM is larger than that of SVM with all features). The number of features selected by the proposed algorithm is significantly smaller than the total number of the features in the original datasets in all of the used datasets.

In the proposed algorithm, we used:

- Heuristic information in calculating the moving probability. This heuristic information indicates to how often a particular feature has been chosen by different ants. There are many ideas that could be used as heuristic information for guiding the search process besides the pheromone values but we see this equation is very useful based on many experiments we have done.
- Different pheromones update equation rather than the usual ones used in ACO for feature selection.
- Pheromone evaporation as in ant colony system.

6 Future Work

Trying other classifiers and additional experiments with other datasets are currently in progress.

Although the initial results are promising, further investigation is required particularly in solving the problem of the big number of parameters that the proposed algorithm suffers from (its parameters besides the parameters of SVM-all of these parameters need to be adjusted especially that the performance of ACO algorithms in general is sensitive to its parameters) in order to enhance its performance.

Another direction for future work is conducting comparisons of the performance of the proposed algorithm with that of other stochastic algorithms used for solving feature selection.

7 Conclusion

In this paper, we solved feature selection problem for classification using an ant system approach on an SVM classifier with several datasets. We used heuristic information in order to guide the search process besides the pheromone values as in most of conventional ACO algorithms. The results we got are promising in terms of the solution quality and the number of selected features.

References

1. Duda, R.O., Hart, P.E., Stork, D.G.: Pattern classification and scene analysis, 2nd edn. Wiley, Chichester (2001)
2. Yang, J., Honavar, V.: Feature subset selection using a genetic algorithm. IEEE Intelligent Systems 13(2), 44–49 (1998)
3. Liu, H., Motoda, H.: Feature Selection for Knowledge Discovery and Data Mining. Kluwer Academic, Norwell (1998)
4. Guyon, I., Elisseeff, A.: An introduction to variable and feature selection. Journal of Machine Learning Research 3, 1157–1182 (2003)
5. Dorigo, M., Bonabeou, E., Theraulaz, G.: Inspiration for optimization from social insect behavior. Nature, 406, 39–42 (2000)
6. Dorigo, M., Stutzle, T.: Ant Colony Optimization. MIT Press, Cambridge (2004)
7. Dorigo, M., Birattari, M., Stutzle, T.: Ant colony optimization- artificial ants as a computational intelligence technique. IEEE Computational Intelligence Magazine (2006)
8. Dorigo, M., Caro, G.D., Sampels, M.: Ant Algorithms. Springer, Heidelberg (2002)
9. Izrailev, S., Agrafiotis, D.: A novel method for building regression tree models for QSAR based on artificial ant colony systems. J. Chem. Inf. Computer Science 41, 176–180 (2001)
10. Izrailev, S., Agrafiotis, D.: Variable selection for QSAR by artificial ant colony systems. SAR QSAR in environmental research 13, 417–423 (2002)
11. Shen, Q., Jiang, J.H., Tao, J.C., Shen, G.L., Yu, R.Q.: Modified Ant Colony Optimization Algorithm for Variable Selection in QSAR Modeling: QSAR Studies of Cyclooxygenase Inhibitors. J Chem. Inf. Model 45, 1024–1029 (2005)

12. Shi, W., Shen, Q., Kong, W., Ye, B.: QSAR analysis of tyrosine kinase inhibitor using modified ant colony optimization and multiple linear regression. European Journal of Medicinal Chemistry 42, 81–86 (2007)
13. Dorigo, M., Maniezzo, V., Colorni, A.: Ant System: optimization by a colony of cooperating agents. IEEE Transactions on System, Man, and Cybernetics 26(1), 1–13 (1996)
14. Dorigo, M., Gambardella, L.M.: Ant colony system: A cooperating leaning approach to the traveling salesman problem. IEEE Transactions on evolutionary computation 1(1), 53–66 (1997)
15. http://www.cs.waikato.ac.nz/ml (viewed January 25, 2010)
16. R: A Language and Environment for Statistical Computing 2006. R Foundation for Statistical Computing, Vienna, Austria (2006), http://www.R-project.org
17. Dalgaard, P.: Introductory statistics with R. Springer, Heidelberg (2008)
18. http://www.cs.waikato.ac.nz/ml/weka (viewed January 25, 2010)
19. Witten, I., Frank, E.: Data Mining: Practical machine learning tools and techniques, 2nd edn. Morgan Kaufmann, San Francisco (2005)

Novelty-Aware Attack Recognition – Intrusion Detection with Organic Computing Techniques

Dominik Fisch, Ferdinand Kastl, and Bernhard Sick

Computationally Intelligent Systems Lab, University of Passau, Germany
{fisch,kastl,sick}@fim.uni-passau.de

Abstract. A typical task of intrusion detection systems is to detect known kinds of attacks by analyzing network traffic. In this article, we will take a step forward and enable such a system to recognize very new kinds of attacks by means of novelty-awareness mechanisms. That is, an intrusion detection system will be able to recognize deficits in its own knowledge and to react accordingly. It will present a learned rule premise to the system administrator which will then be labeled, i.e., extended by an appropriate conclusion. In this article, we present new techniques for novelty-aware attack recognition based on probabilistic rule modeling techniques and demonstrate how these techniques can successfully be applied to intrusion benchmark data. The proposed novelty-awareness techniques may also be used in other application fields by intelligent technical systems (e.g., organic computing systems) to resolve problems with knowledge deficits in a self-organizing way.

1 Introduction

Organic Computing (OC) has emerged recently as a challenging research area dealing with future computationally intelligent systems that will be based on so-called self-x properties such as self-organization, self-optimization, self-configuration, self-healing, self-protection, or self-learning [1,2]. An example for such a system is an intelligent distributed system, e.g., a team of robots, a smart sensor network, or a multi-agent system. Often, the nodes of such a system have to perform the same or similar tasks, or they even have to cooperate to solve a given problem. Typically, these nodes know *how to observe* their local environment and this knowledge is represented by certain rules. However, many environments are dynamic. That is, new rules are necessary or existing rules become obsolete. Therefore, really intelligent nodes should adapt on-line to their environment by means of certain machine learning techniques.

In this article we focus on components—intrusion detection agents (IDA)—of a distributed intrusion detection system (DIDS). These IDA are able to analyze network traffic and to distinguish between "normal" network data (connections) and data originating from certain kinds of attacks (or tools used to prepare an attack). The rules that are used for that purpose are learned from sample data. The challenge is now that an IDA must be able to detect new kinds of attacks as well as new kinds of "normal" data which it had not seen before. This

M. Hinchey et al. (Eds.): DIPES/BICC 2010, IFIP AICT 329, pp. 242–253, 2010.

property is termed *novelty-awareness*. Then, the IDA must support a system administrator in creating new rules. That is, it must present an autonomously learned rule premise to the system administrator who must "label" that rule (i.e., determine an appropriate conclusion). Then, the new rule must be added to the existing rule system. In a future version of our DIDS, new rules will be exchanged between different IDA of the DIDS. Then, an IDA will be enabled to recognize attacks that it had not seen before.

The architecture of an IDA, the DIDS, a framework for large-scale simulations, and techniques for alert aggregation are described in [3,4,5] in more detail. Here, we focus on the novelty-aware attack recognition at the detection layer. This kind of novelty-awareness is very new to the field of intrusion detection. Thus, this article should be seen as a kind of proof of concept, where many of the components will be further improved in the future.

In the following, Section 2 briefly discusses related work in the field of DIDS, Section 3 lays the theoretical and methodological foundations of novelty-awareness, and Section 4 provides some experimental results. Finally, Section 5 summarizes the major findings and gives an outlook to our future work.

2   Related Work

Here, we briefly discuss related work in the field of DIDS. Information about terminology in the field of intrusion detection can be found in [6].

In most cases, the collaborative aspect of DIDS is found in the correlation of distributed data. Classical DIDS research is mostly focused on systems where agents located on network nodes aggregate data and send alerts to a central agent for correlation [7]. [8] proposes a p2p overlay network which allows correlation of attacks across domain borders with the goal of reducing the false positive rate and the reaction time. [9] proposes a system where different agents use different methods for attack detection (misuse or anomaly detection). [10] uses clustering at centralized nodes to perform correlation tasks. [11] describes a distributed fuzzy classifier, where distributed agents perform fuzzification of local data sources. A central fuzzy evaluation engine aggregates the agents findings and generates alerts according to pre-trained rules.

There are only a few proposals for systems which collaborate in some form to improve the performance of attack detection in the distributed agents. These systems are more closely related to our work. [12] describes an artificial immune system based DIDS where a primary IDS generates detectors (negative selection) and secondary IDS on the hosts perform detections and performance evaluation (clonal selection). [13] uses a genetic algorithm (island model) to train decision trees. Individual hosts form islands and work independently, but can exchange individuals among the different islands' gene-pools.

3   Theoretical and Methodological Foundations

In this section our proposed approach for realizing self-adaptive IDA is presented. First, we describe how classification knowledge is represented within the agents. Then, we show how this kind of knowledge can be learned given a set of training data. Finally, techniques for adapting learned knowledge to changes in the environment are introduced.

3.1   Representation of Classification Knowledge

To classify network connections we use a probabilistic approach. That is, for a D-dimensional input sample $\mathbf{x}$ containing information about a specific connection (e.g., duration of the connection or number of transmitted packets) we want to compute the posterior distribution $p(c|\mathbf{x})$, i.e., the probabilities for class membership given an input $\mathbf{x}$. To minimize the risk of classification errors we then select the class with the highest posterior probability (cf. the principle of *winner-takes-all*). According to our previous publication [14], $p(c|\mathbf{x})$ can be decomposed as follows:

$$p(c|\mathbf{x}) = \sum_{j=1}^{J} \underbrace{\frac{\int_{\mathbf{x} \in \mathcal{R}_c} p(j|\mathbf{x}) \mathrm{d}\mathbf{x} \cdot p(c)}{p(j)}}_{p(c|j)} \cdot \underbrace{\frac{p(\mathbf{x}|j)p(j)}{\sum_{j'=1}^{J} p(\mathbf{x}|j')p(j')}}_{p(j|\mathbf{x})}. \tag{1}$$

In this classification approach based on a so-called *mixture density model* $p(\mathbf{x})$, the conditional densities $p(\mathbf{x}|j)$ $(j \in \{1, \ldots, J\})$ are the components of the model, $p(j)$ is a multinomial distribution with parameters π_j (the mixing coefficients or rule "weights"), the $p(c|j)$ are multinomial conditional distributions with parameters $\xi_{j,c}$, and $\mathcal{R}_c$ is the (not necessarily connected) region of the input space associated with class c. That is, we have a classifier (rule set) consisting of J *rules*, where each rule j is described by a distribution $p(j|\mathbf{x})$ (which we call the *rule premise*) and a distribution $p(c|j)$ (which we call the *rule conclusion*). We can state that the former can be trained in an unsupervised way while class labels for patterns are needed for the latter. For a particular sample $\mathbf{x}'$, the values $p(j|\mathbf{x}')$ are called responsibilities (i.e., of the component for the sample).

Which kind of density functions can we use for the components? Basically, our D-dimensional input samples $\mathbf{x}$ describing network connections may have D_{cont} continuous (i.e., real-valued) dimensions and $D_{\mathrm{cat}} = D - D_{\mathrm{cont}}$ categorical ones. Without loss of generality we arrange these dimensions such that

$$\mathbf{x} = (\underbrace{x_1, \ldots, x_{D_{\mathrm{cont}}}}_{\text{continuous}}, \underbrace{\mathbf{x}_{D_{\mathrm{cont}}+1}, \ldots, \mathbf{x}_D}_{\text{categorical}}).$$

Note that we italicize x when we refer to single dimensions. The continuous part of this vector $\mathbf{x}^{\mathrm{cont}} = (x_1, \ldots, x_{D_{\mathrm{cont}}})$ with $x_d \in \mathbb{R}$ for all $d \in \{1, \ldots, D_{\mathrm{cont}}\}$ is modeled with a multivariate *normal* distribution with center $\boldsymbol{\mu}$ and covariance matrix $\boldsymbol{\Sigma}$, i.e.,

$$\mathcal{N}(\mathbf{x}^{\mathrm{cont}}|\boldsymbol{\mu}, \boldsymbol{\Sigma}) = \frac{1}{(2\pi)^{\frac{D_{\mathrm{cont}}}{2}} |\boldsymbol{\Sigma}|^{\frac{1}{2}}} \exp\left(-0.5 \left(\Delta_{\boldsymbol{\Sigma}}(\mathbf{x}^{\mathrm{cont}}, \boldsymbol{\mu})\right)^2\right) \tag{2}$$

with the distance measure (matrix norm) $\Delta_M(v_1, v_2)$ given by $\Delta_M(v_1, v_2) = \sqrt{(v_1 - v_2)^T M^{-1}(v_1 - v_2)}$. Δ_M defines the *Mahalanobis distance* of vectors $v_1, v_2 \in \mathbb{R}^{D_{cont}}$ based on a $D_{cont} \times D_{cont}$ covariance matrix M.

For categorical dimensions we must extend our approach presented in [14] by means of multinomial distributions. We use a 1-of-K_d coding scheme where K_d is the number of possible categories of attribute x_d ($d \in \{D_{cont+1}, \ldots, D\}$). The value of such an attribute is represented by a vector $x_d = (x_{d_1}, \ldots, x_{d_{K_d}})$ with $x_{d_k} = 1$ if x_d belongs to category k and $x_{d_k} = 0$ otherwise. Categorical dimensions are modeled by means of *multinomial* distributions. That is, for an attribute $x_d \in \{x_{D_{cont+1}}, \ldots, x_D\}$ we use

$$\mathcal{M}(x_d | \delta_d) = \prod_{k=1}^{K_d} \delta_k^{x_{d_k}} \tag{3}$$

with a parameter vector $\delta_d = (\delta_{d_1}, \ldots, \delta_{K_d})$ and the restrictions $\delta_{d_k} \geq 0$ and $\sum_{k=1}^{K_d} \delta_{d_k} = 1$.

We assume that the categorical dimensions are mutually independent and that there are no dependencies between the categorical and the continuous dimensions. Thus, the component densities $p(\mathbf{x}|j)$ are defined by

$$p(\mathbf{x}|j) = \mathcal{N}(\mathbf{x}^{cont}|\mu_j, \Sigma_j) \prod_{d=D_{cont}+1}^{D} \mathcal{M}(x_d | \delta_{j_d}). \tag{4}$$

3.2 Knowledge Acquisition Using Sample Data

How can the various parameters of the classifier be determined? For a given training set X with N input samples $\mathbf{x}_n$ and corresponding target classes it is assumed that the $\mathbf{x}_n$ are independent and identically distributed. First, the parameters of $p(\mathbf{x})$ are computed in an unsupervised manner. Let θ be the overall set of model parameters consisting of all μ_j, Σ_j, δ_{j_d}, and π_j. Then, the *likelihood function* of the parameters θ given the data X is defined by

$$p(X|\theta) = \prod_{n=1}^{N} p(\mathbf{x}_n|\theta). \tag{5}$$

We are searching the parameter setting that maximizes this function. In the case of a mixture density model it is not possible to evolve a closed formula for the optimization. However, by introducing the concept of *latent* (i.e., unobserved) variables, iterative methods can be used. For each sample $\mathbf{x}_n$ one of the J components is "responsible". To describe the "assignment" of samples to components, an additional latent random variable $\mathbf{z}_n$ is introduced for each sample. Z denotes the set of all latent variables.

In this work we perform model parameter estimation by means of a technique called variational Bayesian inference (VI) which realizes the Bayesian idea of regarding the model parameters $\boldsymbol{\theta}$ as random variables whose distributions must be trained. This approach has two important advantages over other methods. First, the estimation process is more robust, i.e., it avoids "collapsing" components, so-called singularities whose variance in one or more dimensions vanishes. Second, VI optimizes the number of components by its own. For a more detailed discussion on Bayesian inference, and, particularly, VI see [15]. For the model described in the previous section we need the joint distribution of all random variables (i.e., observations, latent variables and model parameters) which can be decomposed into

$$p(\boldsymbol{X}, \boldsymbol{Z}, \boldsymbol{\pi}, \boldsymbol{\mu}, \boldsymbol{\Lambda}, \boldsymbol{\delta}) = p(\boldsymbol{X}|\boldsymbol{Z}, \boldsymbol{\mu}, \boldsymbol{\Lambda}, \boldsymbol{\delta})p(\boldsymbol{Z}|\boldsymbol{\pi})p(\boldsymbol{\pi})p(\boldsymbol{\mu}|\boldsymbol{\Lambda})p(\boldsymbol{\Lambda})\prod_{d=D_{\mathrm{cont}}+1}^{D} p(\boldsymbol{\delta}_d). \quad (6)$$

where $\boldsymbol{\pi} = \{\pi_j\}, \boldsymbol{\mu} = \{\boldsymbol{\mu}_j\}, \boldsymbol{\Lambda} = \{\boldsymbol{\Lambda}_j\}$, and $\boldsymbol{\delta}_d = \{\boldsymbol{\delta}_{j_d}\}$. Note that for convenience we are using precision matrices $\boldsymbol{\Lambda}_j$ which are the inverses of the covariance matrices (i.e., $\boldsymbol{\Lambda}_j = \boldsymbol{\Sigma}_j^{-1}$). Unfortunately, this approach comes with an infeasible computational effort, and, thus, an approximation must be used. Therefore, it is assumed that the joint distribution of latent variables and model parameters p can be approximated by a function q that can be factorized as follows:

$$q(\boldsymbol{Z}, \boldsymbol{\pi}, \boldsymbol{\mu}, \boldsymbol{\Lambda}, \boldsymbol{\delta}) = q(\boldsymbol{Z})q(\boldsymbol{\pi})\prod_{j=1}^{J} q(\boldsymbol{\mu}_j, \boldsymbol{\Lambda}_j)\prod_{d=D_{\mathrm{cont}}+1}^{D} q(\boldsymbol{\delta}_{j_d}). \quad (7)$$

The distributions of the model parameters on the right hand side are called prior distributions and for an efficient computation their functional form must be chosen in a special way (so called *conjugate* prior distributions, cf. [15]). For the parameters $\boldsymbol{\mu}_j$ and $\boldsymbol{\Sigma}_j$, a Gauss-Wishart distribution must be used as prior distribution [15], i.e.,

$$q(\boldsymbol{\mu}_j, \boldsymbol{\Lambda}_j) = \mathcal{N}(\boldsymbol{\mu}_j|\boldsymbol{m}_j, (\beta_j\boldsymbol{\Lambda}_j)^{-1})\mathcal{W}(\boldsymbol{\Lambda}_j|\boldsymbol{W}_j, \nu_j) \quad (8)$$

where $\boldsymbol{m}_j, \beta_j, \boldsymbol{W}_j$, and ν_j are the parameters of the distribution that are determined during training (see below). The parameters $\boldsymbol{\pi}$ and $\boldsymbol{\delta}_{j_d}$ are assumed to be multinomially distributed and, thus, Dirichlet priors must be used, i.e.,

$$q(\boldsymbol{\pi}) = \mathrm{Dir}(\boldsymbol{\pi}|\boldsymbol{\alpha}) \quad \text{and} \quad q(\boldsymbol{\delta}_{j_d}) = \mathrm{Dir}(\boldsymbol{\delta}_{j_d}|\boldsymbol{\epsilon}_{j_d}). \quad (9)$$

The corresponding parameters $\boldsymbol{\alpha}$ and $\boldsymbol{\epsilon}_{j_d}$ are also infered during training. The VI is conducted iteratively by alternating between two steps. In the first step, the responsibilities $\gamma_{n,j}$ of components j for patterns $\mathbf{x}_n$ are evaluated:

$$\gamma_{n,j} = \frac{\rho_{n,j}}{\sum_{j'=1}^{J} \rho_{n,j'}}, \quad (10)$$

where

$$\ln \rho_{n,j} = \mathbb{E}[\ln \pi_j] + \frac{1}{2}\mathbb{E}[\ln |\boldsymbol{\Lambda}_j|] - \frac{D_{\mathrm{cont}}}{2}\ln(2\pi)$$

$$- \frac{1}{2}\mathbb{E}_{\boldsymbol{\mu}_j, \boldsymbol{\Lambda}_j}[(\mathbf{x}_n^{\mathrm{cont}} - \boldsymbol{\mu}_j)^T \boldsymbol{\Lambda}_j(\mathbf{x}_n^{\mathrm{cont}} - \boldsymbol{\mu}_j)] + \sum_{d=D_{\mathrm{cont}}+1}^{D}\sum_{k=1}^{K_d} x_{ndk}\mathbb{E}[\ln \delta_{jd_k}]$$

with

$$\mathbb{E}[\ln \pi_j] = \psi(\alpha_j) - \psi\left(\sum_{j=1}^{J} \alpha_j\right), \quad \mathbb{E}[\ln \delta_{jd_k}] = \psi(\epsilon_{jd_k}) - \psi\left(\sum_{k=1}^{K_d} \epsilon_{jd_k}\right),$$

where $\psi(\cdot)$ is the Digamma function,

$$\mathbb{E}[\ln |\Lambda_j|] = \sum_{i=1}^{D_{\text{cont}}} \psi\left(\frac{\nu_j + 1 - i}{2}\right) + D_{\text{cont}} \ln 2 + \ln |W_j|,$$

and

$$\mathbb{E}_{\mu_j, \Lambda_j}[(\mathbf{x}_n^{\text{cont}} - \mu_j)^T \Lambda_j (\mathbf{x}_n^{\text{cont}} - \mu_j)] = \frac{D_{\text{cont}}}{\beta_j} + \nu_j (\mathbf{x}_n^{\text{cont}} - m_j)^T W_j (\mathbf{x}_n^{\text{cont}} - m_j).$$

In the second step, the parameters of the prior distributions $q(\cdot)$ are adapted. With $N_j = \sum_{n=1}^{N} \gamma_{n,j}$ being the "effective" number of samples generated by component j, $N_{jd_k} = \sum_{n=1}^{N} \gamma_{n,j} x_{d_k}$ the "effective" number of samples belonging to category k in dimension d generated by component j and the statistics

$$\bar{\mathbf{x}}_j = \frac{1}{N_j} \sum_{n=1}^{N} \gamma_{n,j} \mathbf{x}_n^{\text{cont}}, \qquad S_j = \frac{1}{N_j} \sum_{n=1}^{N} \gamma_{n,j} (\mathbf{x}_n^{\text{cont}} - \bar{\mathbf{x}}_j)(\mathbf{x}_n^{\text{cont}} - \bar{\mathbf{x}}_j)^T$$

the update formulas are given by

$$\alpha_j = \alpha_0 + N_j, \qquad \beta_j = \beta_0 + N_j, \qquad \nu_j = \nu_0 + N_j,$$

$$\epsilon_{jd_k} = \epsilon_0 + N_{jd_k}, \qquad m_j = \frac{1}{\beta_j}(\beta_0 m_0 + N_j \bar{\mathbf{x}}_j)$$

and

$$W_j^{-1} = W_0^{-1} + N_j S_j + \frac{\beta_0 N_j}{\beta_0 + N_j}(\bar{\mathbf{x}}_j - m_0)(\bar{\mathbf{x}}_j - m_0)^T.$$

In the formulas we see some parameters indexed with 0, namely α_0, β_0, ϵ_0, m_0, ν_0, and W_0. These parameters are so-called prior parameters of the VI, which can be used to influence the behavior of the algorithm in a desired way, e.g., to avoid singularities and to cope with sparse data. The values of these parameters represent prior knowledge that can be set depending on the data set or on the specific application.

The VI algorithm is also able to estimate an appropriate number of components for a dataset. The "effective" number of samples N_j for which a component is responsible can be used as a decision criterion. The higher this number, the more "valuable" is the respective component. If a component is not valuable enough (a test criterion is realized with a threshold), it is simply deleted from the model. That is, the VI training approach must be started with a number of components that must be higher than the number that is expected to be required. The training is performed until a given stopping criterion is met (e.g., no or only slight improvements of the likelihood or a fixed number of steps). Point estimates of the model parameters are then obtained by calculating the expected value of the trained distributions.

At this point, we have found parameter estimates for the rule premises ($p(j|\mathbf{x})$, cf. Eq. (1)) in an *unsupervised* manner. Now, we still need the parameters $\xi_{j,c}$ of the rule conclusions $p(c|j)$. These can be obtained in a second, *supervised* step. With I_c we denote the index set of all samples from the overall training set $\mathbf{X}$ for which c is the assigned target class. Then, with $p(j|c) = \int_{\mathbf{x}\in\mathcal{R}_c} p(j|\mathbf{x})d\mathbf{x}$ where $\mathcal{R}_c$ is the region of the input space associated with class c, we get the maximum likelihood estimates

$$\xi_{j,c} = \frac{1}{N_j} \sum_{n\in I_c} \gamma_{n,j}. \tag{11}$$

This supervised step can also be realized in a slightly different way if labeled data are not available: After the unsupervised step, the components (i.e., rule premises) may be labeled by a human domain expert.

3.3   Knowledge Adaptation Based on Novelty-Awareness

In a changing environment agents must be able to detect the need for generating new rules and to handle this situation appropriately. In the case of an IDA, new knowledge is required if events are observed that are not covered by the current set of classification rules. This can either be due to malicious actions such as an hitherto unknown attack taking place or legitimate actions that deviate from the learned profile (e.g., a newly installed application).

First, we will describe our novel approach for detecting the need for new knowledge (i.e., novelty detection). Here, we only use the continuous part $\mathbf{x}^{\text{cont}}$ as an indicator for novelty. The key measure for our technique is the Mahalanobis distance Δ. We exploit the fact that the squared Mahalanobis distances $\Delta_j^2(\mathbf{x}^{\text{cont}}, \boldsymbol{\mu}_j)$ of samples $\mathbf{x}^{\text{cont}}$ generated by a Gaussian component j to the corresponding center $\boldsymbol{\mu}_j$ are approximately χ^2-distributed with D_{cont} degrees of freedom. Knowing the distribution of the Mahalanobis distances, we can define a hyper-ellipsoid around each center $\boldsymbol{\mu}_j$ such that we can expect that a certain percentage κ of the samples produced by the process which is modeled by component j lies within that hyper-ellipsoid. The radius ρ of these hyper-ellipsoids can be determined by means of the inverted cumulative χ^2 distribution. Based on these hyper-ellipsoids we define a novelty status s_{nov} of the overall classifier that can be regarded as the degree of "satisfaction" with respect to the currently observed situation. This status is updated with every new observation. It is rewarded if the observation is inside the hyper-ellipsoid and penalized otherwise. If the ratio of penalty to reward is equal to the ratio of "inside samples" to "outside samples", there is an equilibrium of penalties and rewards and s_{nov} oscillates around its initial value. In this case, our classifier fits the observed data. If, however, we observe more than $1 - \kappa$ percent outside samples (i.e., due to a new process that is not yet covered by the classifier such as a new kind of attack), s_{nov} is penalized more often and, thus, decreases. If it falls below a user-defined threshold τ, novelty is detected.

To compensate the effect of overlapping components we additionally scale the rewards and penalties with the component responsibilities (cf. Eq. 10). Thus, our novelty detection algorithm works as follows:

Novelty Detection:

1. *Set the percentage κ of samples that are expected to be inside the hyperellipsoid (e.g., $\kappa := 0.9$) and penalty ν_{pen} and reward ν_{rew} values with the correct ratio (e.g., $\nu_{rew} := 0.1$, $\nu_{pen} := \frac{\kappa}{1-\kappa} \cdot \nu_{rew}$).*
2. *Determine the set J_{in} of rules for which the sample $\mathbf{x}^{cont}$ is inside the hyperellipsoid and the set J_{out} of the remaining rules by comparing the squared Mahalanobis distance of $\mathbf{x}^{cont}$ to the centers $\boldsymbol{\mu}_j$ to a threshold ρ:*

$$J_{in} := \{j | \Delta_j^2(\mathbf{x}^{cont}, \boldsymbol{\mu}_j) \leq \rho\} \qquad J_{out} := \{j | \Delta_j^2(\mathbf{x}^{cont}, \boldsymbol{\mu}_j) > \rho\}.$$

   The threshold ρ is obtained by evaluating the inverse cumulative χ^2-distribution for the value κ.
3. *Compute an update value for the overall novelty status of the classifier by scaling the rewards and penalties with the corresponding responsibilities:*

$$\Delta_{nov}(\mathbf{x}^{cont}) := \eta \cdot \left(\sum_{j \in J_{in}} \gamma_{n,j} \cdot \nu_{rew} - \sum_{j \in J_{out}} \gamma_{n,j} \cdot \nu_{pen} \right)$$

   with η being the step size controlling the reaction time.
4. *The new novelty status is then*

$$s_{nov} := s_{nov} + \Delta_{nov}(\mathbf{x}^{cont})$$

   where s_{nov} must be initialized appropriately (e.g., with $s_{nov} := 1$).
5. *If s_{nov} sinks below a given threshold τ (e.g., $\tau := 0.2$), there is a need to integrate one or several new rules into the classifier.*

The algorithm can be parametrized to show different behavior, i.e., if new processes are expected to emerge distant to existing ones and the detection delay should be short, larger values for κ (e.g., $\kappa = 0.95$) should be used. A more deliberate behavior can be achieved with smaller values ($\kappa = 0.7$). It is also possible to use multiple instances with different parameterizations in parallel.

Whenever novelty is stated, the rule set must be adapted accordingly by adding new rules. Basically, we use the VI technique on a sliding window of recent samples to find new rule premises. To avoid changes of the already existing premises, the centers and covariance matrices of existing components are fixed and only those of new components are adapted. The mixture coefficients can either be re-estimated based on the sliding window or set to identical values. A rule conclusion, i.e., an estimate of the parameters of the distribution $p(c|j)$ for a new component j, can then be obtained in various ways:

1. Application experts (e.g., system administrators) can be asked to label a set of recently observed samples (e.g., measured within a sliding window). These labels are then used to determine values for the parameters $\xi_{j,c}$.
2. Application experts can be asked to label a new rule j, i.e., to assign it uniquely to one of the classes.
3. In the case of rule exchange between IDA, certain rules, and in particular their conclusions, may be taken over from other IDA.

Altogether, we can state that the adaptation of rule premises can be done in an unsupervised way, i.e., autonomously by the agents themselves. For the rule conclusions we need application experts in some application scenarios, but their effort can be kept as low as possible if rules are taken over from other agents whenever possible and experts are asked to label rules instead of a (often large) number of samples which can be done much more efficiently.

4   Experiments

To analyze the performance of our proposed techniques we use parts of the well-known DARPA intrusion detection evaluation data set [16] that consists of several weeks of labeled network data (i.e., legitimate normal network traffic interleaved with various attacks) which was generated within a simulated environment. The network architecture as well as the generated network traffic have been designed to be similar to that of an Air Force base. We are aware of the various critique of the DARPA data (e.g. [17]). In order to achieve fair and realistic results, we carefully analyzed all known deficiencies and omitted features that could bias detector performance.

We used the TCP/IP network dump as input data for an agent. At the sensor layer TCP connections are reassembled and statistical information (i.e., events) are extracted and handed over to the detection layer. Each event consists of features that are typically used for intrusion detection, i.e., two categorical dimensions (source and destination port) and ten continuous dimensions (e.g., duration, number of transmitted packets, entropy of the exchanged information). We removed all attack connections from the first week of the DARPA data set and used the result to train an initial detection model for the agent that describes the expected normal network traffic. The agent is equipped with two instances of our proposed novelty detection technique (one parametrized with $\kappa = 0.97, \eta = 0.05$ to detect distant and one with $\kappa = 0.80, \eta = 0.1$ to detect close new processes) and it is able to perform self-adaptation. When a new rule premise is generated, a simulated human expert is asked to provide a conclusion (which is calculated here using the labeled connections). We confront the agent with weeks 2 to 5 (attacks with less than 20 connections were left out). After every week, we reset the agent to its initial model to prevent influences between the weeks.

Table 1 (left) shows the classification rate (CR), missing alert rate (MA), false alert rate (FA), the total number of connections (i.e., events), and the number of newly generated rules for week 2. First, note that obviously the normal traffic of week 2 differs from week 1 as two additional rules are generated. The attacks *back* and *ipsweep* are successfully detected with good classification rates. *Guest* and *portsweep* only consist of a few connections and, thus, the delay until a new rule is generated significantly reduces the classification rate. Interestingly, *ipsweep* shows a high rate of false alerts. A closer inspection of the misclassified connections showed, however, that these connections are suspicious (i.e., they are directed at closed ports and consist only of two packets) and should definitely be reported to a system administrator as they indicate an erroneous program configuration.

Table 1 (right) shows the results for week 3. The normal traffic significantly differs from week 1 as the agent learned 18 new rules. All attacks are successfully detected. Again, *portsweep* being a short attack results in a lower classification rate due to the detection delay.

Table 1. Classification Results for Week 2 (Left) and Week 3 (Right)

Type	CR	MA	FA	events	rules
Normal	n/a	n/a	n/a	182 932	2
Back	95.5%	4.6%	1.4%	983	3
Guest	74.0%	26.0%	0.0%	50	1
Ipsweep	89.9%	10.1%	72.1%	855	2
Portsweep	63.6%	36.4%	8.3%	99	4

Type	CR	MA	FA	events	rules
Normal	n/a	n/a	n/a	54 893	18
Back	92.1%	7.9%	0.3%	999	3
Neptune	100%	0.0%	0.4%	185 652	1
Nmap	95.9%	4.1%	9.1%	941	1
Portsweep	70.0%	30.0%	5.6%	100	4

Table 2. Classification Results for Week 4 (Left) and Week 5 (Right)

Type	CR	MA	FA	events	rules
Normal	n/a	n/a	n/a	49 159	10
Neptune	98.9%	1.1%	0.2%	798	1
Portsweep	98.4%	1.6%	5.7%	1 971	3
Satan	16.7%	83.3%	2.4%	4 003	2
Warezclient	72.8%	27.2%	0.2%	419	2

Type	CR	MA	FA	events	rules
Normal	n/a	n/a	n/a	44 130	11
Neptune	100%	0.0%	0.4%	419 832	1
Portsweep	96.4%	3.6%	2.9%	2 238	7
Satan	5.8%	94.1%	1.9%	204	1

The results for week 4 are outlined in Table 2 (left). Obviously, the attack *satan* is very hard to detect for our agent. A closer inspection showed, that the first of the 10 newly generated rules for normal traffic covers a major part of all *satan* connections. We analyzed the events that resulted in the generation of this rule and, again, found a number of unsuccessful connection attempts. However, as they are labeled as being normal connections our simulated human expert provides a "normal" conclusion for the rule. A real human expert would certainly provide a different conclusion for these suspicious connections.

Neptune and *portsweep* are very well detected in week 5 (cf. Table 2, right). Again, such as in week 4, one of the new rules for normal traffic covers most of the *satan* connections.

These experiments showed very promising results of our proposed techniques. Our initial model was trained using only normal traffic but for all attacks corresponding rule premises were generated and for nearly all attacks good classification results were obtained. The classification rates of the *satan* attack suffered from a number of unsuccessful connection attempts contained in the normal traffic that led to the creation of corresponding normal rules. Thus, these misclassifications can be regarded as an artifact caused by our expert simulation.

5   Conclusion and Outlook

In this work we laid the methodological basis for IDA that recognize novel kinds of attacks, react accordingly by creating new rules, and (in the future) collaborate by exchanging these locally learned rules. The self-adaptation of the IDA is performed in a very efficient manner that reduces the need for a human application expert to a minimum: System administrators are confronted with rule premises for which appropriate conclusions must be found. Thus, we try to avoid situations where system administrators must analyze huge amount of alerts to build new rules. We investigated how these techniques perform on some well-known benchmark intrusion data. In the future, we will combine the classifiers presented here with conventional intrusion detection systems such as Snort [18] to improve the classification rates and we will develop DIDS based on OC principles. We will also consider categorical input attributes of a classifier in our novelty-awareness techniques (detection and reaction) and improve the temporal behavior of these techniques.

It is obvious that the proposed novelty-awareness techniques may also be used in other applications to support intelligent technical systems (e.g., in the field of OC) in their task to resolve problems with knowledge deficits in a (partly or completely) self-organizing way. Thus, novelty detection and reaction techniques will become a fundamental OC principle. We will use the techniques for knowledge exchange in intelligent distributed systems, too. This kind of collective intelligence is biologically inspired in the sense that these systems follow the human archetype: Humans not only learn by exchanging information (e.g., observed facts) but also by teaching each other learned knowledge (e.g., rules) and experience gained with the application of this knowledge.

Acknowledgment

This work was supported by the German Research Foundation (DFG) under grants SI 674/3-2 and SI 674/3-3 (priority program Organic Computing).

References

1. Müller-Schloer, C.: Organic computing – on the feasibility of controlled emergence. In: IEEE/ACM/IFIP Int. Conf. on Hardware/Software Codesign and System Synthesis (CODES+ISSS 2004), Stockholm, Sweden, pp. 2–5 (2004)
2. Würtz, R.P. (ed.): Organic Computing. Understanding Complex Systems. Springer, Heidelberg (2008)
3. Buchtala, O., Grass, W., Hofmann, A., Sick, B.: A fusion-based intrusion detection architecture with organic behavior. In: The first CRIS Int. Workshop on Critical Information Infrastructures (CIIW), Linköping, pp. 47–56 (2005)
4. Fisch, D., Hofmann, A., Hornik, V., Dedinski, I., Sick, B.: A framework for large-scale simulation of collaborative intrusion detection. In: IEEE Conf. on Soft Computing in Industrial Applications (SMCia/ 2008), Muroran, Japan, pp. 125–130 (2008)

5. Hofmann, A., Sick, B.: On-line intrusion alert aggregation with generative data stream modeling. IEEE Tr. on Dependable and Secure Computing (2010) (status: accepted), http://doi.ieeecomputersociety.org/10.1109/TDSC.2009.36

6. Axelsson, S.: Intrusion detection systems: A survey and taxonomy. Technical Report 99-15, Chalmers University of Technology, Department of Computer Engineering (2000)

7. Snapp, S.R., Brentano, J., Dias, G.V., Goan, T.L., Heberlein, L.T., Ho, C.L., Levitt, K.N., Mukherjee, B., Smaha, S.E., Grance, T., Teal, D.M., Mansur, D.: DIDS (distributed intrusion detection system) – motivation, architecture, and an early prototype. In: Proc. of the 15th IEEE National Computer Security Conf., Baltimore, MD, pp. 167–176 (1992)

8. Yegneswaran, V., Barford, P., Jha, S.: Global intrusion detection in the domino overlay system. In: Proc. of the Network and Distributed System Security Symp., NDSS 2004, San Diego, CA (2004)

9. Chatzigiannakis, V., Androulidakis, G., Grammatikou, M., Maglaris, B.: A distributed intrusion detection prototype using security agents. In: Proc. of the 6th Int. Conf., on Software Engineering, Artificial Intelligence, Networking and Parallel and Distributed Computing, Beijing, China, pp. 238–245 (2004)

10. Zhang, Y.F., Xiong, Z.Y., Wang, X.Q.: Distributed intrusion detection based on clustering. In: Proc. of 2005 Int. Conf. on Machine Learning and Cybernetics, Guangzhou, China, vol. 4, pp. 2379–2383 (2005)

11. Dickerson, J.E., Juslin, J., Koukousoula, O., Dickerson, J.A.: Fuzzy intrusion detection. In: Proc. IFSA World Congress and 20th North American Fuzzy Information Processing Society (NAFIPS) Int. Conf., Vancouver, BC, pp. 1506–1510 (2001)

12. Kim, J., Bentley, P.: The artificial immune model for network intrusion detection. In: 7th European Conf. on Intelligent Techniques and Soft Computing (EUFIT 1999), Aachen, Germany (1999)

13. Folino, G., Pizzuti, C., Spezzano, G.: Gp ensemble for distributed intrusion detection systems. In: Proc. of the 3rd Int. Conf. on Advances in Pattern Recognition, Bath, U.K, pp. 54–62 (2005)

14. Fisch, D., Sick, B.: Training of radial basis function classifiers with resilient propagation and variational Bayesian inference. In: Proc. of the Int. Joint Conf. on Neural Networks (IJCNN 2009), Atlanta, GA, pp. 838–847 (2009)

15. Bishop, C.M.: Pattern Recognition and Machine Learning. Springer, New York (2006)

16. Lippmann, R.P., Fried, D.J., Graf, I., Haines, J.W., Kendall, K.R., McClung, D., Weber, D., Webster, S.E., Wyschogrod, D., Cunningham, R.K., Zissman, M.A.: Evaluating intrusion detection systems: the 1998 DARPA off-line intrusion detection evaluation. In: DARPA Information Survivability Conf. and Exposition (DISCEX), Hilton Head, SC, vol. 2, pp. 12–26 (2000)

17. McHugh, J.: Testing intrusion detection systems: a critique of the 1998 and 1999 DARPA intrusion detection system evaluations as performed by Lincoln laboratory. ACM Tr. on Information and System Security 3(4), 262–294 (2000)

18. Roesch, M.: Snort – lightweight intrusion detection for networks. In: LISA 1999: Proc. of the 13th USENIX Conf. on System Administration, Berkeley, CA, pp. 229–238 (1999)

Evolutionary-Computation Based Risk Assessment of Aircraft Landing Sequencing Algorithms

Wenjing Zhao[1], Jiangjun Tang[1], Sameer Alam[1], Axel Bender[2],
and Hussein A. Abbass[1]

[1] UNSW@ADFA, Canberra, Australia
{w.zhao,j.tang}@student.adfa.edu.au, h.abbass@adfa.edu.au
[2] DSTO, Edinburgh, Australia
axel.bender@dsto.defence.gov.au

Abstract. Usually, Evolutionary Computation (EC) is used for optimisation and machine learning tasks. Recently, a novel use of EC has been proposed – Multiobjective Evolutionary Based Risk Assessment (MEBRA). MEBRA characterises the problem space associated with good and inferior performance of computational algorithms. Problem instances are represented ("scenario Representation") and evolved ("scenario Generation") in order to evaluate algorithms ("scenario Evaluation"). The objective functions aim at maximising or minimising the success rate of an algorithm. In the "scenario Mining" step, MEBRA identifies the patterns common in problem instances when an algorithm performs best in order to understand when to use it, and in instances when it performs worst in order to understand when not to use it.

So far, MEBRA has only been applied to a limited number of problems. Here we demonstrate its viability to efficiently detect hot spots in an algorithm's problem space. In particular, we apply the basic MEBRA rationale in the area of Air Traffic Management (ATM). We examine two widely used algorithms for Aircraft Landing Sequencing: First Come First Served (FCFS) and Constrained Position Shifting (CPS). Through the use of three different problem ("scenario") representations, we identify those patterns in ATM problems that signal instances when CPS performs better than FCFS, and those when it performs worse. We show that scenario representation affects the quality of MEBRA outputs. In particular, we find that the variable-length chromosome representation of aircraft scheduling sequence scenarios converges fast and finds all relevant risk patterns associated with the use of FCFS and CPS.

Keywords: Algorithms' Behavior, Aircraft Sequencing, Evolutionary Computation.

1   Introduction

Existing demands on the air traffic system routinely exceed the capacity of airports. This leads to air-traffic imposed ground and airborne delays of aircraft. For the majority of U.S. and European airports such delays are estimated to be over 15 minutes per aircraft [4] costing airlines billions of dollars per year [10]. Thus airports are proving to be serious bottlenecks in handling rising air traffic densities. Since constructing

M. Hinchey et al. (Eds.): DIPES/BICC 2010, IFIP AICT 329, pp. 254–265, 2010.
© IFIP International Federation for Information Processing 2010

new airports or additional runways is not a near-term solution, researchers investigate various approaches as how to make the most efficient use of the available runways given safety constraints. Amongst these approaches is the effective scheduling of aircraft landings, which can significantly improve runway throughput capacity as well as safety and efficiency of airports.

It has been shown in the literature that the problem of finding optimal landing sequences – when the constraints of spacing between arrivals depend on the aircraft type as is the case in real-world applications – is NP-hard [6]. Thus it is unlikely that efficient optimisation algorithms exist [6]. Even if there was an accurate schedule optimiser, it would probably lack the speed to respond quickly to operational demands in the high-paced work environment of air traffic controllers (ATC). In the real world, therefore, fast and frugal heuristics are more useful than sophisticated but slow algorithms.

The most commonly used heuristics-based algorithm that generates efficient aircraft landing sequences is First Come First Served (FCFS). The basis of this method is the Estimated Time of Arrival (ETA) of aircraft at the runway and the minimum time separation between aircraft [7]. In FCFS, the aircraft land in order of their scheduled arrival times. ATC add suitable separation times to ensure appropriate spacing between aircraft. FCFS is straightforward and favoured by airlines for its fairness and by ATC for its simplicity that puts little demands on ATC workloads. However, its drawback is that it may lead to reduced runway throughput due to unnecessary spacing requirements [8].

Another common approach is Constrained Position Shifting (CPS) [2] in which an aircraft can be moved forward or backward in the FCFS schedule by a specified maximum number of positions. This approach provides ATC with additional flexibility and helps pilots to better predict landing times and positions [8]. However, it also increases the controller's workload in terms of increased ATC-Pilot communication and controller directives.

Both FCFS and CPS thus have their advantages and disadvantages, which express themselves in variations of algorithmic performance depending on problem situation and context of use. Considering the large amount of money lost because of runway congestions, it makes economical sense to investigate in which aircraft landing sequence scenarios (ALSS) CPS performs better (or worse) than FCFS. Such an investigation will enable airports to identify and understand the risks, both negative and positive, when choosing one scheduling heuristic over another.

In this paper, we make use of the recently introduced Multiobjective Evolutionary Based Risk Assessment (MEBRA) framework [1] to identify positive and negative risks associated with the application of a particular algorithm. Rather than optimising an algorithm, MEBRA explores and evaluates the risk profiles of algorithms. These risk profiles are signatures in the problem space and associated with the performance of a computational algorithm. In its risk assessment, MEBRA employs scenario representation, scenario generation, scenario evaluation and scenario mining. Here the term "scenario" refers to a problem instance in which the computational algorithm under investigation is applied.

So far though, MEBRA has only been applied to a limited number of problems. Here we demonstrate its viability by applying it to the Air Traffic Management (ATM) problem domain. We study performance and identify risks associated with the use of FCFS and CPS in ALSS. Our paper further investigates how scenario representation impacts on algorithm evaluation. We examine three different representations: Fixed Length Chromosome, Variable Length Chromosome, and a Probabilistic Model.

At the start of our application of MEBRA to ATM, random ALSS are generated and encoded in the chromosome representation. Then complex landing sequence scenarios are evolved over many generations by applying genetic operators and using a fitness function that correlates with risk. This imposes selection pressure on the population of scenarios. ALSS that are deemed "fitter individuals" have increased likelihood to survive into the next generation. In the final "scenario Mining" step of MEBRA, the scenario population at the end of evolution is used to identify common characteristics, or "signatures", of aircraft landing sequences that contribute to schedule delays. This aids in understanding those factors that result in technical risks in the generation of landing sequences when using scheduling heuristics such as FCFS or CPS.

The rest of this paper is organised as follows. In Section 2, we describe the aircraft landing sequencing problem along with details of the FCFS and CPS algorithms. Next, we present the MEBRA framework (Section 3) and how it applies to the risk assessment of aircraft landing sequencing algorithms (Section 4). We illustrate the approach in a simple example and describe our results in Section 5. Conclusions are drawn in the final section.

2 Aircraft Landing Sequencing

The U.S Federal Aviation Administration (FAA) has established minimum spacing requirements between landing aircraft to prevent the turbulence from wake vortices [5]. If an aircraft interacts with the wake vortex of the aircraft landing in front of it, it could lose control. To prevent this risk, a minimum time separation between aircraft is mandated. This separation depends on both the size of the leading aircraft and that of the trailing aircraft. The FAA divides aircraft into three weight classes, based on the maximum take-off weight capability. These classes are:

1. *Heavy Aircraft* are capable of having a maximum takeoff weight of 255,000 lbs or more.
2. *Large Aircraft* can have more than 41,000 lbs and up to 255,000 lbs maximum takeoff weight.
3. *Small Aircraft* are incapable of carrying more than 41,000 lbs takeoff weight.

A matrix of the minimum time separations mandated by the FAA is shown in Table 1.

2.1 First Come First Served

FCFS is a prominent scheduling algorithm in Sequencing Theory [9]. It is the most straightforward method to sequence aircraft arrivals in an airport. Much of present technology has some relationship with it or is even based on it [6].

Table 1. Minimum time separation (in seconds) between landings as mandated by the FAA

Leading Aircraft	Trailing Aircraft		
	Heavy	Large	Small
Heavy	96	157	196
Large	60	69	131
Small	60	69	82

FCFS determines the aircraft landing sequence according to the order of its estimated time of arrival (ETA) at the runway. ETA is computed by the control center at the time an incoming aircraft crosses the transition airspace boundary. If the difference between the ETA of two successive aircraft violates the minimum separation time constraints, then the Scheduled Time of Arrival (STA) of the trailing aircraft is adjusted accordingly. The following numerical example illustrates this adjustment.

Given seven aircraft, A, B, C, D, E, F, G, each belonging to one of the three weight classes H (heavy), L (large) or S (small). FCFS orders these aircraft according to their ETA, see third row of Table 2. It then adds time to an ETA, when the separation time between two aircraft is smaller than the allowable minima shown in Table 1. For instance, the ETA of the small aircraft C is only 60 sec later than the ETA of the preceding large aircraft B. Thus 71 sec are added to the ETA of C to achieve a separation of 131 sec as required by the FAA (Table 1). In the example, the STA of all aircraft following C are now determined by adding the minimum separation time to the STA of the leading aircraft because all STA calculated this way happen to be later than the ETAs. The makespan (i.e. the difference between final STA and first STA) in this example is 18m59s - 07m51s = 668 sec.

FCFS scheduling establishes the landing sequence based on predicted landing times. It therefore is easy to implement and does not put significant pressure onto ATC workloads. However, it ignores information which can be used to increase runway throughput capacity.

Table 2. FCFS scheduling example

Aircraft	A	B	C	D	E	F	G
Category	L	L	S	H	L	S	H
ETA	07m51s	10m00s	11m00s	12m00s	13m00s	14m00s	15m00s
AC Order	A:1	B:2	C:3	D:4	E:5	F:6	G:7
STA	07m51s	10m00s	12m11s	13m11s	15m48s	17m59s	18m59s

2.2 Constrained Position Shifting

CPS, first proposed by Dear [3], stipulates that the ETA-based schedule can be changed slightly and that an aircraft may be moved up by a small number of positions. Neumann and Erzberger [8] investigated an enumerative technique for computing the sequence which minimises the makespan, subject to a single position shift (1-CPS) constraint. In the example of Table 2, for instance, the swap of aircraft D and E would result in a reduction of makespan by 23 sec: the STAs of E, D, F and G would be 13m20s, 14m20s, 17m36s and 18m36s, respectively. This is the basic motivation for CPS methods.

Finding the optimal ordering of a set of aircraft through CPS can be seen as a search for the lowest-cost path through a tree of possible aircraft orderings, where the cost is the sum of the time separations required between each pair of aircraft. For the CPS problem, an initial sequence of aircraft is given, along with the list of minimum separation constraints (e.g. Table 1) and the maximum possible time-shifts for each aircraft. In the final sequence shown in Table 3, each aircraft is constrained to lie within one shift from its initial position, and no aircraft must have a time of arrival earlier than permitted by the maximum allowable time shift.

Table 3. CPS scheduling example

Aircraft	A	B	C	D	E	F	G
Category	L	L	S	H	L	S	H
ETA	07m51s	10m00s	11m00s	12m00s	13m00s	14m00s	15m00s
AC Order	A:1	B:2	C:3	E:4	D:5	F:6	G:7
STA	07m51s	10m00s	12m11s	13m20s	14m20s	17m63s	18m36s

3 MEBRA – Multiobjective Evolutionary Based Risk Assessment

The objective of this paper is to demonstrate how evolutionary computation (EC) methods can be used to assess the performance of aircraft landing sequencing algorithms. The approach we take is a simplified version of the Multiobjective Evolutionary Based Risk Assessment (MEBRA) framework that is designed for the purpose of exploring and evaluating computational algorithms under risk [1]. In aircraft landing sequencing problems, risks associated with computational algorithms include production of suboptimal scheduling sequences, i.e. unnecessarily large makespans; computational complexity that results in algorithms taking too long and becoming unresponsive to operational demands; and unnecessary increases of ATC workloads. The occurrence of these risks depends on the specifics of the problem at hand; for instance in an ALSS that requires a large number of aircraft to be scheduled in a very short period of time ATC are more likely to get overloaded than in an ALSS when only a few aircraft need to be sequenced. MEBRA of algorithmic performance is thus concerned with searches on the problem space, also known as the "scenario space", rather than the solution space.

MEBRA comprises four building blocks: Scenario Representation, Scenario Generation, Scenario Evaluation, and Scenario Mining. MEBRA's *Scenario Representation* can be as simple as sampling a parameter space that captures quantitative aspects of a problem, or as complex as narratives that try to capture futuristic strategic uncertainties. During *Scenario Generation* MEBRA makes use of evolutionary computation. Problem instances are evolved over many generations while being exposed to selection pressure. This pressure makes less risky scenarios less likely to survive into the next generation and therefore is part of *Scenario Evaluation*. In this paper, we make use of the single objective version of MEBRA, called SEBRA. In the *Scenario Mining* step, MEBRA identifies risk patterns or "hot spots", i.e. conditions in scenario space under which risk eventuates. Scenario mining techniques can be as simple as descriptive statistics of the evolved scenario population or as complex as a framework that analyses dynamics and network dependencies to unveil the "rules of the game".

4 Application of MEBRA to Aircraft Landing Sequencing Algorithms

4.1 ALSS Representation

In order to capture complex patterns of aircraft landing sequences, we use three different chromosome representations: fixed-length sequence representing a problem instance, a variable-length sequence representing a pattern that is repeated in a problem instance, and a stochastic finite state machine representation representing the probability transition matrix to generate patterns. A detailed description of the three representation is as follows:

1. *Fixed-length chromosome.* In the fixed-length chromosome, each gene represents an aircraft type. The position in the chromosome corresponds to the aircraft's position in the arrival schedule according to ETA. The length of the chromosome is equal to the total number of aircraft whose landing need to be scheduled. In our experiments, the fixed-length chromosome contains 200 genes. At chromosome initialisation, ETA values are spaced with 1 sec and assigned to the aircraft sequence. We use this initialisation condition because having all aircraft arrive "at once" puts the biggest demand on the landing sequencing algorithms and thus will facilitate the search for "hot spots" in ALSS.

2. *Variable-length chromosome.* The variable-length chromosome encodes a pattern. A pattern is a partial sequence of aircraft arrivals. As with the fixed-length chromosome, each gene encodes an aircraft type. With respect to the whole aircraft arrival sequence, the partial sequence has a starting point described by a position in the arrival schedule and a length that is smaller than the total number of aircraft to be scheduled. In our experiments, the starting point is always the first position in the scheduling sequence and the pattern's length varies between 3 and 50. At the time a pattern is evaluated, it is repeated as many times as needed to generate a 200-gene sequence. For example, a pattern of length 50 would need to be repeated four times. This normalises the scale when comparing-variable length and fixed-length chromosome representations. The evolution based on the variable length representation is pushed to find those patterns that optimise the fitness function (see Subsection 4.3). A selection pressure is placed automatically to favour shorter patterns since their frequency in the 200-gene sequence increases.

3. *Stochastic Finite State Machine (SFSM) chromosome.* The SFSM chromosome contains nine genes which encode how likely it is that an aircraft type is followed by another in the schedule. The genes thus represent probabilities of the nine possible SFSM transitions. The initial generation initializes the chromosomes randomly from uniform distributions. Obviously, when the SFSM is used to generate a sequence, transition probabilities out of each node

are normalised. Moreover, it is natural that this stochastic representation would require multiple evaluations (30 in our case) of each chromosome to approximate its fitness.

4.2 ALSS Generation

In the generation of ALSS we make use of evolutionary computation (EC) techniques. In EC, a seed population of scenarios is evolved over many generations (implicit parallelism) to explore the space of possible ALSS. From generation to generation, individuals are subjected to single-point crossover and uniform mutation. Evolution ("search") proceeds to meet a given selection pressure (such as in Equation 2 below) and according to some given rules; e.g. in our experiments (Section 4.5) we apply tournament selection with elitism. Note that evolving ATM problems according to the selection pressure in Equation 2 does not ensure that we always find scenarios for which both FCFS and CPS generate optimal landing schedules. However, for most of the evolved complex scenarios in the final population this actually is the case. It is thus fair to assume that low-risk scenarios evolved with Equation 2 will have features that differ from those of the high-risk problems generated under the selection pressure of Equation 1 (below).

4.3 ALSS Evaluation

To assess both positive and negative risk of inefficiency-based delays in aircraft landing sequencing algorithms we define two fitness functions. The first one is designed to identify those situations where FCFS is inferior to CPS. Therefore, the objective of the first fitness function is to maximise the difference between the FCFS makespan and the CPS makespan. As mentioned earlier, we study worst-case situations, i.e. when all aircraft in a sequence arrive within one second of each other and are ready to be landed. The "negative-risk" objective function can be described formally as follows:

$$\text{Max } \{F = T_{FCFS} - T_{CPS}\} . \tag{1}$$

where T_X denotes the makespan of algorithm X.

As described earlier, in any ALSS the CPS method guarantees an equal or better makespan than the FCFS sequencing approach. By evolving solutions that optimise the function in Equation 1, MEBRA will evolve problem instances for which CPS considerably outperforms FCFS. While we cannot be sure that CPS is a very good algorithm to use in such evolved complex scenarios, we definitely know that FCFS performs very poorly. The evolutionary process thus finds scenario sets for which CPS results in maximum improvements to the FCFS schedule; i.e. we identify scenarios in which FCFS is particularly inefficient.

The second fitness function, the "positive-risk" objective, is to minimise the difference between the two makespans, i.e. we identify low-risk scenarios for which CPS will not result in significantly reduced makespans. Formally,

$$\text{Min } \{F = T_{FCFS} - T_{CPS}\} . \tag{2}$$

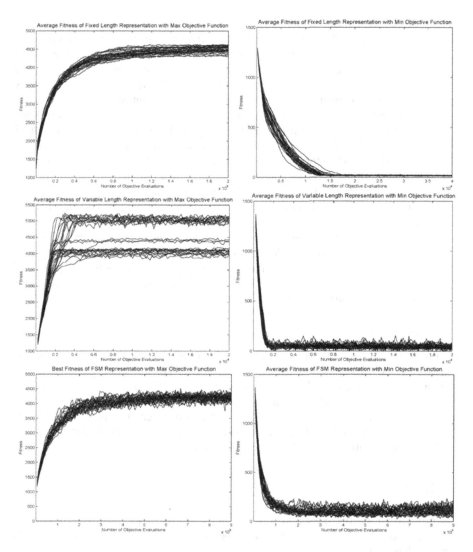

Fig. 1. The progress in fitness values as a function of the number of objective function evaluations. Figures on the left are for the negative-risk objective function while those on right are for the positive-risk objective function. The top figure depicts the evolution of a population of scenarios encoded with fixed-length chromosome representation, the middle one for the variable-length chromosome representation and the bottom one for the SFSM chromosome representation of ALSS.

4.4 ALSS Mining

To compare among the three representations, we use three two-way 2x2 comparison matrices. Each matrix captures the best-best, worst-best, worst-worst, and best-worst overlaps between the solutions found using each representation. Each cell in the matrix is the comparison result between:

1.   Fixed length v.s. Variable Length: the count of matched patterns by sliding the pattern of the variable length and counting its frequency in the fixed length. We start from the first aircraft in fixed length chromosome and slide the variable length chromosome by one aircraft position at each step. We count the number of matches between the partial sequence in fixed length is as same as the whole sequence of variable length chromosome.
2.   Fixed length v.s. SFSM: the distance of probabilities of transitions by transforming the fixed length to a SFSM using the frequency of transitions found in the fixed length chromosome. We calculate the frequency of aircraft transitions in the fixed length chromosome and translate these frequencies into the stochastic finite state machine representation. We obtain nine transition probabilities from the fixed length chromosome with the same format as the SFSM chromosome. The Euclidean distance between the two normalized probability vectors is used to calculate similarities.
3.   Variable Length v.s. SFSM: the distance of probabilities of transitions by transforming the variable length into the fixed length (by repeating the patterns) then transforming the fixed length to a SFSM using the frequency of transitions found in the 200-gene sequence. The calculations are then done in the same way illustrated in the previous step.

4.5 Experimental Setup

We ran each of the 6 SEBRA evolutions 30 times with different seeds and a population size of 200. We apply tournament selection with elitism, single-point crossover with probability 0.9 and uniform mutation with probability equal to the reciprocal of the chromosome length. For the variable length chromosome, the mutation is set to 0.02. Those parameters are chosen carefully after a number of sample runs. We allowed sufficient number of objective evaluations in each run for evolution to become stable (the best solution does not change significantly).

5   Results

The progress in the two fitness functions, "negative-risk" and "positive-risk" objectives, corresponding to each of the six experimental setups and the associated 30 seeds is plotted in Figure 1.

The following observations can be made:

1.   Three types of local optima in the negative-risk objectives can be distinguished when we use a variable-length chromosome representation of ALSS – one with a fitness value of around 5000, a second with a fitness of approximately 4400, and a third one with fitness of about 4000.
2.   Both fixed-length and SFSM chromosome representations appear to have become stuck between two of the three local optima found by the variable-length chromosome.
3.   In the variable-length chromosome representation the number of objective evaluations to convergence is an order of magnitude smaller than the evaluations needed in the other two scenario representations.

This suggests that it is more efficient to evolve pattern (as in the experiments with variable-length ALSS chromosomes) than to evolve whole scenarios.

Table 4. Count of Building Blocks Matches in Fixed-Length vs Variable-Length ALSS

		Fixed	
		best	worst
Variable	best	20196	0
	worst	0	7200

Table 5. Distance of Probabilities for Building Blocks when comparing SFSM vs Fixed-Length and vs Variable-Length ALSS

		Fixed		Variable	
		best	worst	best	worst
SFSM	best	0.718186	1.452852	0.635106	1.827628
	worst	1.898998	0.839643	1.914774	1.079916

We now address the question whether the patterns found by evolving the variable-length representation are also present in the evolved fixed-length and SFSM ALSS. Table 4 shows that the patterns which maximize the difference between FCFS and CPS ("worst"-case scenarios, as of Eq.1) and which are found by evolving variable-length ALSS can be found with high frequency in the evolved fixed-length ALSS. These patterns are not at all present in fixed-length scenarios that minimize the difference between the two makespans ("best"-case scenarios, as of Eq.2). This indicates that the variable-length patterns are some sort of building blocks in this problem and that it is more efficient to evolve building blocks directly than to evolve the solution vector as a whole.

Similar trends are found in Table 5. The normalized transition probabilities found by the fixed and variable length representations are closer to those found by the SFSM representation in corresponding experiments.

Figure-2 depicts two patterns found by evolving SFSM ALSS. Examples of high frequency patterns found by evolving the variable-length representation when looking for worst-case scenarios include: HSHSHSH, HSHSHSS, HLSHS, and SHSHSH. These patterns are not as simple as they may appear. The HSHSHSH pattern, when used as a building block will generate an HH link. Examples of building blocks found in best-case scenarios include: SLLH, LHSL, HHHH, LHHHH, and HHHSS SLLH, LHSL, HHHH, LHHHH, and HHHSS. It is easy to see why each of these patterns would give an advantage to CPS over FCFS.

In summary, we demonstrated that evolutionary computation can be a powerful framework to evaluate the performance of different algorithms. A deeper analysis of the resulting solutions can shed light on the problem patterns that determine strengths and weaknesses of an algorithm compared with another (baseline) algorithm. In the problem domain investigated in this paper, discovering these patterns allows to balance safety risks that can result from an unnecessary increase of ATC workloads and the (economic and ecological) costs that result from unnecessary delays or holdings of aircraft.

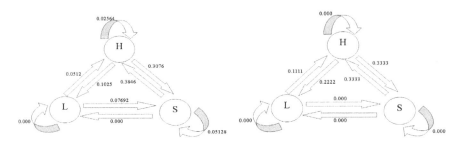

Fig. 2. Two examples of SFSM found in the case of Max objective function

6 Conclusions

For many years, Evolutionary Computation (EC) has been successfully applied to optimisation problems, although almost exclusively to evolve solutions for such problems. In this paper, we showed that EC techniques can be used in a novel way, namely to assist in the assessment of algorithmic performance. We employed the Multiobjective Evolutionary Based Risk Assessment (MEBRA) concept to evolve problem instances in which heuristic algorithms perform particularly poorly or particularly well.

MEBRA can be used as a comparative analysis technique. Through the application of clustering methods, pattern analysis and the like to the population of evolved problem instances, or scenarios, it can detect signatures, or "hot spots", in the scenario space for which an algorithm performs better or worse than a reference algorithm. Thus, MEBRA provides valuable information about when it is best to use one algorithm over another.

We applied a single-objective version of the MEBRA framework – SEBRA – to the comparison of two prevalent heuristics used in the landing sequencing of aircraft arrivals in an airport: the First Come First Served (FCFS) and Constrained Position Shifting (CPS) algorithms. We found indeed that SEBRA could identify hot spots in the problem space for which FCFS performed markedly worse than CPS. We also found patterns in the sequences of estimated time of arrival (ETA), for which FCFS performs equally well as the computationally more complex CPS. The patterns were interesting and could easily be interpreted by making use of the minimum separation time matrix.

Our results indicate that convergence and variance of SEBRA depend on the chromosome representations for the SEBRA problem instances. The fixed-length chromosome and stochastic representations were stable and converged reasonably fast. The variable-length chromosome representation converged the fastest and found all patterns of interest.

References

1. Abbass, H.A., Alam, S., Bender, A.: MEBRA: Multiobjective Evolutionary Based Risk Assessment. Computational Intelligence Magazine, 29–36 (August 2009)
2. Balakrishnan, H., Chandran, B.: Scheduling aircraft landing under constrained position shifting. In: AIAA Guidance, Navigation, and Control Conference and Exhibit (2006)

3. Dear, R.: The dynamic scheduling of aircraft in the near terminal area. Technical report, M.I.T (1976)
4. Donohue, G., Laska, W.: United States and European Airport Capacity Assessment using the GMU Macroscopic Capacity Model (MCM). In: Proc. of the 3rd USA/Europe ATM R&D Seminar, Napoli, Italy (2000)
5. FAA: Aeronautical Information Manual/Federal Aviation Regulation. McGraw-Hill, New York (2003)
6. Hu, X., Chen, W.: Genetic algorithm based on receding horizon control for arrival sequencing and scheduling. Engineering Applications of Articial Intelligence 18, 633–642 (2005)
7. Neuman, F., Erzberger, H.: Analysis of sequencing and scheduling methods for arrival traffic (1990)
8. Neuman, F., Erzberger, H.: Analysis of delay reducing and fuel saving sequencing and spacing algorithms for arrival spacing. Technical report, NASA Technical Memorandum 103880 (1991)
9. Pinedo, M.: Scheduling: theory, algorithms and systems. Prentice-Hall, New Jersey (2002)
10. Wickens, C.D.: Human Operators and Automation. In: The Future of Air Traffic Control. National Academy Press, Washington (1998)

A Collaborative Decision Support Model for Marine Safety and Security Operations*

Uwe Glässer[1], Piper Jackson[1], Ali Khalili Araghi[1],
Hans Wehn[2], and Hamed Yaghoubi Shahir[1]

[1] Software Technology Lab,
School of Computing Science, Simon Fraser University, Burnaby, BC, Canada
{glaesser,pjj,aka52,syaghoub}@cs.sfu.ca
[2] MacDonald, Dettwiler and Associates Ltd., Richmond, BC, Canada
hw@mdacorporation.com

Abstract. Collaboration and self-organization are hallmarks of many biological systems. We present the design for an intelligent decision support system that employs these characteristics: it works through a collaborative, self-organizing network of intelligent agents. Developed for the realm of Marine Safety and Security, the goal of the system is to assist in the management of a complex array of resources in both a routine and emergency role. Notably, this system must be able to handle a dynamic environment and the existence of uncertainty. The decentralized control structure of a collaborative self-organizing system reinforces its adaptiveness, robustness and scalability in critical situations.

Keywords: Coastal Surveillance, Self-Organizing System, Automated Planning, Configuration Management, Abstract State Machines.

1 Introduction

Canada and its allies have identified the vulnerability of sea lanes, their ports and harbors to a variety of threats and illegal activities. With a total length of over 243,000 kilometers (151,000 miles), Canada has the longest coastline of any country in the world [1]. Scarce surveillance and tracking capabilities make it difficult to perform large volume surveillance, keeping track of all marine traffic [2]. A collaborative research initiative by Defence R&D Canada, MDA and three academic partners addresses the design of intelligent decision support systems [3] for large volume coastal surveillance [4]. The NADIF research project [5] expands on the CanCoastWatch (CCW) project [4] by building on realistic marine safety and security scenarios studied in CCW. The aim is to facilitate complex command and control tasks of Marine Security Operation Centres (MSOC) [6] by improving situational awareness and automating routine coordination tasks. The proposed system concept integrates Adaptive Information Fusion techniques with decentralized control mechanisms for Dynamic Resource Configuration Management

* The work presented here is funded by MacDonald, Dettwiler and Associates Ltd. (MDA) and NSERC under Collaborative R&D Grant No. 342503-06.

M. Hinchey et al. (Eds.): DIPES/BICC 2010, IFIP AICT 329, pp. 266–277, 2010.

(DRCM) and task execution management. Autonomously operating agents form an intelligent decision support system through distributed collaboration and co-ordination. The target platforms for this system are dynamically reconfigurable network architectures.

Operating under uncertainty in an adverse environment, as will be explained, the system design presented here strives for resilience through adaptivity, robustness and scalability, building on concepts of collaborative self-organizing systems inspired by biological processes and mechanisms [7]:

> *What renders this approach particularly attractive from a dynamic network perspective is that global properties like adaptation, self-organization and robustness are achieved without explicitly programming them into the individual artificial agents. Yet, given large ensembles of agents, the global behavior is surprisingly adaptive and can cope with arbitrary initial conditions, unforeseen scenarios, variations in the environment or presence of deviant agents.*

Border control and emergency response services deploy a range of mobile sensor platforms with heterogeneous sensor units that cooperatively perform surveillance and rescue missions in the vast coastal areas that constitute the *littoral zone*. Platforms include satellites; airborne vehicles (SAR helicopters, patrol aircraft and UAVs); coastguard vessels(frigates and various smaller boats); and land vehicles.

We distinguish cooperative search (e.g., locating a fishing boat in distress) from non-cooperative search (detecting illegal activities, e.g., smuggling operations). A typical mission involves various tasks and subtasks deploying multiple mobile platforms with diverse capabilities: sensor capabilities, mobility capabilities, extraction and transport capabilities. Situation awareness[1] entails flexible control mechanisms to respond to dynamic changes in *internal conditions* regarding mission requirements (priorities, search areas, medical conditions, time windows) and *external conditions*, such as adverse weather conditions and fading daylight, as well as often unpredictable changes in the operational status of platforms.

The NADIF system concept comprises three main parts: a Decision Support Engine, a Configuration Management Engine, and an Information Fusion Engine. We focus here on the design of a collaborative decision support and configuration management model. Section 2 discusses background concepts. Section 3 outlines the conceptual model, and Section 4 addresses Automated Planning and Tasking. Section 5 illustrates our System Reference Model. Section 6 concludes the paper.

2 Background

This section presents background concepts relevant to the work presented here. We employ these to formulate a model that accurately captures the characteristics, functionality and requirements of the target system.

---

[1] Situation Awareness, a state in the mind of a human, is essential for decision-making activities. It concerns the perception of elements in the environment, the comprehension of their meaning, and the projection of their status in the near future [8].

2.1   Cooperative Models

A Cooperative Multi-agent System in general consists of a number of agents collaborating with each other. Agents are able to use different types of communication in order to fulfill shared goals. Within cooperative systems, there is a wide range of different system architectures with each model defined by some main characteristics.

Different models have been studied (e.g., Swarms, Coalition, Collaboration and Clusters) in [9]. Among these models, *clusters* match the requirements of our system best. In such systems different agents can be combined together to aggregate their capabilities as a group. Clustering also increases the flexibility of the system through dynamic re-organization of the agents. This is beneficial for applications which work in a changing environment. Clustering results in a more complicated structure, which can be costly to manage, but the behavior of each node can be kept simple [10].

2.2   Self-Organizing Systems

The concept of self-organization is used in diverse research areas, such as Biology, Physics and also in social sciences such as Economics. In nature it can be seen, for instance, in flocking by birds and fish. The construction of physical structures by social animals (e.g., bees or ants) is another example. Self-organization is defined as the emergence of global level pattern in a system as a result of many low-level interactions which utilize only local information [11]. The concept of biologically inspired self-organization is becoming increasingly popular in automated systems. In Swarm Robotics, many simple physical robots communicate with each other while interacting with the environment. These communications produce feedback to the system and consequently initiate emergent global behavior in the system. Such behavior is called *Swarm Intelligence* [12]. Swarm behavior can be generated from very simple rules for individual agents.

2.3   Command and Control

In our previous work [13], the DRCM (Dynamic Resource Configuration Management) architecture for the current system was introduced. The topology of the resource configuration network is based on the Command and Control (C2)

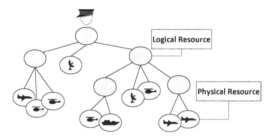

Fig. 1. Organizing Resources: Hierarchical Network Architecture

Hierarchy which is broadly used in the military domain [14]. In such a hierarchy, nodes represent different resources in the network (e.g., platforms, sensors, services and units) and the edges connecting nodes can be seen as relationships (command and control from parent nodes) or connectivity (e.g., link, TCP/IP, radio). In Fig. 1, missions are introduced into the system through the commander. As illustrated, the C2 hierarchy has a decentralized control structure where a parent node (commander) assigns tasks to a group of subordinate nodes and subsequently, local decisions are made in the lower layers.

3   Collaborative Self-Organization

This section introduces the conceptual model and basic design principles shaping the DRCM core, specifically the decentralized control processes that dynamically configure mobile resources into resource clusters and continuously monitor and control the operations and tasks being performed by the cluster components.

Operating under uncertain mission requirements in an unstable physical environment calls for flexible adaptation to new situations. Building on collaborative self-organizing system concepts naturally facilitates reconfigurable applications and dynamic reorganization in response to internal changes in resource requirements and external changes affecting the availability of resources.

The complex command and control structure is realized in a distributed and hierarchical fashion by means of a dynamic ensemble of autonomously operating *control agents* interacting with one another and with their local environment. Intuitively, each agent is associated with an individual resource representing a concurrent control thread of the decentralized system. Agents are created or eliminated at run-time as resources are added to or removed from the system.

3.1   Resource Hierarchy

Missions represent complex tasks and goals that normally exceed the capacity and capabilities of any individual resource; hence, they need to be decomposed into subtasks and subgoals in such a way that the resulting tasks and goals can be performed co-operatively by a resource cluster that has the required capacity and also matches the capabilities. This process is performed by the planning component in several iterative steps until all the resulting tasks are executable tasks. When such tasks are ready to be executed the tasking component then allocates resources depending on resource availability and task priority.

In order to simplify mapping the constituent tasks of a mission onto resources that execute them, the network architecture hierarchically organizes resources in clusters. Control agents are nodes in the network architecture; their organization into clusters is stated by undirected edges (see Fig. 1). Referring to distinct roles of resource entities, there are two different types of nodes:

- *Physical resources* refer to real-world resource entities in the form of mobile sensor platforms. In the hierarchy, only the leaf nodes represent physical resources. Depending on the level of abstraction at which a distributed fusion system is considered, a physical resource may refer to a group of mobile sensor platforms, to a single mobile platform, or even to an individual sensor unit on a given sensor platform. [2]

- *Logical resources* refer to abstract resource entities formed by clustering two or more physical and/or logical resources, each with a certain range of capabilities, into a higher level resource with aggregated (richer) capabilities needed to perform more complex operations. A logical resource identifies a cluster of resources. All non-leaf nodes represent logical resources (Fig. 1).

Resource clusters form collaborative self-organizing command and control units that are configured at run-time to perform specific missions and tasks, where their resource orchestration is subject to dynamic change. For increased robustness and to reduce control and communication overhead, logical resources operate semi-autonomously, making their own local decisions on the realignment and reorganization of resources within a cluster. DRCM policies govern the migration of resources between clusters based on common prioritization schemes for resource selection, load balancing and organization of idle resource pools. Resources may join or be removed from a cluster on demand depending on their sensor capabilities, mobility capabilities, geographic location, cost aspects and other characteristics. The underlying design principles resemble those for improving performance and robustness in mobile ad hoc networks.

3.2   Organization Principles

Specific challenges arise from complex interaction patterns between logical and physical resources and the dependencies between the operations and tasks to be performed in a collaborative fashion. The following organization principles outline some of the aspects that need to be addressed.

- *Resource Clustering Principles* control the arrangement of resources into resource clusters. Composition rules defined over resource descriptors specify the clustering of resources so as to form composite resources with richer behaviors. A resource descriptor is an abstract representation of resource attributes such as physical capabilities (e.g., sensor capabilities, mobility and time constraints), geographic position and workload information.
- *Resource Distribution Principles* refer to the spatio-temporal distribution of mobile resources in the geographical environment. Position information and projections of resource trajectories provide important input for grouping resources into clusters (e.g., keeping resources of the same group in close proximity to each other) and also to satisfy communication requirements (e.g., moving a resource in order to act as a communication proxy).
- *Task Decomposition Principles* define the decomposition of complex tasks (including entire missions) into subtasks based on common patterns and schemes for mapping tasks onto resources. This concept entails an abstract characterization of tasks for specifying their resource requirements and the required orchestration of resources for performing the tasks.

---

[2] Henceforth, we identify physical resources with mobile sensor platforms.

4   Intelligent Decision Support

In order to support the decision making of system operators, it is vital for the system to be able to simulate the entire process of decision making. The focus here is on Automated Planning and Automated Tasking.

4.1   Automated Planning

Generally speaking, any non-trivial objective will require a planning process in order to decide upon the best set of actions to follow. In the domain of Marine Safety and Security, missions introduced by command personnel are stated at an abstract level, establishing a goal without defining a specific manner in which it must be achieved. Expert knowledge and institutional policies can then be invoked in order to select which tasks are likely to be successful. This can be seen as an iterative process, as high level plans are used to generate subplans until an actionable set of tasks is found.

A hierarchical perspective captures this mechanism well: abstract tasks are successively broken down into more refined subtasks. Subtasks requiring more refinement before they can be implemented are also broken down. This continues until all of the resulting subtasks are executable. The set of executable tasks generated this way constitute the elements of the plan. The Hierarchical Task Network (HTN) approach [15] is a prime example of this kind of planning. HTNs use substitution rules called methods to select the right subtasks for each abstract task, generating a tree-like network through this process. The network not only shows the relationship between tasks and subtasks, but also any constraints that exist between tasks. If executable subtasks can be found for all tasks in the network, a solution has been constructed for the problem at hand.

Fig. 2 shows a simplified HTN plan. The top task, *Capsized Boat*, corresponds to the mission introduced to the system. It is too general as stated to be fulfilled, so a method associated with it is used to find three subtasks. In turn, these subtasks require further refinement and other methods are used to find appropriate subtasks for them. Two kinds of constraints are illustrated: precedence and shared resource. The first defines a partial order in which the tasks must be completed, and the second forces a reasonable limitation on the choice of resources to complete the tasks. The leaf nodes of the network correspond to the executable tasks that make up the final plan.

A planning system that interacts with the real world must have the ability to replan in order to adapt task choice to deal with changing conditions or new information. Replanning should cause as little disruption as possible to the existing plan, since tasks may currently be underway. Local replanning aims to do this by making changes in the task network as close to the problem as possible [16]. This entails the requirement to be able to evaluate the current world state in order to recognize when replanning is needed, and what in particular needs to change.

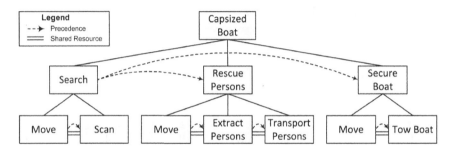

Fig. 2. Hierarchical Task Network (HTN) Example

4.2   Automated Tasking

Once a plan has been decided upon, either in whole or in part, it is still necessary to see that it is successfully completed. This is due to factors outside of the control of the system, as well as imperfect knowledge gathered from sensors. Appropriate resources must be found for the tasks, and they must be performed only when appropriate. Tasks in the midst of execution must be monitored, since they may provide data that must be considered immediately. Tasks can end prematurely, due to resource failure or environmental interference, for example. In these cases the problem may be solved by finding a new resource to assign to the task, or it may be necessary to change the existing plan. The Tasking component in our system is responsible for handling these issues. It also serves as a nexus of interaction between the other components. In this way, it serves as a buffer and conductor for asynchronous events, enabling the system to act in a robust manner in real-time.

5   System Reference Model

In this section, we describe the interactions between the components of the system in terms of an abstract generic scenario indicating their responsibilities and relations. In order to model and analyze system scenarios, a standard notation, *User Requirements Notation (URN)* [17] is used. In 2008, the *User Requirements Notation* was approved as an *ITU-T* standard that combines concepts and notation for modeling goals and scenarios. A *scenario* describes a partial usage of the system. It is defined as a set of partially ordered responsibilities to be performed such that the system reaches its goals. Each scenario has *start points*, represented by filled circles and *end points* illustrated by solid bars. A scenario progresses along *paths* between these start and end points, and the *responsibilities* are represented by crosses on the path. The diamond symbol is called a *stub* and is a placeholder for a sub-scenario. We employ them in our model for complexity management by encapsulating some related and coherent responsibilities as a *subcomponent*. Beyond the above concepts and notations, there are other aspects supported by *URN*, but those are not used here.

5.1   Describing the Abstract Generic Scenario

This system is intended to be implemented in a distributed manner, with all
five services running on each node in the C2 hierarchy. This allows for a truly
decentralized control structure and improves the robustness of the network. We
use *jUCMNav* for modeling different concrete scenarios of the system in various
situations. The *abstract generic scenario* is the result of generalizing the common parts of these concrete scenarios. As shown in Fig. 3, the system has five
components in addition to the Command and Control Center. This section defines the responsibilities of each component and also the communication among
them. It is important to note that Fig. 3 shows the flow of *control* and *information*, and the duties of each element, so some parts of the path can be executed
concurrently for different *missions* and *tasks*.

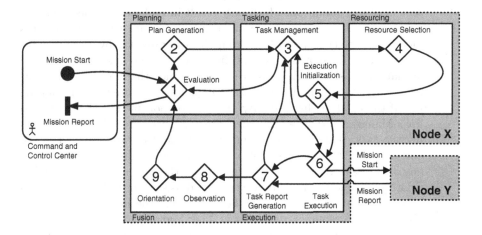

Fig. 3. Abstract Generic Scenario of the NADIF System

The Command and Control Center is outside the boundary of the system
and is considered to be an actor on the system. This component is responsible
for introducing *new missions* to Planning. In addition, it will receive a report
of the finished mission, whether it is successful or not. The decision support
components of each node are modeled as an interacting set of internal services.
The responsibilities of each component and their respective subcomponents are:

Planning is responsible for generating new plans and also replanning previous
   cases when necessary.
   − *Evaluation*(1): This subcomponent is responsible for evaluating finished
      tasks, as well as relevant situation information, such as the output of the
      Fusion component. If the results of a task compromise an active mission,
      it is sent back to Plan Generation for replanning. If instead a mission has

finished (whether successful or not), this subcomponent issues a report to the Command and Control Center.

- *Plan Generation*(2): In this subcomponent, the current plan is decomposed into a set of tasks. Any tasks that are executable are sent to Task Management in order to wait for resource assignment and execution.

Tasking is responsible for managing tasks which are waiting for execution or that have just finished execution.

- *Task Management*(3): This subcomponent maintains the pool of waiting tasks. If a task needs a resource, a request is sent to Resource Selection. When a task is ready to execute, it is sent to Task Execution. It also checks if a task can no longer be executed, due to exceeding its time window, finished status (from the execution report sent by Task Report Generation), or if no resource assignments are possible (i.e., a rejection message from Execution Initialization). In these cases, the task will be sent back to Evaluation, which may result in replanning if necessary.

- *Execution Initialization*(5): Its main duty is to pick the best resources for executing the current task from the list provided by Resource Selection. The decision is based on different parameters such as resource availability, task priority, resource location, and other information. First, resources currently in use by tasks of higher priority are pruned from the list. If the resulting list is empty, this subcomponent sends a message to Task Management; otherwise, there are appropriate resources for executing the task. If the selected resources are idle, they are assigned to the current task, which is then sent to the task pool in Task Management. If any of the selected resources are in use, but the current task has a higher priority, a request to release these resources is sent to the Task Execution subcomponent. Once they have been released, the higher priority task obtains these resources and waits in Task Management for execution.

Resourcing is responsible for monitoring resources available to the current node. It also participates in resource configuration management.

- *Resource Selection*(4): This subcomponent acts as a filter to find the resources that satisfy the required capabilities of a task. In this manner, a list of resources that are able to perform the task is created and sent to the Execution Initialization subcomponent in Tasking.

Execution is responsible for managing and monitoring the tasks during their execution process.

- *Task Execution*(6): This subcomponent is responsible for monitoring the execution of current tasks. There are two different situations: 1) the assigned resources are *physical*, so the execution of the task is controlled by this subcomponent, or 2) the assigned resources are *logical*, so the task can be considered as a *new mission* to be sent to the corresponding node for execution (as shown in Fig. 3, in which Node X sends a task to Node Y as a new mission). In the new node, the new mission passes through the same scenario.

- *Task Report Generation*(7): Whenever task execution has finished, this subcomponent generates a report. In the case that the task has executed in another node (i.e., as a mission), its final report comes into this subcomponent. The report contains the results of performing the task and is sent to the Task Management subcomponent. This report will be used in Task Management to determine whether or not the task has effectively finished execution. Furthermore, Task Report Generation sends regular reports to Observation to provide data required for the Information Fusion process.

Fusion is responsible for the synthesis of high level information from low level data and information. Information fusion is a key enabler of Situation Analysis, a process which leads to Situation Awareness.

- *Observation*(8): This is concerned with getting all of the data produced from executing tasks into the same coordinate frame, i.e., aligning them in space and time, and presenting a coherent and consistent picture across several agents. The output of this effort are fused tracks. This is commonly referred to as Level 1 data fusion. Note that this is a processing function that is distinct from sensing.
- *Orientation*(9): Here conclusions are drawn from the tracks by reasoning about the relationships between objects and making inferences about their intentions, and ultimately analyzing the impact of those intentions on others. This stage is referred to as Level 2 data fusion.

Note that Observation and Orientation inside the Fusion component directly correspond to the first two steps of John Boyd's Observe-Orient-Decide-Act (OODA) loop [4]. The Act step is handled by the Execution component, while the rest of the system model is dedicated to the complexity of the Decision step. The OODA concept has wide acceptance in the military R&D community, and the mapping to an Agent concept emphasizes the distributed nature of the tasks.

5.2 Abstract State Machine Representation

We formally describe the detailed design specifications of the subcomponents comprising the system in terms of Abstract State Machine [18] models. These are executable in principle (for experimental studies) using the CoreASM tool environment [19]. ASM code for the Task Management subcomponent is included in [9]. We present two rules here: (1) Execution Initialization establishes how a resource is assigned using a list of resource candidates provided by Resource Selection, and (2) Task Execution enables self-organization in the system by allowing tasks to be distributed in a recursive manner as missions among subordinate logical resources until they are assigned to a physical resource capable of executing them.

ExecutionInitialization(t : TASK) ≡
    let $prunedList = \{r | r$ **in** $resourceCandidateList(t)$ **with**
                        $priority(t) > MaxPriority(r, time(t))\}$ **in**
      choose r **in** $prunedList$ **with** $cost(r, t) = MinCost(prunedList, t)$ **do**
        if $busy(r, time(t))$ **then**
          Release$(r, time(t))$
        $resource(t) := r$
        $task(r, time(t)) := t$
      ifnone **do**
        $resourceCandidateList(t) := undef$
        add "NO RESOURCE" **to** $exceptions(t)$
    add t **to** $taskPool$

TaskExecution(t : TASK) ≡
    let $r = resource(t)$ **in**
      if $PhysicalResource(r)$ **then**
        $Active(t) := true$
        Execute(t, r)
      else   // r is a logical resource
        add t **to** $missions(r)$

6   Conclusions

Decision support systems have considerable potential in a range of application fields involving situation analysis processes: the examination of a situation, its elements, and their relations, to provide and maintain a state of situation awareness [20]. We contend that this is a sensible choice for Marine Safety and Security. For the considered scenarios the challenge is to manage complex coordination tasks under uncertain mission requirements, operating in a dynamically changing environment adversely affecting mission success. In the presence of uncertainty and frequent change, dynamic replanning and re-tasking constitute the norm.

The NADIF system concept is characterized by adaptiveness, robustness and scalability and thus embraces change. Building on biologically-inspired computing principles, a self-organizing network of intelligent control agents forms the backbone of the Decision Support and Configuration Management engines. Collaboratively agents decompose and distribute complex operations across the network. By deferring decisions on how to operationalize mission requirements and by localizing decisions on resource alignments within a cluster, this organization enhances flexibility by avoiding the bottleneck of central control structures.

References

1. Natural Resources Canada, The Atlas of Canada – Coastline and Shoreline, http://atlas.nrcan.gc.ca/site/english/learningresources/facts/coastline.html (Visited: May 2010)
2. Marine Traffic Project , http://www.marinetraffic.com (Visited: May 2010)

3. Guerlain, S., Brown, D.E., Mastrangelo, C.: Intelligent Decision Support Systems. In: IEEE Intl. Conf. on Systems, Man, and Cybernetics (2000)
4. Li, Z., Leung, H., Valin, P., Wehn, H.: High Level Data Fusion System for Can-CoastWatch. In: 10th Intl. Conf. on Information Fusion, Quebec City, Canada (2007)
5. Net-Enabled Adaptive Distributed Information Fusion for Large Volume Surveillance (NADIF), https://wiki.sfu.ca/research/NADIF/ (Visited: May 2010)
6. Royal Canadian Mounted Police, Marine Security Operation Centres (MSOC), http://www.grc-rcmp.gc.ca/mari-port/msoc-cosm-eng.htm (Visited: May 2010)
7. Biology-Inspired Techniques for Self-Organization in Dynamic Networks, http://www.cs.unibo.it/bison/ (Visited: May 2010)
8. Endsley, M.R.: Theoretical Underpinnings of Situation Awareness: A Critical Review. In: Endsley, M.R., Garland, D.J. (eds.) Situation Awareness Analysis and Measurement. CRC Press, Boca Raton (2000)
9. Glässer, U., Jackson, P., Khalili Araghi, A., Yaghoubi Shahir, H.: Intelligent Decision Support for Marine Safety and Security Operations. In: IEEE Intl. Conf. on Intelligence and Security Informatics, Vancouver, Canada (2010)
10. Arabie, P., Hubert, L.J., De Soete, G. (eds.): Clustering and Classification. World Scientific, Singapore (1996)
11. Camazine, S., Deneubourg, J.L., Franks, N.R., Sneyd, J., Theraulaz, G., Bonabeau, E.: Self-Organization in Biological Systems. Princeton University Press, Princeton (2003)
12. Beni, G., Wang, J.: Swarm Intelligence in Cellular Robotic Systems. In: NATO Advanced Workshop on Robots and Biological Systems, Tuscany, Italy (1989)
13. Farahbod, R., Glässer, U., Khalili, A.: A Multi-Layer Network Architecture for Dynamic Resource Configuration & Management of Multiple Mobile Resources in Maritime Surveillance. In: SPIE Symposium on Defense, Security + Sensing: Multisensor, Multisource Information Fusion, Orlando, USA (2009)
14. McCann, C., Pigeau, R.: Clarifying the Concepts of Control and Command. In: 5th Command and Control Research and Technology Symposium (1999)
15. Ghallab, M., Nau, D., Traverso, P.: Automated Planning: Theory and Practice. Morgan Kaufmann, San Francisco (2004)
16. Ayan, N.F., Kuter, U., Yaman, F., Goldman, R.P.: HOTRiDE: Hierarchical Ordered Task Replanning in Dynamic Environments. In: 3rd Workshop on Planning and Plan Execution for Real-World Systems (2007)
17. Mussbacher, G., Amyot, D.: Goal and Scenario Modeling, Analysis, and Transformation with jUCMNav. In: 31st Intl. Conf. on Software Engineering, Companion Volume, Vancouver, Canada (2009)
18. Börger, E., Stärk, R.: Abstract State Machines: A Method for High-Level System Design and Analysis. Springer, Heidelberg (2003)
19. Farahbod, R., Gervasi, V., Glässer, U.: CoreASM: An Extensible ASM Execution Engine. Fundamenta Informaticae 77(1-2), 71–103 (2007)
20. Bossé, É., Roy, J., Ward, S.: Concepts, Models, and Tools for Information Fusion. Artech House Inc, Boston (2007)

Combining Software and Hardware LCS for Lightweight On-Chip Learning

Andreas Bernauer[1], Johannes Zeppenfeld[2], Oliver Bringmann[3],
Andreas Herkersdorf[2], and Wolfgang Rosenstiel[1]

[1] University of Tübingen, 72076 Tübingen, Germany
bernauer@informatik.uni-tuebingen.de
[2] Technische Universität München, 80290 München, Germany
[3] Forschungszentrum Informatik, 76131 Karlsruhe, Germany

Abstract. In this paper we present a novel two-stage method to realize
a lightweight but very capable hardware implementation of a Learning
Classifier System for on-chip learning. Learning Classifier Systems (LCS)
allow taking good run-time decisions, but current hardware implementations are either large or have limited learning capabilities.

In this work, we combine the capabilities of a software-based LCS, the
XCS, with a lightweight hardware implementation, the LCT, retaining the
benefits of both. We compare our method with other LCS implementations using the multiplexer problem and evaluate it with two chip-related
problems, run-time task allocation and SoC component parameterization.
In all three problem sets, we find that the learning and self-adaptation capabilities are comparable to a full-fledged system, but with the added benefits of a lightweight hardware implementation, namely small area size and
quick response time. Given our work, autonomous chips based on Learning
Classifier Systems become feasible.

Keywords: System-on-Chip, Learning Classifier System, XCS.

1 Introduction

As the number of functions integrated in a single chip increases, the complexity
of a chip grows significantly. Furthermore, increasing transistor variability [4,6],
process variation [1], and degradation effects [18] make it increasingly difficult
to ensure the reliability of the chip [16]. The International Technology Roadmap
for Semiconductors (ITRS) [13] estimates that until 2015, up to 70% of a chip's
design must be reused to keep up with the increasing complexity.

Autonomic System-on-Chip (ASoC) [15] add a logical, autonomous layer to con-
temporary SoCs that helps the designer to manage the complexity and reliability
issues: decisions that are hard to take at design time because many parameters
are uncertain, can be taken at run time by the autonomic layer. Learning Classifier Systems (LCS) have been shown to be able to take the right run-time
decisions [3,2] and even adapt to events that due to the chip complexity have
not been foreseen at design time. LCS use a genetic algorithm and reinforcement

M. Hinchey et al. (Eds.): DIPES/BICC 2010, IFIP AICT 329, pp. 278–289, 2010.
© IFIP International Federation for Information Processing 2010

learning to evolve a set of rules, the interaction of which propose a preferably optimal action to any situation the chip may encounter. Although LCS allow very capable systems for autonomous run-time decisions and self-adaptation, current hardware implementations either require large portions of the chip [5], increasing total chip costs, or have limited learning capabilities [24].

In this paper, we present a novel two-stage method to realize an on-chip Learning Classifier System (LCS) that is small, takes the good run-time decisions, and can adapt to unexpected events. In the first stage at design time, we learn a rule set in software using a particular LCS, the XCS [23]. In the second stage, we use the rule set to initialize the lightweight LCS hardware implementation LCT [24]. The idea is that the XCS learns just enough rules so that the LCT can adapt to the actual manifestation and conditions of a particular chip and even to unexpected events, albeit in a limited way.

We first compare our method to other LCS implementations using the multiplexer problem, a traditional testbed for LCS [23], and then apply it to two chip-related problems, namely task-allocation and SoC component parameterization. We show that the LCT can adequately learn and still react to unexpected events. To the best of our knowledge, this is the first study of a lightweight but still capable hardware implementation of an LCS. We think that our work makes using LCS to control chips conceivable.

This work is structured as follows. Section 2 gives an overview of related work. Section 3 introduces the XCS and the hardware implementation LCT. Section 4 describes our proposed method. Section 5 presents the three benchmarks multiplexer, task-allocation and SoC component parameterization that we use to assess our method. Section 6 shows the results of our assessment and Section 7 concludes this paper.

2   Related Work

Learning Classifier Systems were originally introduced in [12]. The XCS was first presented in [21] and later refined in [23]. The XCS has been used in a large range of learning and classification problems, including controlling a robotic mouse [10], a system-on-chip (SoC) [3], the lights of a traffic junction [17], and for finding suitable partitions in hardware-software codesign [11]. A first hardware implementation of an XCS has been presented in [5], named XCS_i, which uses fixed-point arithmetic. The implementation shows good learning rates of the XCS_i, but is quite large. In [24], the authors present an optimized hardware implementation of an LCS, called the Learning Classifier Table (LCT), which is small but has no mechanism to create new classifiers. Using a hand-crafted initial rule set, the authors show that the LCT can adjust the frequency of a SoC according to a given objective function.

The most popular machine learning algorithms for which hardware implementations exist are neural networks [19,9] and, more recently, support vector machines [14]. Along with the fact that for these systems, "the actual rules implemented [are] not apparent" [19], their implementations are about five times as large as the LCT [14].

3   XCS and LCT

We briefly describe the XCS and LCT and refer to [22,23,7,24] for further details.

The XCS learns a minimal set of *classifiers* (or *rules*) the interaction of which, in the ideal case, provide an optimal response (called *action*) for a given situation. The learning is based on a genetic algorithm and reinforcement learning. Each classifier (or rule) consists of a condition, an action, a reward prediction, the reward prediction accuracy, and some other house keeping values. The condition is a string of bits ('0', '1', and the don't-care symbol '#'). At each learning step, the XCS matches the input signal with the condition of each classifier and notes the actions and accuracy-weighted reward predictions that each classifier proposes. The XCS then selects an action to apply: in the exploit mode, it chooses the action that promises the highest reward, while in the explore mode, it chooses a random action to find new alternatives. After the action has been applied, the XCS receives a reward depending on the new state and updates its reward predictions and classifier set accordingly. After some number of iterations, the genetic algorithm repeatedly creates new, possibly better suited rules.

The LCT consists of a memory, which holds a fixed number of classifiers, and hardware-based mechanisms for action lookup and fitness update. There is no mechanism to generate new classifiers. The classifiers in the LCT consist only of a condition, an action and a fitness, similar to the fitness in the strength-based ZCS [20]. To realize the don't-care bits, the LCT first logically ANDs the monitor signal with a mask before comparing it with the bit value. The LCT selects the action of a matching classifier randomly according to the classifier's relative fitness (roulette-wheel selection) using weighted reservoir sampling to ensure a fixed lookup time. After receiving the reward for a previously applied action, the LCT distributes the reward r to the classifiers of the action set and updates the fitness f according to $f \leftarrow \beta r + (1 - \beta)f$ with the learning rate $0 \leq \beta \leq 1$.

4   Methodology

One major trade-off of hardware-based machine learning lies between the learning capabilities of the implementation and the allotted hardware resources: the system is either very capable but requires a lot of resources or it requires little resources but is less capable. We address this problem with the following two-stage approach:

1. At design time, the software-based XCS learns a (preferably optimal) set of rules to solve a given problem.
2. We translate the XCS rules with our xcs2lct too into a form that is suitable for the LCT. Initialized with these rules, the hardware-based LCT continues to learn at run time.

With this setup, we can use all the resources that are available to a capable software implementation (the XCS) and use the acquired knowledge in a lightweight hardware implementation (the LCT). The idea is that the XCS learns a rule set that allows the LCT to adapt to the actual manifestation and conditions of a particular chip and even to unexpected event, despite its limited learning capabilities.

As the chip area that is necessary to store the classifiers in memory constitutes the largest part of the LCT, we would like to minimize the number of necessary classifiers to keep the chip area requirement small. We therefore consider translating both all XCS rules to corresponding LCT rules (all-XCS translation) and only the top performing rules (top-XCS translation). The xcs2lct translates the rules according to the following algorithm, which ensures that the XCS and the LCT classifiers match the same input values:

```
foreach b ← xcs-rule[i] do
    if b == '#' then lct-rule[i].(mask,bit) ← ('0', '0');
    else            lct-rule[i].(mask,bit) ← ('1', b);
```

To compare our method with the base performance of the LCT, we also consider two more ways to generate LCT rules, full-constant and full-reverse. Both translations provide all possible LCT rules, that is, a complete condition-action table[1] as there is no known method to generate an appropriate rule table for the LCT. The full-constant translation initializes the rule fitness to half the maximum reward (500) and, as it is independent of the XCS rules, represents the bottom line of LCT's own learning capabilities. The full-reverse translation sets the rule fitness to the highest predicted reward of all matching XCS rules, or zero, if no XCS rule matches, and represents the combined learning capability of the LCT and the XCS.

The original action selection strategy for the LCT is roulette-wheel, which selects actions randomly according to the relative predicted reward of the matching classifiers, similar to the explore mode of the XCS. Additionally, we also consider the winner-takes-all strategy, which selects the action whose matching classifiers predict the highest reward, similar to the exploit mode of the XCS. However, unlike in the XCS, in the LCT the accuracy of the prediction does not influence the action selection.

While the XCS is usually configured to alternate between the explore and exploit mode, in our experiments the LCT uses only one of either strategies. We leave the analysis of alternating strategies in the LCT as future work.

5   Experimental Setup

We use three problem types to assess our method: multiplexer [21], task allocation [2], and SoC component parameterization. Additionally, we define an unexpected event for each problem type to explore LCT's learning ability. As the XCS has already been shown to be able to solve these problem types and adapt to unexpected chip events [2], in this work we concentrate on the performance of the LCT.

---

[1] Of course, the memory requirements of the classifiers generated with full-* grow exponentially with the problem size. We use them only for comparison.

The *multiplexer* problem is a typical LCS benchmark [23]. The n-multiplexer-problem is defined over binary strings of length $n = k + 2^k$. The first k bits index a bit in the remaining bits. The correct action for the LCS is the value of the indexed bit. For example, in the 6-multiplexer problem, $m_6(011101) = 0$ and $m_6(100100) = 1$. We define the *inversed multiplexer* as the unexpected event for the multiplexer, that is, the LCS is supposed to return the inversed value of the indexed bit. For example, in the inversed 6-multiplexer problem, $\overline{m}_6(011101) = 1 - m_6(011101) = 1$. We use the same XCS parameters as the full-fledged FPGA implementation of XCS presented in [5] to have comparable results: $\alpha = 0.1$, $\beta = 0.2$, $\delta = 0.1$, $\varepsilon_0 = 10$ (which is 1% of the maximum reward), $\nu = 5$, $\theta_{GA} = 25$, $\chi_{GA} = 0.8$, $\mu_{GA} = 0.04$, $P_\# = 0.3$; GA subsumption is on with $\theta_{GAsub} = 20$, while action set subsumption is off. We do not use generalization or niche mutation. The reported results are averages over 20 runs.

The *task-allocation* problem has been first introduced in [2] and is motivated by the advent of multi-core systems, where tasks can be run on several cores simultaneously to increase overall reliability. In the (L, i)-task-allocation problem, the LCS must allocate i available tasks on $L \geq i$ cores, some of which are known to be occupied and thus not available. The system input is a binary string of length L, where each bit represents the occupation of a particular core. There is one action for each possible allocation plus a special action that indicates that no allocation is possible (e.g., when all cores are already occupied), totaling $\binom{L}{i} + 1$ possible actions. An action is valid and returns the maximum reward if the corresponding allocation only allocates available cores; otherwise the reward is zero. The unexpected event for the task-allocation problem is the unmonitored failure of a core: although reported as available, the core cannot be occupied, and an allocation of that core returns zero reward. For the task-allocation problem, we use the XCS parameters from [2] to have comparable results, which differ from the multiplexer settings only in the following parameters: $\alpha = 1$, $\theta_{GA} = 250$, $\chi_{GA} = 0.1$, $\mu_{GA} = 0.1$, $P_\# = 0.4$; GA subsumption is off. The reported results are averages over 5 runs, due to the longer simulation time for the many problem instances.

The *SoC component parameterization* problem demonstrates the ability of LCS to dynamically parameterize a system-on-chip at run time, similar to [3]. The system consists of a processing core that is subject to random load fluctuations. As the load changes, the LCS is responsible for setting the operating frequency of the core as low as possible (i.e., maintaining as high a utilization as possible), while ensuring that the core can keep up with the workload. The monitor input consists of the core's current frequency as well as its utilization. There are five possible actions: four actions to increase or decrease the core's operating frequency by 10 or 20 MHz over a range from 50 to 200 MHz, and one action to keep the core's frequency unchanged. The reward for each action is calculated by comparing the value of a system-wide objective function before and after the action is applied. The objective function indicates how far from the designer-specified optimum of high utilization and low error rate the system is currently operating and is defined as $f_{obj} = (100\% - \text{utilization}) + \text{error\_rate}$, where a low value indicates that the system is operating near its optimum. A base reward of half the maximum reward (500) is given when the objective function returns the same value before and after the action is carried out. This is the lowest possible reward without actively worsening the system's operating state. The unexpected event for the component parameterization problem is a manufacturing defect that causes critical timing errors for operating frequencies in excess of 100 MHz. As a result, increasing the frequency above 100 MHz causes the core to cease functioning, resulting in wasted cycles for error correction and providing lower rewards to the LCS. With timing errors, the LCT must therefore learn to cap the frequency at 100 MHz, even when the workload would warrant higher operating frequencies. We use the same XCS parameters as for the task-allocation problem, except for $\alpha = 0.8$ and $P_\# = 0.1$. The reported results are averages over 100 runs.

We use the implementation of the XCS in the programming language C as described in [8] as the software version of XCS. We use a SystemC-based simulation model of the LCT hardware implementation described in [24], with the additional winner-takes-all strategy described in Section 4.

We compare the performance of the LCT that has been instructed using our method with the base performance of the LCT, the performance of the full-fledged hardware implementation of the XCS presented by [5], the performance of the XCS reported in [2], and the performance of the software version of the XCS. We also check whether the LCT retains the capability of LCS to adapt to unexpected events.

6   Results

In this section we present the results on the three problem types multiplexer, task-allocation, and SoC component parameterization mentioned previously.

6.1   Multiplexer

Figure 1 shows the correctness rate (x-axis) and population size (y-axis) for the 6-, 11-, 20-, and 37-multiplexer problem for all eight possible combinations of translations and action selection strategies for the LCT. Note that the x-axis starts at 70% correctness rate and that the scales of the y-axes differ. The top-XCS translation uses only classifiers that predict the maximum reward with perfect accuracy. As we aim for a small but correct LCS, in each graph lower right is better. The figures show that in the new winner-takes-all (WTA) strategy (solid symbols), the LCT solves the multiplexer problem perfectly , while in the original roulette-wheel (RW) strategy (empty symbols), it solves only between 80% and 97% of the problem instances. With the winner-takes-all strategy, the LCT shows the same results as the full-fledged XCS implementation presented in [5]. The figure also shows that the population size of the all-XCS translation (square symbol) is about three times the population size of the top-XCS translation (upwards triangle symbol) for all multiplexer problems. As the population sizes

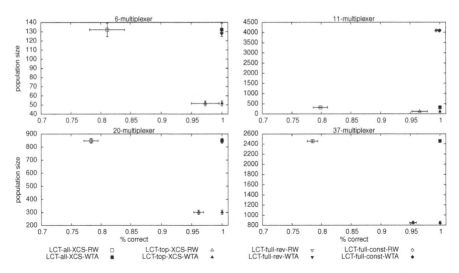

Fig. 1. Performance in the multiplexer problem. *Clockwise from upper left:* 6-, 11-, 20-, and 37-multiplexer. Within each graph, lower right is better. Note that the y-axes differ in scale. Error bars are standard deviations σ in the respective dimension.

for the full-* translations rise exponentially, we excluded them from the 20- and 37-multiplexer problem.

All LCT configurations were able to perfectly adapt to the unexpected event of the inversed multiplexer problem (not depicted), given a rule base that the XCS has learned for the (regular, non-inversed) multiplexer problem. However, the LCT can only adapt to the inversed multiplexer problem, if the XCS was able to solve the multiplexer problem sufficiently well (e.g., because XCS' learning process was terminated prematurely). Otherwise, even if the XCS shows a correctness rate of 100%, not all LCT configurations can adapt to the inversed multiplexer. Figure 2 illustrates the case for $\overline{m}_{11}$. While the configurations all-XCS and full-const solve 80%-100% of the inversed multiplexer problem, the top-XCS and full-rev solve no more than 30%. The correctness rate did not change further until 1 million steps. We assume that the prematurely terminated XCS contains too many high-rewarding rules that are falsely marked as accurate because they were trained on only few problem instances, disturbing the results of the top-XCS and full-rev translations.

From the results in the multiplexer problem, we conclude that with the all-XCS translation the LCT shows both a high correctness rate and retains the capability to adapt to unexpected events. When using the full-const translation, we find similar results. Combining XCS' knowledge and LCT's own learning capabilities in the full-rev translation leads to an LCT whose capability to adapt to unforeseen events is very sensitive to the quality of the XCS rules. Similar is true when using only the top performing XCS rules with the top-XCS translation. As for more real-world problem types the XCS cannot always learn perfectly, we will concentrate on the all-XCS translation in the following experiments.

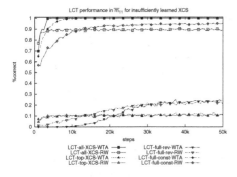

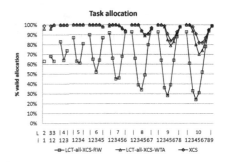

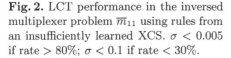

Fig. 2. LCT performance in the inversed multiplexer problem $\overline{m}_{11}$ using rules from an insufficiently learned XCS. $\sigma < 0.005$ if rate $> 80\%$; $\sigma < 0.1$ if rate $< 30\%$.

Fig. 3. Rate R_{LCT} of valid task allocations in the LCT and R_{XCS} for comparison. $\sigma < 11\%$ or better for any setting.

6.2 Task Allocation

Figure 3 shows the rate R_{LCT} of valid task allocations of the LCT for the (L, i)-task-allocation-problems, $1 \leq i < L \leq 10$, and R_{XCS} for comparison. The x-axis shows the problem instances and the y-axis shows run-time R_{LCT} and design-time R_{XCS}. From the figure we note that the LCT uses rule bases for which the XCS correctly allocates more than 90% of the problem instances for $L < 9$ and more than 80% for $9 \leq L \leq 10$, comparable to what has been reported in [2]. We find that the LCT using the winner-takes-all strategy (WTA) has very similar rates to the XCS, with a larger difference only for $L = 10$. Using the roulette-wheel strategy (RW), the LCT finds valid allocations considerably less often; in particular for $1 < i < L-1$, R_{LCT} drops as low as 22%. The reduced performance in the $(10, 5)$ and $(10, 6)$ problem instances concurs with the findings in [2] that these two problem instances are the most difficult for the XCS.

To test LCT's ability to adapt to unexpected events, we initialize the LCT with the all-XCS-translated XCS rules and let the cores fail randomly every 5 000 steps. Note that there is no further rule sharing between the XCS and the LCT besides the initialization of the LCT; we depict the XCS solely for comparison purposes.

Figure 4 shows R_{LCT} and R_{XCS} after the first (left half) and the second (right half) randomly chosen cores have failed. Note that the diagram shows fewer problem instances for the second core failure, as not every instance allows the failure of two cores (e.g., when allocating three tasks out on four cores, the failure of two cores turns the problem unsolvable). We find that the rate of valid task allocations of the LCT increases slightly, on average by about 1 %-point (maximum 10 %-points) after the first core has failed and an additional 1 %-point (maximum 11 %-points) after the second core has failed. Compared to the rates before any core has failed, we find an increase of about 2 %-points on average (maximum 17 %-points). The increase is of about the same amount for any employed action selection strategy, with the roulette-wheel strategy showing

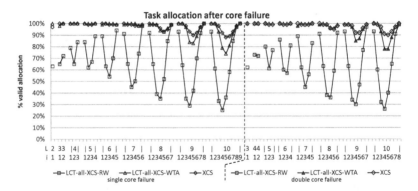

Fig. 4. R_{LCT} after one or two randomly chosen cores have failed, and R_{XCS} for comparison. After one core has failed, $\sigma < 7\%$; after two cores have failed, $\sigma < 5\%$.

a greater variance (not depicted). The results show approximately the same increase that the XCS would show. As reported in [2], the valid task-allocation rate generally increases after a core fails because the probability that the action "no valid allocation possible" is correct increases.

Summarizing, we find that when using the winner-takes-all action selection strategy, the LCT shows rates of valid task allocations which are comparable to what we find in the XCS and to what has been reported in [2]. The LCT also retains the capability to adapt to the unexpected failure of two cores, as previously shown for the XCS in [2]. The roulette-wheel strategy, however, shows high rates of valid task allocations only for some border cases.

6.3   Component Parameterization

Figure 5 shows the reward returned to the LCS in the SoC component parameterization problem before (left) and after (right) the unexpected event of malfunctioning in the core, with 1000 being the maximum reward. The figure shows the results for the first 3000 steps to clearly show the reward's trend over time. We find that the less explorative winner-takes-all strategy (WTA, dashed line) receives the highest reward among the LCT configurations, with the all-XCS translation (square) being on top. While on average the roulette-wheel strategy (RW, solid line with symbols) never actively degrades performance, it is unable to achieve even the level of performance that a static, non-learning winner-takes-all strategy (cross on dashed line) achieves given the XCS-generated rule set as a starting point. The more explorative roulette-wheel strategy is also unable to show a significantly improved learning behavior, clearly making the winner-takes-all strategy a better choice for this problem.

As expected, the initial average reward when using the full-const translation (triangle) is 500, indicating that an equal number of rules benefit and harm the system. Even though the winner-takes-all strategy is quickly able to achieve higher rewards, it is not able to achieve the same level of reward as a system

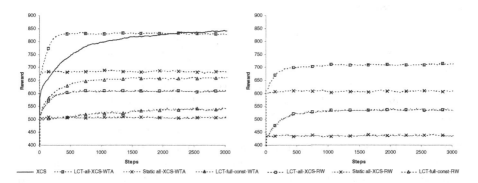

Fig. 5. Reward averaged over 100 runs for component parameterization with fully functional (left) and defective (right) component. After stabilization, $\sigma < 20$. Learning rate of XCS used to generate LCTs' initial rule set included for comparison.

initialized with a design-time generated rule set (all-XCS, square). The roulette-wheel strategy is only able to attain a very slight improvement to its average reward.

Comparing the final reward of the design-time XCS (solid line with no symbols) with the initial rewards of the run-time LCT using all-XCS translation shows a surprising discrepancy. Although the LCT uses the rules learned by the design-time XCS, we find a severe drop in the initial reward (from ∼840 to ∼650). We presume that this is because the LCT does not incorporate the complete functionality of the XCS. For example, the LCT cannot sufficiently represent XCS rules with high accuracy but low prediction, as the LCT does not store accuracy. Thus, the LCT must initially re-learn portions of the design space. Fortunately, the LCT is able to perform this initial re-learning fairly quickly within the first 500 steps.

Figure 5 shows the results of the component parameterization problem with the unexpected event as explained in Section 5. The results are very similar to those of the non-defective system, except that the average reward achieved by the system is somewhat lower than before. In fact, the starting rewards of less than 500 for the roulette-wheel strategy (solid line) indicate that, initially, a majority of actions are taken that disadvantage the system. As before, the learning capabilities of the LCT quickly achieve an increase in the average reward. However, the fact that any frequency above 100 MHz results in timing errors prevents the system from adapting to heavier load scenarios, forcing the system to operate at a lower degree of optimality and generally reducing the achievable maximum rewards.

In summary, we find that the LCT using the winner-takes-all action selection strategy and the all-XCS translation is capable to solve the SoC component parameterization problem, even in the event of a unexpected manufacturing defect.

7   Conclusions

In this paper, we have presented a two-stage method that combines the capability of the software-based XCS with the area efficiency of the LCS hardware implementation LCT. In the first stage at design time, the XCS initially learns a set of classifiers based on a software simulation of a given problem. In the second stage, we translate the classifiers into rules that are suitable for the LCT and apply the LCT to the same problem at run time.

We showed that with our newly introduced winner-takes-all action selection strategy for the LCT, the LCT can solve the multiplexer, the task-allocation and the SoC component parameterization problem, if we initialize it with all rules that the XCS has learned (all-XCS). In addition, the LCT retains the capability to adapt to the unexpected events of the problems, which includes the unexpected failure of two cores and the manufacturing defect of a core. We also found that the performance of the LCT is less sensitive to the performance of the XCS when using the all-XCS translation.

In summary, the results show that our proposed method allows a small and lightweight yet very capable hardware implementation of an LCS, with which the autonomic control of chips using LCS becomes feasible.

In future work, we will investigate alternating between roulette-wheel and winner-takes-all action selection for quicker adaptation to unexpected events in the LCT. We will also examine ways to reflect XCS's knowledge of reward prediction accuracy in the reward of the generated LCT rules, avoiding the initial drop in returned reward, and we will look for a trade-off between the good performance of all-XCS and the smaller classifier set of top-XCS.

References

1. Agarwal, A., Zolotov, V., Blaauw, D.: Statistical clock skew analysis considering intra-die process variations. IEEE CAD 23(8), 1231–1242 (2004)
2. Bernauer, A., Bringmann, O., Rosenstiel, W.: Generic self-adaptation to reduce design effort for system-on-chip. In: IEEE SASO, pp. 126–135 (2009)
3. Bernauer, A., Fritz, D., Rosenstiel, W.: Evaluation of the learning classifier system xcs for soc run-time control. LNI, vol. 134, pp. 761–768. Springer, GI (2008)
4. Bernstein, K., Frank, D., Gattiker, A., Haensch, W., Ji, B., Nassif, S., Nowak, E., Pearson, D., Rohrer, N.: High-performance cmos variability in the 65-nm regime and beyond. IBM Journal of Research and Development 50(4/5), 433 (2006)
5. Bolchini, C., Ferrandi, P., Lanzi, P.L., Salice, F.: Evolving classifiers on field programmable gate arrays: Migrating xcs to fpgas. Journal of Systems Architecture 52(8-9), 516–533 (2006)
6. Borkar, S.: Thousand core chips: a technology perspective. In: DAC, pp. 746–749. ACM, New York (2007)
7. Butz, M., Wilson, S.W.: An algorithmic description of xcs. In: Lanzi, P.L., Stolzmann, W., Wilson, S.W. (eds.) IWLCS 2000. LNCS (LNAI), vol. 1996, pp. 253–272. Springer, Heidelberg (2001)
8. Butz, M.V., Goldberg, D.E., Tharakunnel, K.: Analysis and improvement of fitness exploitation in xcs: bounding models, tournament selection, and bilateral accuracy. Evol. Comput. 11(3), 239–277 (2003)

9. Dias, F., Antunes, A., Mota, A.: Artificial neural networks: a review of commercial hardware. Engineering Appl. of Artificial Intelligence 17(8), 945–952 (2004)

10. Dorigo, M.: ALECSYS and the AutonoMouse: Learning to control a real robot by distributed classifier systems. Machine Learning 19(3), 209–240 (1995)

11. Ferrandi, F., Lanzi, P., Sciuto, D.: Mining interesting patterns from hardware-software codesign data with the learning classifier system XCS. Evolutionary Computation 2, 8–12 (2003)

12. Holland, J.H.: Adaptation. In: Rosen, R., Snell, F.M. (eds.) Progress in theoretical biology, pp. 263–293. Academic Press, New York (1976)

13. International Roadmap Committee. International technology roadmap for semiconductors (2008), http://www.itrs.net/reports.html

14. Irick, K., DeBole, M., Narayanan, V., Gayasen, A.: A hardware efficient support vector machine architecture for fpga. In: FCCM 2008, Washington, DC, USA, pp. 304–305. IEEE Computer Society, Los Alamitos (2008)

15. Lipsa, G., Herkersdorf, A., Rosenstiel, W., Bringmann, O., Stechele, W.: Towards a framework and a design methodology for autonomic soc. In: ICAC (2005)

16. Narayanan, V., Xie, Y.: Reliability concerns in embedded system designs. Computer 39(1), 118–120 (2006)

17. Prothmann, H., Rochner, F., Tomforde, S., Branke, J., Müller-Schloer, C., Schmeck, H.: Organic control of traffic lights. In: Rong, C., Jaatun, M.G., Sandnes, F.E., Yang, L.T., Ma, J. (eds.) ATC 2008. LNCS, vol. 5060, pp. 219–233. Springer, Heidelberg (2008)

18. Schlunder, C., Brederlow, R., Ankele, B., Lill, A., Goser, K., Thewes, R., Technol, I., Munich, G.: On the degradation of p-mosfets in analog and rf circuits under inhomogeneous negative bias temperature stress. In: IEEE IRPS, pp. 5–10 (2003)

19. Widrow, B., Rumelhart, D.E., Lehr, M.A.: Neural networks: applications in industry, business and science. Commun. ACM 37(3), 93–105 (1994)

20. Wilson, S.W.: Classifier systems and the animat problem. Machine Learning V2(3), 199–228 (1987)

21. Wilson, S.W.: Zcs: A zeroth level classifier system. Evolutionary Computation 2(1), 1–18 (1994)

22. Wilson, S.W.: Classifier fitness based on accuracy. Evolutionary Computation 3(2), 149–175 (1995)

23. Wilson, S.W.: Generalization in the xcs classifier system. In: Koza, J.R., Banzhaf, W., et al. (eds.) Genetic Programming Conference, University of Wisconsin, Madison, Wisconsin, pp. 665–674. Morgan Kaufmann, San Francisco (22-25, 1998)

24. Zeppenfeld, J., Bouajila, A., Stechele, W., Herkersdorf, A.: Learning classifier tables for autonomic systems on chip. In: Hegering, H.-G., Lehmann, A., Ohlbach, H.J., Scheideler, C. (eds.) GI Jahrestagung (2). LNI, vol. 134, pp. 771–778, GI (2008)

Collaborating and Learning Predators on a Pursuit Scenario

Nugroho Fredivianus, Urban Richter, and Hartmut Schmeck

Institute of Applied Informatics and Formal Description Methods (AIFB)
Karlsruhe Institute of Technology (KIT)
76128 Karlsruhe, Germany
{Nugroho.Fredivianus,Urban.Richter,Hartmut.Schmeck}@kit.edu
http://www.aifb.kit.edu

Abstract. A generic predator/prey pursuit scenario is used to validate a common learning approach using Wilson's eXtended Learning Classifier System (XCS). The predators, having only local information, should independently learn and act while at the same time they are urged to collaborate and to capture the prey. Since learning from scratch is often a time consuming process, the common learning approach, as investigated here, is compared to an individual learning approach of selfish learning agents. A special focus is set on the performance of how quickly the team goal is achieved in both learning scenarios. This paper provides new insights of how agents with local information could learn collaboratively in a dynamically changing multi-agent environment. Furthermore, the concept of a common rule base based on Wilson's XCS is investigated. The results based on the common rule base approach show a significant speed up in the learning performance but may be significantly inferior on the long run, in particular in situations with a moving prey.

Keywords: Multi-agent learning, predator/prey pursuit scenario, emergent behavior, collaboration, and XCS.

1 Motivation

Due to the increasing scale and complexity of strongly interconnected application systems there is a need for intelligent distributed information processing and control. The design of multi-agent systems (MASs) has addressed this need, using concepts from machine learning and distributed artificial intelligence [1]. MASs have been utilized successfully in a range of application scenarios: Guiding automated machines in collaborative industry scenarios [2], trading energy on market platforms [3], seeking smallest distance routes for delivery services [4], or managing air conditioners in buildings [5], are some examples of problems which are solved (completely or partially) using MAS approaches.

A MAS consists of a collection of agents acting autonomously within their common environment in order to meet their objectives. They take sensory inputs from the environment, match them on actions, and then perform some actions,

M. Hinchey et al. (Eds.): DIPES/BICC 2010, IFIP AICT 329, pp. 290–301, 2010.

which again affect their environment [6]. Here, an agent does not always represent a physical entity. It could be a virtual one, defined by a piece of software, or even some lines of a program. The predator/prey scenario [7] has been shown to provide a generic scenario as a basis for fundamental research on MASs, capturing essential aspects of many potential fields of application (cf. [8]).

In this paper, we investigate different aspects of learning in predator/prey scenarios. Each predator collects experiences while trying to capture the prey and learns from others. We compare a *common (centralized) knowledge approach* where every predator contributes to a centralized rule base to an *individual knowledge approach* where every agent learns on its own and the experiences are stored locally in decentralized rule bases.

The paper is structured as follows: Section 2 summarizes some related work concerning XCS in multi-agent environments. Section 3 explains in more detail the investigated scenario. Section 4 concentrates on collaboration methods, while Sect. 5 discusses the methodology. Section 6 presents the results and comparisons, followed by a conclusion and an outlook in Sect. 7.

2   Learning Classifier Systems in MASs

The field of learning classifier systems (LCSs), introduced in the 1970ies [9], is one of the most active and best-developed forms of genetic-based machine learning. LCSs are rule-based on-line learning systems that combine nature-inspired optimization heuristics and reinforcement learning techniques to learn appropriate actions for any input they get.

A variety of different LCS implementations has been proposed, many are based on Wilson's eXtended Learning Classifier System (XCS) [10], as sketched in Fig. 1. A learning agent senses its environment and sends its detector values to an XCS. The input is compared to all rules (called *classifiers*) in the rule base (*population P*). Matching classifiers enter the *match set M* and are grouped by their actions using the *prediction array PA*, which consists of each action's average of the predicted values. Then, the action with the highest prediction value is chosen, and the related group of classifiers enters the *action set A*. The chosen action is executed and a reward value is received based on the quality of this action with respect to the resulting state of the environment. The reward is used to update the prediction values of the classifiers in the action set and a learning cycle starts again.

In general, *multi-agent learning approaches* using LCSs are based on the idea of several independent LCSs which work in parallel on the same learning problem. Agents administrate individual populations learned locally on the one hand, and contribute to global shared rule sets on the other hand. In multi-agent scenarios, this may be useful, when agents have to cooperate with each other and their local behaviors contribute to a global goal with respect to different roles. In dynamic environments, agents have to cope with changes, which often require different behaviors. This corresponds to different roles an agent can take.

In [11], an XCS approach is investigated by modeling social problems. The *El Farol bar problem* is used as a benchmark for ten up to hundred agents learning

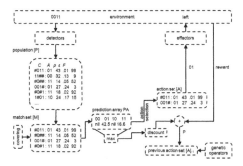

Fig. 1. Schematic overview of the on-line learning in XCS [10]

a cooperative behavior in parallel. XCS is also used in [12], where some agents in forms of various five-square tiles (called *pentominos*) collaboratively manage themselves to cover the smallest possible area by lying side by side. These papers indicate the feasibility of using XCS in multi-agent scenarios with collaborative agents, which is also in the focus of this paper.

3   Predator/Prey Pursuit Scenarios

In the literature, various types of predator/prey pursuit scenarios exist. Typically, some predators follow the goal of capturing a prey in a two-dimensional grid world [13]. Since such a two-dimensional grid world with a team of collaborating agents (i.e., predators) offers many design possibilities, this approach has been adopted for the investigations of this paper. Our special scenario is described as follows.

3.1   Grid World

In this paper, the grid world consists of a borderless two-dimensional array (also known as a torus), some predators, and one or more preys. For example, Fig. 2(a) shows a 10×10 grid world with four predators working as a team to capture one prey (a capturing situation is shown in Fig. 2(b)).

At each simulation tick, predators and prey move to one of the neighboring cells in the von Neumann neighborhood. If the cell at the desired direction is occupied, the agent stays where it is. Also, when more than one agent intends to move on a free cell, only one of them (chosen arbitrarily) will move into the cell while the other ones do not move.

The prey is captured when it has no possibility to move as all four directly neighboring cells are occupied by the predators. Therefore, the quality of the predators' moves is evaluated with respect to their ability to minimize their distance to the prey (measured as the *Manhattan distance*, i.e., the sum of horizontal and vertical distances).

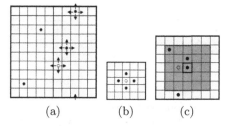

Fig. 2. (a) A borderless grid world with four predators (black dots) and a prey (white dot); (b) The goal is achieved as the prey is captured by the predators. (c) A predator's local observation range (using the Chebyshev distance of two).

3.2 Prey

Since the investigated scenario focuses on collaboratively learning predators, we start with a simple prey which ignores any sensory information except for the status of its four directly neighboring cells. In every tick it moves to one of its von Neumann neighboring cells in an arbitrarily chosen direction, unless stated differently for experimental purposes. If the prey is captured (i. e., it cannot move any more), it is eliminated and another one will appear at a random location within the grid world – to ensure that the simulation is continuously running and predators can learn in several cycles.

3.3 Predators

Every predator is designed to obtain sensory information within a limited observation range determined by a *Chebyshev distance* of two (which refers to the maximum of the horizontal and vertical distances), as depicted in Fig.2(c). There, the predator in the middle of the grid can sense itself, two of its teammates, and the prey. Here, sensing is interpreted as recognizing and knowing the grid coordinates (x, y) of all the currently sensed objects.

Moreover, the location of the prey is broadcasted to all the predators as soon as one of them has sensed it locally. This is intentionally implemented to allow for a local evaluation of the quality of the moves. In other words, without knowing the prey's location, predators cannot learn anything (since possible movements could not be rewarded in a goal-oriented way).

When the prey's location is unknown (for instance, at the beginning of the simulation), all predators move arbitrarily expecting to find it somewhere (Fig.3(a)). When at least one of them has located the prey (e. g., as depicted in Fig. 3(b)), the coordinates of the prey are broadcasted (i. e., (5, 7) in Fig. 3(b), as (0, 0) is the bottom-left corner cell) and retrieved by all teammates at the same tick. If the prey's location is known, the predator uses it for deciding about the next action. This decision is taken at each time step of a simulation run.

Now, conventional non-collaborative predators will individually decide to take their best movement regardless of any information about its teammates' positions. However, it is possible that the set of a predator's movements which

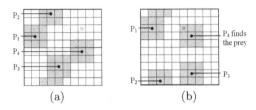

Fig. 3. Two examples of situations with predators having a viewing range of one: (a) No predator sees the prey; (b) The prey is located by predator P_4

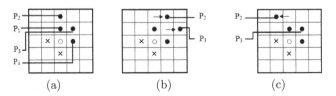

Fig. 4. (a) P_1 and P_4 are denoted as *blocking* predators, P_2 and P_3 as *blocked* predators. (b) The blocked predators cannot get closer the prey. (c) Similar to Fig. 4(b).

minimize the distance to the prey is limited, since it may be blocked by its teammates, as depicted in Fig. 4(a). Then, the desired goal of capturing the prey is not directly achievable.

As depicted in the example, the predators P_1 and P_4 perform a *selfish* behavior and block their teammates P_2 and P_3 as long as they all try to minimize their distance to the prey with each move. Consequently, if P_1 and P_4 remain at their capturing positions, P_2 and P_3 can only follow the option to move around P_1 and P_4 in order to reach the other capturing positions, as marked with crosses. Fig. 4(b) and Fig. 4(c) show the two *blocked predators* P_2 and P_3 could attempt to resolve this by moving away to the east or to the west. This provides possibilities for the blocked predators to have good moves afterwards, but the common behavior of all four predators does not relate to a desirable collaborative behavior. The following section describes ideas to pursue the team task collaboratively.

4   Collaboration Methods

In order to overcome the drawbacks of selfish behavior of non-collaborating predators, we investigate possibilities of learning collaborative behavior which is superior with respect to the global goal of capturing the prey. In a dynamically changing environment, learning is often challenged by the need to adjust the learning speed to the dynamics of the system (as mentioned in [14]). These aspects are focused on in the following.

4.1   Fair Moves

In Fig. 4(a), blocking situations have been discussed which may arise in various ways. Two possible static solutions are explained here:

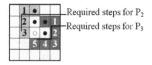

Fig. 5. Required steps to capture the prey starting from a blocking situation

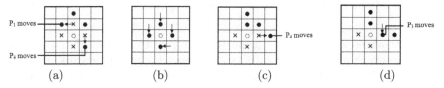

Fig. 6. (a) Fair moves by P_1 and P_4. (b) Goal achieved. (c) Not a fair move. (d) P_3 blocks P_4.

1. The blocked predators move step by step around the other predators to get closer to the prey eventually;
2. The predators collaborate and perform so-called *fair moves*.

As depicted in Fig. 5, the first strategy requires at least five steps for all predators to surround the prey. In contrast, using fair moves as shown in Fig. 6(a) and Fig. 6(b), only two steps are required which is a significant benefit.

The idea behind the fair moves is that blocking predators should move out of their current position to give their teammates a chance to get closer to the prey. This is called a fair move, only if the Chebyshev distance of the moving predator to the prey does not change.

Starting from the situation displayed in Fig. 4(a), an example of fair moves is shown in Fig. 6(a). The fair moves of P_1 and P_4 are allowing P_2 and P_3 to come closer to the prey, as shown in Fig. 6(b). On the other hand, Fig. 6(c) shows a move by P_4 which is not a fair one. This unsurprisingly leads to a situation where P_4 becomes a blocked predator, as depicted in Fig. 6(d). Due to the benefit of fair moves, the agents should get a special reward in the on-line learning cycles, whenever they perform a fair move.

4.2   Common Rule Base

As outlined in Sect. 2, multi-agent learning approaches may use individual rule bases or global shared rule sets. Generally, selfish agents would learn for themselves while collaborative ones do it for the team. In this paper, two different learning architectures (as depicted in Fig. 7) are compared. Figure 7(a) shows an architecture where every agent has its own rule base and the others do not get the benefit of learning from any of their teammates' experience. In contrast to this, the second architecture uses a common rule base for all the agents, as depicted in Fig. 7(b), i. e., every predator decides on its action by using the accumulated experience of the team. Different from centralized learning approaches

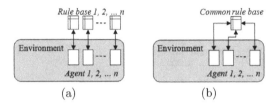

Fig. 7. Learning architectures: (a) Individual rule bases; (b) Common rule base

with a centralized single-learning agent (e. g., in [5]); this approach is based on a rule base which cumulatively collects experience from all predators. In other words, all predators still make decisions autonomously, but store their knowledge in a centralized rule base – accessible to all teammates.

Obviously, a good move for a predator is always a good one for others being in the same situation. If predators act as a set of sensors (or experience collectors for a common rule base), they will presumably have shorter learning times than in scenarios where learning is limited to selfish agent behavior (i. e., a team of four predators can update a common rule base four times faster than a single predator can update its own rule base). Thus, in dynamically changing environments, a quicker converging process of how to behave well seems to be very desirable.

Although these architectures are independent of the specific method of updating the rule bases, in the following it is assumed that XCS is used as the learning method in both scenarios. Following, the predators' algorithm in applying the common rule base is described.

4.3   The Algorithm

At each tick of the simulation, every predator executes the algorithm given in Fig. 8, which does the following: A predator observes its environmental surrounding and takes a decision on an action that specifies the direction of the next movement. Having the prey in the local observation range, the predator broadcasts the location of the prey. Without having the prey in sight, a predator will examine whether any other teammate can sense the prey.

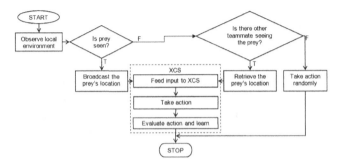

Fig. 8. A flow chart of the predator's algorithm performed at each simulation tick

If the prey's location is available (locally or by broadcast), a learning mechanism is applied based on Wilson's XCS: An action is selected from the local or global XCS rule base. It is triggered and evaluated, and the reward is used to build up the predator's knowledge. Otherwise, the predator performs a random movement without referring to the rule base.

The next section describes how these behaviors are implemented, how the methods affect the results, and how useful they are in achieving the goal.

5 Methodology

In the experimental setting, the predator/prey scenario is performed in a two-dimensional 15×15 borderless grid world. Four predators having a *viewing range* limited to a Chebyshev distance of two have to learn to capture a prey. All rule bases are initialized to an empty population (i. e., no predefined knowledge). New rules are generated using the standard covering operator [15]. The maximum number of rules per rule base is set to 480. This means, whenever the number of classifiers is greater than 480, rule deletions will occur, as specified in [15].

Initially, all entities start at random coordinates. When the prey is captured, a new prey will appear and the old one disappears. The number of capture cycles is then used to compare the performances in different parameterized scenarios.

To adapt the XCS algorithm to the scenario, three things have to be defined: The input string to the XCS rule base, the action encoding, and the reward mechanism. As explained and known from the literature (e. g., in [14]), classifier systems have weaknesses in learning speed due to increasing search spaces. Therefore, an efficient way of learning favors an intelligent coding of input and output values and a proper reward mechanism.

Thus, two sorts of information are used as input to a learning predator: The current relative direction of the prey and the predator's von Neumann neighborhood of range one (denoted as *(direct) neighborhood* afterwards). The direction is used to decide where the predator should move to, while the direct neighborhood is useful for extracting the information whether a neighboring cell is occupied or not.

Figure 9(a) depicts an example derived from Fig. 2(c) and explains the encoding of the chosen XCS input. Firstly, the environment is simplified into eight directions coded into four bits sequentially representing *north, east, south,* and *west,* as shown in Fig. 9(b). For example, the direction *southeast* would be '0110'. Since our investigations are limited to a scenario with one prey, only one of the eight directions will be *true*.

The second part of the input is information concerning the possibility to move to the neighboring cells. Moving to a cell occupied by a teammate is unfavorable, but in contrary, moving towards the prey is a good one. Therefore, no information about the prey's existence is given to this part of the input.

As seen in Fig. 9(b), the first part of the input is '0001' representing west. Then, a neighboring cell is coded to '1' if it is occupied by a teammate, or to '0' otherwise. Starting from the northern cell, going clockwise, and taking one bit

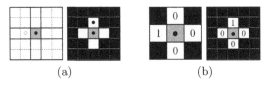

(a)   (b)

Fig. 9. (a) Simplification of the observed area; (b) Encoding of the XCS input

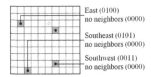

Fig. 10. XCS input of predators not seeing the prey

Table 1. Allocation of rewards

no.	D_{t-1}	D_t	name	condition	basic reward	add. reward
1.	x	$x-1$	closer	any	100	0
2.	x	$x+1$	further	any	10	0
3.	x	x	stagnant	any	1	0
4.	x	$x+1$	fair move	was a blocking predator & unchanged Chebyshev distance	0	140
5.	1	1	staying as a neighbor	moving towards the prey	0	99

for every direction, the neighboring cells are coded to '1000'. The XCS output will be one of four possible directions (*north, east, south,* or *west* are encoded as 0, 1, 2, or 3).

This simple form of input is also applicable to be implemented by the predators not seeing the prey. For instance in Fig. 3(a), P_1, P_2, and P_3 compose inputs using the prey's coordinate broadcasted by P_4, as shown in Fig. 10. Moreover, the encoding is able to represent fair moves. For example, if the prey is located at north ('1000') and a teammate is sensed on the southern neighboring cell ('0010'), then moving east (2) or west (4) will provide a fair move.

Based on the XCS output, each predator moves and gets a reward to the classifiers in the action set according to the mechanism shown in Table 1. The reward is based on the Manhattan distance between a predator and the prey. After moving, each predator checks its current distance to the prey (D_t) and compares it to the previous (D_{t-1}). The standard reward for an input-output-combination (a rule) is 50, and a reward is considered as low if it is less than that. A high reward will be given to a rule if it takes the predator closer to the prey. Otherwise, a low reward will be received. Stagnancy, where a predator fails to change its position, is rewarded very lowly.

A *basic reward* is given to any actions, while an *additional reward* is only given to specific movements. Fulfilling more than one criterion, a move will be awarded by the sum of the basic and additional rewards. For instance, staying at any distance of x is a *stagnant* move deserving the low reward of 1. Additional reward would be given for $x = 1$ which is a *staying as a neighbor* move, deserving the total reward of 100. This value refers to *closer*, since in the rule base both of them are represented by the same classifier denoting *if the prey is in direction z and you are not blocked by your teammate, then go to z*. Finally, a *fair move* is rewarded very highly to encourage predators taking it, testing its effectiveness in achieving the team task.

6   Results and Comparisons

Experiments have been done using two types of prey, a static (not moving) prey and a moving one, having the same speed as the predators. The following figures show averaged experimental results how the agents behave in simulations over time. The horizontal axis denotes the simulation time in a logarithmic scale while the vertical axis depicts the average number of capture cycles from the beginning to the end of the simulations. Data are taken from 20 experiments where each simulation ends after one million ticks – one tick is one simulation step. Due to lack of space we did not include any information on the statistical significance of the results. But a simple statistical analysis indicates insignificant deviations.

Figures 11(a) and 11(b) present the experimental results of the comparison between simulations with and without rewarding fair move decisions in the case of both learning architectures (individual vs. common rule base). Moreover, both figures show some relatively significant increases for the number of average capture times by rewarding fair move decisions, either in capturing a static or a moving prey. Since rewarding fair moves seems advantageous, further comparisons only focus on the two different rule base architectures which are always rewarding fair decisions.

The learning speed, which has been pointed out as a weakness of XCS, is improved slightly by implementing a common rule base. As shown in Fig. 12,

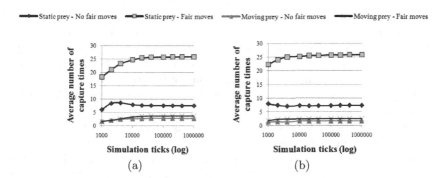

Fig. 11. Comparisons of learning with and without rewarding fair move decisions using: (a) the individual rule base approach; and (b) a common rule base

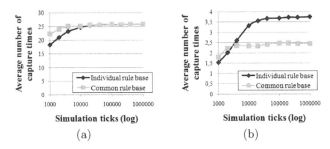

Fig. 12. Comparison of learning using individual and common rule bases in fair mode simulations using (a) a static prey; and (b) a moving prey

simulations using the common rule base approach are superior for some initial period although after some time the individual rule base approach provides better results, especially in capturing a moving prey.

Furthermore, the individual learning approach can benefit from storing individual knowledge for a longer period. Rarely used classifiers are possibly deleted in the common learning approach, since the maximal number of classifiers keeps the population as compact as possible (cf. the mechanism of deleting classifiers, as proposed by [15]).

7   Conclusion and Outlook

This paper has focused on an instance of the generic pursuit scenario where predators should learn to contribute to a common goal - capturing a prey. The usability of Wilson's XCS has specially been investigated in two different approaches. Firstly, all predators individually learn and store their experience in local rule bases. Secondly, the predators share and store their experiences in a common rule base.

Predators have been designed with a local view where they can sense their local environment. If the prey is found, its coordinates will be broadcasted to all other predators. Then, a simple input encoding has been defined, consisting of the direction where the prey has been located and information about the neighboring cells - are the cells occupied with the teammates or not. Finally, a proper reward function for fair moves has been proposed, which enforces collaborative group behavior. These fair moves are based on the idea that moving away from a desirable position and thus giving a chance for a teammate to come closer could be beneficial in some cases.

Experimental results have been achieved using different parameter combinations. The results provide a clear view: The learning approach using a common rule base provides a quicker improvement in the learning behavior but may be significantly inferior on the long run, in particular in situations with a *moving prey*. Nevertheless, the presented idea of collaborative learning by storing the knowledge in a common rule base provides a wide area for further research on multi-agent learning: The complexities of heterogeneous predators, an intelligently acting prey, or more complex goals than capturing a prey give rise to new challenges for learning, which will be tackled by future work.

References

1. Sen, S., Weiß, G.: Learning in multi-agent systems. In: Multi-agent systems: A modern approach to distributed articial intelligence, pp. 259–298. MIT Press, Cambridge (1999)
2. Parunak, H.V.D.: Industrial and practical applications of distributed artificial intelligence. In: Multi-agent systems: A modern approach to distributed artificial intelligence, pp. 377–421. MIT Press, Cambridge (1999)
3. Eßer, A., Franke, M., Kamper, A., Möst, D.: Impacts of consumer response and dynamic retail prices on electricity markets. Future Power Markets 5, 335–341 (2007)
4. Dorigo, M., Gambardella, L.M.: Ant colonies for the traveling salesman problem. BioSystems 41, 73–81 (1996)
5. Huberman, B.A., Clearwater, S.: A multi-agent system for controlling building environments. In: Proceedings of the 1st International Conference on Multi-Agent Systems (ICMAS 1995), pp. 171–176. MIT Press, Cambridge (1995)
6. Wooldridge, M.J.: An introduction to multi-agent systems. John Wiley & Sons, Chichester (2002)
7. Benda, M., Jagannathan, V., Dodhiawala, R.: An optimal cooperation of knowledge sources: An empirical investigation. Technical Report BCS-G2010–28, Boeing Advanced Technology Center, Boeing Computing Services, Seattle, United States of America (1986)
8. Lenzitti, B., Tegolo, D., Valenti, C.: Prey-predator strategies in a multi-agent system. In: Proceedings of the 7th International Workshop on Computer Architecture for Machine Perception (CAMP 2005). IEEE Computer Society, Los Alamitos (2005)
9. Holland, J.H.: Adaptation in natural and artificial systems. University of Michigan Press, Ann Arbor (1975)
10. Wilson, S.W.: Generalization in the XCS classifier system. In: Genetic Programming 1998: Proceedings of the Third Annual Conference, pp. 665–674 (1998)
11. Hercog, L.M., Fogarty, T.C.: Social simulation using a multi-agent model based on classifier systems: The emergence of vacillating behaviour in "el farol" bar problem. In: Lanzi, P.L., Stolzmann, W., Wilson, S.W. (eds.) IWLCS 2001. LNCS (LNAI), vol. 2321, pp. 88–111. Springer, Heidelberg (2002)
12. Takadama, K., Terano, T., Shimohara, K.: Learning classifier systems meet multi-agent environments. In: Lanzi, P.L., Stolzmann, W., Wilson, S.W. (eds.) IWLCS 2000. LNCS (LNAI), vol. 1996, pp. 192–212. Springer, Heidelberg (2001)
13. Stone, P., Veloso, M.: Multi-agent systems: A survey from a machine learning perspective. Autonomous Robots 8(3), 345–383 (2000)
14. Richter, U., Prothmann, H., Schmeck, H.: Improving XCS performance by distribution. In: Li, X., Kirley, M., Zhang, M., Green, D., Ciesielski, V., Abbass, H.A., Michalewicz, Z., Hendtlass, T., Deb, K., Tan, K.C., Branke, J., Shi, Y. (eds.) SEAL 2008. LNCS, vol. 5361, pp. 111–120. Springer, Heidelberg (2008)
15. Butz, M.V.: XCSJava 1.0: An implementation of the XCS classifier system in Java. Technical Report 2000027, Illinois Genetic Algorithms Laboratory, Urbana, United States of America (2000)

SelSta - A Biologically Inspired Approach for Self-Stabilizing Humanoid Robot Walking

Bojan Jakimovski, Michael Kotke, Martin Hörenz, and Erik Maehle

Institute of Computer Engineering, University Lübeck, Germany
www.iti.uni-luebeck.de

Abstract. In this paper we elaborate a study on self-stabilizing humanoid robot that achieves run-time self-stabilization and energy optimized walking gait pattern parameters on different kinds of flat surfaces. The algorithmic approach named SelSta uses biologically inspired notions that introduce robustness into the self-stabilizing functionality of the humanoid robot. The approach has been practically tested on our S2-HuRo humanoid robot and the results from the tests demonstrate that it can be successfully used on humanoid robots to achieve autonomic optimized stabilization of their walking on different kinds of flat surfaces.

Keywords: Self-stabilizing humanoid robot, S2-HuRo, biologically inspired approach, symbiosis, SelSta approach, humanoid robot walking optimization.

1 Introduction

In recent years the trend in robotics research has shifted towards service, field, and entertainment robots as market demand continually rises for these types of robots. Different kinds of humanoid robots are developed nowadays with purpose to serve the elderly people or for entertainment purposes like humanoid robots playing soccer games [1]. Humanoid robots are complex robotic systems exhibiting high degrees of freedom (DOF), consisting of different electronic hardware parts and complex software control architectures [2] [3].

Many surveys have been done on mathematical modeling of biped locomotion mechanisms [4] [5]. Most of the mathematical models are related to dynamic walking models and maintaining the zero moment point (ZMP) inside the support region. The ZMP was first introduced in [6] [7] and since then there are many research studies based on the ZMP method and their combinations with other methods [8] [9].

The control algorithms [10] for humanoid robots should be robust in order to achieve stable walking gait and balance of the humanoid robot without compromising the mechanical stability. Some researchers prefer to use simulations [11] - [14] in order to experiment and predict the outcome of their control algorithms applied on the humanoid robots without sacrificing the mechanical integrity of their real robots. The simulation environments are stated to provide high fidelity rigid body dynamics [15] - [18]. However, the simulation experiments cannot be completely identical with reality experiments because of various factors such as: environmental influences, dynamics, vibrations, sensors noise, etc. present in the second ones. This directly implies that the algorithm developed for the simulation can not be one-to-one mapped to the reality

M. Hinchey et al. (Eds.): DIPES/BICC 2010, IFIP AICT 329, pp. 302–313, 2010.

experiments or a lot of work will be spent on "tuning" some parameters in order to mitigate some problems that come from not identical mapping.

For that reason we have planned in advance on how to set and conduct the self-stabilizing humanoid robot walking experiments (without using simulations) so we can assure that the algorithm will function as intended on a real robot under real circumstances.

In this research we also wanted to overcome the cumbersome traditional dynamic model designing that perhaps fits to only one particular robot, but instead to derive a more generic biologically inspired approach that with small or no adjustments can be used in variety of other humanoid robot research projects. In the search for better algorithms and approaches for achieving better locomotion and dynamics of humanoid robots, researchers, besides the classical mathematical modeling approaches, have also tried to use biologically inspired paradigms for this domain [19] - [22].

Some of them are based on spinal central pattern generators (CPGs) in vertebrate systems [19], others use the CPG in relation with modulation of stiffness [20], reflex based stabilization using SMA muscles [21] or coupled oscillators [22].

The practical usefulness of bio-inspired paradigms in robotic domain has encouraged us to apply biologically inspired notions of mutual interactions seen by biological species for achieving self-stabilizing robot walking over different kinds of flat surfaces (carpets, different types of floors, etc.).

The structure of the paper is organized as follows: In the second chapter we describe our humanoid robot demonstrator S2-HuRo. In the third chapter we describe the self-stabilizing approach SelSta in details. There, we explain also its relation to the biologically inspired notions of mutual interactions seen by biological species. In the fourth chapter we present the experimental test setup and results of experiments done on our humanoid robot demonstrator. In the fifth chapter we give out a conclusion about the research presented in this paper.

1.1 S2-HuRo (Self-Stabilizing Humanoid Robot)

We have used the humanoid robot named S2-HuRo (Fig.1) as robot demonstrator in order to test the self-stabilizing algorithm that we have developed for humanoid robot walking stabilization.

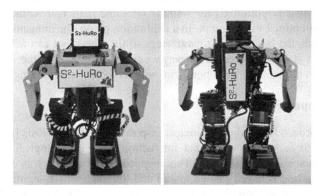

Fig. 1. S2-HuRo (Self-Stabilizing Humanoid Robot)

The humanoid robot is based on the "Robonova" [23] humanoid robot platform with ATmega servo controller. It has been additionally modified by excluding some arm servos (to reduce the weight) and including some other components such as: an embedded system, two dual-axis gyroscopes, voltage convertors, batteries, three contact sensors per foot, etc. Its height is 35 cm, its weight is 1.8 kg.

The contact sensors on the feet are used to acquire information whether the robot leg is touching the ground surface or not. They are also used to detect if the robot has fallen while walking, which is needed for evaluation within self-stabilizing walking experiments.

2   SelSta – A Self-Stabilizing Approach for Humanoid Robot Walking

2.1   SelSta Approach - Overview

Here we elaborate an approach named as *SelSta* which we found will be very useful for the domain of humanoid robots self-stabilized walking. Namely, the research on humanoid robot walking usually is concentrated on finding a control algorithm for humanoid robot walking where the characteristics of the surface on which the robot is walking are often overlooked. However, the surface on which the robot is walking indeed brings different dynamics to humanoid robot walking stability. Here by surface we mean a flat surface from some material like linoleum floor, different types of carpets (soft, medium, hard) and the like. It is often very important that the humanoid robot walking is optimally stabilized and energy-efficient for a particular walking surface. This may also mean difference between the winner and the looser in some RoboCup [1] humanoid robot match. This research objective is how to develop a robust automated method that will achieve optimal and energy efficient stabilized walking of humanoid robots for any kind of flat surface with different material characteristics in a relatively short time.

The *SelSta* method was designed to function under real circumstances on a real robot, since no simulation can replace or perfectly represent the different surface dynamics introduced to a humanoid robot walking on different types of surfaces.

It is built as an add-on module to the already developed humanoid robot walking algorithm (not strictly optimized for walking on some particular surface) with some predefined non-optimal walking gait. In a calibration phase, the humanoid robot using *SelSta* first finds the best walking parameters so that the robot can achieve the best performance in stability, speed, and energy consumption over some given surface. After that, in its normal run, the robot is run with the best found walking parameters.

2.2   SelSta Approach Details

The *SelSta* approach is based on biological inspiration from symbiosis [24] which can be associated to some sort of mutual interaction between biological species from which the both species have benefit. This mapped to our approach is described with "mutual" interaction between robot's lateral and longitudinal (or sagittal) axis stability. Those stabilities are estimated from both gyros axes values and the robot's servos accumulated load during the robot's walking. Before describing the details on how this "mutual" interaction was practically realized in the *SelSta* approach, we are going to describe what the *SelSta* approach consists of. The *SelSta* approach comprises the SymbScore evaluation that codes the "mutual" interaction of the robot's axes (explained later in this chapter), combined with a genetic algorithm that generates lateral and longitudinal balancing movement parameters for the robot's feet - represented with two real type genes. We have chosen a genetic algorithm for optimization purposes, but in general other optimization approaches (PSO, Ant Colony Alg., etc.) can be also considered in combination with *SymbScore*. The balancing movement action of the robot's "ankles" takes place only when the leg starts with its stance phase (foot on the ground). In that impulsive movement the foot moves from its neutral position, assumed with 0 degrees when the foot is parallel to the ground, to some other degree values independently chosen for lateral and saggital directions. These values are chosen by the genetic algorithm in range from -5 to 5 degrees (with resolution 0.5), where forward and right from robot's point of view there are positive values and in other directions there are negative values. Such impulsive movement takes place in the middle of each stance phase. After this movement, the foot is set back to 0 degrees in lateral and saggital planes. The balancing movement is represented with double sided arrow lines in Fig.2 and Fig.3.

One robot's walking period takes 6 robot steps (Fig.2) from which the first and the last steps are "start of walking" and "stop of walking" respectively. The whole evaluation period duration is 4 robot steps. Just for better understanding, this process is sketched in Fig.2. In that period averaged gyro values from both robot's axes and accumulated robot's servo loads are measured. At the end of the robot's walking period a *SelSta* symbiosis score - *SymbScore* is computed which states how stable and optimal the robot's walking was. The *SymbScore* therefore "guides" the optimization, so the robot maintains greater stability while walking. While the robot is standing between two evaluation walking periods a genetic algorithm is run to compute the lateral (A) and longitudinal (B) balancing movement parameters for the next evaluation period of the robot's walking. This computation time for generating the next generation is rather small and can be neglected. The score - *SymbScore* is used in the genetic algorithm's objective function to select the next better generation of parameters for balancing the movement of the foot. In each self-stabilizing run, there may be several such evaluation periods up to the moment where enough optimized self-stabilizing walking of the robot is generated for a particular surface. The parameters for genetic algorithm are presented in Fig. 4. The "Number of generations" and the "Population size parameters" have been experimentally found, so the approach can be still fast and at the same time enough robust to find the optimal solutions. The other GA parameters are selected by default. "*Tournament selection*" was used for selecting the individuals in the population. Each individual in the population of the genetic algorithm has the following format:

A	B

Where A, B represent: lateral (A) and longitudinal (B) leg positioning from the normal robot still standing position and range from -5 to 5 degrees, with resolution 0.5.

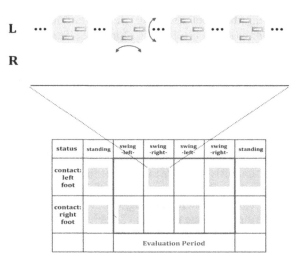

Fig. 2. Evaluation period and the swing and stance phases of the robot's legs; Double sided arrow lines represent the balancing movement of the robot foot during each stance phase; L and R represent the left and right robot's foot on the ground; Right foot (R) in this case is in its swing phase (not on the ground) therefore not shown

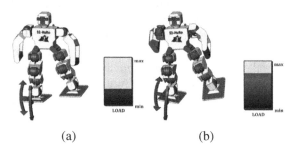

Fig. 3. Balancing movement of the robot's foot during each stance phase; (a) Situation where the robot is better balanced and has smaller load on the servos; (b) Situation where the robot is more unstable and has higher load on the servos

Genetic Algorithm Parameters	
number of generations	15
population size	10
replacement percentage	0.5
convergence percentage	0.99
crossover probability	0.6
mutation probability	0.05

Fig. 4. Genetic algorithm parameters

The resolution can be decreased if needed. The A, B parameters for standing still position are defined as 0, 0. The genetic algorithm is a single point crossover. The replacement percentage is 0.5, meaning one half of the population in every cycle is replaced with a new one.

The genetic algorithm finishes with its search either when the number of generations reaches 15 or the convergence percentage is 0.99. At the end, optimized parameters for balancing movement for robot walking on the particular surface are found.

The symbiosis score - *SymbScore* computation practically is implemented as cascaded fuzzy logic rule base computation (Fig.5) that at the end generates a *SymbScore* value between 0 and 1, a score approaching 1 is the better score, meaning the parameters chosen for the robot's balancing movement action are the best ones for some particular robot walking.

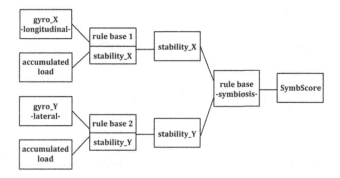

Fig. 5. SymbScore computation - implemented as cascaded fuzzy logic rule base computation

The inputs to the *SymbScore* computation are the two axes gyro values. The gyro values range from -66 to +66 units, and their absolute values were considered for computation. These values are associated to lateral and longitudinal movement; and the averaged accumulated load of all the servos and their values in range from 0 to 70 units. The "rule base 1" and "rule base 2" (Fig.6) have identical rules and compute the "stability_x" and "stability_y" related to robot stability on longitudinal (or sagittal) and lateral axis. Those are intermediate normalized outputs ranging from 0 to 1. Each computed value gives the relationship between the present load on the robot's servos and one axis gyro values. A value closer to 1 means stability computed for that particular axis is better. Those two intermediate values get further "fuzzified" into the "rule base symbiosis" (Fig.7) that computes the *SymbScore* result value between 0 and 1. An exception is when the robot has fallen during the evaluation period, in which case the *SymbScore* is set to 0. The *SymbScore* value is computed continously.

In Fig.7 the rules numbered 3 and 7 represent the "mutual" relationship between "stability_x" and "stability_y" - intermediate computed stabilities for two robot's axes. The meaning of these rules can be interpreted as follows: only when both of their values are *not* drastically different, the computed *SymbScore* can be bigger (closer to 1), i.e. indicating more stable and more energy efficient robot walking. The overall robot's stable walking depends both on the robot's stability in its longitudinal (sagittal) and lateral axis.

#	IF		THEN	
	GYRO_X_LON	LOAD	DoS	STAB_X_LON
1	small	small	1.00	stable
2	medium	small	1.00	medstable
3	big	small	1.00	nonstable
4	small	medium	1.00	medstable
5	medium	medium	1.00	medstable
6	big	medium	1.00	nonstable
7	small	big	1.00	medstable
8	medium	big	1.00	medstable
9	big	big	1.00	nonstable

Fig. 6. Fuzzy logic rule base for "stability_x" and "stability_y" computation; DoS is degree of support for fuzzy rules and is set to 1

#	IF		THEN	
	STAB_X	STAB_Y	DoS	SYMB_SCORE
1	small	small	1.00	small
2	medium	small	1.00	medium
3	big	small	1.00	small
4	small	medium	1.00	medium
5	medium	medium	1.00	medium
6	big	medium	1.00	big
7	small	big	1.00	small
8	medium	big	1.00	big
9	big	big	1.00	big

Fig. 7. Fuzzy logic rule base for SymbScore computation with highlighted rules 3 and 7 representing the "mutual" relationship between the two axes stabilities; DoS is degree of support for fuzzy rules and is set to 1

3   Experiments and Results of SelSta Approach for Self-Stabilizing Humanoid Robot on Different Kinds of Surfaces

3.1   Experimental Test Setup

For performing the experiments with the S2-HuRo we have prepared the following setup as can be seen of Fig.8. The surface on which the robot walks is replaced with another one in every experiment. Therefore we have experimented with self-stabilizing behavior on different kinds of flat surfaces (carpets). For our experiments we have chosen 4 different types of surfaces: hard linoleum surface, soft green carpet, hard green carpet, and orange soft carpet, on which we have tested the *SelSta* method. In each of these tests the robot is connected to power supply cables and a serial connection to PC.

This was chosen only for performing the data logging (which on PC is 2 times faster than on the robot's embedded system) and used for starting/stopping the robot walking. The robot is hung on a steel cable via metal rings. The rings give the robot enough space for performing its walking actions without influencing the walking movement itself. On the other hand, they give support when the robot is falling (due to some improper walking behavior or poorly generated balancing parameters). When this happens a human operator puts the robot to standard standing position first.

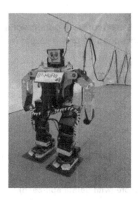

Fig. 8. One of the four test setups - S2-HuRo self-stabilization experiment on orange soft carpet

Then via PC command the robot is instructed to continue with a new cycle of balancing movement parameter generation till the optimal parameters for balancing movements are found. We chose the steel wire rope support approach since we expected a lot of robot falls, however that was probably overcautious.

3.2 Results from Experiments

The experiments were performed on 4 different kinds of surfaces and on each surface (floor or carpet) self-stabilization was performed for 3 different robot walking speeds (slow, medium and fast). Although the speed of the robot is not an objective of an optimization function, we have observed the robustness of our SelSta approach when the robot is trying to get self-stabilizing walking with different walking speeds. The 3 initial robot walking gaits & speeds were manually predefined (but not optimized for any particular surface). During the experiments the *SelSta* approach tried to find the optimal balancing parameters for each of those speeds for every kind of surface on which the robot was walking. The self-stabilizing approach for every evaluation walking section produces a lot of data that can be analyzed later and from where the success of this approach can be recognized. Due to the limited space in this paper, we represent here only a selection of results from the acquired data of all the self-stabilizing experiments on different flat surfaces. The results are related to self-stabilizing experiment by fast speed robot walking on green soft carpet. The results from measurements for this particular surface can be seen as examples on how the results from other self-stabilization runs on other surfaces look like (Fig.9, Fig.10). In Fig.9 the symbiosis score - *SymbScore* generated by *SelSta* approach for 15 generations (evaluation walking sections) is represented. The other two lines in the same figure represent the other types of *SymbScores* evaluated for walking robot stability by standard setup and manual setup for the balancing parameters.

They are given here just for comparison purposes with the value that is reached by the self-stabilization approach, where its value is distinctly better than by the standard and manual setup approaches. In this figure it can be also seen that sometimes the manual setup can be very subjective and not always better performing than the standard setup values. It has to be also kept in mind that manual setup is done once for a particular terrain and that the speed of the robot also has influence on how "performing" are the

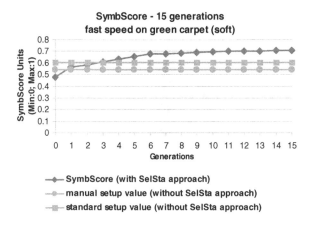

Fig. 9. SymbScore values by self-stabilization by fast walking speed on green soft carpet - 15 generations

setup values. Fig. 10 represents data logged by only one walking evaluation section by self-stabilizing fast speed robot walking on green soft carpet. One walking section contains 4 robot steps, therefore there are a lot of such walking sections within one self-stabilizing walking trial. The "Mode" line on that graph represents the stance and swing phases of the robot's legs and has two values: -25 and +25. The other lines are named as "Gyro_X" with range -66 to +66, "Load" with range 0 to 70, "Stability_X", "Symb-Score" varies in range from 0 to 1 and is computed as previously described. For better clarity of the figure the values for "Gyro_Y" and "Stability_Y" were omitted and values for "Stability_X" and "SymbScore" are normalized between 0 and 20.

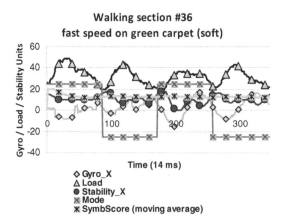

Fig. 10. Representation of data logged for section number 36 out of many walking evaluation sections for each generation by self-stabilizing fast speed robot walking on green soft carpet

Surface	Green Carpet (Hard)								
Method	Autonomous Self-Stabilizing			Manual Values			Standard Values		
Walking Speed	Slow	Medium	Fast	Slow	Medium	Fast	Slow	Medium	Fast
Foot axis (X-Longitudinal; Y-Lateral)	X Y	X Y	X Y	X Y	X Y	X Y	X Y	X Y	X Y
Stabilization parameters (axis degrees)	3.5 1	3 0.5	0.5 -3	1 4	1 4	1 4	0 0	0 0	0 0
Self-Stabilization approach duration	13 min	10 min	11 min	10-14 hrs			/		
SymbScore (average of 5 test sections)	0.8	0.51	0.66	0.72	0.42	0.56	0.69	0.11	0.63
SymbScore (best of 5 test sections)	0.85	0.53	0.72	0.86	0.46	0.65	0.82	0.34	0.71
Robot fallings (in 5 test sections)	0	0	0	0	0	0	0	3	0

Surface	Green Carpet (Soft)								
Method	Autonomous Self-Stabilizing			Manual Values			Standard Values		
Walking Speed	Slow	Medium	Fast	Slow	Medium	Fast	Slow	Medium	Fast
Foot axis (X-Longitudinal; Y-Lateral)	X Y	X Y	X Y	X Y	X Y	X Y	X Y	X Y	X Y
Stabilization parameters (axis degrees)	1.5 0.5	2 4	0.5 -4.5	1 4	1 4	1 4	0 0	0 0	0 0
Self-Stabilization approach duration	16 min	14 min	12 min	10-14 hrs			/		
SymbScore (average of 5 test sections)	0.8	0.28	0.65	0.72	0.3	0.54	0.73	0.22	0.6
SymbScore (best of 5 test sections)	0.85	0.56	0.74	0.79	0.42	0.58	0.83	0.38	0.62
Robot fallings (in 5 test sections)	0	1	0	0	1	0	0	0	0

Surface	Linoleum Surface (Hard)								
Method	Autonomous Self-Stabilizing			Manual Values			Standard Values		
Walking Speed	Slow	Medium	Fast	Slow	Medium	Fast	Slow	Medium	Fast
Foot axis (X-Longitudinal; Y-Lateral)	X Y	X Y	X Y	X Y	X Y	X Y	X Y	X Y	X Y
Stabilization parameters (axis degrees)	-0.5 -0.5	2.5 -0.5	2.5 -1	1 4	1 4	1 4	0 0	0 0	0 0
Self-Stabilization approach duration	11 min	12 min	11 min	10-14 hrs			/		
SymbScore (average of 5 test sections)	0.82	0.62	0.72	0.76	0.62	0.71	0.78	0.61	0.66
SymbScore (best of 5 test sections)	0.86	0.64	0.75	0.85	0.71	0.75	0.81	0.73	0.73
Robot fallings (in 5 test sections)	0	0	0	0	0	0	0	0	0

Surface	Orange Carpet (Medium Soft)								
Method	Autonomous Self-Stabilizing			Manual Values			Standard Values		
Walking Speed	Slow	Medium	Fast	Slow	Medium	Fast	Slow	Medium	Fast
Foot axis (X-Longitudinal; Y-Lateral)	X Y	X Y	X Y	X Y	X Y	X Y	X Y	X Y	X Y
Stabilization parameters (axis degrees)	1 2.5	1.5 4	1.5 0	1 4	1 4	1 4	0 0	0 0	0 0
Self-Stabilization approach duration	16 min	14 min	11 min	10-14 hrs			/		
SymbScore (average of 5 test sections)	0.68	0.36	0.72	0.63	0.24	0.59	0.58	0.09	0.65
SymbScore (best of 5 test sections)	0.77	0.57	0.78	0.72	0.46	0.71	0.67	0.27	0.7
Robot fallings (in 5 test sections)	0	1	0	0	2	0	0	4	0

Fig. 11. Results from humanoid robot self-stabilizing experiments done on different kinds of surfaces, with different testing parameters and three different walking speeds

The results of the tests are shown in Fig. 11. They also include data from performance tests done on 5 walking test sections (each section is 6 robot walking steps as described earlier) of the best found balancing parameters and direct comparison to tests done with manual set values for the balancing parameters and standard set values (feet longitudinal and lateral degree is 0). The comparison includes number of robot fallings by that final evaluation approach.

In comparison with manual set up values, the self-stabilizing *SelSta* approach generates in a relatively short time a more stable, energy efficient walking of the humanoid robot on different kinds of surfaces. This can be clearly seen when comparing the values in rows: *SymbScore* (average of 5 test sections), *SymbScore* (best of 5 test sections) for "Autonomous Self-Stabilizing", "Manual Values" setup, "Standard Values" setup. The bigger values by *SymbScore* indicate more stable and energy efficient walking. Quantitatively and qualitatively better values with Autonomous Self-Stabilizing category in comparison with the "Manual" and "Standard" Values setup categories, indicate that the autonomously found parameters using our biologically inspired approach are better. With this the *SelSta* approach has clearly reached its main projected goals.

4 Conclusion

In this paper we have explained the *SelSta* approach that we have created for self-stabilizing humanoid robot walking on different specific kinds of flat surfaces. The *SelSta* approach is robust since it is built on a modular basis as an addition to the already built control algorithm for humanoid walking. Thus, it can be easily adopted to other humanoid robots and also for creating more optimally stabilized humanoid robots that play soccer on RoboCup[1] matches. Further research will be done on transferring the functionality of this method to stabilize the humanoid robot walking over rough terrains.

References

1. http://www.robocup.org
2. Kopacek, P., Schierer, E., Wuerzl, M.: A Controller Network for a Humanoid Robot. In: Moreno Díaz, R., Pichler, F., Quesada Arencibia, A. (eds.) EUROCAST 2005. LNCS, vol. 3643, pp. 584–589. Springer, Heidelberg (2005)
3. Tsay, T.I.J., Lai, C.H.: Design and Control of a Humanoid Robot. In: IEEE/RSJ International Conference on Intelligent Robots and Systems 2006, vol. 9, pp. 2002–2007 (2006)
4. Vukobratovic, M., Borovac, B., Surla, D., Stokic, D.: Biped Locomotion, Dynamics, Stability, Control and Application, Springer, Berlin (1990).
5. Yang, D.C., Liu, L.: Kinematic Analysis of Humanoid Robot. Chinese J. of Mechanical Engineering 39, 70–74 (2003)
6. Vukobratovic, M., Juricic, D.: Contribution to the synthesis of biped gait. IEEE Trans. Bio-Med. Eng. BME-16(1), 1–6 (1969)
7. Vukobratovic, M.: How to control artificial anthropomorphic system. IEEE Trans. Syst. Man. Cyb. SMC-3(5), 497–507 (1973)
8. Lee, B., Stonier, D., Yong-Duk, K., Jeong-Ki, Y., Jong-Hwan Kim, K.: Modifiable walking pattern generation using real-time ZMP manipulation for humanoid robots. In: IEEE/RSJ International Conference on Intelligent Robots and Systems, IROS 2007, pp. 4221–4226 (2007)
9. Cuevas, E., Zaldivar, D., Tapia, E., Rojas, R.: An Incremental Fuzzy Algorithm for the Balance of Humanoid Robots. Humanoid Robots: New Developments (2007)
10. Lei, X., Su, J.: Feedback Control of Humanoid Robot Locomotion. In: Wang, L., Jin, Y. (eds.) FSKD 2005. LNCS (LNAI), vol. 3613, pp. 890–899. Springer, Heidelberg (2005)
11. Qing, T., Rong, X., Yong, L., Jian, C.: HumRoboSim: An Autonomous Humanoid Robot Simulation System. In: 2008 International Conference on Cyberworlds, pp. 537–542 (2008)
12. Friedmann, M., Petersen, K., von Stryk, O.: Tailored Real-Time Simulation for Teams of Humanoid Robots. In: Visser, U., Ribeiro, F., Ohashi, T., Dellaert, F. (eds.) RoboCup 2007: Robot Soccer World Cup XI. LNCS (LNAI), vol. 5001, pp. 425–432. Springer, Heidelberg (2008)
13. Calderon, C.A.A., Mohan, R.E., Zhou, C.: Virtual-RE: A Humanoid Robotic Soccer Simulator. In: 2008 International Conference on Cyberworlds, pp. 561–566 (2008)
14. Deng, X., Wang, J., Xiang, Z.: The Simulation Analysis of Humanoid Robot Based on Dynamics and Kinematics. In: Xiong, C.-H., Liu, H., Huang, Y., Xiong, Y.L. (eds.) ICIRA 2008. LNCS (LNAI), vol. 5314, pp. 93–100. Springer, Heidelberg (2008)
15. http://www.cyberbotics.com/products/webots/

16. http://playerstage.sourceforge.net/gazebo/gazebo.html
17. http://msdn.microsoft.com/en-us/robotics/default.aspx
18. http://sourceforge.net/projects/usarsim
19. Bartsch, S., Kirchner, F.: Robust control of a humanoid robot using a bio-inspired approach based on central pattern generators, reflexes, and proprioceptive feedback. In: Bartsch, S., Kirchner, F. (eds.) IEEE International Conference on Robotics and Biomimetics, pp. 1547–1552 (2006)
20. Kim, H.K., Kwon, W., Roh, K.S.: Biologically Inspired Energy Efficient Walking for Biped Robots. In: IEEE International Conference on Robotics and Biomimetics, pp. 630–635 (2006)
21. Kratz, R., Klug, S., Stelzer, M., von Stryk, O.: Biologically Inspired Reflex Based Stabilization Control of a Humanoid Robot with Artificial SMA Muscles. In: IEEE International Conference on Robotics and Biomimetics, pp. 1089–1094 (2006)
22. Morimoto, J., Endo, G., Nakanishi, J., Cheng, G.: A Biologically Inspired Biped Locomotion Strategy for Humanoid Robots: Modulation of Sinusoidal Patterns by a Coupled Oscillator Model. IEEE Transactions Robotics 24, 185–191 (2008)
23. http://www.hitecrobotics.com
24. Ahmadjian, V., Paracer, S.: Symbiosis: an introduction to biological associations. Oxford University Press, Oxford (2000)

Appendix

More info, results, and movies about *SelSta* research and self-stabilizing robot S2-HuRo can be found on our web site: www.iti.uni-luebeck.de in sub-section robotics.

Author Index